PRESENTED BY: **Van Wert Elks
Lodge # 1197,
Mr. James Stanley,
Exalted Ruler**

HISTORY

OF THE

ORDER OF ELKS

The first edition of this History, compiled by James R. Nicholson, covered the period from the fraternity's beginning in 1868 to 1952. The second edition compiled by Lee A. Donaldson covered the History to the end of 1967. The third edition compiled by Raymond C. Dobson covered the History to the end of 1978. This fourth edition compiled by George B. Klein continues the History to the end of 1988.

PUBLISHED BY

GRAND SECRETARY'S OFFICE

OF THE BENEVOLENT AND PROTECTIVE ORDER OF ELKS

OF THE UNITED STATES OF AMERICA

2750 N. Lakeview Avenue, CHICAGO, IL 60614-1889

Printed in U. S. A.

Printed by Award Printing Corp., Chicago, IL

CONTENTS

ILLUSTRATIONS

INTRODUCTION

THIS PUBLICATION is designed to be a history
of the Benevolent and Protective Order of Elks from its inception
to the close of the Grand Lodge Session of 1967.

The history of the Order has been only partially written up to
this time.

The Order was nearly thirty years old when in 1897 the Grand
Lodge, assembled in Minneapolis, directed the Grand Exalted
Ruler, Meade D. Detweiler, to

"secure for publication and permanent preservation the minutes of the
Grand Lodge for the years from 1871 to 1878 inclusive."

"It was designed," Detweiler said, "that when these valuable memorials
were obtained there should be published with them a compendium of
the early history of the Order of Elks, which should be so carefully
collated from all reliable sources as to stand forth, for the future, a
permanent and unchallengeably authentic record of the birth and
early struggles of our brotherhood."

But the Detweiler history takes us only to 1878, covering the first
ten years of the Order.

In 1910 Edward Ellis published a History of the Order up to
that date.

Up to the time of the creation of *The Elks Magazine* what
amounted to a running history appeared in the columns of the
various Elks magazines, privately owned.

1

Similarly, since June, 1922, when the first issue of the Order's own publication, *The Elks Magazine,* appeared, it has carried the history of the Order in the fraternal news of its monthly issues.

In *The Elks Magazine,* in the June and July issues of 1938, there appeared an article, "Three Score and Ten," which covered, necessarily briefly, and rather sketchily, the history of the first seventy years of the Order.

At the time of the Order's Diamond Jubilee, there also appeared in *The Elks Magazine* an article written by Mildred Masters French reviewing briefly the activities of the Order up to that time.

Much of the history of the Order can also be found in considerable detail in the annual "Proceedings of the Grand Lodge" which have carried the minutes of the Grand Lodge Sessions with the incorporation therein of the reports of the Grand Exalted Ruler and other Grand Lodge Officers, Commissions and Committees.

The present work results from many days and evenings spent in pleasant research among these documents and publications.

The plan followed has been to divide the history into decades, starting consideration of a subject in the decade in which it originated. However, it has seemed best to complete the treatment of that subject in that decade-section, no matter how many years beyond that particular decade it may have continued to be of interest.

The one exception to this procedure has been made in connection with the subject of The Order and the American Youth. In the case of this subject, while its story is started in the Fifth Decade, such part of that story as refers to the activities following the creation of the Youth Activities Committee of the Grand Lodge is told in the Ninth Decade in which period that Committee was created.

It has been more a work of selection than of creation, and in the following pages the writings and reports referred to have been freely drawn upon for material without, in each instance, indicating the source.

I entertain a deep sense of gratitude to those who have preceded me and made this work possible.

Early in my efforts to compile the information which follows I spoke to Past Grand Exalted Ruler Michael F. Shannon relative to the character of the task.

He suggested that my position was similar to that of another (Michel Eyquem de Montaigne) who wrote of one of his own works:

"I have gathered a posie of other men's flowers and nothing but the thread that binds them is mine own."

It might be added that I not only bring the flowers of other men, but that I have found necessary and have received the assistance of many others in discovering these flowers, selecting those deemed worthy of a place in a History of the Order, clipping them when clipping was indicated and attempting to arrange them properly. Frequent conferences with William M. Frasor, Past President of the Illinois Elks Association and Executive Director of the Elks National Service Commission, have added substantially to the coverage and accuracy of the material used.

Secretary Augustus F. Groll (since deceased), and his successor, Jerry Navarro, assisted by making the early records of New York Lodge No. 1 available.

The chapters on special subjects have been submitted for correction and suggestions to those members of the Order best qualified to pass on their accuracy and proper coverage, as follows:

WORLD WAR I To the two remaining members (aside from the writer) of the Elks War Relief Commission, Past Grand Exalted Rulers Edward Rightor and Bruce A. Campbell.

ELKS NATIONAL HOME To the Chairman of the Board of Grand Trustees, D. E. Lambourne, Salt Lake City, Utah, Lodge No. 85, and to Superintendent of the Home, Robert A. Scott, P. E. R. of Linton, Indiana, Lodge No. 866, and former Chairman of the Board of Grand Trustees.

THE ANTLERS To C. Fenton Nichols, San Francisco, California, Lodge No. 3, who, very definitely, more than any other member of the Order was responsible for the development and the continuation of the Elks Antlers.

CONSTITUTION AND STATUTES To Earl E. James, Oklahoma City, Oklahoma, Lodge No. 417, Chairman of the Committee on Judiciary, 1948 to 1952.

STATE ASSOCIATIONS To Past Grand Exalted Ruler Bruce A. Campbell, who served as Chairman of the Grand Lodge Committee which was responsible for Grand Lodge authorization for such Associations and drafted the laws governing their administration.

3

ELKS MAGAZINE AND ELKS NATIONAL MEMORIAL BUILDING	To Past Grand Exalted Ruler Bruce A. Campbell, Chairman of the Elks National Memorial and Publication Commission.
ELKS NATIONAL FOUNDATION	To Past Grand Exalted Ruler John F. Malley, Chairman, Elks National Foundation.
WORLD WAR II	To Past Grand Exalted Ruler James T. Hallinan, who was Vice-Chairman of the Elks War Commission.
ELKS NATIONAL SERVICE COMMISSION	To Past Grand Exalted Ruler James T. Hallinan, Chairman of that Commission.
RITUAL OF THE ORDER	To Past Grand Exalted Ruler Raymond Benjamin (later deceased), who had served as Chairman of the Ritual Committee of the Grand Lodge, had contributed materially to that Ritual, and probably was better informed relative to its history than any other member of the Order.
	Also, Past Grand Exalted Ruler J. Edgar Masters (Grand Secretary) was consulted in respect to the Ritual material.

During the preparation of this History I have received the fullest possible assistance from the Grand Secretary. His personal knowledge of events and personalities acquired in his long years of membership and service in the Order and the records of his office have provided a wealth of information upon which he has drawn generously to assist in the production of this History.

I am grateful for the interest, consideration and assistance of all the members of the Elks National Memorial and Publication Commission: Past Grand Exalted Rulers Bruce A. Campbell, John R. Coen, Michael F. Shannon, James T. Hallinan and John S. McClelland.

To each of them was submitted, in advance of printing, the entire work, and from them were received suggestions of value.

With gratitude and appreciation is acknowledged the assistance of all who have contributed to the production of this History.

In research and composition suggestions Otho DeVilbiss, Director of Public Relations for the Order, has been of material assistance.

Many among the staff of *The Elks Magazine* have been very helpful.

William H. Magrath, Controller of the Elks National Memorial and Publication Commission, has given his assistance most helpfully to the production of the publication.

John Schmitt, Circulation Manager of the Magazine, has rendered great help in suggestions following his careful and critical reading of the manuscript.

Lee C. Hickey, Editor of *The Elks Magazine,* has lent his knowledge, judgment and experience most importantly to the treatment of various subjects and to the selection and arrangement of illustrations.

Miss Regina Fisher, Associate Editor of the Magazine, has been very helpful in the matter of checking names and dates which her many years with the publication well qualified her to do.

The intelligent cooperation of two successive secretaries to the compiler, Mrs. Janet Tierney and Mrs. Helen Warren, and the assistance of Miss Katherine Anastos and Miss Estelle Levinstone of the Magazine's stenographic staff and of Miss Mildred Schaefer, the secretary to the Director of Public Relations of the Order, has rendered the task much easier.

In the beginning of these introductory remarks I stated that it was to be more a matter of selection rather than of creation, a compilation rather than original writing.

Apparently I succeeded in making it so impersonal that when the History that I regarded as finished was submitted to the members of the Elks National Memorial and Publication Commission and to certain Elks Magazine personnel it was suggested by several that I should editorialize more than I had done.

Suggestions having been asked for it seemed only proper that suggestions made should receive proper consideration.

And so, I decided to accept the suggestions and precede each section of the History by some editorial notes.

I can only hope that I have succeeded in including enough editorial material to satisfy the suggestors and not enough to bore other readers.

James R. Nicholson

REVISOR'S PREFACE

Past Grand Exalted Ruler James R. Nicholson, who compiled THE HISTORY OF THE ORDER OF ELKS 1868-1952, received a moving tribute at the 1965 Grand Lodge session in Miami Beach. The occasion was in honor of the 50th anniversary of his election as Grand Exalted Ruler. Past Grand Exalted Ruler William S. Hawkins, in presenting the resolution on this occasion, said: "This is a unique event in the history of our Order. No other Grand Exalted Ruler has attained to this happy milestone and, such being the nature of things, it is unlikely that any other will do so . . . His is a distinguished record of service without parallel in the history of the Order."

Past Grand Exalted Ruler Nicholson was ill at the time and unable to attend the Convention. He had been requested to record the remarks to be delivered to the Convention and he did so. In his recorded message, Past Grand Exalted Ruler Nicholson said: "From the beginning, the Order of Elks has been dedicated to the welfare of our country and has devoted itself to making the American ideals of liberty, justice, opportunity, and progress a living reality and not just an empty dream. May our patriotism never waver . . . The Order of Elks is a far more powerful force in American life today than it was 50 years ago. It will continue to grow in strength and favor as it remains responsive to new ideas that are soundly conceived, while remaining faithful to the proven values of the past."

It was fortunate that this happy tribute to Past Grand Exalted Ruler Nicholson came at that time for he passed away August 31, 1965 while he was engaged in the work of revising and updating the History originally published in 1952.

At the request of the National Memorial and Publication Commission, publisher of the History, I assumed the responsibility for revising and updating the History.

In so doing, I determined to keep the same plan that Brother Nicholson had followed originally. Furthermore, I decided to follow his example in quoting freely from the writings of various other persons without cluttering up the History with numerous attributions and references.

As a result of my labors, I have gained a better understanding of the demanding task that Brother Nicholson set himself, and a much greater appreciation of his achievement. I hope that, in carrying forward the work begun by him, I have been able in some degree to maintain the standards that he set, and that my revisions will add to the usefulness of this volume.

L. A. Donaldson

SECTION

Origin and General Character of the Order

A very large percentage of the material in Section A comes from the pens of Past Grand Exalted Rulers Detweiler and Harper, Past Grand Trustee Phillips and historian Ellis.

The first three mentioned were all talented writers and eloquent speakers and the last named a tireless, thorough and accurate researcher and a very good writer.

While some of the facts in the Harper "Tribute to the Order" may appear to be dated, the spiritual evaluations are as true and valid as when they were written several years ago.

The Phillips' "Origin of the Order" derives special value from the fact that he was acquainted with some of the actual founders of the Order and had an opportunity to secure his information directly from those participating in the events recorded.

As will be noted, Past Grand Exalted Ruler Detweiler, as the result of the research he made of the early records of the Order under the direction of the Grand Lodge, stated in connection with the Vivian Controversy that it was of the highest importance that full justice should be done to the founder of the Order and that Vivian's

The Founders of the Order

Above appear ten of the fifteen members of the Jolly Corks who founded the Benevolent and Protective Order of Elks. From left to right, they are: E. W. Platt, Frank Langhorne, William Carleton, William Sheppard, Richard R. Steirly, Charles A. Vivian, John T. Kent, Henry Vandemark, Harry Bosworth, M. G. Ash.

G. F. McDonald   W. L. Bowron   Thomas G. Riggs   J. G. Wilton

Above appear the photographs of four more members of the original group of fifteen. Unfortunately, there is no photograph available of John H. Blume, the fifteenth member of the group.

"undoubted claim to the grand distinction should now, and for all time, stand forth in the clear light of day unsullied by a doubt."

The adoption by the Grand Lodge of the Detweiler report could properly be expected to be the final word on this controversy.

However, no attempt has been made in this History to suggest whether or not Charles Algernon Sidney Vivian might properly be referred to as "The Founder of the Benevolent and Protective Order of Elks."

The only purpose and desire I have had has been to place the agreed facts and the controversial statements before readers of this History that each might reach his own conclusion.

A Tribute to the Order

The following is from the pen of Fred Harper, Lynchburg, Va., Lodge No. 321, Past Grand Exalted Ruler:

General Character of the Order

"The Order of Elks is an organization of American citizens who love their country and desire to preserve its cherished institutions; who love their fellow man and seek to promote his well being; and who love the joyousness of life and endeavor to contribute to it, as well as to share it.

"The Order questions no man's religion; nor bars him on account of his creed. It is not concerned with one's political affiliations. And it does not permit either religion or politics to be injected into, or to have any effect upon, its fraternal deliberations, national or local.

"It lures no man to its doors by any promised material benefits which might appeal to his self-interest. It pledges no support to the further-ance of personal ambitions. It has no insurance features to appeal to one's sense of economy. It is beneficent, not merely benevolent, and believes that doing good is better than merely being good. It teaches that it is nobler to serve than to be served; that laughter is better than tears, a kind word more potent than a frown; and that life is all the sweeter for a song.

"It therefore seeks to draw into its fraternal circle only those who delight in wholesome associations with congenial companions; who are deeply imbued with the spirit of patriotic loyalty and devotion; who recognize the obligations of human brotherhood; and who desire, without the fanfare of the trumpets of publicity, to share with their associates in the endeavor to feed the hungry, to shelter the homeless, to relieve those in distress, and to prove themselves true friends to all in need.

"With such a membership, holding such ideals, the Order has grown from a modest but purposeful group of organizers into a great and powerful fraternity whose patriotic services have won for it a high place in national esteem and whose benefactions have smoothed the pathway of countless thousands.

Services Rendered, Charitable and Patriotic

"A primary object of the Order is the practice of charity in its broadest significance, not merely that of alms giving. Its service in this wide field necessarily involves a great diversity of activities which naturally are influenced by local conditions. It therefore early adopted the policy of permitting its subordinate lodges to select for themselves the benevolent endeavors in which they severally desired to engage, rather than to require them to participate in national projects undertaken by the Order as a whole.

"However, throughout practically its entire history as a national fraternity, the Order has endeavored to maintain itself in readiness, as a national body, to extend its aid in cases of major catastrophe and misfortune. Through its official agencies in all parts of the country, it has been able to render such assistance with a promptness, effectiveness and lack of red tape, which have tremendously enhanced the practical helpfulness of its adopted measures.

"A detailed recitation of such activities of the Order would include practically all those calamitous events which occurred in our country during the last half century, and which have necessitated general appeal to our whole people.

"The Order of Elks was the first, and is yet the only national fraternal organization to require each of its subordinate lodges to celebrate Flag Day with appropriate ceremonies. Every year hundreds of thousands of people are thereby reinspired with patriotic zeal and devotion, insuring a better American citizenship.

"Never an altar is erected in all its jurisdiction, but that the first emblem to be reverently placed thereon is the American Flag. No man is permitted to stand in front of that altar and assume the obligation of membership unless he be an American citizen. And at the close of every lodge session he attends he is required to renew his pledge of allegiance to that flag and all for which it stands.

"Every subordinate lodge of the Order is a patriotic watch tower, in which keen minds are alert to discover insidious attacks upon our country's cherished institutions and in which loyal and courageous hearts are promptly mobilized for every appropriate defensive activity.

"The combined influence of these continuing patriotic activities of the Order, operating upon the minds and hearts of its hundreds of thousands of members, and through them upon the minds and hearts of other countless thousands, are beyond calculation.

"For many years the aggregate expenditures of the subordinate lodges for charitable purposes have run into millions of dollars each year, covering humanitarian services of infinite variety. Among the most usual of activities may be mentioned the following: Food to the hungry; shelter for the homeless; clothes and fuel for the needy; milk for the undernourished babies; medical attention to the sick; baskets to the poor at Christmas and Thanksgiving; outings for underprivileged children, entertainment to shut-ins; work for the unemployed; artificial limbs for the maimed; hospital beds; free clinics; night schools and in recent years the care for and entertainment of the members of the Armed Forces. And the list might be indefinitely extended.

"All of the State Associations have undertaken important and extensive charitable works within their own several jurisdictions, determined by the peculiar conditions therein existing and the preferences of their constituent members. They include provisions for scholarships to worthy students, maintenance of orphans, training of the blind, service to hospitalized veterans (and other state-wide projects of similar character and of equal worthiness, which are being carried on as continuing activities). No history of social service in the United States would be complete without an inspiring chapter devoted to the achievements of the Order of Elks in this field.

"In the field of patriotic service, the Order of Elks has likewise proved itself an agency of particular force and effectiveness.

"Organized at a time when the bitterness and rancor of the Civil War left their wounds on every heart on both sides of the Mason and Dixon line, the Order patiently taught its members through the years, drawn as they were from all sections of the country, that bitterness ought to be sweetened; that rancor ought to be assuaged; those wounds ought to be healed.

"Through the widening influence of its members, thus bound together by the ties of brotherhood and thus fraternally schooled, the restoration of national accord was assuredly hastened, and a patriotic service of superlative importance was thus performed."

Origin of the Order

The following article relative to the origin of the Elks was written in 1922 by William T. Phillips, Past Exalted Ruler of New York Lodge and Past Grand Trustee of the Order. He was for many years Secretary of New York Lodge No. 1 and held many official positions in the Grand Lodge. He also was for a few years just preceding his death an editorial writer for *The Elks Magazine*.

Origin of the Elks

BY WILLIAM T. PHILLIPS

"The Benevolent and Protective Order of Elks and New York Lodge No. 1 celebrate their birthday anniversary simultaneously on February 16th of each year, for this was the date that a little coterie of actors styling themselves 'The Jolly Corks,' who for some months had been meeting weekly for social and convivial purposes, decided upon a change of name and the adoption of a more permanent and serious policy than mere conviviality.

"The desire for companionship which brought these men together was also the inspiration for the development of the fraternal instincts which gave birth to America's most distinctive and human brotherhood.

"The object of this brief sketch is to set forth the real facts of the origin of the Order. The story, always interesting, is the story of the expansion of a dream of brotherhood into the greatest of American fraternities.

"On Friday, November 15th, 1867, Charles A. Vivian, an English comic singer, landed in New York via an English trading vessel from Southampton. On the night of his arrival he dropped into the Star Hotel, a 'Free and Easy' kept by John Ireland on Lispenard Street, near Broadway. In spite of its name, the old time 'Free and Easy' was a thoroughly respectable institution. Its specialties were steaks, chops, rarebits and ale, and the patrons were entertained during meals with songs and stories by paid or amateur performers. This form of entertainment, a forerunner of the present cabaret, was a popular institution of that day.

"Richard R. Steirly, also of English birth, was piano player at the Star Hotel. Vivian struck up an acquaintance with him and volunteered to sing a few songs. He made such an impression on John Ireland that the latter sent for his friend, Robert Butler, manager of the American Theatre on Broadway. Vivian sang for Butler, making such a hit that he was engaged for a three weeks' run at the American. When closing time came at the Star Hotel, Steirly took Vivian around to his boarding house at 188 Elm Street, kept by Mrs. Giesman. There he found a collection of congenial spirits, among them William Lloyd Bowron, who afterwards became 'Number One of Number One,' and who had known Vivian in his native land."

The streets in that section of New York have been replotted and their names changed so that the plot known as "188 Elm Street" can now be found on Lafayette Street in the block between Broome and Spring Streets.

In 1939 the Council of the City of New York passed the following resolution: "Be it resolved . . . that the two blocks remaining on Elm Street be known as Elk Street to pay tribute to the famous Order of Elks which was founded on that street in the year 1867."

It was really the Jolly Corks that was "founded" at that address in 1867. Elk Street now extends for two blocks north of City Hall between Chambers and Worth Streets.

"On November 23rd, 1867, Dick Steirly went to the American Theatre to take notes for the purpose of orchestrating some of Vivian's songs. After the matinee, Vivian took Steirly over to 'Sandy' Spencer's place at Broadway and Fulton Street. There they met Hughey Dougherty, Cool Burgess and Henry Vandemark. The latter suggested that the party shake dice for the refreshments.

"Vivian replied that he never handled the cubes, but would show them a new game. Calling for three corks he gave one each to Steirly and Vandemark, keeping the other for himself. He asked Cool Burgess to be the judge, and Dougherty to count '1-2-3.' They rehearsed the trick of each dropping his cork on the bar and picking it up as rapidly as possible, several times, the idea conveyed to the initiated being that the last man to lift his cork was to buy. Vivian then gave the word of command, Dougherty counted. He and Steirly passed their hands over their corks while Vandemark, eager to lift his cork from the bar, was both first and last to pick it up, and consequently was 'stuck' for the round. This was the first introduction of a delectable form of amusement which became popular.

Birth of the Jolly Corks

"At about this time the excise law was being strictly enforced, and Sunday in New York City was a very dry day. Devotees of the cork trick formed the habit of congregating at Mrs. Giesman's on this day to hold social conventions under the inspiring influence of a stock of beer laid in the night before. This little coterie styled itself the 'Corks,' with Vivian as the 'Imperial Cork.'

"The revels of the jolly crew meeting at Mrs. Giesman's became disturbing to the other boarders and she finally required them to forego their Sunday gatherings in her house. Quarters were found at 17 Delancey Street, over a saloon kept by one Paul Sommers, where the meetings were continued. The object of the 'Corks' at this time was entirely convivial. Its membership was composed of professional and semi-professional entertainers with a sprinkling of legitimate actors. Among the latter were Thomas G. Riggs, George F. McDonald, William Sheppard and George W. Thompson, a theatrical agent. When the cork trick was tried on McDonald it amused him so that he called the coterie the 'Jolly Corks,' and as such it has gone down upon the pages of history.

"In a little pamphlet written by Brother Charles W. Young, devoted to the origin of the Order, he says: In the latter part of December—just before the holidays—Charles Vivian, Hugh Egan, Hughey Dougherty, Harry Stanwood and George Guy, returning one afternoon from a funeral of a friend—Ted Quinn, of local concert hall fame—dropped into Tony Pastor's. There they found Billy Gray, Tony and 'Dody' Pastor, John Fielding and William Sheppard, who became interested in the story of the 'Jolly Corks,' and all of them strolled over from Pastor's to 'Sandy' Spencer's, where they found George F. McDonald and others.

"After hearing the story of the funeral the 'Jolly Corks' had attended McDonald suggested that the organization should become 'a pro tective and benevolent society.' During the next week or ten days McDonald broached the idea to a number of 'Jolly Corks' including William Carleton, William Sheppard, Tom Riggs and others.

"At the meeting held on the 2nd of February, 1868, presided over by Charles A. Vivian, George F. McDonald offered a motion to organize 'The Jolly Corks' as a lodge along benevolent and fraternal lines and providing that a committee be appointed to formulate rules and regulations for its government, prepare a suitable ritual, and select a new name. According to Meade D. Detweiler's history, this com mittee consisted of Richard Steirly, Thomas G. Riggs, Henry Vandemark, George F. McDonald and Charles A. Vivian, ex-officio. Vivian having in mind an English organization, 'The Royal Antediluvian Order of Buffalos,' favored the name 'Buffalos' for the new organization, but the majority were desirous of bestowing a distinctively American title upon the new organization.

"It is said that the actual work of the committee was done by George W. Thompson, William Lloyd Bowron and Thomas G. Riggs. Referring again to Brother Detweiler's book we find the suggestion of the name attributed to a fine elk's head which occupied a conspicuous place in 'Barnum's Museum,' then located at Broadway and Ann Street. The committee later visited Cooper Institute Library, where the Brothers found the elk described in a work on Natural History as an animal 'fleet of foot, timorous of wrong, but ever ready to combat in defense of self or the female of the species.' This descrip tion appealed to the committee as containing admirable qualities for emulation by members of a benevolent fraternity and the title 'Elk' was incorporated in its report.

Birth of the Order of Elks

"On February 16, 1868, the committee reported, recommending that the 'Jolly Corks' be merged into the Benevolent and Protective Order of Elks and the recommendation was adopted by a vote of 8 to 7. It is chronicled by Brother Charles W. Young that the following seven voted for the name 'Buffalo':

Charles A. Vivian
Richard R. Steirly
M. G. Ash
Henry Vandemark
Harry Bosworth
Frank Langhorne
E. W. Platt

and the following eight voted for the name 'Elk':

George F. McDonald
George W. Thompson
Thomas Grattan Riggs
William Carleton
William Sheppard
George Guy
Hugh Dougherty
William Lloyd Bowron

"W. L. Bowron was inclined at first to favor 'Buffalo' but changed his mind and became the decisive factor in the final selection of the name 'Elk.' Other historians say that the vote was a tie and that Vivian was finally brought around to favor the name 'Elk' and cast the deciding vote from the chair.

"Brother Young, however, due to a twist of memory, which is quite likely to occur when writing so many years after the meeting described took place, credits George Guy and Hugh Dougherty with being present and voting for the change of name. These two names were not among the original fifteen Elks, though both were members of the 'Jolly Corks,' and their names have been used by Brother Young in place of John H. Blume and John T. Kent.

"With the elimination of the names of Guy and Dougherty and the substitution of Blume and Kent, the names of the founders as given by Brother Young are correct."

While Phillips substitutes John T. Kent and John H. Blume for George Guy and Hugh Dougherty, Detweiler, while agreeing with Phillips in respect to these two names, does disagree with him as to another name. He places on the list the name of J. G. Wilton but does not include George W. Thompson.

As to Thompson, there appears the following reference to him in the Detweiler history:

"After the reorganization of February, 1868, under the title of B. P. O. E., Vivian, as Right Honorable Primo, presided at one session of the lodge in which he conferred the First Degree upon a number of brothers, among them being George W. Thompson, who so informed the writer."

Past Grand Exalted Ruler Detweiler, in his report on the organization of the Order of Elks, states that he secured his information from George W. Thompson, William L. Bowron, Richard R. Steirly, John T. Kent, E. W. Platt, Henry Vandemark, John H. Blume and Harry Bosworth, all members of the Jolly Corks, and R. S. Martin, who became a member shortly after the organization and who later was Secretary of New York Lodge and Grand Secretary of the Order.

Where Phillips secured his information it is impossible to say at this time.

Each of them, however, failed to include among the fifteen original members of the Order the name of the well-known minstrel and manager, George Guy, where Charles W. Young, in his pamphlet, does place him. (Charles W. Young was initiated in New York Lodge in December, 1875.)

It is interesting to note that Guy, in a letter written to members of the Order in a later year, tells about his attendance at meetings of the Jolly Corks and says that he took his first degree as an Elk in May, 1868, and his second degree in August, 1868. He says:

"I think you will find me about tenth in the roll. I can refer you to Brothers R. S. Martin and Tony Pastor.

"Our charter was read, rules and by-laws endorsed, approved and adopted on a Sunday, dating 16th of February, 1868."

This Guy letter was written in protest against any statute prohibiting the holding of lodge meetings on Sunday evenings as unfair to the members of the theatrical profession who founded the Order.

His letter, of considerable length, was printed for broad distribution among members of the fraternity and one of these printed copies is now in the possession of his grandson, Arthur Guy, the guide at the Elks National Memorial Building.

The Phillips article continued as follows:

"At the same meeting the following officers were elected:

> Charles A. Vivian, *Right Honorable Primo*
> Richard Steirly, *First Assistant Primo*
> William Lloyd Bowron, *Second Assistant Primo*
> James W. Glenn, *Third Assistant Primo*
> William Carleton, *Recording Secretary*
> Henry Vandemark, *Tiler*

"A Committee on Constitution and By-Laws was appointed which reported early in March. The Constitution it presented provided for two degrees and the ritualistic work of these two degrees was adopted May 17, 1868. The Committee on Ritual was George W. Thompson,

Charles E. Ellis, in his History, states that the Jolly Corks remained at 17 Delancey Street only for a period of four weeks, when they moved to the top floor of Military Hall at 193 Bowery.

Three days before the 80th birthday of the Order, Grand Exalted Ruler L. A. Lewis, accompanied by a group of Past Grand Exalted Rulers and other important officers of the Order, placed a plaque, of which there is a reproduction to the right, on that building.

Below appears a reproduction of a photograph of those in attendance.

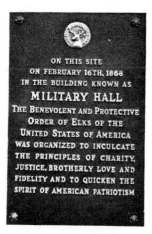

ON THIS SITE
ON FEBRUARY 16TH, 1868
IN THE BUILDING KNOWN AS
MILITARY HALL
THE BENEVOLENT AND PROTECTIVE ORDER OF ELKS OF THE UNITED STATES OF AMERICA WAS ORGANIZED TO INCULCATE THE PRINCIPLES OF CHARITY, JUSTICE, BROTHERLY LOVE AND FIDELITY AND TO QUICKEN THE SPIRIT OF AMERICAN PATRIOTISM

In the above picture there appear the following: Left to right, Past Grand Exalted Ruler Wade H. Kepner, Special Deputy Floyd H. Brown, William M. Frasor, Executive Secretary of the Elks National Veterans Service Commission, Past Grand Exalted Ruler David Sholtz, Grand Esteemed Lecturing Knight H. H. Russell, Past Grand Exalted Ruler James T. Hallinan, Grand Exalted Ruler Lewis, Past Grand Exalted Rulers J. Edgar Masters, Grand Secretary, Henry C. Warner and E. Mark Sullivan, Grand Treasurer Joseph B. Kyle, Past Grand Exalted Rulers Bruce A. Campbell, Frank J. Lonergan, Michael F. Shannon and James R. Nicholson, and Emmett T. Anderson, a member of the Elks National Veterans Service Commission.

17

William Lloyd Bowron, George F. McDonald, Thomas G. Riggs, William Sheppard, James Glenn and Henry Vandemark.

"Most of the work was done by George F. McDonald, who was a fine actor, a man of deep sentiment and possessed of considerable literary ability.

"With the beginning of the Benevolent and Protective Order of Elks a breech was opened between two factions within the ranks, which rapidly developed into a feud. On one hand were the legitimate actors, endeavoring to invest the new organization with principles and ideals in keeping with a benevolent and fraternal institution, while on the other were the semi-professional entertainers more in sympathy with the original purposes of the convivial 'Jolly Corks.' Charles Vivian was leader of the latter faction, and when he appeared for the second degree on June 14, 1868, the professionals who were in command ordered a ballot and he was rejected. At the same time a number of Vivian's friends were barred from the meeting and afterwards declared expelled.

"This incident ended Vivian's connection with the Benevolent and Protective Order of Elks. He died in Leadville, Colorado, March 20, 1880, twelve years later, of pneumonia. His life in the theatrical profession was one of many vicissitudes. He had toured with his own company, stranded, traveled the usual up and down hill road of the strolling player. He was a clever entertainer, a man of charming personality, but improvident, careless of tomorrow, living in the fullness of each day. On April 28, 1889, the remains of Charles Vivian were exhumed and taken to Boston, under the auspices of Boston Lodge No. 10, where they rest in Mt. Hope Cemetery. As far as can be learned from personal friends, Vivian never claimed to have been an Elk. He did claim to have been one of the organizers of the Elks, which he was, but he never took the degrees of the Order, and severed all connections with it a few months after it was born.

"The proceedings of the meeting of June 14th and the expulsion of Vivian and his associates, may have been illegal and perhaps did not square with strict interpretation of the principles of justice, but it must be said in extenuation of those responsible that they considered only the elimination of what they believed an undesirable element. They were actuated by high motives, and desired to establish standards of membership by which they hoped the Order's future would be measured.

'Some of the brothers expelled with Vivian were reinstated by order of the Grand Lodge some years later and became honored members of the Order and were respected citizens of their communities. It is safe to say that none of them realized at the time of their disagreements with the early Elks the import of the movement which merged the 'Jolly Corks' in the Benevolent and Protective Order of Elks, or of the wonderful destiny the Order was to fulfill.

"George F. McDonald, who was responsible for the merger, however, was a man who visualized the future and saw the great possibilities of an Order devoted to the practice of Charity and Brotherly Love, and it is recorded that in the early 70's he predicted to Ben McGinley and Billy Dutton that within fifty years the Elks would have a membership of one million. The first presiding officer of the Benevolent a id Protective Order of Elks was Charles A. Vivian, who, under the title of Right Honorable Primo, occupied the chair from February 18th to May 24th, 1868.

"On May 17th the degree ritual was adopted and election was ordered for May 24th, when Charles Vivian was to be continued as presiding officer. He was absent from New York on that date and the following were elected:

George W. Thompson	Right Honorable Primo and Exalted Ruler
James W. Glenn	First Assistant Primo and Esteemed Leading Knight
William Lloyd Bowron	Second Assistant Primo and Esteemed Loyal Knight
George F. McDonald	Third Assistant Primo and Esteemed Lecturing Knight
William Sheppard	Secretary
Henry Vandemark	Treasurer
Albert Hall	Tiler

"The initiation fee for the two degrees was $2.00.

"The Elks continued to meet in the Delancey Street quarters for about a month after the adoption of the ritual but the membership increased so rapidly that a larger place was made necessary and the organization moved into larger quarters at Military Hall, 193 Bowery.

"With this move the initiation fee was increased to $5.00.

"The first Exalted Ruler — George W. Thompson — was elected May 24th, 1868, when Vivian, who was slated for the office, did not appear. He was succeeded by George J. Green, who was Exalted Ruler for the term of 1870-1871.

The Grand Lodge

"During that year a movement was started by Philadelphia professionals for a lodge in their city. New York Lodge, in the meantime, had become incorporated and it became necessary, if the Order were to expand, for the members of New York Lodge to give up their title

FIRST CHARTER OF THE GRAND LODGE

The first Charter of the Grand Lodge. It was granted to New York Lodge No. 1 at a meeting held on February 19, 1871, but the Charter was dated effective February 12, 1871.

and rights to a Grand Lodge. Accordingly, a Committee was appointed on December 4th, 1870, to devise ways and means for the formation of a Grand Lodge. This Committee reported on January 1st, 1871, the following resolution, which was unanimously adopted:

> 'Resolved that the first Grand Lodge of the Benevolent and Protective Order of Elks consist of the following: The original founders of the Order, together with all the present and past officers of the First and Second Degrees, who are now in good standing with the Order, and that the above take effect immediately.'

"On February 12, 1871, Brother Claude Goldie applied for and received, from the newly organized Grand Lodge, a dispensation for New York Lodge No. 1.

"This brings us to the end of the story of the foundation, and marks the beginning of the great American fraternity which has since spread to every corner of our country's possessions.

"The roster of the Order at its Foundation was a list of leaders of the amusement profession. Today it contains the names of 815,000 American citizens, leaders in all walks of life and of every degree of wealth and influence.

"Out of the heart-throbs of a few actors, fifteen hundred and thirty lodges have been born, each inculcating the principles of the founders, and urging the emulation of the qualities attributed to the animal from which the Order derives its name. In the words of Brother George F. McDonald, the Elks are urged to become "strong of limb, fleet of foot, quick and keen of perception; quick to see or hear the sign or cry of distress, timorous of doing wrong and fleet of foot to aid the unfortunate."

The Vivian Controversy

At the session of the Grand Lodge in Minneapolis in 1897, the Grand Trustees were directed to secure for publication and permanent preservation the minutes of the Grand Lodge from 1871 to 1878 inclusive.

It was designed that these should serve as a permanent and unchallengeable authentic record of the birth and early days of the Order. The Grand Trustees entrusted Grand Exalted Ruler Detweiler with the responsibility of doing that work.

Following consultation with all available participants in the activities of the preceding years of our Order and a complete and exhaustive research, Grand Exalted Ruler Detweiler stated that he regarded it as forever settled that Charles A. Vivian "is the man to whom belongs the honorable title of 'Founder of Elks,' inasmuch as the suggestion of perpetuity was made by him."

At the time Grand Exalted Ruler Detweiler made his report, of the fifteen original "Jolly Corks" the following nine were living:

Richard R. Steirly, *pianist and teacher*

John T. Kent, *clerk*

Henry Vandemark, *clerk*

E. N. Platt, *clerk*

Harry Bosworth, *clothing business*

John H. Blume, *advertising agency clerk*

Frank Langhorne, *photographer*

William L. Bowron, *orchestra leader*

Thomas G. Riggs, *actor*

The deceased members were:

Charles A. S. Vivian, *comic singer*

M. G. Ash, *photographer*

William Carleton, *Irish comedian*

William Sheppard, *black-face minstrel-man*

George F. McDonald, *actor*

J. G. Wilton, *wood-turner*

While there may be some repetition in Grand Exalted Ruler Detweiler's report of facts relative to the early history of the Order and the part that Charles Algernon Sidney Vivian played therein appearing in the Phillips' report, it seems appropriate that in a history of this character both should be included.

The Detweiler History

The following extracts from Grand Exalted Ruler Detweiler's report have a direct or an indirect bearing on the question of whether Vivian was the founder of the Elks and a full-fledged member of the Order.

"After the reorganization of February, 1868, under the title of Benevolent and Protective Order of Elks, Vivian, as Right Honorable Primo, presided at one session of the lodge in which he conferred the First Degree upon a number of brothers.

"Necessitated soon after to leave New York for Philadelphia, in the pursuit of his vocation, Brother Steirly, as the next highest officer, presided in Vivian's absence.

"The first ball under the auspices of the Order was given at Ferraro's Assembly Rooms on April 16, 1868.

"Vivian attended this initial ball and made an address.

"At the time of the adoption of the Ritual for the Second Degree, May 17, 1868, Vivian, who was to have continued as presiding officer, was not present and election was held for new officers with the following results:

George W. Thompson	Right Honorable Primo and Exalted Ruler
James Glenn	First Assistant Primo and Esteemed Leading Knight
William Lloyd Bowron	Second Assistant Primo and Esteemed Loyal Knight
George F. McDonald	Third Assistant Primo and Esteemed Lecturing Knight
Henry Vandemark	Treasurer
William Sheppard	Secretary
Albert Hall	Tiler

"At the next meeting of the lodge, May 24, 1868, Brother Thompson conferred the ritualistic work of the Second Degree upon the First Degree members who had not been members of the Committee on Ritual.

"These included Kent, Steirly, Vandemark, Platt and other friends of Vivian, whose rights as Elks were thus firmly established and fully recognized. Vivian, however, was still absent from the city on professional engagements.

The First Benefit

"The first benefit given for the purpose of augmenting the funds of the new organization was on Monday afternoon, June 8, 1868, at the Academy of Music.

"The wording of the announcements advertising the benefit in the *New York Herald,* which appeared from June 2nd to June 8th, read as shown on the following page.

ACADEMY OF MUSIC

Monday Afternoon, June 8th

THE ENTERTAINMENT OF THE AGE!

COLOSSAL MUSIC FESTIVAL!

FIRST ANNUAL BENEFIT

of the

PERFORMERS' BENEVOLENT AND PROTECTIVE ORDER OF ELKS

"The use of the word 'Performers' in this advertisement to qualify the title of the Order, breathes a hint of factionalism wherein the legitimate actors plotted deliberately to take the Order for their own.

"An incident connected with this benefit was the beginning of an act of injustice to a number of worthy brothers which was never righted until the session of the Grand Lodge in 1893, and then only in the name of a single member.

"From this time also may be dated the efforts which appear to have been set forth to rob Brother Vivian of his well-deserved laurels as the founder of our Order.

"On the occasion of this benefit, Vivian returned from Philadelphia where he was then employed, for the purpose of assisting.

"Before his departure from New York he had been presented by his associates with an elegant gold Elk badge.

"When, therefore, full of zeal and enthusiasm for the success of the society which he had organized, he came back to find that his name did not appear on either programs or posters, he was naturally somewhat angered and his cause was warmly espoused by a number of staunch friends.

The Start of the Break

"What occurred at that time precipitated an unseemly altercation at the next meeting of the lodge, June 14, 1868, when an attempt was made to summarily expel Vivian, but his friends objected.

"So vigorous were the protests of the aggrieved brethren that the meeting adjourned without taking action and no further attempt was ever made in regard to the expulsion of Vivian as he never afterwards sought admission.

"But one week thereafter when Steirly, Kent, Bosworth and other friends of Vivian presented themselves at the lodge room they were met by a number of his opponents, reinforced by a policeman, and notified they could not enter.

"Brother Kent having demanded an explanation from Brother George F. McDonald, received the reply that in future none but professionals would be permitted to enter the Order.

"Later they were informed they could be admitted by giving the new password which had been written on cards which were enclosed in envelopes that were only distributed to those in sympathy with the opposition to Vivian.

"Later, without trial, notice of any accusation, or any opportunity for defense, Vivian, Steirly, Kent, Bosworth, Vandemark, Platt, Ash, Blume and Langhorne were notified that they had been expelled.

"The so-called expulsion of these brethren was illegal and void. In the case of Steirly, the injustice was corrected by the Grand Lodge, at Detroit, in 1893.

"At the risk of appearing prolix, the Grand Exalted Ruler desires to present briefly a resume of a few facts in connection with the idea that has sometimes been advanced that Vivian is not entitled to the credit of being regarded as the founder of the Elks; for he believes it to be of the highest importance that full justice should be done to the memory of our founder and that his undoubted claim to the grand distinction should now, and for all time, stand forth in the clear light of day unsullied by a doubt.

"The trouble hitherto has seemed to be that some few claimed that he was never an Elk. Upon examination it appears that the reason urged for this view was the fact that Vivian had never received the Second Degree and upon the further pretense that the Benevolent and Protective Order of Elks was not fully organized until the work of this degree had been adopted, May 17, 1868.

"In the light of the Constitution already referred to and the name thereon—Benevolent and Protective Order of Elks— this claim is futile and valueless; and after the exhaustive investigation which has now been made and the mass of evidence which has been adduced, it should never be heard again.

"Vivian was the first presiding officer of the original lodge of Elks, but for reasons already given, over which he had no control, never received the Second Degree or perfected ritual.

The Death of Vivian

"Before passing from this branch of the resume of Elks history, it will not be inappropriate to mention the death of Brother Vivian.

"It occurred at Leadville, Colorado, March 20, 1880, the cause of death being pneumonia. Vivian, who was thus cut down at the early age of 34, was one of the most versatile men in his profession, gifted with a wonderful voice and of a genial nature that won for him friends wherever he went.

"His funeral was quite an event in Leadville, which was then the center of those great gold mining enterprises which had produced the wonderful influx of adventurers and wealth seekers from every land. It took place on the Sunday following his decease being under the care of the 'Forty-Niners,' who spared no expense, the casket containing his remains having cost $600. The whole population turned out and with a band of music accompanied to the cemetery the remains of the deceased actor.

"March 17, 1889, the Honorable W. C. VanDerlip, Chairman of the Board of Grand Trustees, called the attention of Boston Lodge to the fact that the grave of the founder of the Order was in neglected condition, only rudely marked by a wooden slab, on which the name had been scratched with a nail.

"To the everlasting credit of Boston Lodge, be it said, that the information was followed by prompt action for the removal of the remains to a more appropriate resting place.

"In this Brother VanDerlip and the Boston Lodge had the prompt cooperation of members of Denver Lodge and of Brother W. F. Bechel of Omaha Lodge.

"April 28, 1889, all that was mortal of Charles Vivian was given an honored place in the beautiful Elks Rest in Mt. Hope Cemetery, Boston, where soon after an artistic and suitable monument was erected in his memory."

Controversy Started Early

The Order had been in existence only three years when the question of who was justified in being recognized as the founder thereof received the attention of the members.

On June 11, 1871, at the Grand Lodge Session held on that date, it was voted that "a committee be appointed to make inquiry as to who founded the B.P.O.E., said committee to have power to call for books, papers, etc."

George F. McDonald, A. H. Mulligan and Thomas G. Riggs were appointed as members of this committee.

Careful reading of minutes of the Grand Lodge Session for the next two years discloses no report of that committee.

Thus, a question and a cause for controversy and dispute, instead of being solved in the early days when necessary facts were available from those who had participated in the founding of the Order, was left for the attempted solutions of those who came in later years and had not the same facilities for solving the problem that were in the possession of or available to the members of the committee appointed in 1871.

New York Lodge Committee

In 1905, New York Lodge No. 1 selected a Vivian Committee composed of the following:

> Champe S. Andrews, *Exalted Ruler*
> Arthur C. Moreland, *Past Exalted Ruler*
> James J. Armstrong, *Past Exalted Ruler*
> Thomas F. Brogan, *Past Exalted Ruler*
> Edward Leach, *Past Exalted Ruler*
> Bernard J. Fagan, *Secretary*

to study the justification for the claim that Vivian was the founder of the Benevolent and Protective Order of Elks.

At a meeting held on February 19, 1905, Richard R. Steirly testified before the Committee. He said that Vivian suggested the "Jolly Corks" and that name.

He also said that when it was voted to change the name to the Benevolent and Protective Order of Elks, Vivian was elected Right Honorable Primo, which was the name that the Exalted Ruler went under at that time. He also testified that Vivian was a member of the Committee that drew up the Constitution, Rules and Regulations and that Vivian presided the night that the Constitution, Rules and Regulations were adopted.

William Lloyd Bowron testified that Vivian was opposed to the change of name. He did say, however, that Vivian acted as presiding officer after the name was changed.

It has been impossible to find the report of this Committee in the records of New York Lodge.

Boston Lodge Committee

Boston Lodge also formed a committee to study the whole Vivian controversy. This Committee consisted of:

George M. Hosmer, *Past Exalted Ruler*, CHAIRMAN
A. C. Smith, *Past Exalted Ruler*
M. Ambrose Hannon, *Past Exalted Ruler*
Edwin A. Perry, *Past Grand Exalted Ruler*
William A. Blossom, *Past Exalted Ruler*

That Committee reported that:

1. Vivian originated the idea of changing the society known as the "Jolly Corks" from a body entirely social in its purpose to a fraternal benevolent society.

2. That he was presiding officer of the "Jolly Corks" and was the first presiding officer of the Benevolent and Protective Order of Elks and that he was the active leader in the creation of the latter body.

3. That he rearranged the first ritual used by the Order which afterwards with slight changes became the ritual of the First Degree and a portion of which continued in use in the Elks work.

The Committee endorsed the stand taken by Past Grand Exalted Ruler Detweiler in his report and said "we agree fully with the deduction made by Brother Detweiler."

In connection with the name of "Jolly Corks" which became the Benevolent and Protective Order of Elks, the Committee reported as follows:

"It was proposed to organize a benevolent order from this society and on Sunday, February 16, 1868, the first meeting was held and the name Elk was adopted by a vote of 8 to 7.

"Brother Vivian favored the name of Buffalo after that of an English Benevolent Order of which he was a member, but was outvoted, but at the same time he was elected as presiding officer and given the title of Right Honorable Primo which title was used in the first degree until 1883. In March, 1868, a Constitution was adopted.

"Provision was made in this Constitution for two degrees and a committee was appointed to prepare a ritual for the same. This Constitution was printed at the time and was used and copies given to initiates as late as 1869. Vivian's name appears on this on the 3rd and 4th and 12th pages as the presiding officer."

The Thompson Pamphlet

In the *Elks-Antler* of July, 1914, Arthur C. Moreland, former Grand Secretary, and editor and publisher of the *Elks-Antler*, carried an article with the title of "The Vivian Myth."

In this he quoted from a pamphlet by George W. Thompson, the First Exalted Ruler, as follows:

"The History published by the Grand Exalted Ruler in statements of facts, is in a great measure correct, but one sentence in his introductory remarks to the History, I cannot in justice to the Order and the Brothers who were instrumental in its foundation permit to pass, without submitting the following facts which I leave to the judgment of the Brothers to determine as to the accuracy of my position.

"The sentence in Brother Detweiler's History to which I take exception is:

'The Grand Exalted Ruler regards as forever settled beyond any cavil or question, the fact that Brother Vivian is the man to whom belongs the honorable title of "Founder of the Elks," inasmuch as the suggestion of perpetuity was made by him, and which he believes will be fully demonstrated by a careful perusal of the following brief epitome of the various steps of evolution accompanying the institution of an Order of which we are proud to be members.'

"In my objections to the position taken by Brother Detweiler I can merely offer the facts within my own knowledge substantiated by competent evidence, and I do not dispute anything but this one particular paragraph, and if, after having told my story, the verdict should be against me, I will bow with submission, but I can hardly believe that the story of Mr. Vivian's connection with the Order, can of itself, give his claim to the title of Founder, which he never, by any possibility while in life, asserted."

GEORGE J. GREEN
1871

CHARLES T. WHITE
1871-72

JOSEPH C. PINCKNEY
1872-74

Exalted Grand Rulers

FIRST DECADE

1868-1878

HENRY P. O'NEIL
1874-76

FRANK GIRARD
1876-78

Note: Ellis, who was an indefatigable researcher, says in his book as to a photograph of Exalted Grand Ruler James W. Powell (1874): "A distant relative states positively that Mr. Powell was never known to have had a picture taken."

S E C T I O N

First Decade

From February, 1868, to January, 1871, the Order of Elks was a single lodge. However, in that first period of time the group had adopted a Constitution, Rules and Regulations and a Ritual providing for two degrees. It had also created the Eleven O'Clock Toast observance and its membership had grown from 15 to 289.

Only a short time passed before the fame of this new fraternal group spread, largely, undoubtedly, because such a large percentage of its membership consisted of people of the theatrical profession who moved from town to town professionally.

Particularly was there a strong interest in Philadelphia in having a similar and associated group in that city.

The idea appealed to the members of the New York group and in January, 1871, the Grand Lodge was formed and Charter Number 1 was issued to New York Lodge and Charter Number 2 to Philadelphia Lodge.

Just at the end of this decade, the Order had its only experience with an insurance auxiliary—a brief one, as is indicated in the story of its temporary adjunct, known as the Elks Mutual Benefit Association.

During this period there was held the first Lodge of Sorrow, the forerunner of the present Elk Memorial Sunday.

In 1877 a meeting of the Grand Lodge was held in Philadelphia. However, the legality of its being outside of New York was questioned and the meeting resumed in New York City and all legislation was repassed in that city.

During this period the original Constitution of February 19, 1871, was followed by that of 1874 and that in turn succeeded by the Constitution of 1878.

This was a period when elaborate regalia was adopted for Grand Lodge officers and subordinate lodge officers and somewhat less striking adornment for the lay members. A meeting in those days must have been a very impressive affair.

By the end of the first decade there were ten lodges with a membership of 820.

First Decade—1868-1878

PRESIDING OFFICERS

CHARLES ALGERNON SIDNEY VIVIAN	Right Honorable Primo February 16, 1868 to May 17, 1868
GEORGE W. THOMPSON	Right Honorable Primo May 17, 1868 to November 13, 1870
GEORGE W. THOMPSON	Exalted Ruler May 24, 1868 to December 4, 1870
GEORGE J. GREEN	Right Honorable Primo November 13, 1870 to February 18, 1871
GEORGE J. GREEN	Exalted Ruler December 4, 1870 to February 18, 1871

The first Grand Exalted Ruler (then called Exalted Grand Ruler) of the Order was George J. Green. He served February 12, 1871, to December 10, 1871. He was succeeded by the following Exalted Grand Rulers: *

CHARLES T. WHITE, New York Lodge No. 1

December 10, 1871 to December 8, 1872

JOSEPH C. PINCKNEY, New York Lodge No. 1

December 8, 1872 to February 1, 1874

JAMES W. POWELL, Philadelphia Lodge No. 2

February 1, 1874 to December 13, 1874

HENRY P. O'NEIL, New York Lodge No. 1

December 13, 1874 to December 10, 1876

FRANK GIRARD, New York Lodge No. 1

December 10, 1876 to December 8, 1878

GRAND SECRETARIES

At the first regular session of the Grand Lodge, held in New York on February 12, 1871, E. G. Browne was elected Grand Secretary. At that meeting William Coffin acted as Grand Secretary *pro tem*.

E. G. Browne served until December 10, 1871, when Alex H. Mulligan was elected Grand Secretary.

At the session of the Grand Lodge held on June 16, 1872, Thomas G. Gaynor was elected "Grand Recording and Corresponding Secretary."

Henry P. O'Neil acted as Grand Secretary *pro tem* at that meeting.

William Coffin was elected Grand Secretary December 8, 1872. He served as Grand Secretary for five years until December 9, 1877. Henry P. O'Neil was elected to that position and served for one year.

MEMBERSHIP

During the first decade the membership of the Order grew to 820. That membership (as of November 3, 1878) was divided as follows:

---

* The title of the presiding officer of the Grand Lodge was changed to Grand Exalted Ruler in 1890.

New York No. 1 263
Philadelphia No. 2 76
San Francisco No. 3 79
Chicago No. 4 82
Cincinnati No. 5 70
Sacramento No. 6 ....Charter Surrendered
Baltimore No. 7 42
Louisville No. 8 51
St. Louis No. 9 56
Boston No. 10 88
Pittsburgh No. 11 13

820

VALUE OF LODGE PROPERTY AND EXPENDITURES FOR RELIEF

At the end of this first decade (1878) the ten lodges reported lodge property valued at $21,048.42.

Expenditures for relief were in the amount of $2,854.65 for the year ending November 3, 1878.

The Early Years

NOVEMBER 15, 1867

Charles Algernon Sidney Vivian landed in New York from England.

NOVEMBER 23, 1867

Vivian introduced the so-called "cork trick" to Richard Steirly, Hugh Dougherty, Cool Burgess and Henry Vandemark which resulted in the creation of the "Jolly Corks." From that time on the group met regularly on Sunday evenings in the boarding house owned by Mrs. Giesman at 188 Elm Street.

Shortly afterward the group, which had grown rather large for Mrs. Giesman's quarters and whose social sessions, it has been reported, Mrs. Giesman finally concluded were a little too noisy, found quarters at 17 Delancey Street.

At this time the initiation fee was increased from 50¢ to $2.00.

At the meeting presided over by Vivian, George F. McDonald made a motion that the original "Jolly Corks" become a fraternity along benevolent and fraternal lines and that a Committee be appointed to make up rules and regulations therefor.

FEBRUARY 16, 1868

The Committee reported and recommended that the "Jolly Corks" be merged into the "Benevolent and Protective Order of Elks." The report was adopted. At that meeting Vivian, who presided, was elected Right Honorable Primo.

A Committee on Constitution and By-Laws was appointed which reported early in March.

The new Order of Elks continued to meet on Delancey Street for about a month after it came into existence.

Membership increased so rapidly that it was necessary to have more extended accommodations and the organization moved to the upper floor of Military Hall, 193 Bowery.

At this time the initiation fee was increased to $5.00.

APRIL 16, 1868

The first ball under the auspices of the Order was held at Ferraro's Assembly Rooms at Broadway and 28th Street.

APRIL 17, 1868

William H. Brown was authorized to close transactions for the occupancy of Masonic (later Clarendon) Hall on 13th Street at the best possible price. This was carried unanimously and Tony Pastor and William Korff were added to the Committee. The Committee reported on April 24th, and the change of location was made May 1, 1870, although the lodge met for a time at 720 Broadway, pending alterations of the Masonic Hall.

At the time of the move to Masonic Hall the initiation fee was raised to $20.00, being $10.00 for each degree.

The more commodious quarters secured and the increase in fee for admission to the Order indicated unmistakably the vigorous growth of the lodge which had now passed the crucial period of its infancy and was rapidly developing into a stalwart and healthy manhood.

MAY 17, 1868

A Constitution providing for two degrees and ritualistic work for the degrees was adopted.

MAY 24, 1868

George W. Thompson was elected Right Honorable Primo (for the First Degree) and Exalted Ruler (for the Second Degree).

MAY 31, 1868

George McDonald suggested a toast "To Our Absent Brothers" and thus created the Eleven O'Clock Toast.

JUNE 8, 1868

The first benefit of the new association was held at the Academy of Music at 14th Street and Irving Place.

JUNE 14, 1868

At a meeting on this date Vivian appeared to take the Second Degree but was rejected.

NOVEMBER 13, 1870

George J. Green elected Right Honorable Primo.

DECEMBER 4, 1870

George J. Green elected Exalted Ruler.

DECEMBER 4, 1870

Antonio Pastor offered a motion that steps be taken to form an "Exalted Grand Lodge."

DECEMBER 25, 1870

The first Ladies' Social in the annals of Elkdom was held as the result of a motion made by Antonio Pastor at the meeting of November 27th of the same year, viz:

> "That the lodge set apart an evening for the purpose of inviting our mothers, wives, sisters and female friends to our social session and that no male friends be admitted on that evening."

When the evening indicated by the lodge for this purpose arrived, the regular order of business was suspended and Tony Pastor was chosen Chairman of the Social Session. The committee having charge of the exercises of the occasion was composed of S. K. Spencer, Harry Thomas and R. Fitzgerald.

JANUARY 1, 1871

Creation of a Grand Lodge approved.

FEBRUARY 12, 1871

It was voted that the lodge be known as New York Lodge No. 1.

MARCH 10, 1871

Charter for Grand Lodge obtained from New York legislature.

The First Constitution, Rules and Regulations

(Adopted by the original lodge three years prior to the creation of the Grand Lodge.)

The First Constitution, adopted in March, 1868, contained 15 articles, which were followed by 21 Rules and Regulations.

The committee which drafted the Constitution consisted of:

> George F. McDonald, Chairman
> William Sheppard
> Charles A. Vivian
> E. N. Platt
> Thomas Grattan Riggs

The preamble, stating the object of the new organization, was signed by the five Brothers mentioned above, as well as by:

> Richard Steirly
> William Carleton
> Henry Vandemark
> William L. Bowron
> M. G. Ash
> John T. Kent
> J. G. Wilton
> Frank Langhorne
> John H. Blume
> Harry Bosworth

TITLE PAGE _____

> The Constitution, Rules and Regulations of the Benevolent Order of Elks
>
>> New York, Press of Wynkoop & Hallenbeck
>> No. 113 Fulton Street, 1868

SECOND PAGE _____

> Elk's Head

The Benevolent and Protective Order of Elks
Organized February 16, 1868

Officers for the year 1868:

Primo ....Charles Vivian
1st Deputy Primo...R. R. Steirly
2nd Deputy Primo...
3rd Deputy Primo..
Honorary Secretary ....William Carleton
Corres. Secretary ....
Treasurer ....Henry Vandemark
Tiler ....William Sheppard

PREAMBLE—The undersigned members of the Theatrical, Minstrel, Musical, Equestrian and Literary
Professions, and others who sympathize with and approve of the object in view (hereinafter stated in the
Constitution), do hereby organize an Order to promote, protect and enhance the welfare and happiness
of each other:

Charles Vivian	M. G. Ash
Richard Steirly	John T. Kent
William Carleton	J. G. Wilton
H. Vandemark	F. Langhorne
William Sheppard	J. H. Blume
E. N. Platt	G. F. McDonald
W. Bowron	T. G. Riggs
H. Bosworth	

CONSTITUTION

Article 1 This Order shall be called the Benevolent
and Protective Order of Elks.

Article 2 There shall be but two degrees in this Order.

Article 3 No member shall be eligible to the Second
Degree until he shall have been a member at
least three months.

Article 4 No person shall be admitted to this Order
under twenty-one years of age.

Article 5 Candidates can only be proposed by members who have received the Second Degree.

Article 6 Members shall be elected only by ballot. Three black balls constitute a negative.

Article 7 The appropriation of all funds for relief purposes shall be in the hands of a committee of duly qualified members of the Second Degree.

Article 8 The R. H. Primo shall appoint all committees from the ranks of the Second Degree.

Article 9 There shall be two sessions of all regular meetings of the Order—one business, the other social.

Article 10 All business transactions of this Order shall be considered strictly private, and any member divulging the same, or any part thereof, shall, on conviction, be expelled.

Article 11 The officers of a lodge of this Order shall consist of the following, viz:—

R. H. Primo
Three Deputy Primos (1st, 2nd, 3rd in order)
Secretary
Corresponding Secretary
Treasurer
Tiler

Article 12 Any officer violating the Constitution or Rules of this Order, or any part thereof, shall be liable to impeachment.

Article 13 The Treasurer shall be required to give bonds in at least two thousand dollars on assuming the duties of his office.

Article 14 It shall require a two-thirds vote of the members of the Second Degree then present to impeach or remove any officer of this Order.

Article 15 The unanimous vote of all the living S. D.'s shall be necessary, in order that an amendment or alteration of this Constitution can be effected.

RULES AND REGULATIONS

1. That the meetings of this lodge shall be held once every week.

2. That it shall be the duty of the Secretary to read the articles of Constitution to the lodge previous to balloting for a candidate or candidates.

3. That the initiation fee be two dollars, and lodge dues twenty-five cents per week, payable in advance.

4. That a fee of one dollar be paid on the proposal of a candidate and the balance on the night of initiation.

5. That a notification of acceptance be sent to each candidate.

6. That the articles of Constitution be read to each candidate prior to initiation.

7. That the balloting for membership shall take place on the next regular meeting after proposition, and his initiation on the following regular meeting.

8. That a member of the Second Degree can propose but one member at each meeting, and no more than five candidates can be initiated at each regular meeting.

9. It shall be the duty of the R. H. Primo to preside at all meetings when he deems it necessary; appoint all committees; have general supervision over all matters pertaining to the lodge; shall see that members conduct themselves properly, and comply with the Constitution and Laws of this Order.

10. It shall be the duty of the Deputy Primos to assist the R. H. Primo in the duties above stated, and officiate for him in his absence.

11. It shall be the duty of the Honorary Secretary to keep correct minutes of all regular meetings; all accounts between the members and the lodge; receive all monies; pay the same over to the Treasurer, and receive his receipt for the same.

12. It shall be the duty of the Corresponding Secretary to issue all certificates appertaining to the business of the Order, and assist the Honorary Secretary, when necessary, in the discharge of his duties.

13. It shall be the duty of the Treasurer to keep a correct account of all monies received and expended by the lodge, and report the state of the funds at the last meeting of each month, or when called upon by the lodge.

14. It shall be the duty of the Tiler to assume sole charge of all the property of the lodge, viz: The rooms and condition of the same, keys of the doors, attend the door at all regular meetings of the lodge, and shall be responsible for the faithful discharge of all duties attending the same. He shall also purchase all property, stationery, etc., at the request of the lodge, and all bills for same to be presented to the R. H. Primo for his signature, prior to the liquidation of the same.

15. Any member neglecting to pay his dues for four successive weeks shall be notified of the fact, and failing to give satisfactory reasons therefor shall be expelled.

16. Seven members shall constitute a quorum for the transaction of business.

17. The funds of this Order shall be appropriated for the following purposes: All necessary expenses attending renting of rooms for meetings, balls, concerts, or exhibitions given by this lodge, printing, books, stationery, for charitable and other purposes conformable with the terms of the charter and consistent with the objects of this Order.

18. The annual election of officers shall take place the last regular meeting of each year.

19. The roll shall be called at the termination of the first session of each regular meeting. Members being absent shall be fined twenty-five cents.

20. It shall be the duty of every member of this Order to attend the funeral of a deceased brother, on receiving notice to that effect, the relatives of the deceased sanctioning the same.

21. That no alteration or suspension of the above rules, or any one of them, be made unless two-thirds of the members of the Second Degree present shall vote in the affirmative.

> George F. McDonald, *Chairman*
> William Sheppard
> Charles Vivian
> E. N. Platt
> Thomas G. Riggs

Ritual

The writing of a history of the Ritual of the Order of Elks presents many problems, one of which is that of avoiding the saying of anything about the secret work of the Order that should not be said.

However, there is information concerning the development of our Ritual, and about those who played the most important parts in that development, that could be and should be collected and included in a history of the Order.

An effort has been made to select those items appearing to be most probable of interest to the members of the Order.

Creation of a Ritual

When the "Jolly Corks" was converted into the Benevolent and Protective Order of Elks in 1868, attention was given immediately to the creation of a ritual.

The Constitution of the Order, adopted in March, 1868, provided for a First and Second Degree.

The adoption of a ritual for the First Degree completed the preliminary steps of organization.

The ritual for the Second Degree was not completed and adopted until May 17, 1868.

The first Committee on Ritual was composed of:

> George W. Thompson, *Chairman*
> George F. McDonald
> William Lloyd Bowron
> Thomas G. Riggs

William Sheppard
James Glenn
Henry Vandemark

The Ritual first created was largely the work of Chairman George W. Thompson and George F. McDonald.

The presiding officer, who in the First Degree was addressed as "Right Honorable Primo," was called, in the Second Degree, "Exalted Ruler."

The terms "Right Honorable Primo" and "First," "Second" and "Third Assistant Primo" were retained in the organization for many years.

In the Ellis History it is stated that they were used in the ritualistic work as late as 1883, when they were eliminated in the Ritual then prepared by Exalted Grand Ruler Edwin A. Perry and Grand Secretary Arthur C. Moreland. It has not been possible to verify this in the Grand Lodge Proceedings, but it may properly be assumed that Ellis wrote authoritatively.

In the early days of the Order the Ritual provided for a password to be changed semi-annually. The word adopted at the meeting of May 29, 1870, for the ensuing term was "Integrity."

The use of a password was continued for many years. At one time it was changed monthly, during another period it was changed annually and in 1899 it was abandoned.

The Grand Lodge and the Ritual

When the Grand Lodge was two months old, it was voted that a committee of five be appointed "to prepare odes for the First and Second Degrees of the Order" referred to as follows:

Opening ode
Closing ode
Installation ode
Funeral ode
Ode for introducing a candidate
Ode to be used previous to a candidate's taking the
obligation
Ode (joyful) to be used on a candidate's being brought to
light.

A Committee was appointed composed of Antonio Pastor, John F. Poole, Harry Stanwood, Henry O'Neil and William Coffin.

The minutes of the Sessions of the Grand Lodge for the next two or three years do not carry any record of a report by this Committee.

――――― 1 8 7 4 ―――――

In 1874, George J. Green urged a special committee be appointed to revise the secret work. George J. Green, Thomas G. Gaynor, Henry P. O'Neil, Franklin Moran, and Alfred Stimmel were appointed.

In December, 1874, there was read to the Grand Lodge by Henry P. O'Neil the Ritual prepared by this committee, and it was adopted.

At that meeting Exalted Grand Ruler O'Neil appointed, as his Committee on Work and Ritual, Cool White, Chairman, R. S. Martin and George J. Green.

――――― 1 8 7 5 ―――――

At a meeting in June, 1875, the Committee on Work and Ritual recommended:

> "That the 'changeable' word (presumably the password) of the First Degree be dispensed with immediately and that the Grand Secretary notify officers of subordinate lodges to instruct candidates accordingly."

This was unanimously endorsed.

Exalted Grand Ruler O'Neil Not Satisfied

In 1875 Exalted Grand Ruler Henry P. O'Neil said:

> "The labor is still to a certain extent incomplete, and I find by experience that it would be well, if no member of the Committee on Work and Ritual could undertake this manual, and, I must confess, tedious labor, to permit that Committee to employ some member of the Order, properly qualified, to do this work at a reasonable salary.

> "With so much talent in the Order, it is, in my opinion, strange that we have been so long wanting what other orders have deemed so necessary and what would certainly enhance to a great degree the beauty of our ceremonies."

He recommended that the Committee appointed to revise the secret work also be requested to prepare a form of opening and closing the Grand Lodge, as well as "sets of odes with appropriate music for the use of subordinate lodges during the ceremonies of opening, closing and initiation."

Exalted Grand Ruler O'Neil Takes a Hand

Apparently the Exalted Grand Ruler decided he would have to take a hand in this work himself, as we find the Chairman of the Committee, in 1876, reporting that "several original odes, adopted for various ceremonies and subordinate lodges, and also for burial services, had been composed by Brother O'Neil and set to appropriate music and arranged by him."

"The Order of Growlers"

In 1882, Messrs. Jones, Goodwin and VanDerlip, of Boston Lodge No. 10, presented a statement to the Grand Lodge, claiming that some persons, among them some former members of the Order, were in possession of its secrets, had banded together under the name of "Order of Growlers" and were holding meetings and using the Elks Ritual.

These Boston Elks submitted for consideration a new Ritual, but at the Grand Lodge Session in 1883, the Grand Secretary reported that the proposed Ritual had been rejected by a majority of the subordinate lodges.

Comments by Exalted Grand Ruler Tindale

In his report that year, Exalted Grand Ruler John J. Tindale had said:

> "In the first place, I do not share the fears expressed by the brethren who prepared and submitted the proposed 'New Ritual' last year that the use of our present Ritual by unauthorized persons not only tends to the destruction of the utility of the same for our purposes, but also affects the stability of the Order itself.

> "On the contrary, I am of the opinion that if our entire work should be published and broadcast through the country, it would not injure the Order to any appreciable degree.

> "I am of the opinion, however, that our Ritual contains objectionable features, 'relics of barbarism,' if I may be allowed to use the expression, which should be eliminated."

The Tindale Suggestions Followed

The Session adopted a recommendation of the Committee, consisting of J. H. Rathbone, Washington Lodge No. 15, E. J. Collins, Providence Lodge No. 14, and J. Cheever Goodwin, Boston Lodge No. 10, that the incoming Committee be directed to "so far revise the present Ritual as to eliminate all objectionable features in the First and Second Degrees."

The Ritual of 1884

Accordingly, in 1884 an amended Ritual was submitted by a Committee composed of W. D. Wetherell, St. Louis Lodge

No. 9; E. J. Collins, Providence Lodge No. 14 and Arthur C. Moreland, New York Lodge No. 1.

This was adopted by the Grand Lodge with only one amendment. It provided that where "a" occurs in the obligation before "Supreme Being" the word "the" be substituted.

This Ritual was written for two degrees.

It is the oldest printed Ritual now in the possession of the Grand Secretary of the Order.

Three Years of Rest

For three years the Order appeared to get along all right with the 1884 Ritual. Then we find Exalted Grand Ruler Will E. English dissatisfied. In 1887 he said:

> "Numerous complaints have, from time to time, reached me as to the faulty construction of the Ritual now in possession of the various lodges, and I warmly recommend that the entire Ritual be referred to a competent committee for revision and that special attention be given to the complete reconstruction of the work of the First Degree in order that it may be more impressive to the candidate and more interesting to the members in attendance."

Nothing appears to have been done immediately about this protest, and the next year, 1888, we find Exalted Grand Ruler Hamilton E. Leach saying:

> "The beauties and impressiveness of the rituals of other orders are within the knowledge of many of our members. The comparison makes us realize that there is a deficiency in this regard with us that can and should be rectified. The ceremonies of initiation should be associated with such beautiful sentiment that it would be a delight to those who confer it and a most gratifying revelation to the candidate who receives a degree."

Exalted Grand Rulers English and Leach
Failed to Get Results

However, the Committee reported at the Session of 1889 that they had sought suggestions of amendments from various Grand Lodge members, but received none and said:

> "We advise retaining our present Ritual, believing its beauty lies in its simplicity."

A New Ritual ——— One Degree

In 1890, a Committee composed of D. T. West, Springfield, Ohio, Lodge No. 51; C. E. Battle, Columbus, Georgia, Lodge No. 111, and H. H. Dodd, Fond du Lac, Wisconsin, Lodge No. 57, submitted a "New Ritual" to the Grand Lodge. This was exemplified and adopted. Three hundred copies were ordered printed.

The following year, 1891, a Committee consisting of Edwin B. Hay, Washington, D. C., Lodge No. 15; J. J. Hayes, Vicksburg, Mississippi, Lodge No. 95, and Peter Rush, Detroit, Michigan, Lodge No. 34, recommended that "the two degrees be combined into one strong degree but that the salient features of the present ritual be preserved in their entirety."

This recommendation was endorsed and the next year, 1892, a Committee comprising George A. Reynolds, Hartford, Connecticut, Lodge No. 19, and J. J. Hayes, Vicksburg, Mississippi, Lodge No. 95, presented a Ritual in which they said, they had "embodied all the essential features of the old, endeavoring to eliminate all inconsistencies and useless repetitions." This Ritual was adopted by the Grand Lodge.

The records fail to show whether or not this Ritual was approved by the subordinate lodges. Whether or not it was, the records show that it did not meet with general favor.

In 1893, the Committee on Work and Ritual, composed of William H. Friday, Brooklyn, New York, Lodge No. 22; J. J. Hayes, Vicksburg, Mississippi, Lodge No. 95, and Charles E. Wolf, Albany, New York, Lodge No. 49, reported that something new in the way of a ritual would be in keeping with the growth of the Order and was in general demand.

The Committee stated that it had prepared a work in which that part of the old Ritual which had proved so successful in the past was retained but that, with this exception, the work was "entirely reconstructed."

With some corrections this Ritual was adopted.

Changes Still Desired

At the 1894 Grand Lodge Session in Atlantic City the Committee on Work and Ritual composed of Arthur C. Moreland, Chairman, New York Lodge No. 1; J. W. Leahy, Tiffin, Ohio, Lodge No. 94, and George W. Falkenstein, McKeesport, Pennsylvania, Lodge No. 136, submitted a report stating that they had read and carefully considered a skeleton manuscript of a new Ritual, entirely original and thoroughly Elk in its conception and workings, but which would need much care and preparation before it could be properly presented and perfected. They said:

> "We recommend that the incoming Committee on Work and Ritual be empowered to take the manuscript, prepared by George W. Ryer, of New York Lodge No. 1, and use the same as a nucleus for a Ritual,

which shall be short, Elk-like in its character, and which will stand
without subsequent changes for all future time."

Grand Exalted Ruler Edwin B. Hay
Asked for a New Ritual

None of the heads of the Order following Exalted Grand Ruler
Leach referred to the Ritual in their reports until Grand Exalted
Ruler Hay did so in 1895, when he said:

"The want of a ritual in keeping with the advance the Order has made
in the past few years is very perceptible.

"For a number of years efforts have been made by various committees
to which the duties have been assigned to present a ritual that would
be impressive and interesting and, at the same time, teach the principles of the Order. At the Detroit meeting it was supposed to have
been accomplished."

He added that it had fallen far short as it was exemplified
before the Grand Lodge, and that the good of the old work had
been omitted and what had been added was not good.

In 1895 a Committee composed of Arthur C. Moreland, New
York Lodge No. 1; J. W. Leahy, Tiffin, Ohio, Lodge No. 94,
and Charles Wolf, Albany, New York, Lodge No. 49, submitted
a new Ritual.

The records do not indicate whether or not the Ryer manuscript was used but a statement by Arthur Moreland in the
Elks-Antler of April, 1912, quoted later in this chapter on Ritual,
indicates that in 1895 the Ritual was amended by extracts from
the Ryer manuscript.

The Committee stated that the ritualistic work submitted by
them was, in their judgment, purely Elk and entirely original
and was not borrowed from any similar organization of which
they had cognizance.

In exemplifying the proposed Ritual for the Grand Lodge,
Arthur Moreland said:

"The Committee on Ritual is very much handicapped. The Chairman
is blind, the second member is sick and the third member, as usual
at the Grand Lodge, has lost his voice. Consequently we are obliged
to call into service the kindly offices of Brother McCarthy, who will
assist us in the reading." (Arthur Moreland had become blind in
1892.)

The new Ritual was unanimously adopted.

The Committee urged upon the Grand Lodge the necessity
of having a distinctive grip of the Order which could not be
mistaken for that of any other organization.

Grand Exalted Ruler Meyers Protests
Against Ritual Changes

In 1896, Grand Exalted Ruler Meyers said:

"It must seem evident to the Grand Lodge that the practice of having a new ritual every two or three years is not a means by which our Order gains prominence as there is nothing which will cause a feeling of dissatisfaction more quickly among the members of the Order than a constant changing of the Ritual and Laws of the Order."

However, that year a special Committee consisting of Moses P. O'Brien, Omaha, Nebraska, Lodge No. 39; William H. Friday, Brooklyn, New York, Lodge No. 22; G. D. Ackerley, Jacksonville, Florida, Lodge No. 221; John T. Sutphen, Middletown, Ohio, Lodge No. 257, and Harvey Meyers, Covington, Kentucky, Lodge No. 314, appointed to cooperate with the regular Committee on Work and Ritual consisting of Arthur C. Moreland, New York Lodge No. 1; Frank Moran, Philadelphia, Pennsylvania, Lodge No. 2, and Julius Straus, Richmond, Virginia, Lodge No. 45, recommended that:

"During the ensuing twelve months and until such time as a new ritual shall be adopted, subordinate lodges shall initiate candidates under the Ritual adopted in 1893 at Detroit, except in cases where subordinate lodges have disposed of their paraphernalia or have not secured it.

"In this event, either the Ritual of 1893 or 1895 may be used, but the regalia of the Order shall be that described in the Ritual of 1895."

This recommendation was adopted.

The Committee on Work and Ritual reported that the Special Committee had recommended that a plan be formulated whereby the author or compiler of the most successful ritual should receive as compensation, if the work was adopted, a prize of $200 and the next most successful the sum of $100.

The Committee recommended, therefore, that the incoming Committee be empowered to act as judges of the work submitted and to cause same to be exemplified before the Grand Lodge, and, if said ritual receives the approval of the Grand Lodge, that it shall be ordered substantially for a period of at least five years.

Detweiler Gives His Views

In 1897 Grand Exalted Ruler Detweiler regarded a new ritual as "absolutely necessary." He said that on all sides he had found dissatisfaction with the present conditions and he referred to the "universal desire for a new ritual."

That year the Grand Lodge voted that a committee of five be appointed to prepare a ritual which they should, within six months, submit to the various lodges for adoption.

This Committee consisted of George R. Perry, Grand Rapids, Michigan, Lodge No. 48; C. L. Bunting, Bristol, Tennessee, Lodge No. 232; J. W. Cherry, Norfolk, Virginia, Lodge No. 38; Arthur C. Moreland, New York Lodge No. 1, and A. M. Knox, St. Paul, Minnesota, Lodge No. 59.

In 1898, Grand Exalted Ruler Detweiler said that a special committee which had been appointed for the purpose had submitted to the regular Committee on Work and Ritual a ritual which had been forwarded to the various lodges for approval, and that nearly two-thirds of the lodges had adopted the work.

He stated that the new Ritual very properly continued the innovation of the Ritual of 1895 in discarding all paraphernalia.

He later referred to the fact that, under the methods of the 1895 Ritual, candidates would pass through portions of the initiation which they regarded as distasteful or frivolous, would refuse to proceed further and would fail to become members of the Order. He favored doing away with "horse-play."

Grand Exalted Ruler Galvin

During his year in office (1898-1899) Grand Exalted Ruler Galvin found that considerable disturbance and discord had grown up around the use of "horse-play" in initiation.

In the previous year all "horse-play" had been prohibited. He had advised all lodges that this action by the Grand Lodge must be respected.

He stated that, personally, he would not object to such a change as would permit "certain features to be introduced"— such features to be designated specifically by the Grand Lodge or by the Grand Exalted Ruler and the Board of Grand Trustees, but he felt that the law should be even more stringent with reference to anything improper.

The amendment of 1898 to which he referred, after providing that there should be only one degree, also provided as follows:

"The use during initiation of any device, appliance, property or paraphernalia which may, by any possibility, endanger the safety of the candidate, and any and all conduct during the initiation suggestive of vulgarity or obscenity, or which tends to subject the candidate to any indignity, or which might give offense to any gentleman is expressly prohibited."

Grand Exalted Ruler Galvin had referred in his First Official Circular to the fact that the Special Committee on New Ritual, appointed by Grand Exalted Ruler Detweiler the preceding year, did excellent work and the result of that work had been sent to all subordinate lodges.

He said that it was then submitted to the regular Committee on Work and Ritual and the two committees revised the work with the result that a completed and well-rounded ritual was submitted to the Grand Lodge, which, with a few changes, was adopted by that body. He said that it was a matter of congratulations to the Order that there would now be a uniform ritual in use in all lodges.

Five Years of Ritual Rest

No action looking to alteration of the Ritual was taken in the five years from 1899 to 1904. The one Grand Exalted Ruler of those serving in the first four years of that period, B. M. Allen (1899-1900) who referred to the Ritual, confined his reference to ritualistic work to caution against unacceptable or unauthorized deviations from the Ritual and warned against what he referred to as "exuberant desire for 'fun' at the expense of the inexperienced faun."

G.E.R. Fanning Seeks Another Change

Grand Exalted Ruler Joseph T. Fanning, in his report in 1904, said:

"The Committee on Work and Ritual will have something both of interest and importance to offer for your consideration.

"Frankly, let it be confessed that our Ritual, beautiful and moving as it is, is not everything it might and should be—that is to say—an up-to-date composite of intellectual dignity and sublimity of sentiment; illustrative, sermonic; a supreme enrichment in liberality of mind and portrayed as a prose poem that is a musical caress to the ear and making the heart teem and kindle with high resolves before undreamed."

At that Session the Committee recommended that the succeeding Committee be instructed to prepare and submit at the next Grand Lodge Session an entirely new ceremony of initiation.

The new Committee consisted of Thomas F. Brogan, New York Lodge No. 1; James L. King, Topeka, Kansas, Lodge No. 204, and Warren G. Sayre, Wabash, Indiana, Lodge No. 471. Its recommendation was adopted.

Also, at the 1904 Session the Grand Lodge eliminated the grip and substituted a test word for the sign of recognition.

It also took positive action for eliminating the alleged humorous or "horse-play" features, and the old rule of "harmless deviation from the regular ritualistic ceremonies" was fully abrogated.

"Horse-play" Still a Problem

In his report in 1905, Grand Exalted Ruler William J. O'Brien, Jr., said:

> "It is apparent to me that Section 64, as it now stands, is not regarded with universal favor. My visitations among the subordinate lodges during the year have convinced me that the rank and file of our membership desire the introduction of amusing features.

> "I am convinced to favor the incorporation in the Ritual of a number of special features described and the paraphernalia and so forth to be used in each and giving lodges permission to use any, all or none of said features as they may deem advisable."

The Committee on Work and Ritual, consisting of Alfred T. Holley, Hackensack, New Jersey, Lodge No. 658, Chairman; James L. King, Topeka, Kansas, Lodge No. 204, and William Hickman Moore, Seattle, Washington, Lodge No. 92, stated that it found itself handicapped in attempting to carry out the mandate of the previous Grand Lodge Session for the Committee to prepare and present an "entirely new ceremony of initiation."

The reason for this, the Committee stated, was that so many of the prominent members of the Order desired more, instead of less, "horse-play" and that some District Deputies attributed the decline of attendance at subordinate lodge meetings to the absence of the customary amusing incidents.

The Committee, therefore, referred the matter back to the Grand Lodge, saying:

> "Yielding to this sentiment, your Committee is of the opinion that new features must be introduced. We would respectfully recommend that the Committee on Work and Ritual be instructed to select from numerous articles of paraphernalia a number not to exceed five and also to prepare a short ritual setting forth the language to be used in connection therewith and that they shall submit the same to the Grand Exalted Ruler and the Board of Grand Trustees for their approval and that when so approved the Grand Exalted Ruler shall promulgate the same to the subordinate lodges in the Official Circular and the same shall become part of the present initiatory ceremony."

When Chairman Holley moved the acceptance of the report of the Committee, Champe S. Andrews offered the following as a substitute:

"That the incoming Committee on Ritual be instructed to devise a ritual complete in its character, having in mind the present officers and their duties and the present members of the Order, so that the ritual formulated by the Committee on Ritual can be exemplified at the next Grand Lodge Session, and that the Grand Lodge set aside the sum of $1,000 to be given as a premium to the Brother or member who presents us a Ritual which is finally accepted by the Grand Lodge."

This was adopted.

At the same Session the Committee on Laws recommended that Section 64 of the Grand Lodge laws be repealed and the following be enacted:

"In conferring the degree the form of ritualistic work approved and prescribed by the Grand Lodge and none other shall be used. Provided, however, that permission to introduce harmless and proper deviations from ritualistic work may be granted to Subordinate Lodges by the Grand Exalted Ruler, which authortiy and power cannot be delegated by the Grand Exalted Ruler to any officer or member of the Order. Those Lodges desiring to avail themselves of such privileges must first designate to the Grand Exalted Ruler the particular features which they desire to introduce or confer upon the candidate, together with a description of the paraphernalia or appliance expected to be used, and the language expected to be expressed, in connection therewith by the officers of the lodge. Provided further, that all paraphernalia of every kind and nature, used in the initiatory ceremony shall be purchased and procured through the office of the Grand Secretary."

This recommendation was adopted by the Grand Iodge.

Ritual Divided into Two Parts

Grand Exalted Ruler Robert W. Brown, in his report in 1906, said:

"For several years past it has been conceded that our Ritual imperfectly represented the mental attainment of the Brotherhood; that its beautiful teaching was here and there disenchanted by verbal atrocities and expressions to a degree befogged and that the ceremony and the sentiments were not presented with the desired and required symmetry and dignity and the classic grace and power in spiritualizing effect.

"At Buffalo, the Grand Lodge directed a sweeping change, the production and exemplification of a new Ritual, preserving the mottoes and ideals of the old and adhering to the present officers and their duties."

He added:

"I cannot refrain from the statement that while all you have anticipated may not be brought to fruition, the project of the Committee is so

53

transcendentally an improvement upon the old, your admiration will be challenged. Superior literary culture is manifest throughout and rare appreciation of our ennobling principles distinguishes every line of the composition."

In making its report at Denver in 1906, the Committee on Work and Ritual, consisting of R. L. Holland, Colorado Springs, Colorado, Lodge No. 309; John H. Holmes, St. Louis, Missouri, Lodge No. 9, and P. A. Shanor, Sisterville, West Virginia, Lodge No. 333, said:

"We have divided the Ritual into two parts, being designated as Part I and Part II, the two together constituting the complete Ritual. In Part II has been placed all the work of a comic nature.

"This plan has been adopted for several reasons. The serious work is thus left in compact, concise form so that it may be printed in a book of convenient size. The comic work, under the arrangement, may also be printed in compact, concise form, making it easy to supplement it by circular.

"Part II bears no relation to Part I and its use is entirely optional. In this way we have sought to solve the vexing question of the introduction of comic work. Lodges desiring that it be eliminated are privileged to disregard Part II and they will still have a complete Ritual, while those lodges desiring to enliven their meetings by comic work, will, we hope, find ample provision has been made therefor in Part II. All old work has been retained and speaking parts and instructions provided for some thirty additional appliances."

Part I was known as the "Blue Book" and Part II as the "Red Book."

The Committee gave careful consideration to each manuscript submitted and recommended that $25 be paid to one Brother and $100 paid to another.

The Ritual presented was adopted with some amendments.

Grand Exalted Ruler Melvin Disturbed

What Grand Exalted Ruler Henry A. Melvin was quite concerned about when he wrote his annual report in 1907, had to do with Part II of the Ritual.

At that time the Statutes provided that the lodges could introduce harmless and proper deviations from the ritualistic work upon permission granted by the Grand Exalted Ruler.

He was disturbed by the misunderstanding and confusion that resulted from this Statute. The Ritual prescribed definitely just what might be used in the way of deviation and subordinate lodges were strictly limited to the devices and dialogue set out in the Ritual.

He held that the Ritual and instructions therein constituted the higher law and that the above-referred-to Statute was superseded by the adoption of the Ritual and, therefore, the Grand Exalted Ruler had no power to grant special permission.

He then recommended that the law be amended by striking out the section referred to, and emphasized that lodges were strictly limited to the use of the devices and dialogues set out in Part II of the Ritual.

There was an entire revision of the Statutes at the 1907 Session of the Grand Lodge and that part of the Statutes to which the Grand Exalted Ruler objected was eliminated.

Another Five-Year Period Of Rest

Not until the Grand Lodge Session of 1911 was the Ritual further changed.

That year the Committee consisted of James L. King, Topeka, Kansas, Lodge No. 204; Fred Harper, Lynchburg, Virginia, Lodge No. 321, and Charles E. Lown, Saginaw, Michigan, Lodge No. 47.

They reported that they had altered and amended the following items as recommended, in part, by the previous Committee

1. The entire elimination of Part II.
2. The abandonment of the preliminary obligation.
3. The abandonment of the test oath, because it was generally disregarded.
4. The omission of the Chaplain's recitation.
5. The shortening of the obligation.
6. The simplification and shortening of the charges of the station officers.
7. Making optional the rendition of a part of the present Esteemed Leading Knight's charge.
8. The omission of the eulogy of the flag in the Exalted Ruler's charge.

Aside from that, they stated that they had contented themselves merely to simplify and shorten the Ritual then in use and, at the same time, preserve the beauty and effectiveness of the service.

They had reduced the Ritual from 5,708 words to 3,610 words.

The Exalted Ruler's Tribute to the Flag

All the recommendations of the Committee were adopted, with the exception of the one calling for the omission of the eulogy of the flag in the Exalted Ruler's charge.

The circumstances under which the Committee's recommendation for the elimination of the eulogy of the flag in the Exalted Ruler's charge failed of adoption were rather dramatic.

When the adoption of the recommendation was moved, Walter P. Andrews, Atlanta, Georgia, Lodge No. 78, afterwards Grand Exalted Ruler, addressed the Chair as follows:

> "Insofar as the report of the Committee referred to the charge of the Exalted Ruler, I am unalterably opposed to it. I would regret exceedingly to see the eulogy of the flag eliminated from that charge. It is the most beautiful thing in the whole ceremony of initiation in Elkdom. I move to amend the recommendation by leaving it as it now is."

Past Grand Exalted Ruler English said:

> "Before we vote on that I would suggest that Brother Andrews give us the eulogy of the flag."

Brother Andrews then delivered the charge and his rendition was followed by prolonged applause.

Brother Harper then said:

> "I think I may speak for the Ritual Committee and state that, in view of the demonstration you have just had in approval of the eulogy of the flag, that it would be willing to accept the amendment that the eulogy of the flag be reinstated in the charge of the Exalted Ruler."

Part II Dies Hard

In 1912, the Committee on Work and Ritual, composed of Fred Harper, Chairman; Charles Beecher Lahan, Chicago, Illinois, Lodge No. 4, and John C. Futrall, Fayetteville, Arkansas, Lodge No. 1104, reported a very general complaint against the changes made in the charges of the station officers. The Committee's recommendations for meeting these complaints were adopted.

Chairman Harper said that in some quarters there was a desire for the restoration of the old Part II, but that for the very cogent reasons set forth in the Committee's report, they had declined to recommend its restoration.

A question brought forth a statement from Raymond Benjamin, Chairman of the Committee on Judiciary, that a former Chairman of Judiciary had ruled "that upon the conclusion of the services of the lodge, it might adjourn into a social session at which time this character of material may be utilized."

A motion was offered that Part II be "entirely eliminated." The Grand Exalted Ruler ruled that if that motion were adopted it would entirely eliminate "horse-play" and overrule the decision of the Judiciary Chairman referred to.

The motion was adopted.

Arthur Moreland on the Ritual

Arthur C. Moreland, P.E.R., New York Lodge No. 1, and at one time Grand Secretary of the Order, had a great deal to do during a long period of years with the development of the Ritual of the Order. He was the owner, editor and publisher of the *Elks-Antler*. In the April 1912 issue of that publication there appeared the following interesting and enlightening article on the Elks Ritual:

The History of Our Ritual

"The Grand Exalted Ruler, in his Official Circular No. 2, called upon the members of the Order to assist the Committee on Work and Ritual in revising and amending the present Ritual, and while this writer does not feel that he has either the ability or the time to offer the suggestions necessary to be of assistance, he can in a general article help the committee by narrating the history of the ritual of the Order of Elks from the time of its institution, and thus afford them an outline that can be used in the preparation of a ritual closely identified with the best thoughts of the past and present.

"When the 'Jolly Corks' changed their name to the Benevolent and Protective Order of Elks on February 16th, 1868, they were utterly without any form of initiation beyond requiring the applicant for admission to pay his quota of the refreshments which were the *sine qua non* of that social gathering's existence. This state of affairs continued until May 31st, 1868, when the Committee on Ritual, consisting of Brothers George W. Thompson, George F. McDonald, William Sheppard, Thomas G. Riggs, and William Lloyd Bowron, brought before the body a ritual in two degrees, the first utilizing some of the tricks played upon the unsuspecting initiate in the Corks, and the second the real ritual of the Order of Elks.

"The first degree, as it was called, was all that the Corks ever received, and of which they were already possessors; the second degree was not conferred until four weeks of probationary condition in the first degree had been completed. The rupture by which the membership of the Order was reduced to just seven members on June 14th, 1868, gave the opportunity to those who were left in the body to perfect the ritualistic work.

"The floor work, as it was called, of both degrees was evolved by Brother Hugh P. O'Neil, and the majority of the lectures and explanation of the purposes and objects of the Order were the work of Brother George F. McDonald, with the assistance and suggestions of the other members of the committee.

"This ritual, with two degrees and four weeks' probationary period was in existence and used as originally presented until 1881, when it was amended by Past Exalted Grand Ruler Thomas E. Garrett, of St. Louis, by the addition of another officer named as the Esquire, who took over a large portion of the work of the Fourth Chair, then called

Grand Lecturer, but whose title was at the same time changed to that of Esteemed Lecturing Knight.

'In 1884 Past Exalted Grand Ruler Edwin A. Perry, and the writer, revised, or, to use a better expression, edited this two-degree ritual, the only substantial change in the form of the work being an amplification of the obligation practically in the shape of the present-day obligation. This ritual remained in force and effect until 1891, when, in accordance with a resolution adopted at Cleveland in 1890, a new ritual was presented, being a combination of the two degrees into one degree.

"In 1893 a new ritual was submitted to the Order, eliminating most of the work of the old ritual and substituting paraphernalia of various kinds, considerable rough-house and borrowing many features of obsolete degrees of other fraternities.

"This remained in effect until 1895, when the late Brother George W. Ryer, in conjunction with the writer, prepared the ritual of 1895, returning to most of the original thoughts beautified by poetical expressions from the pen of Brother Ryer. This not being entirely satisfactory, a sub-committee was appointed by Past Grand Exalted Ruler Meade D. Detweiler in 1897, who reported in 1898 the ritual which continued in force until 1906. The committee of 1898 were Brothers P.G.E.R. Charles E. Pickett; C. L. Bunting, of Bristol, Tenn.; George R. Perry, of Grand Rapids; George A. Reynolds, of Saginaw, and the writer. The ritual of 1906 we are familiar with, and it has been altered, changed and amended at nearly every subsequent Grand Lodge Session until the present time.

"The addenda to the ritual which have been most vital were the introduction of the flag as the covering of the altar at the suggestion of this writer in 1896, the instructions in secret work taken from the Loyal Knight to the Esquire, the elimination of the apron 1895, of the badge 1902, of the grip 1904, and the test oath 1911, together with the abolition of all except the dignified and monitory character of the present ritual. The rock upon which most ritual committees founder is the inability of the committee to grasp the thought that mere words without suggestive action are of little avail. Words themselves can be piled up like Ossa upon Pelion, but unless they contain the germ of thought and beauty, are but weeds in the field of phraseology. The ritual committee that desires to bring a work to the Grand Lodge that will stand for all time must also remember that the basic principle for any ritual of this Order is the blending of the thought that the animal whose name we bear can be, as it was by Brother George F. McDonald, made to assimilate, with human virtues, that without hyperbole, reverence and devotion to patriotic thought can be typified in the idealization of the flag, that it is the purpose of this fraternity to inculcate by moral education respect for its laws and rights of our fellow men without the threat of retributive punishment in case of failure, that the aim of the organization should be to make men better and to confirm in all the lectures the impression that the candidate is worthy of the honor bestowed by membership."

Grand Exalted Ruler Benjamin Calls
for Grand Lodge Rituals

In 1914, Grand Exalted Ruler Benjamin appointed as a Ritual Committee: P.G.E.R. Henry A. Melvin, Oakland, California, Lodge No. 171; James L. King, Topeka, Kansas, Lodge No. 204, and William T. Phillips, New York Lodge No. 1.

He charged that Committee with the responsibility of preparing a "special and impressive ritualistic service" for the opening and the closing of the Grand Lodge Sessions and for the inducting into office of the incoming Grand Lodge officers and, further, that a ritualistic service should be provided for the Memorial Service of the Grand Lodge.

Suggestion for Substitute for Old Part II

In his report to the Grand Lodge in 1915, Grand Exalted Ruler Benjamin said that under the comprehensive resolution adopted by the Grand Lodge at Denver, it was within the power of the Committee to solve for all time the question of Part II, which, he said, was not a question of returning to, or using, old Part II and the features it contained, but merely a question of introducing into our Ritual something of a light or less somber character.

No action taken by the Committee on Work and Ritual in respect to the initiatory ritual.

At that Grand Lodge Session, 1915, the Committee reported the creation of ritualistic services for the opening and closing of the Grand Lodge, a ritual for dedication of a public building, a memorial service and funeral service.

The recommendations of the Committee were adopted.

The ritual for opening and closing of the Grand Lodge was used at this session.

Past Exalted Rulers' Night and the Ghost of Part II

The Ritual Committee in 1917, consisting of James L. King, Topeka, Kansas, Lodge No. 204; William T. Phillips, New York Lodge No. 1, and James C. Futrall, Fayetteville, Arkansas, Lodge No. 1104, recommended:

> "That the first meeting night of February of each year be designated as Past Exalted Rulers' Night."

This recommendation was adopted.

The Committee also offered a substitute for the old Part II (Red Book) of the Ritual, saying that there seemed to be a minority demand for something more than the work of Part I. It was designated, the Committee said:

"To provide something that would prove entertaining and at the same time be dignified and impressive and teach in a way other than morally to an Elk."

The Committee said:

"The tests which are here mentioned in this report are to be those of the old ritual, and now provided for in the Red Book, with more emphasis. The ceremony is to precede the regular initiation. Its use is optional with the lodge but in no case is it to be substituted for the regular form of initiation and when used it must be preliminary to such initiation."

The recommendations of the Committee were adopted. These recommendations included the elimination of all of the Exalted Ruler's charge coming after the presentation of the flag and the elimination of the word of recognition.

New Membership Committee Succeeds Committee on Work and Ritual

In 1918, Grand Exalted Ruler Bruce A. Campbell created a New Membership Committee and appointed as members Past Grand Exalted Rulers John P. Sullivan and John Galvin and Grand Esteemed Leading Knight Thomas L. Reilly.

For the next three years a New Membership Committee with Past Grand Exalted Ruler Sullivan as Chairman took the place of a Committee on Work and Ritual but offered no recommendations for material changes in the Ritual.

Social and Community Welfare Committee Succeeds New Membership Committee

At the Grand Lodge Session in 1922 the New Membership Committee was discontinued and it was provided by the Grand Lodge Statute that any proposal to change or alter the Ritual of the Order be referred to the Committee on Social and Community Welfare.

Past Grand Exalted Ruler Sullivan was made Chairman of this Committee. (See Ritual—Special Services.)

Ghost of Part II Finally Dissolved

A resolution to "reinstate a wholesome second-degree initiation as part of the Ritual for the playgrounds of Elkdom" was not adopted.

And thus, after many years of controversy, the "second part" of the initiation was definitely and, undoubtedly, for all time, eliminated.

Ritualistic Committee Is Created

Grand Exalted Ruler John F. Malley, in 1928, suggested that a Grand Lodge Ritualistic Committee be created to supervise initiatory work of subordinate lodges, to promote inter-lodge ritualistic contests and to foster proficiency in the rendition of the Ritual.

A committee of five with powers suggested by him was created by Statute. It was further authorized to recommend to the Grand Lodge changes in the Ritual when "deemed urgently necessary."

This Committee was composed of W. C. Robertson, Chairman, Minneapolis, Minnesota, Lodge No. 44; William T. Phillips, New York Lodge No. 1; David Sholtz, Daytona Beach, Florida, Lodge No. 1141; C. Fenton Nichols, San Francisco, California, Lodge No. 3, and James H. Gibson, Houston, Texas, Lodge No. 151.

In 1929 the Committee recommended several minor changes in the initiatory Ritual. They recommended that exemplification of the Ritual be made mandatory on the part of a lodge at the time of the official visit of the District Deputy. The Statutes were amended in accordance with this recommendation.

In reporting on ritualistic contests, the Committee stated that it had done everything possible to encourage contests between subordinate lodges for the purpose of promoting ritualistic efficiency and that the interest already manifested in ritualistic contests held under the auspices of State Associations encouraged the Committee to believe that they would eventually lead to national competition for a trophy awarded by the Grand Lodge.

They also recommended that the report forms used by District Deputies be so amended as to require them to report whether or not each officer had memorized his part of the Ritual.

Second Year of Ritualistic Committee

This year, 1930, the Ritualistic Committee, composed of W. C. Robertson, Chairman, Minneapolis, Minnesota, Lodge No. 44; David Sholtz, Daytona Beach, Florida, Lodge No. 1141; J. C. Dallenback, Champaign, Illinois, Lodge No. 398; George W. Crane, Aberdeen, South Dakota, Lodge No. 1046, and George W. Denton, Gloversville, New York, Lodge No. 226, reported that very definite progress had been made in improving the rendition of the Ritual. Some changes in Ritual were made.

The Committee stated that, through the cooperation of the District Deputies and the officers of State Associations, inter-lodge contests had been held in a number of states, other states had signified their intention of staging similar contests, and reports from all sides indicated that there had been a general improvement in the ritualistic work.

A national contest was held that year at the Grand Lodge Session in Atlantic City. This was the first Grand Lodge Ritualistic Contest ever held. The winners were:

Wilmington, Ohio, Lodge No. 797 — 1st
Norwood, Massachusetts, Lodge No. 1124 — 2nd
Cocoa, Florida, Lodge No. 1532 — 3rd

Later Ritualistic Contests

These Contests continued to be run under the direction of a Ritualistic Committee of the Grand Lodge for the years 1931, 1932 and 1933.

In these years the Championship Ritualistic Teams were the following:

Year	Lodge	Percentages
1931	Ottawa, Illinois, Lodge No. 588	99.92
1932	New Smyrna Beach, Florida, Lodge No. 1557	99.40299
1933	Newton, Massachusetts, Lodge No. 1327	99.39

From 1933 to 1949 inclusive these contests were held under the direction of the State Associations Committee. Beginning 1950 these contests have been held under the direction of a newly-created Ritualistic Committee of the Grand Lodge. The first prizes in these years were awarded to the following:

Year	Lodge	Percentages
1934	Newton, Massachusetts, Lodge No. 1327	Percentage not reported in the Proceedings
1935	Newton, Massachusetts, Lodge No. 1327	98.57
1936	West Palm Beach, Florida, Lodge No. 1352	97.67
1937	Lincoln, Illinois, Lodge No. 914	98.72
1938	Lincoln, Illinois, Lodge No. 914	93.21
1939	Elizabeth, New Jersey, Lodge No. 289	94.76
1940	Inglewood, California, Lodge No. 1492	97.512
1941	Decatur, Georgia, Lodge No. 1602	97.1913
1942	Riverside, California, Lodge No. 643	98.35
1943	Lyndhurst, New Jersey, Lodge No. 1505	98.87
1944	Fitchburg, Massachusetts, Lodge No. 847	96.03
1945	Contest dispensed with on account of World War II	

Year	Lodge	Percentages
1946	Wakefield, Massachusetts, Lodge No. 1276	96.70
1947	Everett, Massachusetts, Lodge No. 642	97.7996
1948	Pocatello, Idaho, Lodge No. 674	98.424
1949	Fort Lauderdale, Florida, Lodge No. 1517	95.9760
1950	Greeley, Colorado, Lodge No. 809	96.1471
1951	Greeley, Colorado, Lodge No. 809	95.853
1952	DeKalb, Illinois, Lodge No. 765	96.8144
1953	Greeley, Colorado, Lodge No. 809	95.0849
1954	Atlanta, Georgia, Lodge No. 78	93.1269
1955	Sonora, California, Lodge No. 1587	93.1025
1956	Chattanooga, Tennessee, Lodge No. 91	94.5089
1957	Rock Hill, South Carolina, Lodge No. 1318	93.1937
1958	Phoenix, Arizona, Lodge No. 335	95.990
*1959	Decatur, Georgia, Lodge No. 1602	97.270
1960	Tacoma, Washington, Lodge No. 174	93.211
1961	Albany, Georgia, Lodge No. 713	96.169
1962	Rock Hill, South Carolina, Lodge No. 1318	96.146
1963	Rock Hill, South Carolina, Lodge No. 1318	96.141
1964	Puyallup, Washington, Lodge No. 1450	95.743
1965	Kingsport, Tennessee, Lodge No. 1833	95.049
1966	Wellington, Kansas, Lodge No. 1167	96.500
1967	Laconia, New Hampshire, Lodge No. 876	95.436

* At the 1959 Grand Lodge Convention, the Ritualistic Committee divided the competing teams into an Eastern and a Western Group with the two top teams in each section competing for the National Championship. This venture proved to be so popular and successful that it has been continued.

No changes were made in the Ritual during the time that the State Associations Committee had charge of that matter.

During the Grand Lodge Sessions of the years 1934 to 1940 there was no action in respect to changes in the Ritual.

In 1941 a minor change was made and in 1943 there was the change of a single word.

Interest in a revival of the so-called "horse-play" had died and interest had been strongly developed in an attempt to attain perfection in rendition of the Ritual.

The year before the ritualistic work was turned over to the State Associations Committee, Grand Exalted Ruler Coen probably had expressed the sentiment of the members of the Order generally when he said that he did not believe in constant tinkering with rituals and thought that a Committee should confine its efforts to stimulating proper rendition of the Ritual.

Special Ritual Commission Appointed

At the Grand Lodge Session of 1944 the following resolution was adopted:

"Resolved — that a Special Ritual Commission of three members be appointed by the Grand Exalted Ruler to review and revise the Rituals of the Order and to provide any additional ritual that may seem advisable."

In 1946 the Special Ritual Commission, appointed in 1944, which consisted of Past Grand Exalted Rulers Benjamin and Malley and P.E.R. William T. Phillips of New York Lodge No. 1, presented and exemplified a revised Ritual for initiation. In some respects it differed considerably from the Ritual then in use.

After the exemplification Chairman Benjamin moved the adoption of the revised initiatory Ritual.

There followed a great deal of discussion, at the close of which a motion to lay on the table prevailed.

Later a motion was carried that the word "God" be substituted for the words "Supreme Being" whenever such words appeared in the present Ritual.

There were adopted the following new rituals submitted by Chairman Benjamin:

Ritual for installation of Grand Lodge officers.

Ritual for installation of subordinate lodge officers.

Ritual for institution of a new lodge.

A Ritualistic Committee Takes Over

At the Grand Lodge Session in 1949 the Statutes were amended to provide for the appointment of a Ritualistic Committee of five. Section 47A of the Statutes was amended to provide that:

"The Ritualistic Committee shall foster efficiency in the rendition of the Ritual; shall promote inter-lodge ritualistic contests and shall, at every Grand Lodge Session, conduct among the winners of state contests ritualistic contests in such a manner as it deems necessary and expedient according to the discretion of the Committee and shall have referred to it and make recommendations as to all changes or modifications of any or all rituals of the Order."

The Chairmen of this Committee from 1949 to date have been:

1949 —Arthur M. Umlandt, Muscatine, Iowa, Lodge No. 304

1950-1952—W. A. Wall, West Palm Beach, Florida, Lodge No. 1352

1952-1953—Arthur J. Roy, Willimantic, Conn., Lodge No. 1311.

1954-55-56—Edward W. McCabe, Nashville, Tennessee Lodge No. 72

1957-1958—Ronald R. Bringman, San Fernando, Cal. Lodge No. 1539

1959   —Leo P. Ronan, Decorah, Iowa Lodge No. 443

1960-1961—Marston S. Bell, Columbia, S. C. Lodge No. 1190

1962-1963—John Frakes, Tucson, Arizona Lodge No. 385

1964-1965—Raymond J. Quesnel, Montpelier, Vermont Lodge No. 924

1966-1967—Lloyd Chapman, Eldorado, Kansas Lodge No. 1407.

Use of Blindfold Discontinued

At the Grand Lodge Session of 1952 it was voted unanimously to discontinue the use of the blindfold in initiation.

Ritual—Special Services

Funeral Ritual
——— 1871 ———

Nothing seemed to baffle the founders of the Order of Elks as much as the preparation of a satisfactory funeral ritual.

In 1871, four months after the Grand Lodge came into existence, Exalted Grand Ruler George J. Green said that he hoped the Grand Lodge "would fix upon some appropriate ceremonies to be used when a deceased Brother is buried under the auspices of the Lodge."

The suggestion was referred to a Committee on Odes.

Apparently nothing was done about this for some time, as we find that at a Grand Lodge meeting in 1874 it was voted that the Committee on Work and Ritual be instructed to prepare a burial service.

——— 1875 ———

Exalted Grand Ruler Henry P. O'Neil said in his report in 1875:

"FUNERAL RITUAL"

"I would recommend that the same committee be requested to report as soon as practicable the result of their deliberations upon the matter of a funeral service for the Order which was referred to them at our last annual communication.

"The extremely beautiful and extraordinarily successful display of New York Lodge No. 1 on the occasion of the Lodge of Sorrow held in Irving Hall during the term naturally occurs to me as I make this suggestion and I cannot avoid saying that the same master hand that guided that undertaking to its triumphant close will evolve from the material then used an appropriate funeral service which will have as profound an effect upon the public at large as the ceremonies upon the occasion referred to."

1876

In December, 1876, the Grand Lodge adopted a funeral service prepared by a special committee headed by George J. Green.

1879

Apparently, the work of the special committee which prepared the funeral service in 1876 was not satisfactory to Past Exalted Grand Ruler O'Neil, as we find him, in 1879, securing the creation of a special committee consisting of the Exalted Grand Ruler, the Grand Secretary and the Grand Treasurer to prepare a funeral service.

1880

At this Grand Lodge Session the Committee on Burial Service reported progress and was continued.

1882

In 1882, the Committee on Work and Ritual, which was composed of Will E. English, Indianapolis Lodge No. 13, Chairman; J. Cheever Goodwin, Boston Lodge No. 10, and Arthur C. Moreland, New York Lodge No. 1, submitted a new funeral ritual and recommended that it be forwarded to all subordinate lodges with instructions to cause the same to be read at two regular communications, at the conclusion of the latter of which a lodge vote should be taken upon its adoption or rejection.

The recommendation of the Committee was adopted by the Grand Lodge, but was rejected by a majority of the subordinate lodges.

1908

At Dallas, in 1908, the Committee on Work and Ritual, composed of James L. King, Topeka, Kansas, Lodge No. 204; William M. Hargest, Harrisburg, Pennsylvania, Lodge No. 12, and C. B. Lahan, Chicago Lodge No. 4, reported a new funeral service to be substituted for the one then in use.

1909

Notwithstanding this action, however, it was voted at the Grand

Lodge Session at Los Angeles in 1909 that a special committee of three be appointed to draft a funeral ritual which should be "Both original and permanent."

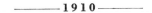

————— 1910 —————

The Committee was not prepared to make a report in 1910, and recommended that the preparation of a funeral ritual be referred to the incoming committee.

————— 1911 —————

This year a Committee composed of James L. King, Topeka, Kansas, Lodge No. 204; Charles E. Lown, Saginaw, Michigan, Lodge No. 47, and Fred Harper, Lynchburg, Virginia, Lodge No. 321, reported that with such material as there was before them they considered it impossible to formulate a final ritual that would meet all the objections raised against the two funeral services the use of which was then permitted by the Grand Lodge.

This referred to the funeral ritual in existence in 1908 and the one adopted that year. Many lodges had failed to accept the latter and had continued to use the earlier one.

The Committee felt that it would be impossible to harmonize the varying expressions of opinion as to what the new service should contain and finally had decided upon a ritual possessing, at least, the qualities of brevity and simplicity.

They said that they considered the proposed new ceremony as fully meeting the requirements of such an occasion and adapted to any locality or any lodge.

It was voted to submit to the subordinate lodges the question of adopting either one of the old rituals or the new one submitted.

————— 1912 —————

In his report to the Grand Lodge meeting in Portland, Oregon, in 1912, Grand Exalted Ruler Sullivan said:

"The Grand Lodge having submitted to the subordinate lodges the selection of one of the three funeral rituals, known as 'One,' 'Two' and 'Three,' the vote of the lodges (representing the membership of the lodges) resulted as follows:

For the adoption of Funeral Ritual No. 1	139,474
For the adoption of Funeral Ritual No. 2	88,183
For the adoption of Funeral Ritual No. 3	64,121

"Funeral Ritual No. 1, having received the largest vote of the subordinate lodges, I have declared the same adopted, and the Funeral Ritual known as 'No. 1' has become the Funeral Ritual of the Benevolent and Protective Order of Elks of the United States of America."

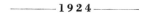

Special Services

At the Grand Lodge Session in Los Angeles, in 1915, a committee composed of Past Grand Exalted Ruler Melvin, James L. King, Topeka Lodge No. 204, and William T. Phillips, New York Lodge No. 1, submitted a ritual for laying a cornerstone of a public building. This was adopted by vote of the Grand Lodge. The Committee also recommended a service for opening and closing of the Grand Lodge, a new installation service for Grand Lodge officers, a new Memorial Day service and a practically new funeral service.

———— 1 9 2 4 ————

At the Grand Lodge Session which was held in Boston in 1924, the Committee on Social and Community Welfare was vested with authority to "revise and rewrite, wherever necessary, all the public rituals of the Order."

The Committee was composed as follows:

> Past Grand Exalted Ruler John P. Sullivan, *Chairman,*
>   New Orleans Lodge No. 30
> Murray Hulbert, New York Lodge No. 1
> John C. Karel, Milwaukee Lodge No. 46
> William J. Sinek, Chicago Lodge No. 4
> Lloyd Maxwell, Marshalltown Lodge No. 312

The result of the labors of this Committee was a complete set of rituals for the following services:

> Laying the cornerstone of a public building
> Dedication of a public building
> Laying the cornerstone of an Elks Temple
> Dedication of a Lodge Room
> Dedication of an Elks' Rest
> Funeral Services
> Memorial Service
> Mother's Day Ritual
> Flag Day Ritual

———— 1 9 2 5 ————

The preceding new and revised rituals were further revised and adopted by the Grand Lodge in 1925.

There have been no changes of a substantial nature in the Special Services Ritual since that time, but minor changes have been made in the 1925, 1958 and 1964 reprinting.

The Elks and the Theater

When the First Constitution, Rules and Regulations of the Benevolent and Protective Order of Elks was adopted, on May 17, 1868, the preamble read as follows:

> "The undersigned members of THE THEATRICAL, MINSTREL, MUSICAL, EQUESTRIAN AND LITERARY professions and others who sympathize with, and approve of, the object in view, do hereby organize an Order to promote, protect and enhance the welfare and happiness of each other."

And so the Order of Elks started as a fraternity of men of the theatrical profession or of other activities closely related thereto.

For many years the Order had this limitation of membership. Slowly, however, its membership broadened until now members of the theatrical profession are no more prominent than those of any other business or vocation.

The departure from the original precept and purpose of the founders has been slow and at times impeded by a reluctance on the part of the early members to see its original character and limitations changed.

However, the debt the Order owes to "The Theatrical, Minstrel, Equestrian, Musical and Literary professions" responsible for its creation and early development, has never been forgotten or lacked appreciation by the informed members of the Order.

A Tribute by Exalted Grand Ruler English

In his report at the Grand Lodge Session in 1887 Exalted Grand Ruler English said:

> "At your last communication a movement was inaugurated looking to a change in the date of holding the Grand Lodge Session to some more convenient time during the summer months. I cordially approve your present adjournment.

> "It would be especially gratifying to the theatrical members of our organization, who are now largely unable to be in attendance by reason of necessary absence in the performance of professional duties. During the year just closed as always before in the history of our Order we have been placed under renewed obligations to the theatrical profession, who have ever willingly volunteered their valuable services to aid in swelling our charity fund by means of benefits and entertainments given under the auspices of the various lodges of the brotherhood.

> "To them we are most deeply indebted for generous and timely assistance, cheerfully and eagerly rendered. Ours is essentially a theatrical

Order, formed by theatrical people in the theatrical center of our country, New York City, and ever nurtured and maintained by members of the theatrical profession, their friends and intimate associates.

"This noble and generous profession has ever been foremost in the cause of sweet charity, and I trust the day will never come when our Order shall drift away from its distinctive theatrical character, or attempt to occupy a field for which it was never intended by those who gave it existence, and whose labor and devotion through many a trying hour have finally brought it to its present eminence, prosperity and success."

Evidence of Continuing Association

In the issue of The Social Session of January, 1892, there were at least twenty items similar to the following:

"On the evening of January 18th the members of Waco, Texas, Lodge attended the performance of Frederick Warde. From the theater they repaired to the Elks Club House where Mr. Warde presided over a delightful social session."

"Newport, R. I., Elks' Benefit February 23rd, with Frank Daniels and his company in 'Little Puck' as the attraction."

"Kingston, N. Y., Lodge held their first social session on the evening of December 31st. They had for their guests the members of George Wilson's Minstrel Company. Brother George Wilson acted as Chairman."

"After the performance of Daniel Sully in 'The Millionaire' at Trinidad, Colorado, the evening of December 9th, the gentlemen members of the troupe were escorted by the members of No. 181 to their hall, where a social session was held."

Grand Exalted Ruler Hay Pays Tribute

In his report to the Grand Lodge in 1895, Grand Exalted Ruler Hay said in respect to the dramatic profession:

"The question often arises among the uninitiated, concerning the status of the dramatic profession, with regard to the Order. It is true that to the profession the Order is indebted for its existence, but for its perpetuation and for the glory of its members today it depends upon the interest manifested in it by contributions from every walk of life.

"The fraternal feeling towards, and the appreciation of, the members of the profession is not decreased with the growth and development of the Order but the tie is stronger today than it has ever been. The profession itself has outlived foolish prejudices and in the world today is recognized as a loved art among all the arts and sciences that make up the great school of enlightenment and the proof of it is that the most popular and faithful exponents are classed among the great men and women that are figuring in the history of our own and other countries.

"But a few weeks since the degree of Doctor of Letters has been conferred upon Mr. Winter (Ed. William Winter, the leading theatrical critic of that day) by one of the leading educational institutions of this country; and Henry Irving, the leader of the drama in England has kneeled before the Queen to receive the honor of knighthood. Therefore the Order is heartily and sincerely in sympathy with the profession and I but utter the sentiment of the entire Order when I say that everything that should be done to encourage the affiliation that should exist between the profession and the lodges in the Order and without placing upon record any promise to promote in advance the interest of the profession, it should be an unwritten law that will tend toward the upholding, maintaining, encouraging and respecting an art that was espoused by our honored founders."

A Tribute by the Grand Lodge

At the Grand Lodge Session in 1895 there was adopted the following resolution presented by James J. Armstrong for New York Lodge:

"Whereas, the Grand Lodge of the Benevolent and Protective Order of Elks, and the Order itself, had its origin and its infancy fostered by the amusement profession, and for many years the treasuries of the various subordinate lodges have been augmented by the efforts of the same profession; and

"Whereas, the natural growth and development of the Order, and the accession to its ranks of a majority other than those in the theatrical profession, has completely obliterated the distinctive character of the Order and formed in its stead a more universal fraternity; and

"Whereas, the Grand Lodge feels that such a transformation should not be effected without a suitable recognition of the services of the amusement profession, in originating and maintaining the fundamental growth of the Order, and the fact that so large a proportion of said profession is maintained on its roll of membership; therefore be it

"Resolved, that the Grand Lodge of the Benevolent and Protective Order of Elks desires to assert that, while it is not a 'Theatrical Order' (for the reasons above given) yet, it is heartily and sincerely in sympathy with said profession, and earnestly desires the affiliation of all reputable male members of said profession with the various subordinate lodges, and requests all lodges to extend all possible hospitality to the members of the profession from which our Order originated.

"Resolved, that the Grand Lodge of the Benevolent and Protective Order of Elks desires to place itself on record as promising to do all in its power to promote and advance the interests of the amusement profession and, as far as compatible with its laws, to be a factor in relieving distress in said profession, thus carrying out the primary object of its institution."

The Address of Frederick Warde

Thirty-five years after the birth of the Order, Frederick Warde, one of the leading legitimate actors of the day, a member of St. Louis Lodge No. 9, spoke at the dedication of the National Elks Home, representing the theatrical profession.

Incorporated in a very beautiful and eloquent address was a reference to the origin of the Benevolent and Protective Order of Elks as follows:

"It is to the Drama and the actors of the Drama that the Benevolent and Protective Order of Elks owes its existence, and if the many faults and frailties with which we are charged were true, that fact would be an extenuating plea in their favor.

"A small coterie of actors recognizing that the itinerant character of their profession necessitated some bond or union for their mutual protection and entertainment as well as care in times of sickness and distress, formed a small society that met weekly, usually on Sunday evenings, when wit and witticism, song and story, served to illume their leisure hours while anecdoting experiences of mutual interest bound them in ties of common sympathy.

"These weekly meetings became so attractive and their number increased so rapidly that finally a permanent organization was established, with the principles of friendship, charity, justice and fidelity as its function; a complete ritual was composed; solemn ceremonies of initiation introduced and a new secret fraternal society came into existence under the name of the Benevolent and Protective Order of Elks."

Later in his address Mr. Warde said:

"The Order has ever been in sympathetic union with the Guild of the Drama. It is proper that it should be so because the Drama is in complete sympathy with the Elks.

"The Drama teaches charity in the broadest sense. You have sworn to practice it.

"The Drama advocates impartial justice to all—that is your cornerstone.

"The Drama illustrates the virtues of fidelity—you claim it as your motto.

"The Drama teaches the doctrine of human love and friendship— human love is your cardinal principle.

"The Drama teaches by example as well as by precept the noblest lessons of manhood and integrity—your ritual does the same.

"Chivalry and the defense of virtue is an omnipresent pennant of the Drama—with you it is a solemn obligation.

"The Drama is Non-Sectarian—so are you and so ad infinitum."

The reputation of the Elks nationally as royal entertainers was built largely upon the willingness of Elks in theatrical road companies to appear at banquets and social sessions of subordinate lodges wherever they were billed, supplying a measure of talent and entertainment not otherwise available excepting in the largest cities.

As this History was originally being compiled, there came to life an interesting story of the relationship between the stage and the fraternity which indicates that three-quarters of a century after the founding of the latter it found an opportunity to pay part of its long indebtedness to the former.

On September 30, 1951, during an interview between Mr. Ed Sullivan and Miss Helen Hayes on television, Mr. Sullivan said:

"You know; I suppose that you have been asked this question before; Miss Hayes, how did you ever become an actress?"

Miss Hayes replied as follows:

"Well, possibly I never would have been an actress if my father hadn't been an Elk; certainly if he hadn't been indirectly connected with the theater as Chairman of the entertainment committee of his lodge in Washington.

"Certainly, I doubt that my mother ever could have talked him into giving us round-way tickets to New York and $50 for a week there. Gee, $50 was an awful lot of money in those days, but my mother was convinced that if her eight-year-old daughter could make audiences laugh in Washington, she could make them laugh on old Broadway."

Early Officers

In 1870, the time for election of officers was changed from the Spring to the first Sunday of November. The officers elected in the First Degree, in accordance with this change, who were installed, November 13, 1870, were:

RIGHT HONORABLE PRIMO, George J. Green
FIRST DEPUTY PRIMO, Antonio Pastor
SECOND DEPUTY PRIMO, Hugh P. O'Neil
THIRD DEPUTY PRIMO, Samuel K. Spencer

GRAND TREASURER, Charles T. White
GRAND SECRETARY, Alex. H. Mulligan
CORRESPONDING SECRETARY, Ed G. Browne
TILER, George B. Dalton
INSIDE GUARD, Charles Darrow

The Second Degree officers, chosen on December 4th of the same year were:

EXALTED RULER, George J. Green
ESTEEMED LEADING KNIGHT, Louis Nevers
ESTEEMED LOYAL KNIGHT, Claude Goldie
GRAND LECTURER, Cool White
SUPREME JUDGE, T. G. Riggs

Mementoes of the Early Years

An Interesting Historic Relic

Grand Exalted Ruler Detweiler, in his report to the Grand Lodge in 1898, made the following reference to interesting mementoes of the early years of the Order:

"During the investigation made by the Grand Exalted Ruler into our early history, it was discovered that the original gavel used by Brother Vivian, as Right Honorable Primo in presiding over the sessions of the first lodge of Elks in 1868, was still in existence. It has been neatly made of ebony by J. G. Wilton, a woodturner, who was one of the original 'Jolly Corks,' and who, as stated in the history prefixed to the minutes of the Grand Lodge from 1871 to 1878, has not been heard from for fifteen years.

"The gavel was in the possession of Brother Richard R. Steirly, now a member of Hoboken Lodge. The Grand Exalted Ruler felt that a relic of this character would be of great interest and value to all Elks, and the most appropriate custodian of it would be the Grand Lodge of the Order, accordingly, through the kindness of Brother Steirly, the venerable gavel has been secured by the Grand Exalted Ruler for perpetual preservation amongst our cherished treasures, and is now made the property of the entire Order in the custody of the highest legislative body.

The First Banner of the B. P. O. E.

"It having been ascertained that the first Elk banner ever used was still in existence and in the possession of New York Lodge No. 1, steps were taken to acquire this interesting and valuable memento of the past, for the use and ownership of the Grand Lodge. Through the kind liberality of New York Lodge these efforts were successful. Although it was the last remaining relic of the olden time in their possession, the brothers of No. 1 have generously donated this valuable banner that it may become the property of the high legislative body which represents the entire Order.

"Appreciating their disinterested sacrifice, the Grand Exalted Ruler now places it in the care of its future custodians, at the same time joining most heartily in the expressed wish of Lodge No. 1 that it shall be prominently displayed at every future Grand Lodge session. To do this will be eminently right and proper, and cannot fail to be a source of inspiration to the loyal and fraternal hearts that in the future will assemble beneath its time-consecrated folds.

"Your Grand Exalted Ruler gratefully acknowledged this precious relic as per letter herewith appended."

These mementoes are now in charge of the Grand Secretary of the Order at the Elks Memorial Building in Chicago, Illinois.

Eleven O'Clock Toast

Early Elk annals attest that George F. McDonald, as referred to on page 35, was the first on record to propose the sentiment "To Our Absent Brothers," since then spiritualized into a golden essence of our liturgy. The official records show that this first eleven o'clock toast was delivered at a social session May 31, 1868.

Regular meetings of subordinate lodges have always been held at night. In the earlier days they were usually held on Sunday nights and were concluded about eleven o'clock. As the participants departed, they naturally made inquiries about the absentees and expressed sympathetic interest in the causes of their absence. It soon became a custom, when the members had repaired to some other place, for some of them to propose a toast to the Brothers who were not present. And in the course of time this custom was quite generally observed whenever a group of Elks were together at eleven o'clock.

Eventually the Grand Lodge specifically provided for such a ceremonial to be observed during lodge sessions, and designated it as "The Eleven O'Clock Toast." Under this provision, whenever a lodge is in session at that hour, the regular order of business is suspended for a few moments while the Exalted Ruler recites the beautiful ritual prescribed, concluding with the words: "TO OUR ABSENT BROTHERS."

Upon other strictly fraternal occasions this "golden hour of recollection" is generally observed in somewhat the same manner. A designated brother, with or without a few preliminary remarks, proposes the toast, to which all members respond with the words, "To our absent brothers," and by uniting and singing "Auld Lang Syne." Even when small groups of Elks are together at this hour, although it be not a formal fraternal occasion, it is not inappropriate to recall the sentiment with a moment of dignified silence.

The Official Elks Eleven O'Clock Toast

At the Grand Lodge Session in 1919 Past Grand Exalted Ruler Fred Harper referred to a statement made by Grand Exalted Ruler Campbell that the tribute to the Absent Brothers in that part of the Ritual relative to our duty at eleven o'clock was being continuously used by members of the Order at banquets and other gatherings where some who are not Elks were present; that there was no objection to its being done on proper occasions and to the Grand Exalted Ruler's request that a resolution authorizing such use be adopted, he then offered the following resolution:

"Resolved: that the rendition upon proper public occasions of that part of the Elks Ritual known as the Eleven O'Clock Toast be permitted by the Grand Lodge."

This resolution was adopted.

The Toast

"My Brothers, you have heard the tolling of eleven strokes. This is to impress upon you that with us the hour of eleven has a tender significance. Wherever an Elk may roam, whatever his lot in life may be, when this hour falls upon the dial of night, the great heart of Elkdom swells and throbs. It is the golden hour of recollection, the homecoming of those who wander, the mystic roll call of those who will come no more. Living or dead, an Elk is never forgotten, never forsaken. Morning and noon may pass him by, the light of day sink heedlessly in the West, but ere the shadows of midnight shall fall, the chimes of memory will be pealing forth the friendly message: 'To our absent Brothers.'"

The Phillips Toast

The following is an Eleven O'Clock Toast delivered by William T. Phillips, P.E.R. New York Lodge No. 1:

"ELEVEN O'CLOCK! The Elks' session of sweet, solemn thought; the moment which bridges the chasm 'twixt Time and Eternity with a golden span of love!

"Oh, Spirit of this Sacred Hour! So Clarify our vision that we may look backward down the pathway of time, and behold in the white light of understanding the trials and vicissitudes of years agone.

"Teach us to appreciate the heart-hunger and longing for companionship which inspired men, doomed by their profession to wander, to lay the foundation for the religion of sympathy and kindness we call Elkdom.

"Help us to contemplate with reverence and love, the Fidelity which gave our founders and their successors of days gone by, courage to beat down the barriers of prejudice and doubt, which fell across the pathway of our Order's present glory.

"Keep alive the sublime truth that the Golden Rule is the foundation of our Order today, as it was many years ago, lest we forget that only while we remain true to its precepts shall our course continue onward and upward.

"Lead our thoughts to those kept from this gathering by suffering and sorrow, that they may feel the healing sympathy of our common brotherhood, enter the hearts of those abroad and comfort them with the constancy of our love; rise upon the music of the bells which toll this hour into the realms of Eternity, so that our brothers gone, even amid the perfect peace they now enjoy, may know we are reading from the tablets of love and memory.

"Remain with us always, to recall at this hour those who wander, those who will come no more, and with hearts attuned to the melody of 'Auld Lang Syne,' may we ever when eleven strokes proclaim the approaching end of day, pledge in the mellowness of Friendship, the memory of Our Absent Brothers."

Lodge of Sorrow and Memorial Day

The record book of New York Lodge for the year 1870 affords much interesting material in regard to the origin and first observance of a Memorial Day of the Order.

On February 16, 1870, Brother George E. Farmer died. At the next meeting of the lodge Brother Coffin suggested the following session be modified out of respect to the deceased brother.

On February 26, 1870, Brother John W. Glenn died. At the meeting of February 27th, Brother Green moved that a Lodge of Sorrow be held on March 20th.

The motion was adopted and a committee appointed.

The session was held in Masonic Hall on the afternoon of the day appointed.

The Hall was appropriately draped and an excellent program was rendered. Music was a prominent feature. An appropriate eulogy was delivered.

The following is a copy of the printed program of a "Lodge of Sorrow" held September 4, 1870, in consequence of the death of Brothers Preston and Lingard.

B. AND P. ORDER OF ELKS

Lodge of Sorrow

MEMORIAL SERVICES

1. Voluntary on the Organ by Brother F. C. Alden.

2. Anthem, by Brothers Brandise, Rockefeller, Russell and Shattuck.

3. Prayer by Rev. Samuel B. Willis.

4. Pleyel's Hymn by Brandise, Rockefeller, Russell and Shattuck.

5. Eulogy on the late Brother Frank Preston by Brother Cool White.
   (Written by Brother J. Green)

6. Quartet, Sacred, "Rock of Ages" by Brothers Brandise, Rockefeller, Russell and Shattuck.

7. Eulogy on the late Brother James W. Lingard by Brother Willard.
   (Written by Brother T. Alston Brown)

8. General remarks by Brethren of the Order.

9. Closing hymn "Old Hundred" by the congregation.

George W. Thompson, R. H. P.

A. H. Mulligan, Secretary.

In later years the term "Lodge of Sorrow" was applied by Statute of the Grand Lodge to the Funeral Services held for individual Elks at the time of their death.

At the Grand Lodge Session of 1889, Exalted Grand Ruler Leach, in his address to the Convention, recommended that it be made an established custom to be observed annually by every lodge, to hold a memorial or "Lodge of Sorrow."

At the same Convention, Allen O. Myers, of Columbus, Ohio, Lodge, and member of the "Laws and Supervision Committee," offered the following resolution:

> "Resolved, that the first Sunday in December annually is hereby designated and dedicated as a day to be celebrated as a 'Lodge of Sorrow' by all Lodges of Elks."

This resolution was unanimously adopted.

At the Grand Lodge Session of 1890 a new constitution and new statutes were adopted.

Section 78 of the new statutes read as follows:

> "The first Sunday in December of each year is hereby designated and dedicated as a day on which shall be commemorated by every Lodge of Elks, the memorial of our departed Brothers and shall be known as 'The Elks Memorial Day.'
>
> "The funeral services of a departed Brother shall be known as a 'Lodge of Sorrow.' "

Later the Section of the statute referring to this matter became Section 226, reading as follows:

> "The first Sunday in December of each year is dedicated as a day on which shall be commemorated by every Lodge of Elks in sacred session the memories of departed Brothers, and shall be known as 'Elks Memorial Day.' It shall be incumbent upon every Lodge to hold such Services upon that and no other day. The Grand Exalted Ruler may, in exceptional cases and for good cause, grant a dispensation to any two or more Lodges to hold such services jointly."

An effort was made in 1930 to amend the statute to provide that the annual Elks Memorial Day Services might be held on the regular meeting night of the lodge nearest to the first Sunday in December.

This amendment was not adopted.

In 1953, Section 226 was amended by striking from the Statute the words "on that day and upon no other day" and adding the following paragraph:

> "The District Deputy Grand Exalted Ruler may, upon written request and for good cause, grant permission to a Lodge to hold such service on a designated day during the week immediately preceding or following the first Sunday in December."

The Grand Lodge (Creation of)

During the year 1870 a movement was started by Philadelphia theatrical professionals for a lodge in that city.

Accordingly, a committee of the Order was appointed, December 4, 1870, to devise ways and means for the formation of a Grand Lodge.

This committee reported on January 1, 1871, the following resolution which was adopted:

"Resolved, the first Grand Lodge of the Benevolent and Protective Order of Elks consist of the following:

"The original founders of the Order together with all the present and past officers of the First and Second Degrees, who are now in good standing in the Order and that the above take effect immediately."

At a meeting held on February 12, 1871, motions were made and carried that the Lodge then existing be known as New York Lodge No. 1, B.P.O.E. and that application be made immediately to the Grand Lodge for a charter. At the same time the petition from the Philadelphia applicants was referred to the Grand Lodge for a dispensation.

The following is the text of the first Grand Lodge meeting:

PROCEEDINGS OF THE FIRST REGULAR

COMMUNICATION OF THE

Grand Lodge B. P. O. Elks

NEW YORK, February 12, 1871

A meeting of the members of the Grand Lodge B.P.O.E. was held this afternoon at 4:15 o'clock at the lodge room, 114-116 E. 13th Street.

Ten members were present, as follows:

Brothers George J. Green, Antonio Pastor, J. C. Pinckney, Claude Goldie, A. H. Mulligan, Hugh P. O'Neil, Fernando Pastor, S. K. Spencer, Henry P. O'Neil and E. G. Browne.

Brother G. J. Green presided and Brother E. G. Browne acted as Secretary.

The matter of effecting an organization was discussed, and it was finally agreed that the Chair appoint a Committee of three to frame a set of rules for the organization of the Grand Lodge B.P.O.E.

First Grand Lodge Rules

The Chair appointed Brothers Henry P. O'Neil, Antonio Pastor and S. K. Spencer, who, after consulting a few minutes, presented the following rules, which were adopted by sections:

1st. That all those, now members of the Grand Lodge, who have not previously filled the position of Exalted Ruler in any subordinate lodge, be now constituted and ever hereafter recognized as Past Exalted Ruler, with all the privileges and rights appertaining to the position.

2nd. That the Grand Lodge immediately proceed to elect Brothers to fill the following positions in the Grand Lodge, to hold such positions until the second Sunday in December, 1871, said election to be governed by the objects of the Second Degree of the Order.

    1st.   Exalted Grand Ruler.

    2nd. Esteemed Leading Grand Knight.

    3rd. Esteemed Loyal Grand Knight.

    4th. Grand Lecturer.

    5th. Grand Secretary.

    6th. Grand Treasurer.

    7th. Grand Tiler.

    8th. Judiciary. Three in number.

3rd. That upon the election and installation of the officers, as above provided for, the Exalted Grand Ruler immediately appoint a committee of five, whose duty it shall be to draft a set of by-laws, rules and regulations to govern the business of the meetings of the Grand Lodge, and to submit such rules, etc., as soon as practicable, such committee to hold office until the next regular election.

4th. That the Exalted Grand Ruler shall also appoint a committee of three whose duty it shall be to inspect the credentials of delegates from subordinate lodges and report thereon to the Grand Lodge, such committee to hold office until the next regular election.

5th. That until such time as the Grand Lodge shall adopt a permanent set of rules, etc., a quorum to transact business shall consist of at least seven, after proper notification by the Grand Secretary, such notification to be considered valid if given at least fifteen (15) days prior to the date for which the meeting may be called.

On motion the meeting resolved itself into a Committee of the Whole to make nominations for officers to serve until the next regular election.

Brother S. K. Spencer was appointed Chairman of the Committee.

Brothers A. H. Mulligan and Fernando Pastor were appointed Tellers. The Committee arose and reported the following nominations:

For Exalted Grand Ruler, Brothers G. J. Green and William Coffin

For Esteemed Leading Grand Knight, Brother Antonio Pastor

For Esteemed Loyal Grand Knight, Brother S. K. Spencer

For Grand Lecturer, Brother Cool White

For Grand Secretary, Brother E. G. Browne

For Grand Treasurer, Brother Hugh P. O'Neil

For Grand Tiler, Brother Fernando Pastor

For Judiciary, Brothers T. G. Riggs, J. C. Pinckney and William Korff

The meeting then resolved itself into a Committee of the Whole to go into election for officers and then arose and reported that Brother George J. Green had been elected Exalted Grand Ruler. There being no opposition to the other officers, they were all declared elected.

On motion the Tellers were discharged with thanks.

On motion Brother J. C. Pinckney, of the Judiciary, was called to the Chair for the purpose of administering the oath of office to the officers-elect.

All the officers, with the exception of Brother Cool White (who is absent from the city) were duly installed in their several positions.

The Exalted Grand Ruler appointed Brothers Hugh P. O'Neil, Henry P. O'Neil, J. C. Pinckney, Claude Goldie and E. G. Browne a Committee on Rules, Regulations, etc., in accordance with Rule 3rd.

Brothers A. H. Mulligan, Antonio Pastor and S. K. Spencer, a Committee on Credentials.

On motion that when we adjourn, we adjourn to meet on next Sunday afternoon, 19th inst., at 3 o'clock.

Agreed to.

Brother Claude Goldie, as representative from the Mother Lodge, asked for a dispensation for that lodge to work.

On motion the same was granted.

There being no further business, on motion the lodge took a recess until Sunday, February 19, at 3 P.M.

Attest:

E. G. BROWNE
Grand Secretary

A charter was obtained from the Legislature of the State of New York, on March 10, 1871, incorporating the Grand Lodge of the Benevolent and Protective Order of Elks of New York, with power to issue charters to subordinate lodges throughout the country. Accordingly, the Grand Lodge thus legally constituted a charter, the same day to New York, No. 1.

March 10, 1871, therefore marks the legal commencement of the Grand Lodge of the Benevolent and Protective Order of Elks and the beginning of New York Lodge No. 1, as existing by that distinctive title under a charter of the Grand Lodge.

Two days later, March 12, 1871, Philadelphia Lodge No. 2 was chartered. The work of drafting a Constitution and Laws and of perfecting the organization of the Grand Lodge was largely performed by Brother Henry P. O'Neil, subsequently Exalted Grand Ruler of the Order.

The first money of the Grand Lodge Treasury was loaned by Tony Pastor, March 5, 1871. This was used to buy a Grand Lodge seal. This money was returned June 11, 1871.

On March 31, 1871, Tony Pastor loaned the Grand Lodge $175 to make certain purchases. This money was returned to Brother Pastor by William Coffin who assumed the debt and was afterwards reimbursed by the Grand Lodge.

Original Incorporation

There follows a copy of the act of incorporation:

ACT OF INCORPORATION

Chapter 88

An Act

To Incorporate the Grand Lodge of the Benevolent and Protective Order of Elks.

PASSED MARCH 10, 1871

The people of the State of New York represented in Senate and Assembly, do enact as follows:

Sec. 1. George J. Green, Elmer J. Post, Claude G. Conner, John Hodges, Thomas G. Riggs, Joseph C. Pinckney, William Korff, Antonio Pastor, Hugh P. O'Neil, Samuel K. Spencer, A. H. Mulligan, William Coffin, E. G. Browne, George B. Dalton, George W. Cumberland, George F. McDonald, William L. Bowron, William Sheppard, G. W. Rockefeller, W. Hallam Brown, Charles T. White, John H. Korff, Thomas G. Gaynor, Henry P. O'Neil and Fernando Pastor, and their successors, and all such persons as are or may be associated with them, are hereby created a body corporate and politic, under and by the name of the "Benevolent and Protective Order of Elks," and as such shall have perpetual succession, with the right to sue and be sued. And the said corporation hereby created, is authorized to buy, purchase, take by devise or otherwise, real and personal estate, to the value of two hundred thousand dollars, and to hold, sell or dispose of the same, and to have and use a common seal, and also to establish branch organizations.

Sec. 2. The said corporation shall have power from time to time to make, constitute, ordain and establish, alter and amend such by-laws, rules and regulations, as they shall judge proper for the management of the said corporation and its members.

Sec. 3. The general business and objects of said corporation shall be to protect and aid its members and their families, and to accumulate a fund for that purpose, which said fund shall be used and appropriated for no other purposes whatsoever.

Sec. 4. The persons particularly named in the first section of the Act shall be the first Trustee of said corporation; and hereafter at each and every annual meeting of said corporation, there shall be elected by ballot five Trustees who shall have charge of all property and effects belonging to said corporation; the said Trustees to hold office until the next succeeding annual meeting, and the affirmative vote of at least three of the said Trustees shall be requisite for the purpose of making any order for or authorizing the investment of any money or monies, or the sale or transfer of any stock, securities or property belonging to the said corporation.

Sec. 5. All vacancies in the board of Trustees caused by death, resignation or otherwise, shall be filled by the said corporation by ballot without unnecessary delay. The said Trustees shall hold a regular meeting at least once in each month to receive reports as to the business and affairs of said corporation, and to transact such business as may be necessary; and any Trustee neglecting to attend any of the meetings of the board for three successive months may thereupon, at the option of the said corporation, be considered as having vacated his position and a successor may be elected to fill the same. The said Trustees shall not, as such, directly or individually, receive any pay or emolument for their services.

Sec. 6. The corporation hereby created shall possess the general powers of and be subject to the restrictions and liabilities prescribed in Title three, Chapter eighteen, of the Revised Statutes.

Sec. 7. This Act shall take effect immediately.

State of New York
Office of the Secretary of State } ss.

I have compared the preceding with the original law on file in this office and do hereby certify that the same is a correct transcript therefrom, and of the whole of said original law.

Given under my hand and seal of office at the city of Albany, this sixteenth day of March in the year one thousand eight hundred and seventy-one.

D. Willer, Jr.

Dep. Secretary of State

(Seal)

Grand Lodge Sessions

First to Thirtieth (1871-1878)

The word "Sessions" is used here because the meetings of the Grand Lodge in recent years have been called "Sessions." In the early days, however, the regularly called meetings were called "Communications" while both the original meeting and those following through "recess" or "adjournment" were referred to as "Sessions." And so, since, in those days they had many "recesses" or "adjournments" by the time of the "Fifth Communication" while there had been held previously only "Four Communications" there had been thirteen "Sessions" so that the Grand Lodge Proceedings designated the "Fifth Communication" as the "Fourteenth Session."

That was held on June 8, 1873, and "recessed" to June 15, "adjourned" to June 22 and "recessed" to December 7 and the meeting of the last-named date was referred to as the "17th Session."

The use of the term "Session" for each of the individual meetings of the "Communications" was continued until the meeting of December 10, 1876, which was the "Twelfth Communication" and the "Twenty-eighth Session." It was at that meeting that it was decided to hold "Communications" of the Grand Lodge once a year and on "the second Sunday in December of each year."

The annual meetings of the Grand Lodge continued to be referred to in the printed proceedings as "Communications" until the proceedings of the meeting of May 19, 1891, in Louisville, Kentucky, which was referred to as "Twenty-seventh Annual" and "Forty-third Session." From then on until 1904 the annual meetings in the proceedings were referred to as "Annual Sessions," not "Communications." For example, the meeting of 1892 was referred to as the "Twenty-eighth Annual Session."

This, of course, was not correct for while it was the Twenty-eighth Session, it was not the Twenty-eighth "Annual" Session, for the reason that in the first six years of the life of the Grand

Lodge sessions or "communications" as they then were called were held twice each year so that the number of any session after that year would be six figures greater than the number of years of the life of the Grand Lodge.

This practice of referring to the annual meetings of the Grand Lodge as Thirtieth or Fortieth Annual Sessions was continued until the Proceedings of 1904 when the title was changed to "Session" rather than "Annual Session" so that in the proceedings of that year the meeting was referred to as "The Fortieth Session" and this practice has since been followed.

The foregoing will explain why, although the Grand Lodge was 81 years old in 1952, the meeting of that year is referred to as the "Eighty-eighth Session."

What are now called "Sessions" were, up to 1891, referred to as "Communications." If the word "Session" were used now as it was in the early days of the Order, the 1952 Meeting would be referred to as the One Hundred and Fourth Session.

At the meeting of February 19, 1871, the Committee on Rules and Regulations presented a Constitution of 26 articles, evidencing that its members had done a great deal of work in one week.

The Constitution

The points in the 26 articles of the original Constitution which might be of interest to the present-day Elks are:

A. The Grand Lodge shall hold an annual session during the second week in December, and a semi-annual session during the second week in June.

B. At the annual session the officers for the ensuing year shall be nominated, elected, and installed.

C. Special sessions may be called by the Exalted Grand Ruler when he deems necessary, and he shall call special sessions when requested to do so by one-third of the members of the Grand Lodge or two-thirds of the members of any subordinate lodge.

D. The elective officers shall be:

> Exalted Grand Ruler
> Esteemed Leading Grand Knight
> Esteemed Loyal Grand Knight
> Esteemed Grand Lecturer
> Grand Secretary

Grand Treasurer

The Judiciary—Supreme Judge, First Associate
Judge, Second Associate Judge

Grand Tiler

The appointive officers to consist of the District Deputy
Exalted Grand Rulers, Grand Chaplain, and such officers
as the Grand Lodge may direct.

E. The Exalted Grand Ruler to appoint the following committees to serve for one year:

> Committee on Laws and Supervision
> Committee on Appeals and Grievances
> Committee on Returns and Credentials
> Committee on Warrants
> Committee on Printing and Supplies

F. That the Exalted Grand Ruler shall officially, at least once during his term of office, visit each subordinate lodge in the district in which he resides.

G. The Exalted Grand Lecturer shall act as Chairman of the Committee on Returns and Credentials, and be prepared to assist in all ceremonies appertaining to the Grand Lodge, officiating as Grand Marshal at such ceremonies as may require the same.

H. At the semi-annual meeting in June each lodge shall pay to the Grand Lodge as dues not less than 25¢ per capita tax for each Devout Elder in good standing.

I. Seven members of the Grand Lodge, or of a subordinate lodge, to constitute a quorum.

J. Each lodge entitled to one vote (cast by its Exalted Ruler or his properly authorized representative) for every twenty-five Devout Elders in good standing on the following subjects:

1. Questions affecting the existence of a lodge.

2. Subjects affecting changes in the charges made by the Grand Lodge for charters, dispensations, rituals, codes, affiliative cards and withdrawal cards, and other modes of revenue received by the Grand Lodge from subordinate lodges.

If a lodge has less than 25 members, it shall still have one vote on these questions.

K. Provision was made for the election of five trustees each year, and their duties were defined.

L. The duties of the several officers and committeemen were quite fully enumerated.

M. Reports from subordinate lodges were provided for, and their rights and limitations set forth.

A charter was granted to New York Lodge No. 1 to date from February 12, 1871, and a charter was granted to the D.E.'s in Philadelphia empowering them "to perform all the secret and other work" of the Order; such charter to date from February 19, 1871.

The meeting of February 19, 1871, recessed until February 26, at which meeting there was the following action:

Lodge Charter form adopted.

The meeting again recessed, this time to March 5, 1871.

At this session the Committee on Examination of the Work of the Second Degree submitted a form for examination and a form for installation of officers and institution of lodges which were accepted.

The Exalted Grand Ruler appointed the following committees to serve until the next semi-annual meeting:

> Laws and Supervision
>
> Appeals and Grievances
>
> Returns and Credentials
>
> Warrants
>
> Printing and Supplies

He appointed William Coffin as Chaplain to the Grand Lodge.

Antonio Pastor offered to advance the funds to purchase certificates of membership and seal for the Grand Lodge and his offer was accepted.

A committee was appointed to arrange for a benefit for the Grand Lodge "in the city of Brooklyn."

The meeting of March 5 was adjourned to March 19 and that meeting was adjourned to April 9, and this first and formative Communication of the Grand Lodge, which consisted of a series of five meetings held respectively on February 12-19-26, March 5 and April 9, was brought to a close.

Second Regular Communication

The Second Regular Communication of the Grand Lodge was held on June 11, 1871. There were ten members present.

Third Regular Communication

The Third Regular Communication of the Grand Lodge was held on December 10, 1871. This was also referred to as the "Second Session"; presumably because it was the second annual session.

Recess was taken until December 17, when Charles J. White was elected Exalted Grand Ruler and A. Hamilton Mulligan was elected Grand Secretary.

Fourth Regular Communication

On June 9, 1872, the Fourth Regular Communication was held.

At practically all the meetings up to this time, as the Grand Lodge was still in its formative stage, amendments to the Constitution were adopted.

At this meeting it was voted that no officer of the Grand Lodge could hold an official position in a subordinate lodge.

It was voted that a subordinate lodge shall have the power to vacate the position of any officer who shall have been absent during three consecutive months of his year of office.

After electing Thomas G. Gaynor as Grand Secretary to fill the position formerly occupied by A. Hamilton Mulligan, the meeting was adjourned to June 23, 1872.

At the adjourned meeting the action taken was largely routine.

The next Annual Communication was held on December 8, 1872.

The resolution adopted at the previous meeting providing that no officer of the Grand Lodge should hold an official position in a subordinate lodge was rescinded.

Joseph C. Pinckney was elected Exalted Grand Ruler and William Coffin was elected Grand Secretary.

After a recess, the Grand Lodge reassembled on December 15, 1872.

At that meeting it was voted:

"That the Right Honorable Primo of Subordinate Lodges be instructed to order the Committee on Initiation to adhere strictly to the ritual and avoid all liberty and rough usage to candidates taking the First Degree."

Voted:

"That each Subordinate Lodge be instructed to elect five representatives for the session in June, and subsequent to that, five representatives at each annual election to be chosen to represent said Lodge in the Grand Lodge."

Note:

"While the meeting of June 9, 1872, was referred to as the 'Fourth Regular Communication,' and therefore it would appear that the meeting of December 6, 1872 should be referred to as the 'Fifth Regular Communication,' that designation was given to the meeting of June 8, 1873, so that this must have been considered a part of the 'Fourth Regular Communication.' "

──────1873──────

The Grand Lodge recessed to March 9, 1873, and reconvened with eight present. At this meeting was announced the death of William Sheppard, who was one of the fifteen "Jolly Corks" and founders of the Order of Elks.

At the "Fifth Regular Communication" (14th Session) of the Grand Lodge, held on June 8, 1873, a communication was received from ten Elks then residing in San Francisco, requesting that they be granted a charter to "form a branch lodge" in that city.

The request was granted.

The "Sixth Regular Communication" was held on December 14, 1873 (18th Session).

At this meeting the following Order of Business was adopted:

    1st Roll Call.

    2nd Reading of minutes of the previous Communication.

    3rd Good of the Order.

    4th Reports from subordinate lodges.

    5th Treasurer's report.

    6th Reports of committees by seniority.

    7th Reading communications.

    8th Bills against the Grand Lodge.

    9th Unfinished business.

    10th New business.

    11th Reading of minutes of the present Communication.

It was voted that "A compensation be allowed to the Grand Secretary for his services of five dollars for each session of the Grand Lodge, the amount of compensation so allowed shall not exceed the sum of fifty dollars per annum."

February 1, 1874 (19th Session)

The Committee on Regalia made an extensive report; the salient recommendations of which were:

"Exalted Grand Ruler — Collar of purple velvet, with small roll of fawn-colored velvet, the front to have an outline five-pointed star, with an elk's head and crossed gavels behind it, two stars on each side, graduated in size, with vine entwined around them, the fawn-colored roll also to have a vine, edges braided, the emblems, stars, vines, and braid, etc., to be embroidered in gilt, with gilt fringe around the collar."

With some modifications, similar regalia was presented for all the officers of the Grand Lodge, while the members had to be content with "Royal purple collar, edges braided, without emblem or vine."

SUBORDINATE LODGE REGALIA

"Exalted Ruler — Collar of fawn-colored velvet, with small roll of royal purple velvet, the front to have an outline five-pointed star, with an elk's head and crossed gavels behind it, two stars on each side, graduated in size, with vine entwined around them, royal purple roll also to have vine. Edges braided, the emblems, stars, vines, braidings, etc., to be embroidered in silver, with silver fringe around the collar."

Similar regalia, with appropriate modifications, was to be required for other subordinate lodge officers, while the Devout Elders (Second Degree) were to have "fawn-colored velvet collar, edges braided without vine or emblem."

James M. Powell was elected Exalted Grand Ruler and William Coffin was continued as Grand Secretary.

A committee composed of George J. Green, Thomas G. Gaynor, Henry P. O'Neil, Frank Moran, and Albert Stimmel was appointed to revise the secret work of the Order.

Henry P. O'Neil, George J. Green, and Hugh P. O'Neil were appointed to a Committee on Revision of Constitution.

The following resolution was adopted:

"That the Grand Lodge positively prohibits the use of any obscene or indecorous language, or actions, during the Social Sessions of the subordinate lodges."

The meeting recessed to meet the second Sunday in March, 1874.

At that meeting, March 8, 1874 (20th Session), the "Constitution of 1874" was adopted, as were the "Statutes of 1874" and the "Rules of Order."

Constitution and Statutes, 1874

CONSTITUTION

Article I   Of the Grand Lodge.
"   II   Of the Powers of the Grand Lodge.

STATUTES

The revenue of the Grand Lodge from subordinate lodges shall be as follows:

1. Annual tax from Lodges, as provided hereafter.

2. Fees for charters, not less than $20.00.

3. Fees for dispensations to form new Lodges, not less than $10.00.

4. Fees for Rituals, not less than $5.00.

5. Fees for Affiliation Cards, not less than $1.00.

6. Fees for dispensations of the following kinds:

   (1) To allow a Lodge to ballot for, and, if elected, to confer the first degree upon a candidate on the day of his proposition, fee $2.50.

   (2) To allow a Lodge to ballot for a candidate, and, if

elected, to confer both degrees upon him at a Communication of the degree of Devout Elder, fee $5.00.

(3) To allow a Lodge to ballot for, and, if elected, to confer upon a brother of the first degree, the degree of Devout Elder, at a Communication of the same, before the expiration of the probationary period, fee $2.50.

(4) To allow a Lodge to grant a dimit to a brother of the first degree for the purpose of affiliating with a sister Lodge, fee $2.50.

" 34 First Degree meetings may be omitted between last week of June and third week of September

" 35 Exalted Grand Ruler may not preside at Subordinate Lodge meetings, except for installation, conferring degree, or exemplifying the Standard Work

" 36 Lodge may not be excused from voting on candidates through black ball reject

" 37 Ballot shall be inviolate

Article VI — Salary and Security of Grand Officers, and Mileage

Section 38 Grand Secretary and Grand Treasurer to give security as Grand Lodge may require

" 39 Grand Secretary to receive for services $5.00 per session of Grand Lodge, but not to exceed $50.00 per year

" 40 Grand Tiler to receive $1.00 per session

" 41 Representatives to Grand Lodge to receive such mileage as Grand Lodge may direct.

The meeting adjourned to April 12, 1874 (21st Session) when only routine matters were considered.

———— 1874 ————

The "Seventh Regular Communication" of the Grand Lodge was held on June 14, 1874 (22nd Session). Routine matters were considered and the meeting adjourned to June 28, 1874, and again no action out of the usual order was taken (23rd Session).

The "Eighth Regular Communication" was held on December 13, 1874.

———— 1875 ————

The "Ninth Regular Communication" was held on June 13, 1875 (25th Session).

Several amendments to the Constitution and to the Statutes were adopted at this meeting, none of which were of historical importance.

The "Tenth Regular Communication" was held on December 12, 1875 (26th Session).

Henry P. O'Neil was re-elected Exalted Grand Ruler and William Coffin was re-elected Grand Secretary.

Upon recommendation of the Committee on Laws and Supervision, it was voted:

"That, after the expiration of the year 1876, this Grand Lodge shall hold but one regular communication annually."

It was voted:

"That the opening and closing of a lodge at every communication should be accompanied by appropriate prayers, and that the Chaplain should have some definite work to perform, as well as in the initiation, in the higher degree, and in our forthcoming burial service."

————— 1 8 7 6 —————

The "Eleventh Regular Communication" was held on June 11, 1876 (27th Session). Exalted Grand Ruler O'Neil reported a dispensation for a lodge in San Francisco. The following recommendations in his report were adopted:

That a charter be granted to San Francisco Lodge No. 3.

That a joint committee, composed of the Committee on Laws and Supervision and the Committee on Printing, be empowered to embody the changes required to permit the holding of membership, in addition to one in a chartered lodge, in as many lodges under dispensation as they may see fit, but for a given period.

That hereafter an apron be worn instead of a collar.

That the Joint Committee on Laws and Supervision and the Committee on Printing and Supplies be empowered to amend the laws so as to do away with the election annually of delegates to the Grand Lodge and substitute a provision conferring permanent membership in the Grand Lodge on all four of the working (chair) officers of subordinate lodges and also on the Treasurer and Secretary, provided they have served a complete term from date of annual election to subsequent date of same.

The "Twelfth Regular Communication" of the Grand Lodge was held on December 10, 1876 (28th Session).

Voted "that the regular communication of the Grand Lodge be convened at 12 o'clock on the second Sunday in December of each year."

Frank Girard was elected Exalted Grand Ruler and Henry P. O'Neil was elected Grand Secretary.

Voted to grant a charter to Chicago Lodge No. 4.

————— 1 8 7 7 —————

The "Thirteenth Regular Communication" was held on December 9, 1877 (29th Session) in Philadelphia.

Amended Constitution, Statutes, and Rules of Order (known as Constitution 1878) were adopted.

The following resolution was adopted:

"Resolved: that the only legal place for the communications of the Grand Lodge, under our laws, is the city of New York, and that, therefore, the next communication should be there held."

It was also determined by vote of the Grand Lodge that the Grand Lodge communication be resumed in New York City in order to cure any illegalities or objections that might hereafter arise; and that all the legislation recorded herein be repassed. (This was therefore done after the return of a constitutional number to New York.)

At the close of the minutes of this meeting, signed by Henry P. O'Neil, Grand Secretary, there appears this paragraph:

"The minutes here given are as full as the rough minutes of the outgoing Grand Secretary rendered possible, and are submitted with the reservation indicated."

This probably accounts for the fact that the minutes carry no reference to the creation of new lodges, while the following items appear in the report of the Grand Treasurer; and indicate the existence of Lodges Nos. 5-6-7-8 either under dispensation or charter.

"April 18, 1877 from Cincinnati Lodge No. 5, for jewels...........$13.75

November 6, 1877 dispensation fees and ritual from Sacramento Lodge No. 6 .... 15.00

April 2, 1877 dispensation to Baltimore Lodge No. 7................ 10.00

April 18, 1877 dispensation to Louisville Lodge No. 8............. 10.00"

———1878———

The "Fourteenth Regular Communication" (30th Session) of the Grand Lodge was held on December 8, 1878.

Charters were granted to St. Louis Lodge No. 9 and Boston Lodge No. 10.

Sacramento Lodge No. 6 surrendered its charter.

The Exalted Grand Ruler reported that he had granted a dispensation to Pittsburgh Lodge No. 11 on September 13, 1878.

George R. Maguire, of Philadelphia Lodge No. 2, was elected Exalted Grand Ruler and R. S. Martin was elected Grand Secretary.

Voted that the title of the fourth officer in subordinate lodges be changed from Grand Lecturer to Esteemed Lecturing Knight.

Elks Mutual Benefit Association

Probably very few present-day Elks ever heard that the Order, at one time, sponsored an insurance branch. Such was the case, however, and the name of that branch was Elks Mutual Benefit Association.

While the minutes of the Grand Lodge Sessions do not carry any information relative to the creation of the Association, a "Sixth Annual Report" thereof, recorded in the printed proceedings of the 1884 Session, would indicate that it was established in 1878.

The first reference to the Association found in the records of the Grand Lodge appears in the minutes of the Grand Lodge Session of December 12, 1880.

At that Session Henry P. O'Neil presented a memorial from the Association as the result of which the Grand Lodge Statutes were amended as follows:

"Resolved, that the statutes be amended by adding to Article 2 on page 34, a new section, to be known as Section 9 of said article as follows:

"Section 9. The Committee on Supervision of the Elks Mutual Benefit Association shall be located in the City of New York; shall consist as far as practicable of non-members of said Association; shall examine its accounts and report thereon in writing to the Grand Lodge at its annual Communication. They shall have power to call upon the officers of said Association at any time and to demand such books, etc., as they may desire to examine, in order that the rights of the members of this Order connected with said Association may be protected.

"In return for the patronage and endorsement of the Grand Lodge, the officers and board of directors in said Association shall give such facilities for examination to the Committee on Supervision, etc., as they may require; and said board of directors shall present at each annual communication of the Grand Lodge a full and complete report of the condition and transactions of said Association for the preceding year."

————— 1881 —————

In December, 1881, Joseph F. Waring, the Secretary, reported 117 members, an increase of three members during the year. The report stated that the membership fee was $3.00 and assessments of $1.10 were levied upon the death of a member.

The Secretary reported that during the year there had been 240 applications for membership which brought the total membership to 372.

He stated that 35 had been dropped and one had died, leaving the membership at 336.

Cash in treasury was $524.28.

———— 1 8 8 4 ————

At the Grand Lodge Session in December, Exalted Grand Ruler Perry said that he was glad to state that the Elks Mutual Benefit Association was in a flourishing condition.

He stated that its membership had reached 474 at the time of the annual report and was steadily increasing. He added that there were sufficient funds in the treasury to pay another assessment without a call upon the members if such a course should be found necessary. Cash on hand—$832.55.

In the ritual of 1884, after a candidate had been initiated and received by the lodge, the Exalted Ruler said to him:

> "My brother, before taking your seat in the Lodge, it is my duty, as the presiding officer of an organization devoted to practical charity, to call your attention to the insurance branch of our Order, known as the Elks Mutual Benefit Association. This society was organized for a two-fold purpose, first, to assist the family of a worthy deceased D. E., and second, to relieve the lodge of a portion of the burden entailed upon it by such a demise.

> "For further information upon this subject, I refer you to the Secretary who will afford you all necessary details."

The most thorough information in the Grand Lodge records relative to the character of the operations of the Association is found in the Sixth Annual Report thereof appearing in the printed proceedings of 1884.

The report gives the following information (here condensed):

Deaths: two were reported. One in November, 1883, and one in January, 1884. One, a Past Exalted Ruler of New York Lodge, had paid a membership fee of $4.00 and six assessments amounting to $6.60, total $10.60.

His widow received $300.

A member of Philadelphia Lodge. He had paid a membership fee of $3.00 and seven assessments amounting to $7.70, total $10.70. This widow received $337.

Last report	336
Added	162
	——
Total	498

Dropped for non-payment	66	
Died	2	
	——	
Total	68	
Reinstated	43	
	——	
Net loss		25
Present members		473

———— 1885 ————

Exalted Grand Ruler Sanderson said in his report:

"This useful branch of our work is growing in favor of our members and increasing in usefulness."

However, at the same Session, the Committee on Elks Mutual Benefit Association, consisting of John H. Meech, J. D. Plunkett, and David B. Hilt, reported that they had made as thorough an examination of the books of account of the Association as the circumstances would admit and found that the business of the Association had been conducted in a careless and inefficient manner with almost an entire absence of the adoption and enforcement of proper safeguards for the protection of the assets of the organization, as evidenced by the failure to properly sign and endorse orders upon the treasurer or affix the seal of the Association to said orders as the prerequisite to the payment of the same.

They recommended that a committee of five be appointed by the incoming Exalted Grand Ruler to consider the reorganization of the Elks Mutual Benefit Association and after consultation with the Board of Directors to report at the next meeting of the Grand Lodge such a detailed plan as would graft the organization upon the working of the Order.

———— 1886 ————

The Committee created for the examination of the Elks Mutual Benefit Association reported that they had made an examination of the books of account of the said Association and found the treasurer's books to be correct and with proper vouchers.

They reported that the receipts of the Association from all sources appeared to have been $2884.30 and the expenditures $2371.87, the difference between which, added to the amount now in the hands of the secretary and that on deposit at the time of the last report, amounted to $1276.20.

The Committee further reported that while they had been charged with the formation of a plan for the reorganization of the Association the members of the Committee were located at such remote points from each other that it was impossible for them to meet for proper consultation.

Apparently there was considerable difference of opinion among the members of the Committee relative to the Association.

In his report at that Session of the Grand Lodge, Exalted Grand Ruler Daniel A. Kelly stated that the insurance branch of the Order had not kept pace with the growth of the fraternity, and he expressed the hope that the subordinate lodges would exhibit more interest in that work.

Apparently, Antonio Pastor had a different opinion. Following the report, he offered a motion to strike from the ritual all reference to the Elks Mutual Benefit Association.

This was referred to the Committee on Ritual. The Committee recommended the adoption of the Pastor motion, and the recommendation was accepted by the Grand Lodge.

1887

At the Grand Lodge Session of this year, the report of the Association was read and was referred to the Committee on Supervision of the Elks Mutual Benefit Association to "report at the next Communication."

Also at this Session, M. Mullone offered the following resolution:

> "Resolved — that a committee of three be appointed by the Exalted Grand Ruler to inquire into the feasibility and practicability of instituting in lieu of the Elks Mutual Benefit Association an insurance fund in the Order from which the heirs of a deceased brother, or such other person or persons as he may designate by will, shall be paid a sum not less than $500.00, or more than $1,000.00, and report thereon at the next meeting of the Grand Lodge."

The Grand Secretary moved to amend by referring the whole subject to the incoming Committee on Elks Mutual Benefit Association.

The amendment was carried and the reference to that Committee was made.

At the Grand Lodge Session in 1887 an Elks Mutual Benefit Association Committee was appointed, consisting of the following:

> M. Mullone, New York Lodge No. 1
> William Harris, Boston Lodge No. 10
> Fred Quintard, New Haven Lodge No. 25

The records of attendance of the Grand Lodge Session of 1888 do not indicate that any of the members of the Committee were in attendance.

Minutes of the 1888 Session of the Grand Lodge (July 10, 11 and 12) show that when that Committee was called it failed to answer.

The report of the Committee was then made a special order of business for July 11, at 2:30 o'clock.

On motion it was decided to increase the Committee on Elks Mutual Benefit Association to five members, and E. H. Warker and H. P. O'Neil, of New York Lodge No. 1, were appointed as the additional members.

On motion of H. P. O'Neil the Elks Mutual Benefit Association was directed to give the Committee all the assistance and information possible in connection with the insurance business of that Association.

———— **1 8 8 9** ————

Exalted Grand Ruler Hamilton E. Leach, in his report to the Grand Lodge in July, 1889, said:

> "We need no partnership or connection with any other society or company, insurance or otherwise, to either give us our strength or identity. We shall centralize all our strength of purpose solely upon the faithful observance of the grand objects of our Order, and any Association or connection of this Order with any other company or Order diverts the attention and efforts of the brothers from theirs."

At this Session, the Grand Secretary, Arthur C. Moreland, of New York Lodge No. 1, submitted a plan of insurance for the consideration of the Grand Lodge which was referred to the Committee on Laws and Supervision.

On recommendation of this Committee, consideration of this matter was postponed until the next regular session.

The Committee on Distribution said:

> "We concur with the views of the Exalted Grand Ruler as to the impracticability of associating this Order with any insurance or benefit association or the adoption of any features of this character as a part of the business of the B.P.O. Elks."

At the Grand Lodge Session of 1892, Joseph Williams, of Denver Lodge No. 17, offered a plan for creating an Elks Mutual Benefit Association.

This was referred to the Committee on Laws and Appeals.

This Committee reported it back to the Grand Lodge without recommendation and it was laid on the table.

——— **1893** ———

In the Grand Lodge Session of 1893, the Committee on Laws and Appeals, consisting of L. E. Griffith, of Troy, New York, Lodge No. 141, and Edmund B. Fuller, of Haverhill, Massachusetts, Lodge No. 165, made the following report which was adopted:

"Your Committee, to whom was referred at the last session of this Grand Lodge papers and correspondence concerning a system of insurance in connection with this Grand Lodge, would respectfully report as follows:

"That no system of insurance be endorsed or adopted by this Grand Lodge."

——— **1907** ———

In the constitution proposed in 1906 and adopted in 1907 it was decreed:

"There shall be no branches or degrees of membership in the Order, nor any insurance or mutual benefit features, nor shall there be other adjuncts or auxiliaries other than the optional organization and maintenance of State Associations and Past Exalted Rulers Associations."

Sunday Meetings

That there was very strong sentiment in the early days of the Order favorable to continuing to hold all meetings of subordinate lodges on Sunday evenings is evidenced by the fact that when, in 1873, Philadelphia Lodge petitioned the Grand Lodge for authority to change its meeting night from Sunday night of each week to Friday night, that request being referred to a committee composed of T. G. Gaynor, G. J. Green and Charles T. White, that committee reported as follows:

"To the Exalted Grand Ruler of the Grand Lodge:

"Your Committee appointed for the purpose of considering a request of Philadelphia Lodge No. 2, in reference to the proposed change in their time of meeting, respectfully report that they disapprove of the proposed change, inasmuch as it strikes at the fundamental principles upon which the Order is based; all of which is respectfully submitted."

The Grand Lodge adopted the report.

Hay Opposes Sunday Meetings

In his report in 1892 Grand Exalted Ruler Hay said:

"When the Order was instituted it was composed mainly of a membership selected from a profession allowing no other than Sunday evening for meetings and the early lodges in institution, by force of habit, followed the custom."

He added that "of late years it is rather the exception and not the rule and new lodges are selecting the week days upon which to meet."

The Grand Exalted Ruler took the position that such action was right, and expressed the sentiment that District Deputies should, at the institution of a new lodge, discourage the idea of fixing Sunday as a regular meeting day.

He felt that respect of public opinion called for discouragement of Sunday meetings.

Anti-Sunday Meeting Resolution

As the result, presumably, of the Grand Exalted Ruler's statements, H. R. Littlefield, Portland, Oregon, Lodge No. 142, offered the following resolution:

"Resolved — all Subordinate Lodges are prohibited from holding their sessions on Sunday; also reunions, picnics and gatherings of like character."

Percy G. Williams, Brooklyn Lodge No. 22, moved an amendment providing that such rule should not take effect until after January 1, 1893.

This was adopted.

The Reaction

In his report to the 1893 Grand Lodge Session, Grand Exalted

Ruler Hay stated that:

> "Several, namely Boston, Philadelphia, Washington and Norfolk, applied for dispensations to continue Sunday meetings from January 1, 1893, until the meeting of the Grand Lodge in June."

He said that he understood that an attempt would be made to rescind the action of the Grand Lodge barring Sunday meetings, and took the position that the Order could not recede from "any high stand it has taken."

He urged that if it were necessary to make the rule stronger by incorporating it into a law, it should be done at once.

The Committee on Distribution reported as follows:

> "Your Committee recommends the valuable suggestion of the Grand Exalted Ruler in relation to giving future Grand Exalted Rulers the power to grant dispensation to certain lodges of our Order in large cities to hold meetings on Sundays.

> "In two or three lodges there is a larger element who can only attend on that day, and we feel that they should not be deprived of that right.

> "The proceedings and ritual of our Order are as sacred as man can conceive and cannot offend the religious community, being mainly for the dispensation of charity. We recommend this to the Grand Lodge for their consideration."

The proceedings of that Session do not record any action by the Grand Lodge.

However, that was the Session at which appeared the bitter feeling between individuals and groups that resulted in the developments recorded here under the heading *The Jamestown Controversy.*

It is possible that the discussion on this subject may have been among the items eliminated from the proceedings under the provision of the following motion which was adopted:

> "That the Board of Trustees be authorized to expunge and eliminate from the proceedings of this body, and from all papers presented to this body, anything of a personal nature or of a vituperative character, reflecting upon any member of the Grand Lodge."

S E C T I O N

Second Decade

In this Decade the Order continued to grow, its membership increasing over ten-fold and the number of its lodges increasing over nine-fold.

It was during this period that attention was first given to developing a degree of care in selecting new members.

It was not until 1886, however, that the laws of the Order were amended to provide that an application for membership should be referred to a committee to "carefully examine into the character of the applicant."

During this entire Second Decade there was no other requirement for membership excepting that of age.

When one thinks of the responsibilities of the Grand Secretary of the Order at the present time, it is interesting to note that at the beginning of the Second Decade the salary of the Grand Secretary was "raised" to $80 per year.

In 1880, the members of the Grand Lodge—growing very liberal—decided that the Exalted Grand Ruler should receive "what

GEORGE R. MAGUIRE
1878-79

CHARLES E. DAVIES*
1879

LOUIS C. WAEHNER
1879-80

THOMAS E. GARRETT
1880-82

JOHN J. TINDALE
1882-83

Exalted Grand Rulers

SECOND DECADE

1878-1888

EDWIN A. PERRY
1883-84

HENRY S. SANDERSON
1884-85

DANIEL A. KELLY
1885-86

WILLIAM E. ENGLISH
1886-87

HAMILTON E. LEACH
1887-89

*Filled unexpired term of Exalted Grand Ruler Maguire

he may expend as personal mileage when officially visiting any subordinate lodge."

Probably they felt that the lodge visited would provide the sustenance.

During this period the first step was taken to guard against "commercialism" when the Statutes were amended to prohibit any member from using his "certificate of membership" or exposing any emblem of the Order as a sign in his business transactions.

At the Grand Lodge Session in 1886 a motion for an amendment to the Constitution providing for State Grand Lodges and a Supreme Lodge, offered by Philadelphia Lodge, was defeated by a vote of 168 to 105.

Up to 1887 there was no provision for a District Deputy in the district where the Exalted Grand Ruler resided.

Second Decade——1878-1888

EXALTED GRAND RULERS

GEORGE R. MAGUIRE, New York Lodge No. 1	1878-1879
CHARLES E. DAVIES, Chicago Lodge No. 4,	1879
Esteemed Leading Grand Knight (Filled out the	
unexpired term of George R. Maguire, who died in office)	
LOUIS C. WAEHNER, New York Lodge No. 1	1879-1880
THOMAS E. GARRETT, St. Louis Lodge No. 9 (2 yrs.)	1880-1882
JOHN J. TINDALE, New York Lodge No. 1	1882-1883
EDWIN A. PERRY, Boston Lodge No. 10	1883-1884
HENRY S. SANDERSON, New York Lodge No. 1	1884-1885
DANIEL A. KELLY, Baltimore Lodge No. 7	1885-1886
WILLIAM E. ENGLISH, Indianapolis Lodge No. 13	1886-1887
HAMILTON E. LEACH, Washington Lodge No. 15	1887-1888
(Served also	1888-1889)

GRAND SECRETARIES

At the Session of the Grand Lodge held in December, 1878, R. S. Martin, who was for many years Secretary of New York Lodge No. 1, was elected Grand Secretary. He served until December, 1879, when George J. Green succeeded him. Green served in 1880, but was not in attendance at the Session in 1881 and for that Session R. S. Martin was acting Secretary.

In December, 1881, Arthur C. Moreland, of New York Lodge No. 1, was elected Grand Secretary, and for the first time the Grand Secretary had an office and suitable records.

He served until 1890.

MEMBERSHIP AND CHARITABLE EXPENDITURES

In the Second Decade the membership increased from 820 to 8,952.

The number of lodges increased from 10 to 92.

YEAR	MEMBERSHIP	CHARITABLE EXPENDITURES
1878-1879	929	No Record
1879-1880	1,060	No Record
1880-1881	1,339	$ 4,440.64
1881-1882	1,806	5,553.01
1882-1883	2,400	5,073.30
1883-1884	3,051	8,163.65
1884-1885	3,949	10,085.73
1885-1886	5,511	8,246.57
1886-1887	7,334	9,336.75
1887-1888	8,952	11,716.77

At the end of this Decade the assets of the 92 lodges amounted to $203,024.61.

Grand Lodge Sessions

Thirty-First Session

The "Fifteenth Regular Communication" of the Grand Lodge—Sunday, December 14, 1879—31st Session—76 present:

All of the printed proceedings of Grand Lodge meetings up to and including the one for this meeting carried on the front cover the following notice:

"To be read in all lodges for the information of the Brethren."

The compensation of the Grand Secretary was increased to $80 per year.

A charter was granted to California Lodge No. 12, which lodge had been granted a dispensation by the Exalted Grand Ruler upon the petition of some who were, as the District Deputy reported, "displeased with the government of the (San Francisco) Lodge."

Upon motion of Henry P. O'Neil, a committee consisting of the Exalted Grand Ruler, Grand Secretary, and Grand Treasurer was appointed to prepare within three months a Burial Service for the Order.

The "Sixteenth Regular Communication" of the Grand Lodge— December 12, 1880—32nd Session—68 present:

L. C. Waehner, Exalted Grand Ruler, recommended "that provision be made to defray the actual traveling expenses (of the Exalted Grand Ruler), at least for mileage."

As a result, the Grand Lodge voted an amendment to the Statutes, providing that the Exalted Grand Ruler receive what he may expend "as personal mileage when officially visiting any subordinate lodge."

He also recommended that, because of the increased work of the Grand Lodge, "especially the correspondence of the Grand Secretary," there be established a "business office for the Grand Lodge."

The Grand Lodge authorized the Exalted Grand Ruler to appoint a committee of three, "of which the Grand Secretary shall be a member," to provide proper accommodations for the Grand Secretary during the following year.

The Constitution was amended by providing that "a Deputy Exalted Grand Ruler at large" be appointed each year.

The Constitution was amended by adding:

"The Deputy Exalted Grand Ruler at large shall be the accredited representative of the Exalted Grand Ruler throughout the United States, whose duty it shall be to advance and promulgate the interests of the Order, without, however, the privilege of interfering with the duties of the District Deputies in their respective districts, except by and with their consent."

The "Seventeenth Regular Communication" of the Grand Lodge —Sunday, December 11, 1881—33rd Session—68 present:

Charter granted to Indianapolis Lodge No. 13.

The Constitution was amended by striking out certain provisions and substituting the following:

"The Grand Lodge shall be composed as follows:

"1. Those who, by virtue of the provisions of our Constitution, as existing prior to December, 1882, shall have been duly placed upon the roll of permanent membership of the Grand Lodge, shall so continue.

"2. Those who, in Lodges under dispensation, shall have filled the position either of Exalted Ruler, Est. Ldg. Knight, Est. Loyal Knight, Est. Lec. Knight, Secretary or Treasurer during the term for which they shall have been chosen, shall be placed upon the roll as permanent members and shall, pending the completion of the term for which they may have been elected, be considered temporary members of the Grand Lodge.

"3. Those who, in chartered Lodges, shall have completed a full Lodge year (i.e., the period between the date of annual election in November of any year and the annual election in November of the year following) as Exalted Ruler of said chartered Lodge, shall be permanent members of the Grand Lodge and shall, pending the completion of said full Lodge year, be recognized as temporary members. Carried."

Exalted Grand Ruler Garrett appointed Frank Girard as Deputy Exalted Grand Ruler at large, as he was active in the organization of several lodges.

Thirty-Fourth Session

The "Eighteenth Regular Communication," of the Grand Lodge— December 10, 1882—34th Session:

Exalted Grand Ruler Garrett in his report said:

"I was applied to for a dispensation to start a new lodge in Chicago. The petition was signed and the new lodge recommended by the highest authorities of our Order resident in the state of Illinois. I made inquiries and was answered that the movement for a new lodge was in the best interests of the Order. Emulation was the alleged object, and fraternal emulation is known to be a good thing to cultivate and practice. Upon the supposition that our brethren of Chicago knew what was wanted for the general good in that jurisdiction better than I could know, I granted the petitioners a dispensation to organize Illinois Lodge, the number of which would have been 16 under charter. I am informed that the new lodge, which was duly organized by Exalted Brother Simon Quinlin, E.G.R. for Illinois, has held only a few informal meetings and done no work under dispensation. It has had plenty of time to prove its right to live, and has failed to produce one argument. The movement appears not to have been in good faith, and looks like trifling with the dignity of a noble Order which has become national in its design and growth, to accomplish a local and petty purpose. Such little schemes must hereafter be discouraged and, if possible, prevented. Illinois Lodge U. D. was a mistake, and the dispensation lapses under our laws, by limitation. I recommend the

Grand Lodge to call it in, and demand the properties of which the lodge may have become possessed."

It was voted that the suggestion of the E. G. R., in the case of Illinois Lodge No. 16 U. D., be adopted, and that the Committee on Charters be directed to demand the dispensation granted and all property, etc., of which said lodge may have become possessed from the Grand Lodge.

CHARTERS

Charters were granted Providence Lodge No. 14, Washington Lodge No. 15 and Denver Lodge No. 17.

The Exalted Grand Ruler on Districts:

"The subject of district jurisdiction, state or territorial, is now thrusting itself upon our attention, and will demand regulation sooner or later. Already complaints have been made that applicants for the degrees have ignored the lodge already established in the city of their residence, applied for admission to a lodge in another city and state, and have been accepted and made members of the Order—when they would have been rejected, had they applied at home. This naturally creates dissatisfaction, and if permitted, will eventually work a wrong to the Order. At present the jurisdiction of all the lodges, in the selecting and making of members, is concurrent. I suggest and would recommend that we draw the lines of district jurisdiction around the lodge or lodges in each district, confining them to the state or territory for their initiates; except as regards applicants from districts where there is no lodge established, and those whose business or profession involves traveling—leaving them without a settled home. Over these exceptions the jurisdiction of the lodges should remain concurrent as heretofore."

The charter of Louisville Lodge No. 8 was declared forfeited.

Thirty-Fifth Session

The "Nineteenth Regular Communication" of the Grand Lodge —December 9, 1883—35th Session:

CHARTERS

Upon recommendation of the Committee, charters were granted to: Cleveland Lodge No. 18, Hartford Lodge No. 19, Peoria Lodge No. 20, Newark Lodge No. 21 and Brooklyn Lodge No. 22.

The charter of Louisville Lodge No. 8 was restored.

The salary of the Grand Secretary was raised to $1,000 per annum.

The office of Grand Marshal was abolished, and the office of Grand Esquire was created.

COMMERCIALISM

The following resolution was adopted and made part of the Grand Lodge Statutes:

"No Brother shall use his Certificate of Membership nor expose any emblem of the Order as a sign in his business transactions."

Thirty-Sixth Session

The "Twentieth Regular Communication" of the Grand Lodge —December 14, 1884—36th Session:

The Committee on Work and Ritual submitted an amended Ritual, which was adopted.

CHARTERS

Charters were granted to Buffalo, New York, Lodge, No. 23; New Haven, Connecticut, Lodge, No. 25; Kansas City, Missouri, Lodge, No. 26; and Memphis, Tennessee, Lodge, No. 27.

The charter of Cleveland Lodge was surrendered.

Authorization was voted for the appointment of an Assistant Grand Secretary at a salary of $400 per year.

Thirty-Seventh Session

The "Twenty-first Regular Communication" of the Grand Lodge —December 13, 1885—37th Session:

Exalted Grand Ruler Henry S. Sanderson, in his report, advised that he had caused Cleveland Lodge to surrender its charter because of lack of interest, but that he was transmitting to his successor a charter for a new lodge in Cleveland. (A charter for a new lodge in Cleveland was granted the next year.)

The Exalted Grand Ruler advised that he had united San Francisco Lodge No. 3 and California Lodge No. 12 into one Lodge to be known as Golden Gate Lodge No. 6.

The following resolution relative to the revision of the Constitution and Statutes was adopted:

"Resolved: That the incoming Exalted Grand Ruler, Grand Secretary and Chairman of the Committee on Laws and Supervision for the ensuing year be appointed a Special Committee to revise the Constitution and Statutes of the Order, embodying in such revision all alterations and amendments heretofore adopted, or that may be adopted at the present session, and that such revision, when completed, shall be printed by and under the direction of the Printing Committee and furnished to subordinate lodges at the actual cost thereof."

CHARTERS

Charters were granted to the following lodges: Golden Gate Lodge No. 6, Rochester Lodge No. 24, Wheeling Lodge No. 28, Little Rock Lodge No. 29, New Orleans Lodge No. 30, Marion Lodge No. 32, Utica Lodge No. 33, Detroit Lodge No. 34, Bridgeport Lodge No. 36 and Columbus Lodge No. 37.

Thirty-Eighth Session

The "Twenty-second Regular Communication" of the Grand Lodge—December 12, 1886—38th Session:

Grand Lodge Constitution, Statutes and Rules of Order:

The Special Committee on the Revision and Codification of the Grand Lodge Constitution, Statutes and Rules of Order reported that it had completed its labors and was presenting to the Grand Lodge a volume comprising the laws.

CHARTERS

The following charters were granted: Cleveland Lodge No. 18, Syracuse Lodge No. 31, Meriden Lodge No. 35, Norfolk Lodge No. 38, Omaha Lodge No. 39, St. Joseph Lodge No. 40, Little Falls Lodge No. 42, Minneapolis Lodge No. 44, Richmond Lodge No. 45, Milwaukee Lodge No. 46, *East Saginaw Lodge No. 47, Grand Rapids Lodge No. 48, Albany Lodge No. 49, Springfield Lodge No. 51, Toledo Lodge No. 53, Youngstown Lodge No. 55, Mansfield Lodge No. 56, Fond du Lac Lodge No. 57 and Dayton Lodge No. 58.

* In 1892 the name of this Lodge was changed to Saginaw.

DATE OF GRAND LODGE MEETING

Two members of a committee appointed to consider the advisability of changing the date of the meeting of the Grand Lodge recommended that the date be changed to the first Sunday in July, while a minority of one recommended that a special committee of three be appointed "to present a well-considered scheme for such change, including therein all necessary amendments to the Constitution, Statutes and Rules of Order, and report such schemes at our next communication."

These reports were referred to the Committee on Laws and Supervision, which Committee recommended a committee of five to be appointed to report on the matter at the next meeting. This recommendation was adopted.

DISTRICT DEPUTY DISTRICTS

It was voted to amend the Constitution to provide as follows:

"Each State and Territory of the United States and the District of Columbia shall constitute a District, as Lodges may be found therein, or as charters or dispensations may be granted to form lodges therein."

PLACE OF MEETING

"An amendment was offered providing for the annual meetings to be held at such place as may be determined upon a majority vote of the Grand Lodge, instead of its place of meeting being confined to the City of New York."

This failed to receive the necessary two-thirds vote.

A motion was later made to amend the Constitution so that Grand Lodge meetings could be held somewhere besides New York. This motion was lost by a vote of 85 nays to 60 ayes.

Thirty-Ninth Session

The "Twenty-third Regular Communication" of the Grand Lodge—December 11, 1887—39th Session:

Exalted Grand Ruler English recommended that the law be so amended to authorize the appointment of a District Deputy for each jurisdiction, the law having previously provided that the Exalted Grand Ruler himself should act as a District Deputy of the district in which he resided.

The Exalted Grand Ruler recommended a revision of the Ritual, and that "special attention be given to the complete reconstruction of the work of the First Degree in order that it may be made more impressive to the candidate and more interesting to the members in attendance engaging in the Degree."

CHARTERS

Charters were granted to the following lodges: Lockport No. 41, Kalamazoo No. 50, Chillicothe No. 52, Lima No. 54, St. Paul No. 59, Paterson No. 60, Springfield No. 61, Elmira No. 62, Cumberland No. 63, Rockford No. 64, Lawrence No. 65, Logansport No.

66, Canton No. 68, New Castle No. 69, Binghamton No. 70, Nashville No. 72, and New Bedford No. 73.

Fortieth Session

The "Twenty-fourth Regular Communication" of the Grand Lodge—July 10, 1888—40th Session:

Exalted Grand Ruler Leach, in his report, stressed the importance and necessity of providing an office for the Grand Secretary.

ANNUAL REUNIONS

In respect to the annual reunions, the Exalted Grand Ruler stated that he was in favor of the Grand Lodge being a migratory body, pointing out that then its annual meeting could be the reunion of the Order, and from every section organized bodies would go as escorts to the Grand Lodge delegates.

The following proposition was submitted to the Grand Lodge:

"In the matter of the amendment to the Constitution, proposed by George W. Andrews and others, a committee of Chicago Lodge No. 4, to amend Section 5 of the Constitution by striking out after the word 'annually' the words 'in the City of New York,' and inserting in the place thereof the words 'at such place as may be determined by a majority vote of the Grand Lodge members present at each annual communication, upon the location of place of meeting for the following year.' "

The amendment was adopted by a vote of 228 ayes to 47 nays, and it was voted that the amendment be submitted to the subordinate lodges for their action, which was favorable.

CHARTERS

Charters were granted to the following lodges: Erie No. 67, Dallas No. 71, Hoboken No. 74, Delaware No. 76, Circleville No. 77, Lincoln No. 80, Glens Falls No. 81, Upper Sandusky No. 83, Burlington No. 84, Salt Lake City No. 85, Bay City No. 88, Pueblo No. 90 and Seattle No. 92.

Constitution and Statutes

It is not practicable or worthwhile to incorporate in a history of this character a detailed story of all the manifold changes that have taken place in the Constitution and Statutes of the Order.

It does seem desirable, however, to treat of the general trend in the development of the Constitution and Statutes and the most important changes.

Trends and Changes

One of the first steps taken by the members of the Order at its birth was to adopt a Constitution and Rules and Regulations. This was done in March 1868.

Following the creation of the Grand Lodge there was adopted, on February 19, 1871, a new Constitution.

In 1874 a Committee composed of Henry P. O'Neil, Chairman, George J. Green and Hugh P. O'Neil submitted a Constitution and Statutes and Rules of Order. The report was adopted.

There was another revision of the Constitution and Statutes, in December, 1877, known as the Constitution of 1878.

In 1885 a resolution was adopted appointing a special committee to revise the Constitution and Statutes, consisting of Exalted Grand Ruler Kelly, Grand Secretary Moreland, and Chairman W. C. VanDerlip of the Committee on Laws and Supervision.

In 1886 Grand Secretary Moreland reported that the codification was entirely the work of Chairman VanDerlip and that he merely corrected proof and attended to its publication. This, it appears, was not really a revision but rather a codification.

The same year Philadelphia Lodge offered a constitutional amendment providing for State Grand Lodges and a Supreme Lodge. On this subject 28 lodges cast 128 ayes, and 15 lodges, 83 nays. A roll call by members resulted as follows: Ayes 168, nays 105. Not having the necessary two-thirds the amendment was not adopted.

Exalted Grand Ruler Leach, in his report of 1889, called attention to the fact that many amendments had been made to the Constitution since it was last printed and asked for a "speedy revision." A special committe of five was appointed to revise, compile and publish the Constitution and Statutes of the Grand Lodge.

This Committee consisted of W. C. VanDerlip, Boston, Mass., Lodge, No. 10; A. J. Wolff, Youngstown, Ohio, Lodge, No. 55; William L. Parslow, Hoboken, N. J., Lodge, No. 74; William G. Meyers, Philadelphia, Pa., Lodge, No. 2, and W. J. Watson, Fond du Lac, Wis., Lodge, No. 57.

The proceedings of the Grand Lodge Session in 1890 do not indicate that any report was made by this Committee on Revision of the Constitution and Statutes. However, Grand Exalted Ruler Quinlin said in his report to the Grand Lodge that year that what was needed was a new Constitution and Statutes.

At the same Grand Lodge Session the Committee on Laws and Supervision, consisting of Charles A. Wilson of Providence Lodge No. 14, and Allen O. Myers and L. M. Hadden of Cincinnati Lodge No. 5, submitted a draft of a Constitution, Laws and Rules of Order. This was unanimously adopted and was endorsed by the subordinate lodges.

In 1897 in his annual report, Grand Exalted Ruler Detweiler said that, in his opinion, the present laws were too unwieldy, defective in many vital points, inconsistent and contradictory, and submitted a proposed Constitution which was referred to a special committee.

In 1898, Chairman E. M. Bartlett, of Omaha, Nebraska, Lodge, No. 39, said that his Committee was submitting a new Constitution that retained all the main features suggested by the Grand Exalted Ruler.

J. C. Nethaway, Stillwater, Minnesota, Lodge, No. 179, and D. Solis Cohen, Portland, Oregon, Lodge, No. 142, could not be present and the Grand Exalted Ruler appointed in their places C. S. Bartram, St. Paul, Minnesota, Lodge, No. 59, and George A. Clugston, Mansfield, Ohio, Lodge, No. 56.

The Chairman then spoke about the attempt of this Committee to simplify the laws and criticized the system existing at that time in respect to controversies, stating that the vast network of appeals provided for had no parallel in his history of jurisprudence.

He said:

"It appeals from the Exalted Ruler to the lodge, from the lodge to the District Deputy, from the District Deputy to the Grand Exalted Ruler, from the Grand Exalted Ruler to the Committee on Laws and Appeals and from the Committee on Laws and Appeals to the Grand Lodge, and no Brother could ever get justice in such an extensive system of appeals."

The Committee proposed in this amended Constitution to organize a Court of Appeals in the Grand Lodge and a trial court of general jurisdiction in the subordinate lodges.

The Committee proposed holding the election of the Grand Lodge officers on the first day of the Session and also changing its Memorial Day from December to May.

There were several amendments to the report and it was adopted by the Grand Lodge. However, it was rejected by the subordinate lodges.

THE CAUSE OF REJECTION

As soon as this Constitution was submitted to the subordinate lodges a number of prominent members of the Order and several lodges began an attack upon it.

New York Lodge adopted resolutions rejecting its proposals, stating the reasons for its opposition to such proposals and sent a copy of the resolution to all of the subordinate lodges.

The proposals objected to were the following:

1. Authority for the Grand Exalted Ruler to appoint a Court of Appeals whose decisions should not be reversible by the Grand Lodge.

2. Provision that a two-thirds vote of the Grand Lodge should be necessary for the infliction of punishment upon a subordinate lodge or upon a member of the Grand Lodge.

3. The creation of a permanent court in each subordinate lodge for the trial of all offenses.

4. Authority for the Exalted Ruler of a lodge to appoint secretly a committee on investigation of an applicant, this committee to report to him.

5. Provisions during the pendency of an appeal by a member expelled or suspended, the appellant should continue as a member of a lodge.

MORELAND ARTICLE

An article in the April, 1899, issue of Arthur C. Moreland's *The Elks-Antler* stated that while New York Lodge had been largely instrumental in defeating the ratification of the entire Constitution because of certain defects, it recognized that the merits of the proposed Constitution far outweighed its defects.

Therefore, the lodge had appointed a Committee to draft amendments to those sections to which it objected.

The article paid tribute to E. M. Bartlett, George A. Clugston and C. S. Bartram for their able and conscientious work, and stated that the Constitution presented by New York Lodge would be their work, with the exception of a restoration of most of the features in regard to the powers of the Committee on Laws and Appeals in the Constitution at that time.

The article further stated that there was so much good and so little to be corrected that it would be a graceful act on the part of the Grand Exalted Ruler to appoint the same committee to receive from the representatives of New York Lodge the result of their labors and present it in their own names to the Grand Lodge.

Grand Exalted Ruler Allen in his report in 1899 said: that the Committee had concluded that the action of the subordinate lodges in rejecting the Constitution evidenced a sense of satisfaction throughout the Order with the existing Constitution.

However, Moreland stated that, in view of the fact that New York Lodge felt the Grand Lodge was entitled to at least some work from that lodge in return for the circular it issued causing the rejection of the new Constitution, he had prepared a substitute for that document.

He then offered a motion that a committee of five be appointed and that the Constitution as presented by him be considered by such Committee.

This motion was adopted and a Committee was appointed consisting of George A. Clugston of Mansfield, Ohio, Lodge, No. 56; C. S. Bartram, St. Paul, Minnesota, Lodge, No. 59; Scott Holmes, Cincinnati, Ohio, Lodge, No. 5, and Arthur C. Moreland and Thomas F. Brogan of New York Lodge, No. 1.

The amended Constitution and Laws were adopted.

AN IMPORTANT REVISION

At the Grand Lodge Session in Buffalo in 1905, Morse Rohnert, Detroit Lodge No. 34, offered a resolution on behalf of the Michigan Association of Elks, that a Committee of five be appointed to consider a substitute for the Constitution of the Order.

A Committee was appointed consisting of Past Grand Exalted Ruler Pickett, Past Grand Exalted Ruler Galvin; Morse Rohnert; Warren G. Sayre, Wabash, Indiana, Lodge, No. 471, and J. A. Sullivan, Richmond, Kentucky, Lodge, No. 581.

In making the report for the Committee, at the Grand Lodge Session at Denver in 1906, Chairman Pickett said that it was the opinion of the Committee that a new system of government was demanded as the current form of government had been adopted when there were but few lodges and but a few members of the Grand Lodge.

Accordingly, the Committee had in mind, in making its recommendations for revision of the Constitution, the desirability of dividing the powers then vested in the Grand Lodge.

The resulting recommendation was that all legislative powers be vested in the Grand Lodge, the same as in our Congress; that all executive powers be vested in the Grand Exalted Ruler, the same as in our President, and all judicial powers be vested in the Grand Forum, the same as in the Supreme Court of the United States.

The report of the Committee was adopted and later ratified by the subordinate lodges.

The revised Constitution took effect upon the convening of the Grand Lodge in Philadelphia in 1907.

The Committee made its report in respect to revised Statutes at the next Grand Lodge Session in 1907 and the amended Statutes were regularly adopted and became in force and effect on and after September 1, 1907.

Since that time, and up to the date of publication of this History, there has been no general revision of the Constitution and Statutes of the Order.

During that period, however, one or two amendments of the Constitution have been adopted at about two-thirds of the intervening Grand Lodge Sessions and at practically every Session amendments to the Statutes have been adopted.

ELECTIVE OFFICERS (GRAND LODGE)

The Elective Officers in 1871, as provided for by the Constitution of that year, were the following:

Exalted Grand Ruler	Grand Tiler
Esteemed Leading Grand Knight	Judges (three in number)
Esteemed Loyal Grand Knight	Supreme Judge
Grand Lecturer	Associate Judge
Grand Secretary	Second Associate Judge
Grand Treasurer	

When the Constitution and Statutes of 1874 were written the Judges were dropped and five Trustees added.

The Esteemed Grand Lecturer was changed to Esteemed Lecturing Grand Knight in 1886.

In 1892 the names of the Chair Officers were changed to the following:

Grand Exalted Ruler (changed in 1890)
Grand Esteemed Leading Knight
Grand Esteemed Loyal Knight
Grand Esteemed Lecturing Knight

The Grand Trustees were reduced from five to three in number.

APPOINTIVE OFFICERS (GRAND LODGE)

In 1871 the only Appointive Officers were the District Deputy Exalted Grand Rulers and the Grand Chaplain.

By 1874 there was added a Grand Inner Guard, and it also was provided that a District Deputy be named for each District except that in which the Exalted Grand Ruler was located.

In the Constitution of 1886 it was provided that a Deputy Exalted Grand Ruler at Large should be appointed, and a Grand Esquire was added to the list of Appointive Officers.

A few years later the Deputy Exalted Grand Ruler at Large was eliminated.

GRAND LODGE VOTES

The Constitutions of 1871, 1874 and 1886 provided that a majority of the legal votes of the members present should decide all questions except such as would affect the Constitution, involve expenditure or appropriation of moneys, suspend a lodge or remove a Grand Officer; to determine either of which should require a two-thirds vote of the members present entitled to vote on such a subject.

In 1892 the corresponding provision in the Constitution was that a majority of votes should decide all questions except those involving an expenditure of money, not provided for by law; inflict punishment upon a lodge, or remove a Grand Officer; to determine either of which should require a two-thirds vote.

In a separate section there was a provision in the 1892 Constitution requiring that amendments to the Constitution should have a two-thirds vote.

The present Constitution provides that a Grand Lodge Officer shall not be convicted and removed on impeachment without a two-thirds vote. All other questions, except amendments to the Constitution, granting a pardon, and acting upon a proposed amendment to the Statutes wherein the fifteen-day clause of Section 12, Article III, has not been complied with, shall be decided by a majority vote.

RESIDENCE OF THE GRAND SECRETARY

In 1886 there was adopted a provision that the Grand Secretary should be a resident of the City of New York and should have his office there.

In 1892, the Constitution simply provided that the Grand Trustees should provide an office in the city the Grand Secretary may designate to transact the business of the Order.

VOTES OF LODGES IN GRAND LODGE

In 1871 the Constitution provided that each lodge be entitled to one vote for every 25 Devout Elders on the following subjects:

1. Questions affecting the existence of a lodge.

2. Subjects affecting changes in the charges made by the Grand Lodge for charters, dispensations, rituals, oaths, affiliate cards

and withdrawal cards, and other modes of revenue received by the Grand Lodge from subordinate lodges.

In 1874 this provision was changed to provide that each lodge should be entitled to one vote for every 25 Devout Elders, or fraction thereof, in good standing, as shown by its last report to the Grand Lodge, on any question of imposing punishment upon a lodge for offenses against our laws or on the adoption of any alteration, amendment or addition to the Constitution.

In 1886 the words "for offenses against our laws" were omitted, and the words "or to the Statutes" were added to the second clause.

In 1892 it was provided that each lodge be entitled to one vote in the Grand Lodge upon any provision to amend the Constitution and Laws for each 50 of its members or fraction thereof.

The Constitution of 1906 included no such provision.

PER CAPITA TAX

In 1871 the per capita tax was not less than 25 cents for each Devout Elder in good standing. By 1967 the per capita tax had been increased to $2.00.

Of this amout one dollar was for subscription to *The Elks Magazine;* 20 cents for the expenses of the Elks National Service Commission, and the remainder for the expenses of the Grand Lodge, including the maintenance of the Elks National Home and the National Headquarters.

GRAND LODGE SESSIONS – TIME AND PLACE

The Constitution of 1871 provided that the Grand Lodge should hold an annual Session during the second week in December and another Session during the second week in July.

In 1874 it was provided that the Session be held in New York City, and in 1898 it was provided that the Grand Lodge should meet at such time and place as it may determine.

At the Grand Lodge Session in 1950 it was provided that the Grand Exalted Ruler, with the approval of the Board of Grand Trustees, shall fix the time and place of holding the regular Session.

QUORUM

Up to 1892 the Constitution provided that seven members of the Grand Lodge should be necessary for a quorum.

That year the requirement was changed to 50 and in 1907 to 100, of whom at least two had to be elective officers. There it remains at the present day.

EXALTED GRAND RULER AND GRAND EXALTED RULER

In 1890 the title of Exalted Grand Ruler was changed to Grand Exalted Ruler. A similar change was made in the title of the other Grand Lodge chair officers.

SPECIAL SESSIONS

From 1871 to 1892 it was provided that special sessions might be called by the Grand Exalted Ruler whenever he deemed the same necessary and it should be his duty to call such session when requested to do so by one-third of the members of the Grand Lodge, or on the written application of two-thirds of the members of any subordinate lodge.

The Constitution of 1892 simply stated:

"The Grand Exalted Ruler may call a special session of the Grand Lodge."

At present, the Statutes provide as follows:

"The Grand Exalted Ruler shall have power, with the approval of the Board of Grand Trustees, in case of an emergency, to call a special session of the Grand Lodge; said call shall state the business to be considered, fix the place where and the time when the session shall be held, which time shall not be within 30 days from the issuance of the call. No business other than that stated in the call shall be considered."

DISTRICT DEPUTIES

In 1886 it was not required that a District Deputy be appointed for the District where the Exalted Grand Ruler lived, but it was required that the Exalted Grand Ruler make an official visit to each lodge in this District.

By 1892 this requirement was eliminated and a provision made for the appointment of a District Deputy for each District.

FORFEITURE OF CHARTERS

The 1871 Constitution provided as follows:

"Any lodge may be suspended or dissolved, and its charter or dispensation forfeited to the Grand Lodge for the following breach of discipline:

"First. Improper conduct.

"Second. Wilfully neglecting or refusing to conform to the Constitution and Laws of the Grand Lodge or the general laws, regulations, and objects of the Order.

123

"Third. Neglecting or refusing to make its returns, or for non-payment of dues to the Grand Lodge, but the charter or dispensation shall not be forfeited in either of the above cases until the lodge shall have been duly notified of its offense by the Grand Secretary and suitable opportunity given its members to answer the charges made against their lodge.

"Fourth. Neglecting to hold the regular stated meetings as provided by law unless prevented from doing so by some unforeseen circumstances, the validity of which as an excuse shall be determined by the Grand Lodge.

"Fifth. Its membership diminishing so that less than a constitutional quorum may be left."

There were many changes made during the years as new Constitutions were written.

In 1907 the causes were increased to nine. Since that time another has been added so that now there are the following ten causes:

(a) Contumacy to the authority of the Grand Lodge, the Grand Exalted Ruler, or any superior officer or tribunal.

(b) Departure from the Standard Work.

(c) Violation of the Constitution or Statutes of the Order or the laws of the community in which such lodge is situated.

(d) Conduct on the part of the members, either in the lodge room or in public places, tending to bring the Order into disrepute.

(e) The use by such lodge of any name indicating any part of the deer or elk, except in legitimate work of the Order within the lodge room.

(f) Failure to pay taxes levied by the Grand Lodge.

(g) Failure to hold meetings for three months.

(h) Failure to make reports required by law.

(i) Refusal to proceed to a trial of charges preferred against any member for an offense.

(j) Being in such a condition, financially or otherwise, that, in the opinion of the Grand Exalted Ruler and the Board of Grand Trustees, it is for the best interest of the Order that such a charter or dispensation be taken away or forfeited.

AMENDMENTS

In 1886 a Constitutional Amendment having been adopted at one Grand Lodge Session by a two-thirds vote, had to be similarly adopted at the next Grand Lodge Session or approved by a majority of the subordinate lodges.

In 1892 the alternate provision of the adoption of an amendment at a second Grand Lodge Session was eliminated.

The present Statutes provide that an amendment to the Constitution must be approved by a two-thirds vote of the members of the Grand Lodge present and voting, and that it shall be submitted to all subordinate lodges for adoption or rejection at a time fixed when the subordinate lodges shall vote upon the same.

The Statutes further provide that a true copy of every proposed amendment to the Constitution which has been adopted by the Grand Lodge shall be forwarded by the Grand Secretary to each subordinate lodge on or before the 15th day of August following, and that every lodge shall vote on it at its first regular session in September.

GRAND LODGE BUDGET

The desirability of a budget system of operation was first recognized in 1907 when it was provided that:

"Sec. 37. The Board of Grand Trustees shall, on the first day of the Grand Lodge Session, introduce a bill, to be known as the 'Budget,' making appropriations for the purposes therein stated.

"After the first day, the Board of Grand Trustees shall call up said bill for passage.

"When such bill shall be enacted into law, it shall be the measure of expenditure of money for the purposes therein specified by the Grand Lodge."

The present Statute covering the Budget is practically the same in effect, although worked out in considerably more detail.

The principal differences are that the present Statute requires that the Budget shall be called up by the Board of Grand Trustees for adoption, modification or rejection immediately before the adjournment of the Grand Lodge and that in the interim between its introduction and its final representation, the Board of Grand Trustees shall amend the original Budget to cover every action of the Grand Lodge then in session insofar as expenditures for the coming Grand Lodge year are concerned.

Requirements for Membership in the Order

There appear to have been no Grand Lodge requirements for membership in the Order in its early days, except that the applicant be 21 years of age or over.

As late as 1886 the only requirements for membership in the subordinate lodges were that a candidate must be proposed in writing by a Devout Elder and that the proposition should state the name, age, business, birthplace, residence and references of the proposed person and also whether he had been proposed in any lodge of the Order and with what results.

It was also provided that the application should be referred to a committee, three in number, whose duty it should be to examine into the character of the applicant, and ascertain if he had ever been rejected.

CITIZENSHIP REQUIREMENT

The first appearance in the Statutes of the requirement that an applicant for membership be a citizen of the United States was in 1890 where there appeared the following:

> "Any white male citizen of the United States, of sound mind and body and good reputation, over 21 years of age, who desires initiation in a lodge, must be proposed in writing by an Elk of the lodge; said proposition shall state the name, age, business, birthplace, residence and references of the person and also whether he has ever before been proposed by any lodge of the Order and with what result, over the signature of the applicant."

BELIEF IN A SUPREME BEING

At the Grand Lodge Session of 1892 the following amendment to the Statutes was offered:

> "After '21 years of age,' insert 'with a belief in a Supreme Being.' "

This was referred to as essential "because otherwise no oath would be considered binding."

No action was taken thereon.

In 1912, the Grand Lodge adopted an amendment requiring an applicant to be "a believer in the existence of a Supreme Being."

POSSESSION OF THE FIVE HUMAN SENSES

The Section of the Statutes covering the requirements for membership in the Order contained in the Revised Statutes of 1907 provided as follows:

> "The membership of the Order shall be confined to white male citizens of the United States of America, of sound mind and body, of good character, not under the age of 21 years and in possession of the five human senses."

BELIEF IN GOD

At the Grand Lodge Session of 1946 an amendment was adopted substituting for the words "the existence of a Supreme Being" the word "God."

At the Grand Lodge Session in Philadelphia in 1948, upon the recommendation of Grand Exalted Ruler Lewis, the following provision was added:

> "No person shall be accepted as a member of this Order who is directly or indirectly a member of, or in any way connected with, the Communist Party, or who believes in the overthrow of our Government by force. The official form of application blank shall contain such questions necessary to disclose past or present affiliations with said party or adherence to such belief."

Up to the date of the printing of this History no further changes, except slight changes in phrasing, have been made by the Grand Lodge in the statutory requirements for membership in the Order.

The present Statutes relating to the subject are as follows:

> "Sec. 144.

> "No person shall be accepted as a member of this Order unless he be a white-male citizen of the United States of America, of sound mind and body, of good character, not under the age of 21 years, and a believer in God.

> "No person shall be accepted as a member of this Order who is directly or indirectly a member of or in any way connected or affiliated with the Communist Party, or who believes in the overthrow of our Government by force.

> "The official form of membership application shall be prepared, approved by the Chairman of the Judiciary Committee, and shall contain such questions as are necessary to disclose past or present affiliations to such party or adherence to such belief."

Requirements for Membership in the Grand Lodge

On January 1, 1871, there was offered and adopted the following resolution:

> "That the first Grand Lodge of the Benevolent and Protective Order of Elks consist of the following:

> "The original founders of the Order, together with all past and present officers of the First and Second Degrees who are now in good standing in the Order."

At a meeting on February 12, 1871 it was voted:

> "That all those, now members of the Grand Lodge, who have not previously filled the position of Exalted Ruler in any subordinate lodge, be now constituted and ever hereafter recognized as Past Exalted

Rulers, with all the privileges and rights appertaining to the position."

On February 19, 1871 the Committee on Rules and Regulations presented a Constitution for consideration of the members and it was unanimously adopted.

This Constitution provided that the Grand Lodge should be composed of all the Past Exalted Rulers in good standing in the subordinate lodges from which they hail.

CONSTITUTION OF 1874

The Constitution of 1874 provided for the following membership in the Grand Lodge:

1. All those who, at the primary organization of the Grand Lodge, were constituted Past Exalted Rulers.

2. All those who have since regularly passed the Exalted Ruler's chair in the subordinate lodges.

3. All those who may hereafter properly become Exalted Rulers of subordinate lodges.

4. Such delegates from subordinate lodges as may, under the Constitution and Statutes, be admitted to temporary membership.

This Constitution also provided as follows:

"Article 1, Section 18.

"Each member of the Grand Lodge shall have, as such, one vote on all questions."

It also provided that:

"Whenever the Exalted Ruler of a lodge shall be unable to attend a regular communication of the Grand Lodge, he shall order an election in his lodge of a representative to act in his place; such representative must be a Past Exalted Ruler of some subordinate lodge."

In the Statutes it was provided that:

"Each lodge shall at its annual meeting elect five delegates to the Grand Lodge, who shall act as temporary members of the Grand Lodge during the ensuing year."

MORE CHANGES

Amendments to the Constitution adopted in 1881 had the following requirements for membership in the Grand Lodge:

"1. Those who, by virtue of the provisions of our Constitution as existing prior to December, 1882, shall have been duly placed upon the roll of permanent membership of the Grand Lodge shall so continue.

"2. Those who, in lodges under dispensation, shall have filled the position either of Exalted Ruler, Esteemed Leading Knight, Esteemed Loyal Knight, Esteemed Lecturing Knight, Secretary or Treasurer during the term for which they shall have been chosen, shall be placed upon the roll as permanent members and shall, pending the completion of the term for which they may have been elected, be considered temporary members of the Grand Lodge.

"3. Those who, in chartered lodges, shall have completed a full lodge year (i.e., the period between the date of annual election in November of any year and the annual election in November of the year following) as Exalted Ruler of said chartered lodge, shall be permanent members of the Grand Lodge and shall, pending the completion of said full lodge year, be recognized as temporary members."

The Constitution of 1886 carried the preceding provisions and also provided, as did the Constitution of 1874, that:

"Each lodge, provided said lodge be properly represented in the Grand Lodge, shall be entitled to one vote, cast by its representative, for every 25 Devout Elders, or fraction thereof, in good standing, as shown by its report to the Grand Lodge, on the following subjects:

"1. On any question of imposing punishment upon a lodge.

"2. On the adoption of any alteration, amendment or addition to this Constitution or to the Statutes."

In 1891 the Constitution was amended to read as follows:

"The legislative powers shall be vested in the Grand Lodge, which shall consist of all present members of the Grand Lodge, all lodge Secretaries who have served or may hereafter serve as such for a period of three or more consecutive years and all Exalted Rulers who have become permanent members of the Grand Lodge and shall be representatives of the various lodges in the Grand Lodge at the first annual Session after they have served a lodge year.

"Each lodge shall be entitled to one vote in the Grand Lodge upon any proposition to amend the Constitution and Laws for each 50 of its members or fraction thereof, which must be cast by the representative of the lodge."

At the Grand Lodge Session in 1895, the provision relative to Grand Lodge membership was amended to read as follows:

"The legislative powers shall be vested in a Grand Lodge which shall consist of all present and future members of the Grand Lodge. All

Exalted Rulers who have served a full lodge year under charter and the first Exalted Ruler serving in lodges under dispensation shall become members of the Grand Lodge.

"Each lodge shall elect a representative and an alternate representative from its own or any other Grand Lodge members at its regular annual election to serve at the ensuing Grand Lodge Session."

(It will be noted that this eliminated the provision for making Secretaries, who had served three years, members of the Grand Lodge.)

"Each lodge shall be entitled to one vote in the Grand Lodge upon any proposition to amend the Constitution or Laws for each 50 of its members or fraction thereof which must be cast by the representative of the lodge, and each member of the Grand Lodge shall be entitled to a vote upon all questions."

In the Constitution printed in 1901 which was the Constitution adopted at St. Louis in 1899 and amended in 1901, there appears the following:

"Each lodge shall elect a representative and an alternate representative from its own or any other Grand Lodge members at its regular annual election to serve at the ensuing Grand Lodge Session. Each lodge shall be entitled to one vote in the Grand Lodge upon any proposition to amend the Constitution for each 50 of its members or fraction thereof which must be cast by the representative of the lodge; and each member of the Grand Lodge shall be entitled to a vote upon all questions."

At the Convention in 1905 the following amendment was made to the Constitution:

"Section 1. The legislative powers shall be vested in a Grand Lodge which shall consist of all duly-qualified elected delegates of the various subordinate lodges, all Exalted Rulers who will have served for the full lodge year under charter, or one year under dispensation or charter, and the first Exalted Ruler serving lodges under dispensation (and in case of death or disability of such officer, the brother elected to serve the unexpired term) shall be eligible to become members of the Grand Lodge.

"Each lodge shall elect one representative and an alternate representative from each 100 of its members or a fractional part thereof, from its own or any other Grand Lodge members, at its regular annual election to serve at the ensuing Grand Lodge Session.

"Each lodge shall be entitled to one vote in the Grand Lodge upon any proposition for each delegate or representative present."

This was adopted by the Grand Lodge by a vote of 298 to 171, indicating that there was considerable division of sentiment about it.

The Committee on Revision of the Constitution reporting in 1906 was perplexed by the problem of the composition of the legislative body.

Every Past Exalted Ruler became a member of the Grand Lodge for life.

There were then something like 10,000 members of the Grand Lodge; there was something over 1,000 lodges, so that the Grand Lodge membership was being increased at the rate of about 1,000 a year.

Chairman Pickett of the Committee attacked this system as creating a body unrepresentative of the subordinate lodges, a body composed of Past Exalted Rulers not answerable to their lodges.

He also stressed the point that a lodge 20 years old having a membership of only 100 would have 20 times the representation in the Grand Lodge of a lodge of 500 members but only one year old.

That the rights of the current members of the Grand Lodge might not be disturbed and yet that body be made more representative of the subordinate lodges, the Committee proposed that the Grand Lodge be composed of its present members and a representative of each subordinate lodge who, when his term expired, ceased to be a member of the Grand Lodge.

The Committee proposed that the term of service of a lodge representative be two years and that one-half of the lodges elect in one year and the other half of the lodges in another year so that one-half of the Grand Lodge would always have seen service.

The revised Constitution submitted by the Grand Lodge Committee on Revision at Denver in 1906 carried the following provisions:

"ARTICLE III

"LEGISLATIVE DEPARTMENT

"Section 1. The legislative powers shall be vested in a Grand Lodge which shall consist of:

"1. Its Past Grand Exalted Rulers in good standing in their respective lodges.

"2. Its officers, members of committees and District Deputy Grand Exalted Rulers.

"3. The members of the Grand Lodge at the time this Constitution shall take effect who shall retain their membership as hereinafter provided."

(In 1908 Sub-Section [3] was amended by adding the following:

"All Past Exalted Rulers who are in good standing in their respective lodges.")

"4. The representatives of subordinate lodges.

"Section 4. Each subordinate lodge shall be entitled to one representative to the Grand Lodge who shall be elected from the Past Exalted Rulers in good standing on its rolls.

"The term of office of representatives shall be two years; provided, however, that at the annual election of subordinate lodges in 1908, the odd-numbered lodges shall select representatives for one year, and the even-numbered lodges for two years. Thereafter, the election for representatives shall be held in the odd-numbered lodges in the odd-numbered years, and the even-numbered lodges in the even-numbered years.

"A lodge under charter shall, at its first election, elect a representative for one or for two years, as the case may be, to conform the term of its representative to the rule herein prescribed.

"A lodge acting under dispensation shall have the right to elect a representative from any of its past or present officers, provided, however, that the right or privilege of such representative shall, until the charter is authorized to his lodge, be limited to questions pertaining to his lodge.

"Section 5. If any member of the Grand Lodge, as it shall be constituted at the time this Constitution shall take effect, shall thereafter fail to attend the Grand Lodge Sessions for four consecutive annual Sessions, or shall be stricken from the rolls of the subordinate lodge, he shall forfeit his Grand Lodge membership; provided, however, that the Session or Sessions of the Grand Lodge held while a member is absent from the country in the service of the Government shall not be counted."

The foregoing was adopted at the 1906 Grand Lodge Session and made effective at the convening of the Grand Lodge Session in July, 1907.

SEVERAL PROPOSALS FOR AMENDMENTS

At the Grand Lodge Session in 1907, Chairman Pickett of the Committee on Revision stated that there had been referred to the Committee certain proposed amendments to the Constitution. They were the following:

"First. An amendment changing the term of office of representatives from two years, as provided in the Constitution, to one year.

"Second. An amendment striking out that clause in the Constitution which provides that if any of the present members of the Grand Lodge failed to attend for four consecutive years, that is, if they are not here during any one of the four consecutive years, they forfeit their membership in the Grand Lodge.

"Third. Another amendment, the effect of which was to make all Past Exalted Rulers life members of the Grand Lodge."

The first amendment was adopted by the Grand Lodge. The second amendment was not adopted. The third amendment was also lost.

SUBORDINATE LODGES TAKE A HAND

In his report to the Grand Lodge at Dallas in 1908, Grand Exalted Ruler Tener said, under the heading of "The Constitutional Amendment":

"At the last Session of the Grand Lodge, an amendment was adopted that the term of the representatives of the subordinate lodges should be one year instead of two. Provision was made that this amendment should be submitted to the subordinate lodges for action at the first regular meeting in November. A very appropriate circular of instructions was issued at the proper time from the office of the Grand Secretary, and the vote taken by lodges resulted as follows:

"In favor of amendment   215,346
"Against the amendment   7,320"

AN IMPORTANT REPEAL

At the same Session, Chairman J. U. Sammis of the Judiciary Committee submitted for the Committee a recommendation making all Past Exalted Rulers members of the Grand Lodge, an amendment which had been killed in 1907. It was now adopted.

Also at this Session the Constitutional provision that if a member of the Grand Lodge failed to attend for four consecutive annual Sessions he would forfeit his Grand Lodge membership, was repealed.

This was another amendment that had failed of adoption in 1907.

By these actions in 1907 and 1908 much that had been done in respect to the requirements for membership in the Grand Lodge in 1906 was undone.

Let us now see what we have left in the Constitution in respect to requirements for Grand Lodge membership.

The Constitution in 1909 provided as follows:

"ARTICLE III

"LEGISLATIVE DEPARTMENT

"Section 1. The legislative power shall be vested in a Grand Lodge which shall consist of:

"1. Its Past Grand Exalted Rulers in good standing in their respective lodges.

"2. Its officers, members of Committees and District Deputy Grand Exalted Rulers.

"3. All Past Exalted Rulers who are in good standing in their respective lodges and all others who were members of the Grand Lodge at the time of the taking effect of this Constitution, while they remain in good standing in their respective lodges.

"A Past Exalted Ruler shall be one who has served his lodge, if under charter, for a full lodge year as such officer, or who has served the unexpired term of one who from any cause failed to complete the term for which he was elected.

"4. Representatives of subordinate lodges.

"Section 4. Each subordinate lodge shall be entitled to one representative to the Grand Lodge, who shall be elected from the Past Exalted Rulers or other Grand Lodge members in good standing on its rolls: And at the same time that such representative is elected, an alternate representative possessing the same qualifications shall be chosen in the same manner to serve in the place and stead of the representative should he for any reason fail to attend the Session of the Grand Lodge for which he was elected. Such representative and alternate representative shall be elected at the same time and in the same manner as the officers of the lodge. The term of office of the representative shall be one year."

At the Grand Lodge Session in 1912 an amendment was adopted which provided that in the case of a lodge acting under dispensation, the Exalted Ruler who served the lodge under dispensation should become a Past Exalted Ruler and member of the Grand Lodge if a charter was granted to such lodge.

PROVISION FOR MILITARY SERVICE

In 1919 the Constitution was amended out of consideration for an Exalted Ruler entering the military, naval, hospital or marine service of the United States so that Sub-Section 4 of Section 1 of Article III should read as follows:

> "A Past Exalted Ruler shall be one who has served his lodge, if under charter for a full lodge year, as Exalted Ruler, or one who, during period of war, resigned his office and entered the military, naval, hospital or marine service of the United States, or who has served the unexpired term of one, who, from any cause, failed to complete the term for which he was elected, or who has in like manner, rendered service to a lodge acting under dispensation if such lodge shall subsequently receive a charter from the Grand Lodge."

A VERY IMPORTANT AMENDMENT

The next change in the Constitution was in 1932. At the Grand Lodge Session that year, upon the recommendation of Grand Exalted Ruler Coen, the Committee on Judiciary proposed an amendment to Article III of the Constitution providing that the representative of a subordinate lodge to the Grand Lodge shall be the Exalted Ruler of such lodge. This was adopted.

From that date (1932) to this writing, no change has been made in respect to the requirements for membership in the Grand Lodge.

Judicial Department

The first reference to any judicial procedure in the Constitutions of the Grand Lodge appears in the Constitution adopted in 1871 and it reads as follows:

> "The Grand Lodge shall have jurisdiction over all subordinate lodges of the B.P.O.E.; possessing the right and power of granting charters, of suspending or taking away the same upon proper cause, of receiving and hearing all appeals, of redressing grievances and complaints arising in subordinate lodges, and of enacting laws for its government and support."

Later in the Constitution there was provision for the election of a Supreme Judge, a first Associate Judge and a second Associate Judge.

In setting forth the duties of the Grand Lodge Officers there is a statement that the Judiciary Committees shall always hold themselves in readiness to receive and decide questions regarding the proper interpretation of the objects of the Order, their decision thereon being final, but it does not say anything about their acting in a judicial capacity in connection with complaints or charges.

It provided that the Committee on Appeals and Grievances should hear all appeals and grievances from lodges and members of lodges referred to them by the Grand Lodge or the Exalted Grand Ruler and report their decisions with the utmost dispatch to the Grand Lodge or to the Exalted Grand Ruler during the recess, and that it should consist of three members.

It further provided that a subordinate lodge might suspend or expel a member, after a fair trial, for conduct prejudicial to the Order, but any such suspended or expelled member should have the right to appeal to the Grand Lodge.

There were no important changes in judicial procedure in succeeding Constitutions until 1906, although some had been attempted.

In his report to the Grand Lodge in 1906 Chairman Pickett of the Committee on Revision of the Constitution submitted the following provisions:

"ARTICLE V

"THE JUDICIAL DEPARTMENT.

"Section 1. The judicial power shall be vested in one Grand Forum, in such Intermediate Forums as the Grand Lodge may from time to time establish, and in Judicial Assemblies.

"Section 4. The Judicial Assemblies shall consist of subordinate lodges acting under the order of business 'Judicial Assembly.' They shall have original jurisdiction in all matters involving charges against a member of a subordinate lodge. Appellate jurisdiction of these matters, and original jurisdiction in other matters, shall be vested in the Grand Forum, or in such Intermediate Forums as may be created by the Grand Lodge."

At the Grand Lodge Session in 1912 the Constitution was amended so that Section 1 and Section 4 read as follows:

"Section 1. The judicial power shall be vested in one Grand Forum, in such Intermediate Forums as the Grand Lodge may from time to time establish, and in Subordinate Forums. The decisions of the Supreme Court of the United States construing the words 'judicial powers,' as used in the Constitution of the United States, shall be binding upon the Grand Forum in construing the words, 'judicial powers' herein.

"Section 4. The Subordinate Forums shall consist of five members of each subordinate lodge who shall be appointed by the Exalted Ruler. Subordinate Forums shall have original jurisdiction in all matters involving charges against a member of a subordinate lodge. Appellate jurisdiction over judgments rendered by Subordinate Forums, and original jurisdiction in all matters shall be vested in the Grand Forum, or such Intermediate Forums as may be created by the Grand Lodge."

There has been no change in these sections of the Constitution up to this date.

Grand Lodge Committees, Commissions and Trusteeships

The changes in Grand Lodge Committees, Commissions and Trusteeships during the years help to indicate those projects and activities which appear to have been considered most demanding or worthy of attention at the various periods of the Order's existence.

THE ORIGINAL COMMITTEES

For the first three years, following the creation of the Grand Lodge, 1871-1872 and 1873, the Committees were: 1. Laws and Supervision; 2. Appeals and Grievances; 3. Returns and Credentials; 4. Printing and Supplies and 5. Warrants.

———— 1 8 7 4 - 1 8 8 2 ————

In 1874 there was added a Committee on Work and Ritual. And so, from 1874 to 1882 there were the six Grand Lodge Committees just named.

Let us see what lasting qualities these several Committees had.

There has remained until this day a Committee of the Grand Lodge dealing with legal matters but it has had its name changed several times.

From 1871 to 1891 it continued to be known as the Committee on Laws and Supervision.

In the latter year the name was changed to Laws and Appeals. It held that name until 1899 when it became simply the Committee on Laws.

Committee on Laws it continued to be up to 1907 and from that date it has been the Committee on Judiciary.

APPEALS AND GRIEVANCES

This Committee continued under that name until 1891 when the Appeals part was absorbed in Laws and Appeals, and Grievances went on by itself. When, in 1901, Laws and Appeals became just Laws, Appeals was out altogether.

GRIEVANCES

Grievances, which started out on its own (after being divorced from Appeals in 1891) continued to be a Committee until 1901 when it also disappeared.

APPEALS AND GRIEVANCES AGAIN

However, in 1903 Appeals and Grievances appeared again as partners. This Committee on Appeals and Grievances lasted this time until 1906 when it was again abolished.

RETURNS AND CREDENTIALS

This relationship continued from 1871 to 1907 when it was succeeded by Credentials and has since continued to be known by that name up to the present day.

PRINTING AND SUPPLIES

This Committee had a rather short life, existing only from 1871 to 1890.

WARRANTS

Warrants lasted three years, when it was succeeded by Charters. Charters continued to 1911 when it was discontinued.

WORK AND RITUAL

Work and Ritual continued as a committee name until 1908 when the word Work was dropped and the Committee became Ritual. It carried that name up to 1918 when the responsibility previously imposed upon the Ritual Committee was taken over by the newly-appointed Committee on New Membership.

As reported in the Ritual section of this History, there was created in 1928, upon the recommendation of Grand Exalted Ruler Malley, a Ritualistic Committee designed primarily to improve the rendition of the Ritual by subordinate lodge officers, but also was authorized to recommend changes in the Ritual when "deemed urgently necessary."

From 1933 to 1949, ritualistic work was under the direction of the State Associations Committee and in 1950 there was recreated the Ritualistic Committee of the Grand Lodge.

There was a special Ritual Commission of three members appointed in 1944 which served until 1946.

The Ritualistic Committee has continued to the present time. Having thus followed the history of original Committees of 1871 and 1874, let us see how Committees created later fared.

COMMITTEE FOR SUPERVISION OF THE ELKS
MUTUAL BENEFIT ASSOCIATION

In 1883 a Committee was appointed under the above name. It lasted only to 1889 when, apparently, the Elks Mutual Benefit Association itself passed out of existence. (See subject in this History under that title.)

AUDITING COMMITTEE

At the Grand Lodge Session in 1897 the Laws were amended by adding to the list of Standing Committees an Auditing Committee. Such a Committee has been continued to the present day.

ELKS HOME COMMITTEE

This Committee was created in 1899. It served until 1902 when it had completed its work, which was the purchase of suitable quarters for use as a national home for aged and indigent members of the Order. (See subject *Elks National Home* in this History.)

PRESS COMMITTEES

The Constitution and Laws adopted in 1899 provided as follows:

> "The Grand Exalted Ruler shall appoint from the members of the Grand Lodge present at each annual Session, a Committee of three to be known as the Press Committee.

> "It shall be the duty of said Committee, with the sanction of the Grand Exalted Ruler, to furnish the newspapers, during the Session at which they were appointed, such information regarding the proceedings of the Grand Lodge as it may be deemed proper to make public."

This provision of the laws was eliminated when the Constitution and Statutes were revised in 1907.

COMMITTEE ON GOOD OF THE ORDER

In 1902 Grand Exalted Ruler Pickett stated that, in his opinion, there were many subjects of vital interest that could not be referred to any of the then present Standing Committees.

He therefore recommended that a new Committee be created to be known as the Good of the Order Committee to consider and act on "subjects and questions pertaining to the Order in general."

The following amendment to the Grand Lodge Laws was adopted:

"A Committee on Good of the Order is hereby constituted which shall consist of all Past Grand Exalted Rulers of the Grand Lodge and shall have original jurisdiction in all matters having reference to the state of the Order and the consideration of subjects which by their nature are not assignable to the consideration of other standing Committees.

"This Committee shall hold its meetings annually at each Session of the Grand Lodge but shall be subject to the call of the Grand Exalted Ruler, in cases of emergency, at such time and place as he may designate."

This was eliminated in the revision of the Constitution and Laws of 1906 which was adopted in 1907.

A Committee of the same name was recreated by the Grand Lodge in 1917. The Chairman was William M. Abbott of San Francisco Lodge No. 3 and the other two members were Lawrence H. Rupp, Allentown, Pennsylvania, Lodge No. 130, and M. A. Tierney, Troy, New York, Lodge No. 141.

It was continued to 1932.

COMMITTEE ON JUDICIARY

The Committee on Constitutional Revision of 1905-6-7, having provided for the establishment of the Grand Forum, recommended the abolition of the Committee on Appeals and Grievances and the Committee on Laws.

In the place thereof they recommended the creation by statutes of a Committee on Judiciary to perform the same duties in the Grand Lodge as the Judiciary Committee in Congress.

The Committee on Judiciary then created has continued to function to the present day.

GRAND TRUSTEES AND GOVERNORS OF THE ELKS NATIONAL HOME

Each of these boards was composed of three members. The Committee on Revision of the Constitution in 1906 proposed to do away with the Board of Governors of the Elks National Home and to give its powers and responsibilities to a Board of Grand Trustees composed of five members.

This was done.

COMMITTEE ON CHARITY AND EMERGENCY

In 1907 the following statute was adopted and has continued to this day:

"The Grand Esteemed Leading Knight, the Grand Esteemed Loyal Knight, and the Grand Esteemed Lecturing Knight shall perform the duties pertaining to their office respectively and shall, together with the Grand Exalted Ruler, constitute a Standing Committee on Charity and Emergency of which the Grand Exalted Ruler shall be the chair man."

COMMISSION ON PROTECTION OF NAME AND EMBLEM

The above Commission was created in 1907 and made its final report in 1909. (See subject, *Protection of Name and Emblem,* in this History.)

COMMITTEE ON PRESERVATION OF THE ELK

Such a Committee was created in 1907 and served for three years. Another Committee of the same name was created in 1911 and also served for three years. Still another Committee of the same name was created in 1916 and served for only one year. (See subject, *Preservation of the Elk* in this History.)

COMMITTEE ON TUBERCULOSIS SANITARIUM

(See subject under that title in this History.)

BIG BROTHER COMMITTEE

In 1913 there was created a Big Brother Committee which continued in operation until 1919 when the work of the Committee was turned over to the Committee called the Social and Community Welfare Committee.

ELKS WAR RELIEF COMMISSION

This Commission was created at the Grand Lodge Session which was held at Boston in 1917, three months after the entry of our country into the first great World War, and continued to serve until the conclusion of its efforts in 1921. (See subject in this History, *Elks War Relief Commission.*)

NEW MEMBERSHIP COMMITTEE

The New Membership Committee was another short-lived Committee, lasting from its creation in 1918 until 1922 when it was discontinued.

SOCIAL AND COMMUNITY WELFARE COMMITTEE

The Social and Community Welfare Committee was created in 1919 and it continued in existence until 1928. (See subject *Community Welfare* in this History.)

NATIONAL HEADQUARTERS COMMITTEE

This Committee was created in 1920 to consider the recommendation of Grand Exalted Ruler Rain of the erection of a headquarters building. (See subject *National Headquarters and Memorial Building* in this History.)

NATIONAL MEMORIAL HEADQUARTERS COMMISSION

In 1921 this Commission, following the receipt by the Grand Lodge of the report of the National Headquarters Committee, was created and empowered to proceed with the erection of a National Headquarters and Memorial Building and the publication of a National Journal. (See subject under that title in this History.)

NATIONAL MEMORIAL AND PUBLICATION COMMISSION

In 1931 there was created the National Memorial and Publication Commission succeeding the National Memorial Headquarters Commission.

NATIONAL FOUNDATION COMMITTEE

This Committee was created in 1927 and concluded its labors and reported to the Grand Lodge Session in 1928. Following its report to that Session there was established by the Grand Lodge the Elks National Foundation.

ELKS NATIONAL FOUNDATION

The Elks National Foundation was brought into existence in 1928 and has continued its work until the present day. (See *Elks National Foundation* in this History.)

ANTLERS COUNCIL

The Antlers Council was instituted in 1930. That continued in existence until 1946. (See subject of the *Elks-Antlers* in this History.)

LODGE ACTIVITIES COMMITTEE

In 1932, upon the recommendation of Grand Exalted Ruler-elect Floyd E. Thompson, there was created a Lodge Activities Committee. An amendment to the Statutes provided that "The Committee on Lodge Activities shall have charge and supervision of such matters as may be referred to it by the Grand Exalted Ruler pertaining to the Good of the Order and all subordinate lodge activities, interlodge relations and similar matters."

The first Lodge Activities Committee consisted of John R. Coen, Robert S. Barrett, Charles S. Hart, Edward J. McCormick and Emmett T. Anderson. John R. Coen was the retiring Grand Exalted Ruler and each of the others was afterwards Grand Exalted Ruler. That Committee has been continued to the present day.

NATIONAL DEFENSE AND PUBLIC RELATIONS COMMISSION

This Commission was established in 1940. Upon the entrance of our country into World War II the name of this Commission was changed to Elks War Commission.

ELKS WAR COMMISSION

The Elks War Commission continued to serve until 1946 when it made its final report and there was created the Elks National Veterans Service Commission.

ELKS NATIONAL VETERANS SERVICE COMMISSION

The Elks National Veterans Service Commission took over the hospital and fraternal center work which had been carried on by the Elks War Commission during the war while the public relations activities of the Elks War Commission were turned over to the Elks National Memorial and Publication Commission.

ELKS NATIONAL SERVICE COMMISSION

In 1949 the name of this Commission was changed to Elks National Service Commission, which is continuing to function.

YOUTH ACTIVITIES COMMITTEE

In 1949 there was established the Youth Activities Committee and that Committee has continued in existence and operation up to the present time.

ADVISORY COMMITTEE

At the Grand Lodge Session at Cleveland in 1949 the Grand Lodge Statutes were amended to add to the list of Committees an Advisory Committee to be composed of all Past Grand Exalted Rulers.

This action of the Grand Lodge was similar to that taken by the Grand Lodge of 1902 in creating a Committee on Good of the Order to be composed of the Past Grand Exalted Rulers. It was similar recognition of the importance of assuring the continued services of those of long experience in the affairs of subordinate lodges that caused the Grand Lodge in 1943 to authorize the organization of Past Exalted Rulers' Associations.

CONVENTION COMMITTEE

In 1953 there was established a Convention Committee which is still functioning.

PENSION COMMITTEE

In 1954 a Pension Committee was created. It was abolished in 1962 and its duties assigned to the Grand Trustees.

MEMBERSHIP AND NEW LODGE COMMITTEE

In 1958 a Membership and New Lodge Committee was added to

our Grand Lodge Committees. In 1960 the name of this Committee was changed to the New Lodge Committee and has continued to the present.

AUDITING AND ACCOUNTING COMMITTEE

In 1960 the name of the Auditing Committee was changed to the Auditing and Accounting Committee.

Since that action in 1960 no new Committees have been created and the Grand Lodge Committees at present consist of the following:

Charity and Emergency	New Lodges
Judiciary	Ritualistic
Lodge Activities	Youth Activities
Credentials	Auditing and Accounting
State Association	Advisory
Americanism	

S E C T I O N

Third Decade

In the latter part of the preceding Decade there was started a movement to make the Grand Lodge migratory—that is, to amend the Constitution by eliminating the provision therein that all Grand Lodge Sessions be held in New York City. This question was put to a vote unsuccessfully at the Grand Lodge Sessions of 1886 and 1887.

In 1888, however, a favorable vote prevailed (228 to 47) and, at the Grand Lodge Session in 1889, it was voted that the Session of 1890 be held in Cleveland.

This resulted in a temporary cleavage in the Order, Grand Secretary Moreland leading a legal battle to secure a ruling that the action of the Grand Lodge in meeting anywhere except in New York was illegal.

New York Lodge and Moreland, personally, were expelled from the Order.

However, the legal steps proved unsuccessful and New York Lodge, seeking a restoration of its charter, and Moreland, seeking

Grand Exalted Rulers

T H I R D   D E C A D E

1888-1898

SIMON QUINLIN
1889-91

EDWIN B. HAY
1891-93
1894-95

ASTLEY APPERLY
1893-94

WILLIAM G. MEYERS
1895-96

MEADE D. DETWEILER
1896-98

a restoration of his membership, action to that end was taken at the Grand Lodge Session of 1893 and Grand Exalted Ruler Hay said:

> "The tie that was severed is reunited; the link that was missing is once more in its place; the mother returns to her children."

In this Decade further steps were taken in the matter of requirements for membership in the Order.

In 1890, the Statutes were amended to provide that an applicant must be "a citizen of the United States of sound mind and body, good reputation and over 21 years of age."

It is in the proceedings of this Decade, in 1889, that we find the first record of the Order's participation in national movements in giving relief in cases of local disaster.

Those first participations were in connection with a fire in Seattle, Washington, and the celebrated Johnstown, Pennsylvania, flood.

The development of the Order's magnificent record through the years in such beneficent activities is covered in this History under the heading of *Disaster Relief*.

This Decade saw the adoption of the "forget-me-not" as the floral emblem of the Order and the approval of the use of royal purple as the official color of the Order.

For a period of two years of this Decade it looked as though the Order might be wrecked as the result of the greatest internal controversy.

This resulted from a battle between the Grand Exalted Ruler and the Board of Grand Trustees. Fortunately, the two years of strife ended with a reunited and a stronger Order.

Probably there never was a more dramatic moment in any Session of the Grand Lodge than when, in Atlantic City in 1895, Meade D. Detweiler, who had been elected Grand Exalted Ruler by the group which had met in 1894 at Jamestown, and in 1895 at Buffalo, appeared at that Convention saying in the course of his remarks to Grand Exalted Ruler Edwin B. Hay and the members of the Grand Lodge:

> "My dear Brothers, this is the proudest and most glorious moment of my life; to be able to lead back this vast herd of Elks by the side of the still waters of peace, and, with you, write all faults on yonder count-less sands and all virtues on the tablets of love and memory."

A new Constitution was adopted at the Grand Lodge Session of 1890. Another Constitution with some rather drastic changes was adopted by the Grand Lodge in 1898 but was turned down by the subordinate lodges, largely as the result of a campaign against it by New York Lodge under the leadership of Arthur

Moreland of that Lodge, who had served as Grand Secretary from 1881 to 1890.

Exalted Grand Ruler Leach said in his report at the Grand Lodge Session in 1889 that since the Order was adding to the Grand Lodge membership at the rate of 125 members per year it would take only a few years to make this body unwieldy.

Such fears have never been realized.

This Decade saw the change of the title of the head of the Order from "Exalted Grand Ruler" to "Grand Exalted Ruler."

Only one man ever carried the two titles. Simon Quinlin was elected by the first title in 1889 and by the second title in 1890.

This Decade saw the birth of the practice of placing the Flag on the Altar of the Order, resulting from the recommendation of a Committee on Work and Ritual headed by Arthur C. Moreland of New York Lodge, for some years Grand Secretary of the Order and for many years the owner of the publication called *"The Elks-Antler."*

The Third Decade, like its two predecessors, showed an increase in membership each year with 400 per cent in growth for the period.

Third Decade—1888-1898

EXALTED GRAND RULERS

HAMILTON E. LEACH, Washington, D. C., Lodge, No. 15	1888-1889
SIMON QUINLIN, Chicago, Ill., Lodge, No. 4	1889-1890

GRAND EXALTED RULERS

SIMON QUINLIN, Chicago, Ill., Lodge, No. 4	1890-1891
EDWIN B. HAY, Washington, D. C., Lodge, No. 15 (2 yrs.)	1891-1893
ASTLEY APPERLY, Louisville, Ky., Lodge, No. 8	1893-1894
EDWIN B. HAY, Washington, D. C., Lodge, No. 15	1894-1895
WILLIAM G. MEYERS, Philadelphia, Pa., Lodge, No. 2	1895-1896
MEADE D. DETWEILER, Harrisburg, Pa., Lodge, No. 12 (2 yrs.)	1896-1898

GRAND SECRETARIES

At the beginning of this period Arthur C. Moreland, of New York Lodge No. 1, was Grand Secretary. He served until 1890.

Allen O. Meyers, of Cincinnati Lodge No. 5, succeeded him in office in that year and served until 1894.

In 1894, George A. Reynolds, of Saginaw, Michigan, Lodge No. 47, was elected Grand Secretary and continued to serve until the Grand Lodge Session of 1904.

Membership and Charitable Expenditures

In this Decade the membership of the Order grew from 8,952 to a membership of 44,252. The number of lodges increased from 92 to 442.

YEAR	MEMBERSHIP	CHARITABLE EXPENDITURES
1888-1889	10,549	$ 7,761.64
1889-1890	13,067	16,427.22
1890-1891	15,472	13,131.74
1891-1892	18,424	14,978.63
1892-1893	21,844	28,339.27
1893-1894	22,068	28,962.17
1894-1895	27,610	53,385.46
1895-1896	32,025	32,893.08
1896-1897	36,515	35,810.99
1897-1898	44,252	47,138.71

The Grand Lodge Sessions were held in the following cities:

1889	New York	1894	Atlantic City
1890	Cleveland	1895	Atlantic City
1891	Louisville	1896	Cincinnati
1892	Buffalo	1897	Minneapolis
1893	Detroit	1898	New Orleans

At the end of this Decade the assets of the 442 lodges amounted to $1,005,600.94.

Grand Lodge Sessions

Forty-First Session

The "Twenty-fifth Regular Communication" of the Grand Lodge —July 9, 10, 11, 1889—41st Session:

At this Session, Exalted Grand Ruler Hamilton E. Leach, in his report, offered for consideration the feasibility of amending the Constitution to permit the establishment of more than one lodge in the cities of the first class.

He commended the lodges for their contributions to the relief of the Johnstown flood and the Seattle fire. He also recommended that the custom be established of lodges holding an annual Lodge of Sorrow, and suggested the last Sunday in January as the date.

He asked for a "speedy revision" of the Constitution. A Committee was appointed to perform such a service.

GRAND SECRETARY

There was adopted an amendment to the Grand Lodge Statutes to read as follows:

"The Grand Secretary shall receive for his services the sum of $2,500 per annum, to be paid monthly.

"He may appoint an assistant, if he deems it necessary, who shall be a member of this Order, and the said assistant's services must be paid for by the Grand Secretary."

CONSTITUTION AND STATUTES

The following resolution was adopted:

"Resolved: that a special committee of five be appointed by the Exalted Grand Ruler whose duty it shall be to have revised and compiled a suitable volume and publish a constitution and statutes for the Grand Lodge, which revision and composition shall be submitted at the next regular communication of the Grand Lodge. The Committee shall be paid by the Grand Lodge a reasonable expense while engaged in this work, and in addition thereto, a reasonable compensation for their services, and shall have the right of access to all the records of the Grand Lodge, and may hold their meetings at such time and places as they deem most expedient."

LODGE OF SORROW

The following resolution was offered and unanimously adopted:

"Resolved: that the first Sunday in December, annually, is hereby designated and dedicated as a day to be celebrated as a Lodge of Sorrow by all lodges of Elks."

The following charters were granted:

Birmingham No. 79	Lowell No. 87	Tiffin No. 94
Rome No. 96	Des Moines No. 98	Los Angeles No. 99
Quincy No. 100	Amsterdam No. 101	Altoona No. 102
Newport No. 104	Trenton No. 105	Keokuk No. 106
Gallipolis No. 107	Mobile No. 108	Wilkes-Barre No. 109
Franklin No. 110	Columbus No. 111	Sioux City No. 112
Jackson No. 113	Zanesville No. 114	Reading No. 115
Evansville No. 116	Lynn No. 117	Fall River No. 118
Danbury No. 120	Easton No. 121	Shreveport No. 122
Scranton No. 123	Fort Worth No. 124	Sedalia No. 125
Galveston No. 126	Urbana No. 127	Asbury Park No. 128

Forty-Second Session

CONSTITUTION AND STATUTES

At the Grand Lodge Session of 1890 in Cleveland, Ohio, the rank of "Devout Elders," or second degree, was abolished, and thereafter all members were to be known as "Elks."

MEMORIAL TABLETS

Also, a resolution was passed at this Grand Lodge Session requiring all lodges to erect a memorial tablet in their lodge rooms in honor of their dead.

CHANGE OF OFFICIAL TITLES

The titles of the four chair officers were changed to the following: Grand Exalted Ruler, Grand Esteemed Leading Knight, Grand Esteemed Loyal Knight and Grand Esteemed Lecturing Knight.

Forty-Third Session

At the Session of 1891 the proposition to extend the Order beyond the confines of the United States was rejected.

A new form of traveling card was adopted at this Session.

It was enacted that thereafter lodges must confine their name titles to the name of the city where located and that the numbers of the new lodges must ascend serially and that no lodge should take the old number of a defunct lodge.

CONSOLIDATION OF DEGREES

The proposition to consolidate the two degrees into one strong, fine degree, was adopted in this communication of the Grand Lodge in 1891. In the consolidated one degree, the four chair officers were named as they now exist.

Forty-Fourth Session

In 1892, at the Grand Lodge Session in Buffalo, the royal purple was finally adopted as the official color, and the "forget-me-not" was adopted as the flower of the Order. (See section *Floral Emblem and Color,* of this History.)

Forty-Fifth Session

The Grand Lodge of 1893 met in Detroit, Grand Exalted Ruler Edwin B. Hay presiding.

During this year provision was made for a lodge registry book, to be kept in the anteroom of each lodge home, in which all visiting Brothers must sign their names so that the Tiler might compare their signatures with those on the traveling cards.

Disaster Relief

Johnstown and Seattle — 1889

The first record of the Order's participation in disaster relief, other than of local importance only, appears in the report of Exalted Grand Ruler Hamilton Leach given at the Grand Lodge Session in 1889.

He referred to the flood at Johnstown, Pa., and a fire at Seattle, Wash., and stated that the Order suffered in both instances but that, notwithstanding, everywhere the members responded to calls for aid, he having called for contributions for a fund to be sent to the sufferers.

Louisville — 1891

In the Grand Lodge Proceedings of 1891 there appeared the following:

> "A statement in detail was submitted on behalf of Louisville Lodge No. 8, showing that $1,491.50 had been contributed by the Order for the relief of the sufferers from the cyclone of March 27, 1890.

> "Of this amount, $1,181.88 had been distributed. The balance of $309.62 was turned over to the Treasurer of Louisville Lodge and was subject to the order of the Grand Lodge.

> "John H. Dee, of Boston Lodge No. 10, moved that, with the approval of Louisville Lodge, the surplus money be donated to the family of Henry Smith, who had been accidentally killed during the day while removing reunion decorations."

Russia — 1892

There was a severe drought and resulting famine in Southern Russia in 1892, for the relief of the sufferers of which the American Red Cross sent grain and other foodstuffs and medicines.

In Grand Exalted Ruler Hay's report to the Grand Lodge that year, he referred to the famine and made an appeal to the representatives of the lodges for small contributions.

In his 1893 report, Grand Exalted Ruler Hay said that many lodges responded, not in large amounts, as only small contributions had been requested, and that $695 was turned over to the fund.

San Francisco Earthquake — 1906

In his report to the Grand Lodge in 1906, Grand Exalted Ruler Robert W. Brown reported on the matter of San Francisco relief.

The total contributions were $109,140.60. At the time of the Grand Exalted Ruler's report there had been disbursements of $61,703.25, leaving a balance in the hands of the Grand Secretary on June 11, 1906, of $47,437.35. The Grand Exalted Ruler said:

"As I turn to the chapter of our California relief, the thrill and spell of that labor of love is still upon me.

"A blessed distinction of the Elk is that he has practiced in the heavenly art of charity, and so it came to pass on that April morning when the world was staggered and aghast by news of the earthquake and fire calamity in California, the Elk was quick to respond and foremost and prodigal, as a matter of habit, in charming the darkness out of wreck and ruin and grim despair. He knew precisely what to do and how to do it, and had been taught to act upon the instant."

Immediately upon hearing about the calamity, the Grand Exalted Ruler issued a circular asking for contributions for a fund for relief in California, in the meantime, with the cooperation of the Board of Grand Trustees, sending $10,000 for immediate relief.

He then boarded a train for California.

Oakland was the base of relief operations. An Elks Relief Committee of 1,000 was organized under the leadership of Exalted Ruler Harrison Clay. Governor Pardee stated that the Elks were the first to render assistance and had continued valiantly to head the relief procession; that within twelve hours following the disaster, the Elks of Oakland had equipped a tented city, and hospitals were taking care of upwards of 2,000 people; that their provision wagons were the first to enter San Francisco and that everything that could be done by union of money and stout hearts and willing hands had been done and was being done.

On his arrival, Grand Exalted Ruler Brown assumed personal charge of the relief measures and appointed a commission consisting of Henry A. Melvin, Oakland Lodge No. 171; Percy V. Long, San Francisco Lodge No. 3, and Ralph Hagan, Los Angeles Lodge No. 99, and stated that from this main body the organization extended to every subordinate lodge where there was a chance to help.

The Grand Exalted Ruler said that only half of the amounts of contributions offered by many of the lodges was accepted, while in nearly every instance there was a postscript that, if it were needed, twice the sum would be sent.

In a letter later sent to the Grand Exalted Ruler by Governor Pardee, he said:

> "As I have endeavored to make plain to you, the generosity of the Order of Elks, in placing in the hands of the Governor of the State such a large sum of money for the relief of the sufferers from our great calamity, without any restrictions whatever as to how the relief should be expended, was most generous on the part of your Order. It has relieved many worthy people whose thanks and appreciation are loud and great.

> "Hoping that the expenditure of the fund has met with the approval of yourself and your Order, I am, with renewed assurances of my esteem,

Very truly yours,
George C. Pardee"

1906——1907

The only other request for help was in connection with a dynamite explosion at Jellico, Tenn. In this instance only a small contribution was found necessary.

1907——1908

CHELSEA, MASS. FIRE

Here hundreds of homes were destroyed and millions of dollars of property laid waste. Many Elks lost their homes.

John D. Shea, Grand Esteemed Leading Knight, spent several weeks in Chelsea at the request of Grand Exalted Ruler Tener, distributing the $2,500 contributed from Grand Lodge funds.

PENNSYLVANIA AND WEST VIRGINIA MINE DISASTERS

More than the usual number of mine disasters in Pennsylvania and West Virginia occurred that year. Two of the most appalling ones were those in Jacobs Creek, Pennsylvania, and Fairmont-Monongah, West Virginia. Contributions of $500 and $1,000, respectively, were made in these instances.

1908——1909

EARTHQUAKE IN SOUTHERN ITALY

Three disasters deemed worthy of action by the Order occurred during this year of the Grand Exalted Rulership of Rush L. Holland.

The first of these was an earthquake in Southern Italy. Spontaneous offers of contributions were made by many lodges but the Grand Exalted Ruler returned them, saying that "the joy of giving should be shared by all."

Stating that the Elks refused to recognize boundary lines as a limit to their benefactions, he secured the consent of the Committee on Charity and Emergency and, the Grand Trustees concurring, the sum of $5,000 was forwarded to the American Red Cross to be used in assisting the victims of this tragedy.

ARKANSAS AND GEORGIA

The town of Brinkley, Ark., was completely destroyed by a tornado. A contribution of $500 was made for relief there and $250 was sent to Augusta, Ga., for flood relief.

1909——1910

Grand Exalted Ruler Sammis' report of 1910 referred to a contribution of $1,000 which was made for assistance in connection with a mine explosion disaster at Palos and Malaga, Ala.

This was a catastrophe in which it was reported that between 200 and 300 persons lost their lives almost in an instant.

1911——1912

A great calamity befell the people in the towns of Austin and Costello, Pa. The bursting of a dam resulted in great destruction of property and the loss of 75 lives. The sum of $1,000 was appropriated for assistance in this calamity.

$1,000 was also forwarded to assist the flood-stricken people of Black River Falls, Wis.

There was also a disaster in Briceville, Tenn.—a coal mine explosion. By way of relief, Grand Exalted Ruler John P. Sullivan and the Board of Grand Trustees authorized a contribution of $1,000.

In the same year there was a Mississippi River flood which brought great calamity to Hickman, Ky. A contribution of $500 for relief was made in that instance.

There was also a contribution of $250 for relief of suffering caused by a Mississippi flood at Vicksburg, and $750 for the same cause at New Orleans.

1912——1913

In this year, during the Grand Exalted Rulership of Thomas B. Mills, there occurred floods on the Ohio River, affecting Henderson, Ky.

Also during this year there was cyclone damage in Nebraska and serious floods affecting the states of Illinois, Indiana, West Virginia, Ohio, Kentucky and other Mississippi Valley states. The loss of life and property was extremely heavy.

Grand Exalted Ruler Mills called a meeting of the Standing Committee on Charity and Emergency, the Board of Grand Trustees, and Past Grand Exalted Rulers Galvin, Brown and Herrmann, and Samuel Perrott of Indianapolis. As a result there was donated for assistance the sum of $25,000.

This fund was distributed under the direction of Past Grand Exalted Rulers Galvin and Herrmann in Ohio, Past Grand Exalted Ruler Robert W. Brown in Kentucky and Southern Indiana, and Samuel Perrott in other portions of Indiana.

In West Virginia the distribution was made through Grand Trustee Holley, while the distribution in Southern Illinois and Nebraska was under the direction of Grand Trustees Faulkner, Clay and Applegate.

1914——1915

During this Grand Lodge year there were no catastrophes of a national nature calling for relief contributions from the Grand Lodge.

However, Grand Exalted Ruler Benjamin found it in order to contribute $1,000 for relief in connection with the holocaust at Hot Springs, Ark.; $500 for flood relief in Texas, and $2,500 to relieve suffering resulting from a disastrous fire in Salem, Mass

1915——1916

The following contributions were made:

Erie, Pa., flood	$1,000
Newport, Ark., flood	500
Louisiana and Mississippi hurricane and flood	1,000
Ardmore, Okla, gasoline car explosion	500
Great Bend, Kans., tornado	100
Paris, Tex., fire	500
Kemp City, Okla., cyclone sufferers	250

1916——1917

Contributions were made as follows:

North and South Carolina, flood sufferers	$ 500
Pittsburgh, Kans., mine explosion	500
New Castle, Ind., tornado	500
New Albany, Ind., tornado	500
Mattoon and Charleston, Ill., tornado	750
Coalgate, Okla., tornado	1,000

1917——1918

Grand Exalted Ruler Fred Harper was able to report that in this year only one call had been made upon him for a relief contribution and that was in connection with an ice flood at Lock Haven, Pa. He met this call with a donation of $500.

1918——1919

During this year, Grand Exalted Ruler Campbell received only two requests for contributions from the Emergency Charity Fund.

One was in respect to a disastrous forest fire in Minnesota. In this instance the Grand Exalted Ruler sent a contribution from the Order in the amount of $2,500.

The other was an appeal from Fergus Falls, Minn., for assistance in connection with the destruction caused by a terrific cyclone followed by fire. In that instance a contribution of $1,000 was made.

1919——1920

Grand Exalted Ruler Rain received a request from the Exalted Ruler of Corpus Christi, Texas, Lodge for a contribution to care for the victims of a hurricane which struck that city. The sum of $1,000 was appropriated.

There were also requests from Montgomery, Ala., and Hattiesburg, Miss., for assistance to those who had suffered great property loss on account of floods; $500 was appropriated.

1920——1921

In this year, the Pueblo, Colorado, vicinity was visited by a devastating flood. There was tremendous loss of life and destruction of millions of dollars worth of property.

Grand Exalted Ruler Abbott, checking the situation, appropriated $10,000 from the Emergency Charity Fund to assist in this situation.

1922——1923

In the period of the Grand Exalted Rulership of J. Edgar Masters, the following contributions were made:

New Bern, North Carolina, fire sufferers $500
Astoria, Oregon, fire sufferers 500
Cleveland, South Carolina, fire sufferers 250

1923——1924

The Grand Secretary's report for this period shows a contribution of $500 for the relief of sufferers from a cyclone in Oklahoma.

1924——1925

Grand Exalted Ruler John G. Price, at the conclusion of his term of office, reported an appropriation of $5,000 for assistance to the victims of a disastrous tornado in the district surrounding Lorain, Ohio; $1,000 for the victims of a disastrous flood in Georgia; $500 in connection with a coal mine disaster in Sullivan, Indiana, and $5,500 for relief work following a tornado in Indiana and Illinois.

1925——1926

During this year contributions were made as follows:

Santa Barbara, California, earthquake sufferers $1,500
Wilburton, Oklahoma, mine disaster victims 500
Mackinac explosion victims 1,000

Florida Hurricane——1926

At the time of the Florida hurricane in 1926, Grand Exalted Ruler Grakelow appealed to the lodges of the Order for contributions to assist in that disaster, and following an immediate response by the lodges he selected Past Exalted Ruler Louis N. Goldsmith of Philadelphia Lodge to carry the fund to Miami and cooperate in the launching of the Elk relief work there.

At the Grand Lodge Session in 1927, Past Grand Exalted Ruler Nicholson, Chairman of the Elks Florida Hurricane Relief Activities, reported that the total responses of the lodges of the Order for the Florida Hurricane Fund amounted to $70,837.15. There was expended $41,116.83, leaving a balance of $29,720.32.

This balance was transferred by the Grand Lodge to the Emergency Charity Fund.

The funds expended in Florida were distributed largely through the cooperation of Miami Lodge No. 948, Fort Lauderdale Lodge No. 1517, and Sebring Lodge No. 1529, as follows:

Miami Lodge No. 948	$27,243.25
Fort Lauderdale Lodge No. 1517	9,500.00
Sebring Lodge No. 1529 (not then instituted)	4,000.00
Miscellaneous	373.58
Total	$41,116.83

MISSISSIPPI FLOOD

At the Grand Lodge Session in 1927, Grand Exalted Ruler Grakelow reported that there had been collected for assistance to the sufferers from the Mississippi flood a total of $89,734.68.

Of this there had been expended $68,835.80, leaving a balance of $20,898.88.

Grand Exalted Ruler Malley reported at the next Grand Lodge Session that this amount which was turned over to him had been augmented by further contributions up to a total of $23,109.51.

1927——1928

During the Grand Exalted Rulership of John F. Malley, there were several very serious disasters.

Torrential rainstorms caused the waters of the Connecticut River to flood the entire district in its course through Vermont, New Hampshire and western Massachusetts. Great property damage, loss of life and suffering resulted.

The following contributions were made:

Red Cross in Vermont	$5,000.00
Burlington, Vt., Lodge	500.00
Sufferers in the vicinity of Montpelier	644.65
Rutland area	500.00
Northampton, Mass., Lodge	557.20
Sufferers in the North Adams district	500.00
Becket, Mass.	500.00
Assist in the relief work of Springfield, Mass., Lodge	500.00

Bicknell, Ind., Lodge reported that economic conditions were such that for a long period of time a very large percentage of the people had been unemployed and destitution had resulted. Bicknell Lodge had exhausted its resources in extended relief. $500 was appropriated for assistance there.

To assist the victims of a cloudburst, $500 was forwarded to Shawnee, Okla., and $3,000 was sent to McCook, Neb., to assist the victims of a cyclone.

$7,500 was forwarded to be distributed through Past Grand Exalted Rulers John P. Sullivan and Edward Rightor, among the subordinate lodges in the Sugar Bowl District of Louisiana for flood relief work. This was followed by an additional subscription of $3,500.

To the Committee on Flood Relief and Rehabilitation of Jackson, Miss., $1,500 was forwarded.

1928——1929

During the Grand Exalted Rulership of Murray Hulbert there was returned, out of previous donations for Mississippi flood relief, the following:

Kentucky State Elks Association	$ 234.60
Vicksburg, Miss., Lodge No. 95	3,450.26
Jackson, Miss., Lodge No. 416	960.00
McCook, Neb., Lodge No. 1434	1,210.31
Total	$5,855.17

There was also returned by Vicksburg, Miss., Lodge $4,410.26, the unexpended balance of the money which had been forwarded by the Grand Exalted Ruler in 1927.

$10,000 was forwarded for the victims of the Florida hurricane; of this sum there was returned an unexpended balance of $915.13.

$5,000 was forwarded to San Juan, Puerto Rico, Lodge for relief to the victims of the same hurricane.

From 1929 to 1937 inclusive the following donations were made:

1929——1930

Coal mine explosion, McAlester, Okla.	$ 300
Nashua, N. H., fire	2,500

1930——1931

$260 for relief in Eastland, Texas, fulfilling a recommendation made by Past Grand Exalted Ruler Hulbert.

$500 to Panama Canal Zone Lodge No. 1414 for relief of Nicaragua earthquake refugees.

1932——1933

Florence, Colo., flood	$ 250
San Juan, P. R., cyclone	500
Southern California earthquake	1,000
Central Tennessee tornado	250
Northern Alabama tornado	100
Auburn and Ellsworth, Me., fires	350
Northern Louisiana tornado	100

1934——1935

Ashland, Ky., flood	$ 500
McCook, Neb., flood	1,000

1935——1936

Helena, Mont., earthquake	$ 500
Watkins Glen, N. Y., flood	400
Houston, Texas, flood	400

1936——1937

Grand Exalted Ruler Sholtz appealed to the Elks National Foundation for assistance in connection with relief for the victims of great floods in the Valleys of the Ohio and Mississippi Rivers, and received from that source a donation of $5,000.

The Grand Exalted Ruler reported that the subordinate lodges contributed directly to the American Red Cross in connection with this catastrophe approximately $100,000, and, in addition, sent $22,186.63 to the Grand Exalted Ruler.

1938——1939

During this year New England was visited by a terrific hurricane and tidal wave. Property damage was high, although, fortunately, the loss of life was small. The need for action to alleviate human suffering and to give food, clothing and medical attention and shelter was urgent. Relief in the amount of $1,450 was expended.

Also, during the year, Southampton, New York, was the center of a storm-stricken area, and $500 was forwarded for relief there.

A request from Ashland, Kentucky, for $100 for flood relief in the Big Sandy Valley was complied with.

1939——1940

The Emergency Charity Fund was resorted to but once. That was in connection with a serious tornado at Albany, Georgia. For the relief there, $400 was forwarded.

1941——1942

The only request received for assistance from the Emergency Charity Fund was one from Brawley, California, to assist the lodge in rehabilitation necessitated by a damaging earthquake that visited that community; $400 was forwarded.

1944——1945

A hurricane and tidal wave caused great damage along the New Jersey coast; $5,000 from the Emergency Charity Fund was forwarded as a contribution to help repair the damage.

To assist in relieving the situation resulting from an epidemic of infantile paralysis and the burden it imposed on the Ithaca, N. Y., Reconstruction Home for Crippled Children, a check for $1,600 was forwarded.

1946——1947

During this year, Oklahoma and Texas were visited by a tornado with a loss of life well over 100, and hundreds of others injured.

The property damage in Woodward, Oklahoma, wiped out a goodly portion of the town. Contributions of $2,000, payable $1,000 to Amarillo, Texas, Lodge, and $1,000 to Woodward, Oklahoma, Lodge, were made.

For the relief of the sufferers in the explosion and fire in Texas City, $2,000 was forwarded.

1947——1948

During this year Grand Exalted Ruler L. A. Lewis was called upon for assistance in the relief of suffering caused by terrible fires in New Hampshire. As a result he ordered that $3,000 be used for that purpose.

1949——1950

The only appeal that was made for assistance from the Emergency Charity Fund of the Grand Lodge resulted from floods in northern Minnnesota which had brought havoc and distress to the community of Crookston and vicinity.

On investigation by Grand Exalted Ruler Emmett T. Anderson, a contribution of $1,000 for relief of the victims of that catastrophe was forwarded.

1951——1952

In the summer of 1951, following disastrous floods in the Kansas-Missouri River Valley regions of Kansas, Nebraska and northern Oklahoma, appeals came to the Grand Exalted Ruler for assistance.

Grand Exalted Ruler Davis asked William M. Frasor, Executive Secretary of the National Service Commission, to become his special representative in the flooded area, and authorized the immediate expenditure of $2,000 from the Grand Lodge Emergency Charity Fund for use in Ottawa, Kansas, where the damage was acute.

As a result of a report made by Mr. Frasor, the Grand Exalted Ruler asked all Elk lodges for contributions, not to exceed $100 a lodge, for flood relief work in the area affected.

BEFORE AND AFTER

(Inset photograph) Main street of Ottawa, Kansas, as water was starting to cross the street, with cars still able to move. Photograph of destruction of buildings was taken from approximately the same location after flood waters receded.

More than 1,100 lodges responded, contributing a total that, with some individual gifts, amounted to over $64,000. Of this amount $57,636.28 was expended for relief and the balance of $11,860.35 was transferred to the Grand Lodge Emergency Charity Fund. More than 100 other lodges gave directly to the Red Cross in answer to an earlier appeal from that organization.

The Grand Exalted Ruler's report on this disaster, and the relief extended by the Order, revealed the following:

Direct cash contributions to 12 lodges	$54,000.00
Telegrams, telephone calls, postage, etc.	2,460.22
Travel and expenses (Wm. M. Frasor, 6 weeks)	1,176.06
	$57,636.28
Unexpended balance	11,860.35
Total	$69,496.63

The Grand Exalted Ruler expressed his deep appreciation of the cooperation of the subordinate lodges and members of the Order, and of the service rendered by Mr. Frasor under extremely trying conditions.

1952——1953

Texas Tornado	$ 2,000.00
Michigan Tornado	1,500.00
Mississippi Tornado	1,000.00

1955——1956

Five emergencies arose during the year to which we responded with assistance to relieve the distress of our fellow citizens in the East, the South and the West, who were victims of floods. In order to provide this assistance, it was necessary to make a special appeal to lodges for contributions. The total amount contributed was $58,912.86. The unexpended balance was placed in the Emergency Charity Fund:

Pennsylvania Flood Relief	4,500.00
Ellenville, N.Y. Flood Relief	1,125.00
California Elks Assn. Flood Relief	12,500.00
New Jersey Elks Assn. Flood Relief	10,100.00
Connecticut Elks Assn. Flood Relief	12,500.00

1957

Kentucky Flood Relief	1,000.00
Kansas Tornado Relief	2,881.48
North Dakota Tornado Relief	2,500.00
Chaffee, Kansas Disaster	1,000.00

1959——1965

Roseburg, Oregon Disaster	500.00
Hollister, Calif. Earthquake	2,000.00
Louisiana-Texas Storm Disaster	3,593.80
Agana, Guam Storm Relief	2,000.00
Alaska Earthquake & Tidal Wave Disaster	155,000.00

1965——1967

Colorado Flood Disaster	5,000.00
Erwin, Tenn. Disaster	500.00
Louisiana Flood Relief	500.00
Harlingen, Tex. Flood Relief	15,000.00
Fairbanks, Alaska Flood Relief	1,000.00

Grand Lodge Becomes Migratory

In 1886 there began a movement to make the Grand Lodge migratory. At the Grand Lodge Session in 1887 there was wide dispute over this proposition. The motion to make the Grand Lodge migratory was defeated by a vote of 85 to 60.

It should be remembered that the early control of the Order was in the hands of the "professionals," as theatrical people were called; they did not want any city to have a lodge except big cities where many "professionals" live. They also kept the Grand Lodge Session permanently in New York for the same reason.

They hotly opposed migrations of the Grand Lodge. These two subjects of the "professionals" and migration were the cause of constant strife and bitter contention.

The matter of migration was brought up again at the Grand Lodge Session in 1888 and a resolution favoring such a change was carried by a vote of 228 to 47. This amendment to the Constitution was ratified by the lodges.

At the Grand Lodge Session in 1889 it was voted to hold the next Session (1890) in Cleveland, Ohio.

In his report at Cleveland, Exalted Grand Ruler Quinlin said:

"The lodge year just closing is eventful, and were it not for one event to be mentioned later on, the year would have closed as successful in all respects as any previous year in the history of our noble Order."

Exalted Grand Ruler Quinlin stated that he had received information that an attempt had been made by a few members of New York Lodge No. 1 to prevent the Grand Lodge from holding its annual Communication of the current year in Cleveland as previously enacted at the annual meeting in July, 1889, and that New York Lodge had adopted a resolution that the courts of law be appealed to for the purpose of setting at defiance the will of the Grand Lodge.

He reported that he had suspended the charter of New York Lodge No. 1 and had authorized Frank Girard, District Deputy, to take charge of all funds, books, papers and properties of the Lodge; had ordered the suspension of Grand Secretary Arthur C. Moreland and appointed John W. White as Secretary, *pro tem,* and had directed the Loyal Grand Knight Frank Wright to formulate charges against New York Lodge.

On May 1, 1890, Exalted Grand Ruler Quinlin wrote to the Exalted Ruler, officers and members of New York Lodge No. 1. He stated that the adoption of the resolution referred to above had been brought to his attention and that court proceedings had begun. He referred to the fact that this action was in defiance to the Constitution and Laws of our Order and in contumacy of the authority of the Grand Lodge. Furthermore, it was to the jeopardy of the discipline, peace and good name of the Order, and in violation of the obligation taken by every good Elk.

He then advised that he was suspending the charter of New York Lodge No. 1 and forbade any of its members "to meet or transact any business until said lodge had answered at the Grand Lodge in regular session at Cleveland, Ohio, July 8, 1890."

He directed the officers of New York Lodge No. 1 to deliver to Frank Girard, Deputy at Large, the "charter, books, papers, jewels, funds, emblems, regalia, or other property and effects."

In his report the Exalted Grand Ruler had said:

"We shall have before us for consideration the 'event' named above, viz., the contumacy and insubordination of Lodge No. 1 and Arthur C. Moreland, former Grand Secretary.

"Some time in the latter part of April, 1890, I received information from an authentic source that an attempt would be made by a few members of New York Lodge No. 1 to prevent this Grand Body from holding its annual communication of this year in the city of Cleveland, Ohio, as previously enacted by the Grand Lodge at its annual gathering in July, 1889.

"In direct violation of their sacred obligations, these misguided Brothers did, at their last meeting in the month of March of the present year, in lodge assembled, adopt a resolution that the courts of law be appealed to, and their aid sought and obtained for the purpose of setting at defiance the will of the Grand Lodge of the Order."

He advised the Grand Lodge that he had received certain papers from the Supreme Court, City and County of New York, forwarded through the mail by Arthur C. Moreland, whom he referred to as "former Grand Secretary of our Order."

The "papers" referred to were a certified copy of an injunction granted by Abraham R. Lawrence, Justice of the Supreme Court of the State of New York, upon application of one Louis Mendel, "restraining the Benevolent and Protective Order of Elks and the Grand Lodge thereof:

"(a) From holding any meeting or communication for the transaction of the business of the Benevolent and Protective Order of Elks, or the said Grand Lodge, outside the State of New York.

"(b) Restraining Arthur C. Moreland from removing the seal, books, papers and property of, belonging, appertaining or relating to defendant, the Benevolent and Protective Order of Elks, or its said Grand Lodge, from this State, or from parting with or disposing of the same in any manner whatsoever."

On motion of L. M. Hadden of Cincinnati Lodge No. 5 it was ordered that "A. C. Moreland, late Grand Secretary, be expelled from the B.P.O. Elks and be forever debarred from its rights and benefits."

This was carried by a unanimous vote.

A Trial Commission was appointed to take under advisement the charges and specifications against New York Lodge No. 1, formulated and presented by the Esteemed Loyal Grand Knight, and report thereon at once.

This Commission offered the following resolution:

"Resolved, that the charges preferred against New York Lodge No. 1 are fully sustained by the proof; and that the Grand Lodge do now proceed to the infliction of such penalties as in its wisdom it may deem proper."

It was thereupon voted unanimously that "the Charter of New York Lodge No. 1 is hereby forfeited."

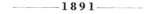

1891

This Grand Lodge Session was held in Louisville, Kentucky.

The Grand Exalted Ruler, in his report, advised of further developments in "the case of New York Lodge."

He referred to the attempt of Arthur C. Moreland, claiming still to be Grand Secretary of the Benevolent and Protective Order of Elks, to prevent Brooklyn Lodge No. 22 from using the name "Elk" or "Cervus Alces" and to secure a court order for that lodge to surrender all property, moneys, etc., to him as the representative of the Grand Lodge which he claimed to be.

(This claim was based on the theory that, since the Order of Elks was chartered in and by the State of New York, it was not legal for the Grand Lodge to convene or operate outside that State.)

A decision in the Brooklyn Lodge phase of this case was rendered by Judge Lawrence, of the New York Supreme Court, which, condensed, was as follows:

> "Courts should not interfere in cases of this character by issuing injunctions restraining benevolent organizations from conducting their business in accordance with the determination of a majority of the members of the organization, unless it is made to appear most clearly upon the papers that the Constitution and By-Laws of the organization have been violated, and that thereby the property of the organization and the rights of its members have been put in jeopardy. No such case is presented on this motion."

Judge Lawrence held that the annual meeting of the Order in Cleveland in 1890 had been properly held; that Arthur C. Moreland was expelled from the office of Grand Secretary before action in this case had commenced, and therefore had no right to speak for the Order; that there were 191 lodges of the Order reporting to Grand Secretary Meyers. He denied the motion.

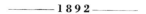

1892

Grand Exalted Ruler Edwin B. Hay, in his report to the Grand Lodge in connection with this case, advised that, following Judge Lawrence's denial of the motion for a preliminary injunction, the case rested until it could be called for final hearing.

He charged that when the case was on the list for November, 1891, the plaintiff pleaded the absence of an important witness, and the case went over and was set for the 6th of June, 1892.

Finally, in November, 1892, the case was heard before Judge

Ingraham who in January, 1893, handed down his decision in favor of the defendant, Peter Roeder, as Secretary of Brooklyn Lodge No. 22. Judge Ingraham said in his decision:

"This action appears to have been brought by Mr. Moreland, using the name of the corporation of which he had ceased to be an officer, and I know of no principle that allows a deposed officer, by such an action to determine the validity of the act which deposed him.

"If the action deposing him was illegal, he can test that action in a proper proceeding, but not in the manner attempted in this action."

————— 1 8 9 3 —————

In March, 1893, advances were made by the Grand Trustees of the Order to New York Lodge No. 1 for the arrangement of a conference looking to the settlement of the question at issue. As a result, a conference to settle the matter was held on the 21st of May, 1893.

There were present Grand Exalted Ruler Hay and Grand Trustees W. C. VanDerlip, Boston Lodge No. 10; Peter J. Campbell, Baltimore, Maryland, Lodge No. 7, and Joseph W. Laube, Richmond, Virginia, Lodge No. 45, with Percy G. Williams, District Deputy for the State of New York, and John J. Shannon, William L. Bowron, Nick Engel, Thomas Dare, H. Chegnay, Edwin Tubbs and Frank Whitmarsh, New York Lodge No. 1, and John J. Collins, Baltimore Lodge No. 7.

The meeting was successful.

Grand Exalted Ruler Hay said in his report:

"It was half doubt and half fear as to the outcome, but at half-past nine o'clock, with joy beaming in every face and seemingly filled with some uncontrollable delight, the committee from New York Lodge came to the Trustees and the Grand Exalted Ruler, and said:

" 'Come, the work is done; the victory is won; New York Lodge has pledged its allegiance to the Grand 'Lodge of the Benevolent and Protective Order of Elks of the United States and are waiting to receive you.'

"It was not then a moment of technical consideration of law nor for hesitation upon any quibbles.

"The time had come, and while it was hard to believe, yet it seemed really true, and at the doors of New York Lodge, when the announcement was made, a sensation impossible to describe seemed to be present.

"Down the long line of Brothers, for that night they all had come out, the Grand Exalted Ruler and the Grand Trustees were escorted to the altar, and when the Exalted Ruler, James J. Armstrong, saluted

169

and extended to the Grand Exalted Ruler of the Benevolent and Protective Order of Elks the welcome, there was a shout that went up that might have been heard for squares.

"It was the outburst of the pent-up feelings of Brothers that had been so long and so patiently waiting.

"Though in that limited circle, and in that room in New York, yet the sound found an echo from the meeting place of every lodge in the country, and the beating of those hearts found its reverberating sentiment in the heart of every Brother wherever he existed.

"It seemed like a dream, and yet it has proved to be a happy reality.

"The 21st of May, 1893, will always be a red-letter day in the history of New York Lodge, and in the history of the Order, and will always be an ever-memorable page in the recollections of all who were present.

"For fraternally they were 'souls with but a single thought and hearts that beat as one.' "

At the Grand Lodge Session of that year (1893) the Committee on Returns and Credentials reported that they had found on file, in regular form, the report of New York Lodge No. 1, together with a copy of resolutions "affirming their allegiance to the Grand Lodge" and asking the restoration of their charter.

The Committee recommended that:

"The action of the Grand Lodge at Cleveland in July, 1890, be and is hereby rescinded and that the charter of New York Lodge is restored and her title as provided by law is hereby confirmed in all of the properties belonging to said Lodge."

The Committee also recommended that all of the members of New York Lodge who had been members of the Grand Lodge be restored to such membership excepting Arthur C. Moreland who, they stated, had been expelled from the Grand Lodge, after due trial, and had failed to make application for restoration to membership.

The Grand Lodge unanimously adopted the report and recommendation of the Committee, and a committee was appointed to conduct the New York representatives into the hall.

The proceedings of the Grand Lodge then record the following:

"The Committee retired, and, in a short time, returned with the New York representatives, and as they entered the Grand Lodge members rose to their feet and sang 'Auld Lang Syne.'

"The old banner of the Grand Lodge was carried in front and the banner of the New York Lodge in the rear.

"The New York representatives were escorted to the stage and welcomed to the Grand Lodge. After congratulations from both sides, during which the Grand Lodge banner that had been in the possession of New York Lodge was presented to the Grand Lodge, the New York representatives were invited to take seats on the floor of the Grand Lodge."

There was then presented to the Grand Lodge the following petition from Arthur Moreland:

"Your petitioner having, as he avers, upon information and belief, been by resolution declared expelled in the month of July, 1890, at meeting of Grand Lodge of the Order held in the City of Cleveland, Ohio, and your petitioner being now a life member of New York Lodge No. 1 and said lodge having, upon May 21, 1893, reunited itself with the Grand body, and in view of the promised general harmony and in accordance with the general principles of the Order, your petitioner tenders his submission to your authority, and in token of his allegiance respectfully requests the reconsideration of the resolution of expulsion and the restoration of his name to the roll of membership of the Grand Lodge with all the rights and privileges appertaining thereto and for which your petitioner will ever pray.

(Signed) A. C. Moreland"

The motion to rescind was carried and Arthur C. Moreland was declared restored to membership in the Order and thus given the opportunity in the following years to perform important services to his lodge and to the Order of Elks.

Grand Exalted Ruler Hay closed "The Case of New York Lodge" with the following words in his report to the Grand Lodge at this Session:

"Patience is good, but joy is best. We have endured one, but today we must reap such profound joy, that has not come to us for several sessions. The tie that was severed is reunited; the link that was missing is once more in its place; the mother returns to her children and New York Lodge today will be officially restored to its chronological position, at the head of all the lodges in the country, No. 1."

Floral Emblem and Color

In his report to the Grand Lodge in 1892 Grand Exalted Ruler Hay said:

"While the memory of our departed Brothers is a strong tie in our fraternity and the 'absent Brother' the subject of many expressions of feeling, and the music of 'Auld Lang Syne' touches a responsive chord in our natures, I step aside a moment from the consideration of suggestions necessary for our welfare to intrude a matter of sentiment, which, if nothing more, is most appropriate.

"The Order has adopted no color as being distinctive. Purple is generally used. Might we not adopt the simple 'Forget-Me-Not' as our flower and make its heaven-born blue our color? The 'Forget-Me-Not' in life, the 'Amaranth and Ivy' in death.

"That blue and bright-eyed floweret of the brook—hope's gentle gem, the sweet 'Forget-Me-Not,' is so deliciously beautiful and expresses in its silent eloquence the sentiment that occupies so large a place in the hearts of all our Brothers."

The suggestion of the Grand Exalted Ruler was referred to the Committee on Work and Ritual.

That Committee reported that while they would not recommend a change in the color of Royal Purple generally used in the Order they would recommend that the

Forget-Me-Not

be adopted by the Grand Lodge as the Floral Emblem of the Benevolent and Protective Order of Elks, as recommended in the address of the Grand Exalted Ruler.

The recommendation of the Committee was adopted.

The Amaranth and Ivy

The Amaranth as used at Elks' funeral services which the attending members of the Order deposit on the casket of a departed Brother, is an imaginary flower which never fades. It is of purplish color, a hue similar to that of the corn flower.

It is regarded by the Elks as emblematic of the immortality of the soul, while the ivy tenderly placed with it on the departed Brother's casket is a symbol of the fidelity of his Brothers' devotion.

Jamestown Controversy

At the Grand Lodge Session in Detroit in 1893 there appears to have been much bitter feeling both between factions and between individuals.

It was very evident that there was bad feeling between Grand Exalted Ruler Hay and Grand Secretary Allen O. Myers.

The printed Proceedings of this Session do not carry much evidence of this for the reason that the following resolution was adopted:

"Resolved: That the Board of Grand Trustees be authorized to expunge and eliminate from the proceedings of this body, and from all papers presented to this body, anything of a personal nature or of a vituperative character reflecting upon any member of the Grand Lodge."

There do appear in the minutes as printed some rather slighting remarks by the Grand Exalted Ruler and the Grand Secretary regarding each other, and the Grand Exalted Ruler did recommend the reduction of the salary of the Grand Secretary from $2,500 per annum to $1,500 and succeeded in having that salary reduced to $2,000.

As the Session drew to a close, however, a motion was offered and adopted that as the per capita tax had been, at the Session, raised ten cents, which would give ample funds to pay the Grand Secretary the same salary he received the previous year, the action reducing his salary be rescinded.

Whether or not the bad feeling or misunderstanding started between individuals, it soon extended to groups, with the newly-elected Grand Exalted Ruler, Astley Apperly, of Louisville Lodge No. 8, and Grand Secretary Allen O. Myers, of Cincinnati Lodge No. 5, leading one group, and retiring Grand Exalted Ruler Hay and the Grand Trustees respresenting the other group.

In the printed Proceedings of that Session there appears the following:

"The next regular order of business was the selection of the time and place for the next meeting of the Grand Lodge in 1894.

"Several places were named, but no selection was made. After the presentation of views upon the subject, and suggestions that a time and place be selected that would be most convenient to the largest number of members, and one that would offer the best inducements and secure the lowest hotel and railroad rates, and that said Grand Lodge meeting should precede any reunion, and not be held in connection therewith."

On motion of Daniel A. Kelly, of Baltimore Lodge No. 7, the whole matter was referred to the Board of Grand Trustees, "with full power to select the time and place for the next annual Session of the Grand Lodge."

This was done by unanimous vote.

The Grand Trustees Fix Time and Place
for Grand Lodge Session

The Grand Trustees were W. C. VanDerlip, Boston Lodge No. 10, Peter J. Campbell, Baltimore Lodge No. 7, and Joseph W. Laube, Richmond, Virginia, Lodge No. 45.

Under date of August 8, 1893, the Trustees wrote to the Grand Exalted Ruler a letter which covered several matters. In that letter they said that in response to several letters asking for action in regard to the next place of meeting of the Grand Lodge and "in accordance with the vote of the Grand Lodge that the Grand Trustees fix the time and place for the next annual meeting, it was voted that it be held on the third Tuesday of June, 1894, at Atlantic City, New Jersey, at ten o'clock a.m., as we are fully convinced that better rates can be obtained at this place than at any other."

The Grand Exalted Ruler Consults the Committee on Laws and Appeals

On December 16, 1893, Grand Exalted Ruler Apperly issued a call to the Committee on Laws and Appeals to meet to consider certain matters he desired to submit to them.

He stated that at the Grand Lodge Session in Detroit in 1893 the Grand Trustees were ordered to secure bids for hotel and railroad rates, and, some time after the first of December, to locate a place for the next meeting of the Grand Lodge, and that in selecting Atlantic City before the December date set they had exceeded their authority.

The Committee on Laws and Appeals was composed of Lewis E. Griffith, Troy, New York, Lodge No. 141; M. A. Foran, Cleveland, Ohio, Lodge No. 18, and T. B. Felder, Atlanta, Georgia, Lodge No. 78.

The only member of the Committee answering the call of the Grand Exalted Ruler was T. B. Felder. Lewis E. Griffith resigned, and M. A. Foran failed to appear. The Grand Exalted Ruler appointed in their place Ensign N. Brown, Stillwater, Minnesota, Lodge No. 179, and P. L. Berry, Hamilton, Ohio, Lodge No. 93.

The Committee thus composed found:

"That the Proceedings of the Grand Lodge showed that the Grand Lodge unanimously ordered that the Grand Trustees should select a time and place that would be most convenient to the largest number of members, the place selected to be one that would offer the best inducements and secure the lowest hotel and railway rates."

However, the Committee referred to the fact:

1. That they could not find from the Grand Trustees that any competition whatever was raised.

2. That they could not find any evidence before them that the Grand Trustees considered any location except Atlantic City.

3. That they did find, however, that the Grand Trustees, within six weeks after the closing of the Grand Lodge Session at Detroit, made and fixed the date as above stated, and for that reason they were forced to the opinion that the Board of Trustees "did not act within the scope of their authority" and that their action "must of necessity be null and void."

Under date of January 14, 1894, Grand Exalted Ruler Apperly issued a call for a "Special Annual Session of the Grand Lodge" to be held at Jamestown, New York, on June 18, 1894.

The Two Sessions

At the Atlantic City Session there were in attendance 193 members of the Grand Lodge, representing 80 lodges.

At the Jamestown Session there were in attendance 138 members of the Grand Lodge, representing 85 lodges.

At the former meeting Grand Esteemed Leading Knight William G. Meyers, Philadelphia, Pennsylvania, Lodge No. 2, presided and Past Grand Exalted Ruler Hay was selected again for that office while George A. Reynolds, of Saginaw, Michigan, Lodge No. 47, was elected Grand Secretary.

The Jamestown Session chose William H. Friday, Brooklyn, New York, Lodge No. 22, as Grand Exalted Ruler and Clate A. Smith, Youngstown, Ohio, Lodge No. 55, as Grand Secretary.

The Atlantic City faction voted to meet again the following year in Atlantic City, while the Jamestown group selected Savannah, Georgia, as its next meeting place.

Past Grand Exalted Rulers Present

In attendance at Atlantic City were the following Past Grand Exalted Rulers:

Daniel A. Kelly	Baltimore Lodge No. 7
John J. Tindale	New York Lodge No. 1
William E. English	Indianapolis Lodge No. 13
Edwin B. Hay	Washington Lodge No. 15

At Jamestown the only Past Grand Exalted Ruler in attendance was Simon Quinlin, Chicago Lodge No. 4.

Future Grand Exalted Rulers

At Atlantic City, among those present who were later to become Grand Exalted Rulers of a united Order were:

William G. Meyers	Philadelphia Lodge No. 2
B. M. Allen	Birmingham Lodge No. 79

Jamestown had the following Grand-Exalted-Rulers-to-be in attendance:

Meade D. Detweiler	Harrisburg Lodge No. 241 (later No. 12)
Jerome B. Fisher	Jamestown Lodge No. 263
	(not then a member of the Grand Lodge but
	Exalted Ruler of the host lodge.)
George P. Cronk	Omaha Lodge No. 39

The Legal Phase

On the day of the Special Session, the Jamestown faction caused to be procured a temporary injunction to prevent the meeting in Atlantic City and the removal of books, etc., from Jamestown.

The Grand Trustees had an answer filed. The injunction was dissolved, the court ruling that the power to select the time and place of the Grand Lodge Session for 1894 had been, by the Grand Lodge, made the responsibility of the Board of Grand Trustees.

An appeal was taken.

The Atlantic City Grand Lodge
Starts Court Action

In the name of Grand Secretary Reynolds, elected at Atlantic City, proceedings were instituted against Clate A. Smith, elected Grand Secretary at Jamestown, for the purpose of gaining possession of the paraphernalia, books, rituals and belongings of the Order in his hands.

A Compromise Move

Omaha Lodge No. 39 and Lima Lodge No. 162 issued circular letters suggesting a meeting for the purpose of "bringing about harmony and reconciliation."

Grand Exalted Ruler Hay answered this appeal with a statement that the place to settle all differences would be Atlantic City, where the Grand Lodge would hold its regular Session.

A meeting resulting from the Omaha and Lima appeal was held in Chicago on March 18, 1895, and adjourned to meet at Buffalo on May 20.

The attendance at this meeting in Chicago appears to have been almost, if not entirely, made up of members of the Jamestown faction.

The Buffalo meeting assumed the character of a Grand Lodge Session. At that meeting a committee, consisting of Meade D.

Detweiler, Harrisburg Lodge No. 241; Eugene L. Lewis, Cincinnati Lodge No. 5, and Charles M. Bedell, Syracuse Lodge No. 31, was appointed to confer with the officers of the Grand Lodge relative to a reconciliation. (Meade D. Detweiler was elected Grand Exalted Ruler.)

Referring to the proceedings instituted against the Grand Secretary selected at Jamestown, Grand Exalted Ruler Hay said, in his report to the 1895 Grand Lodge Session, that:

"The opinion of His Honor, Judge Hammond, in charging the jury, not only established clearly the legality of this Grand Lodge, but in referring to it he said that it was 'the masterful superior of everybody in the Order.'

"The jury unfortunately disagreed upon the question of facts."

On June 24th, the Supreme Court of the State of New York handed down an opinion written by Justice Lewis of that Court sustaining the dissolution of the injunction secured by the Jamestown faction.

The Court said.

"The action of the Grand Exalted Ruler in assuming to change the place of meeting from Atlantic City to Jamestown was without jurisdiction and void."

Under date of July 10, 1895, the Grand Trustees, Willard C. Van-Derlip, Boston Lodge No. 10, Peter J. Campbell, Baltimore Lodge No. 7, and James W. Laube, Richmond Lodge No. 45, reported that they had met with the Committee created at the Buffalo meeting and had agreed to submit the following:

1. The constitution as it existed in Detroit, and was amended at Atlantic City, be reenacted by a reunited Grand Lodge.

2. That the lodges instituted by William H. Friday and Meade D. Detweiler be considered as being regularly instituted.

3. That all subordinate lodges which had paid per capita taxes in 1894 and 1895 to whomsoever paid be exonerated from any further payments on account of same.

4. That all suits and litigation now pending in the courts be discontinued and all Grand Lodge property being held by Clate A. Smith be turned over to the proper officers of the Grand Lodge and that parties represented by the Buffalo Committee release all claims they have to funds in the hands of the Grand Treasurer.

5. That all Grand Lodge members of any subordinate lodge that had paid its per capita taxes for 1894 and 1895 be entitled to admission to the Grand Lodge.

6. That all financial differences and indebtedness be referred to the incoming Board of Grand Trustees with power.

This report was received and its recommendations adopted.

Grand Exalted Ruler Hay appointed Willliam E. English, P.G.E.R.; George W. Thompson, P.G.E.R.; W. J. Toomer, Jacksonville; Harry Mears, Baltimore; Joseph T. Fanning, Indianapolis; A. A. Cleveland, Astoria; John Coogan, Hartford; Charles Jewett, New Albany, and William G. Meyers, Grand Esteemed Leading Knight, to escort Messrs. Detweiler, Bedell and Lewis and those accompanying them before the Grand Lodge.

What followed was most dramatic.

On the arrival of the delegation, Thomas F. McNulty, Baltimore Lodge No. 7, sang "Auld Lang Syne," and the entire membership of the Grand Lodge rose and joined in the singing.

Meade D. Detweiler Speaks

Meade D. Detweiler, who was an outstanding orator, spoke for the delegation and the group it represented. A few extracts from his talk, addressed to the Grand Exalted Ruler and the Grand Lodge, follow:

"Believe me when I say that I feel too sensibly this high and unmerited compliment to make any other return than the simple expression of my gratitude. In coming here today there was no purpose in my mind to make a speech, but the enthusiasm of this meeting thrills me so that I cannot refrain from expressing a few sentiments in this reunited Grand Lodge of the Benevolent and Protective Order of Elks.

"An Order such as ours, my Brothers, of noble views and exalted aims, is greater than any individual. The perpetuation of its beneficent influence and its precious legacy to humanity is far beyond any personal aspirations or preferments.

"The present moment teems with weighty responsibilities and wondrous opportunities. It is a turning point for weal or woe, not for individuals, but for our magnificent Order.

"My Brothers, this is the proudest and most glorious moment of my life; to be able to lead back this vast herd of Elks by the side of the still waters of peace, and, with you, write all faults on yonder countless sands and their virtues on the tablets of love and memory.

"Unity and harmony being fully restored upon terms that must at once be acceptable to all Elks, I here and now declare my willing surrender to the reunited Order the office that was given to me at Buffalo and pledge my most sacred honor to use every effort at my command to urge everybody to yield a loyal and unswerving support to the Grand Exalted Ruler and officers to be elected in this Grand Lodge.

"There will be but one Grand Lodge; there is and there shall be but one Grand Exalted Ruler and his title will never be questioned I hope in the future.

"The humblest private in the victorious army, keeping step to the thrilling music that heralds an advance to new conquests and future fields of glory, is greater than the commander of a disorganized host. The principles taught by our Order must and will live, for it is the mission of the B.P.O.E., in the fullness of time, to elevate its members, to actuate them to nobler thoughts, grander impulses and loftier aspirations, that will lift them far above the sordid things of this life and crown them with the dignity, the luster and the honor of a full and perfect manhood."

Grand Exalted Ruler Replies

Let us close this account of the "Jamestown Controversy" with extracts from the reply of Grand Exalted Ruler Hay:

"Brother Detweiler says that this is the happiest moment of his life. Truly, what must it be to us, and what must it be to your Grand Exalted Ruler!

"When I grasped Brother Detweiler's hand the magnetic flash which united us here created a current that went around this entire country, and brought into touch all the Brothers of our Order who have taken our solemn obligation.

"He may have had political honors thrust upon him, and preferment in his own community; but he has never received such an ovation from the heart and from the soul as was tendered him here today in your midst.

"We but echo the sentiments in all the lodges of the country, and those who are not represented here today will welcome him again with all that he represents into our midst.

"God bless our reunited Order, and I cannot better conclude what I have to say than by asking our Grand Chaplain to invoke the blessing of the Deity upon us all."

National Incorporation

After the subject of migration of the Grand Lodge Sessions was introduced, changing the original idea of the Grand Lodge meeting annually in New York City, the question of incorporation had come up in all litigation.

At Cleveland, the Grand Lodge decided that the meeting in that city was legal, and that its incorporation in New York State did not mean that all of its meetings had to be held in that State.

In Detroit, in 1893, it went farther, and adopted Constitution and By-Laws in which the title of the Order was designated as "The Benevolent and Protective Order of Elks of the United States of America."

At the Convention in Atlantic City in 1895, Grand Exalted Ruler Hay stated that the Grand Trustees and the Committee on Laws and Appeals had deemed it wiser that the Order should have a charter that would thereafter prevent all cavil upon the subject of where the Grand Lodge could hold its meetings.

He reported further that an Act of Congress to permit the organization to be chartered under the laws of the District of Columbia was proposed in the House of Representatives, but it being near the close of the session, and since some objection had been raised by certain constituents of a member of Congress, it was not insisted upon nor was there a need absolutely for a national enactment, as the statutes of the United States particularly provide for the incorporation of benevolent and religious bodies, and under this Act, the Benevolent and Protective Order of Elks of the United States of America had been incorporated and granted all the rights and privileges under the law so made, and provided especially the right to hold its annual meeting whenever and wherever it pleases as provided by its own By-Laws.

He then presented to the Grand Lodge a copy of the following certificate of incorporation:

CERTIFICATE OF INCORPORATION OF THE

BENEVOLENT AND PROTECTIVE ORDER OF

ELKS OF THE UNITED STATES OF AMERICA

We, the undersigned, Edwin B. Hay, Joseph Y. Potts, John C. Maxwell and Thomas J. King, all of the District of Columbia, Willard C.

VanDerlip, of Boston, Mass., Peter J. Campbell, of Baltimore, Md., and Joseph W. Laube, of Richmond, Va., being persons of full age, all of whom are citizens of the United States, and a majority of whom are citizens of the District of Columbia, pursuant to and in conformity with Section 545, 546, 547, 549, 550, 551 and 552, of the Revised Statutes of the United States relating to the District of Columbia, do hereby associate ourselves together for benevolent, charitable, educational and literary purposes and for mutual improvement, and we do hereby certify that:

FIRST: That the name of this organization shall be the "Benevolent and Protective Order of Elks of the United States of America."

SECOND: The term for which it is organized is twenty (20) years.

THIRD: Its objects shall be and are benevolent, social and altruistic; to promote and encourage manly friendship and kindly intercourse; and to aid, protect and assist its members and their families.

FOURTH: The number of its Trustees shall be three (3) viz: Willard C. VanDerlip, Peter J. Campbell and Joseph W. Laube and they shall hold office during the first year of its existence or until their successors are elected, and the said organization, by the name above, may have and use a common seal and may meet annually or oftener at such time and places and in such manner as may be specified in its By-Laws. In testimony whereof, we have hereunto set our hands this nineteenth day of June, in the year of our Lord, one thousand eight hundred and ninety-five.

Edwin B. Hay
Joseph Y. Potts
John C. Maxwell
Thomas J. King
Willard C. VanDerlip
Peter J. Campbell
Joseph W. Laube

——— 1915 ———

In 1915 Grand Exalted Ruler Benjamin, noting that the charter of the Grand Lodge under the laws of the District of Columbia obtained in 1895 would expire in June, 1915, prepared a certificate of perpetual continuance of that charter which was duly executed by the Grand Exalted Ruler as President of the Corporation, Grand Secretary as Secretary of the Corporation and the Grand Trustees as Grand Trustees and Trustees of the Corporation.

Flag on the Altar

The placing of the American Flag on the altar of our lodges had its inception in the report of the Committee on Work and Ritual rendered to the Grand Lodge which convened in Cincinnati, July 7, 8 and 9, 1896. This Committee convened jointly with a special committee appointed at the Session, and on July 8, a joint report was submitted by Arthur C. Moreland, Chairman, recommending the present arrangement on the altar of the Flag, the Bible and the Antlers.

The members of the Committee on Work and Ritual were:

Arthur C. Moreland	New York Lodge No. 1
Frank Moran	Philadelphia Lodge No. 2
Julius Straus	Richmond, Va., Lodge No. 45

The Special Committee was composed of:

Moses P. O'Brien	Omaha, Neb., Lodge No. 39
William H. Friday	Brooklyn Lodge No. 22
G. D. Ackerly	Jacksonville, Fla., Lodge No. 221
John T. Sutphen	Middletown, Ohio, Lodge No. 257
Harvey Meyers	Covington, Ky., Lodge No. 314

The placing of the American Flag on the altar of our subordinate lodges was a significant and far-reaching act. It was a great factor in the successful growth of the Order, for it put the visible stamp of patriotism upon every lodge and associated the banner of our country, the Bible and our Order's emblem in an immortal trinity.

——————1 9 3 0——————

The report of the Ritualistic Committee in 1930 contained the following:

"Last September, Brother H. R. McCann, Secretary of Sandpoint, Idaho, Lodge No. 1376, raised the question as to whether our present custom of permitting the Bible to rest upon the Flag of our country was not in violation of the code prescribed by the War Department.

"Since that time we have received two or three similar inquiries.

"In order to get a clear ruling, our Committee placed the matter before Colonel W. C. Sweeney, Commander of the 3rd U. S. Infantry, who had his adjutant, Captain Townsend, confer with the War Department which issued a circular setting forth clearly that the Flag should never be used as a decoration or a drapery by military organizations but should always be left flying free.

"The department makes it clear, however, that it does not seek to establish rules and regulations for civilian practice or to interfere with any use of the Flag by civilians so long as that use is generally respectful.

"For that reason, in the opinion of Col. Sweeney and Captain Townsend, there would be no objection to placing the Bible reverently upon the Flag."

——————— 1 9 4 0 ———————

In December, 1940, Past Grand Exalted Ruler Holland, replying to an inquiry relative to the use of the Flag on the altar, wrote as follows:

"Many years ago, I should say at least twenty, the question was raised as to whether or not the use made of the American Flag in Elk lodge rooms could reasonably be construed as showing disrespect for the National Emblem. I took the matter up with the officers of the Army and the Navy and with the United States Flag Association, fully explaining how the Flag was used on the altar in Elk lodge rooms and that the desire of the Order was at all times to show respect for the Flag, and that if the use being made of it was considered as showing disrespect, the custom which had maintained for many, many years would be considered by the officers of the Grand Lodge with a view of discontinuing the practice."

He said further that it was a unanimous opinion of those consulted that the use which the Order was making of the Flag on the altar was evidence of the great respect shown the Flag and that it could not be construed as showing disrespect.

——————— 1 9 5 2 ———————

The following is an extract from a memorandum on the subject of the use of the Flag on the altar, prepared by Past Grand Exalted Ruler E. Mark Sullivan:

"The Elk symbols of this love of God, of country and of countrymen, are the Bible, the Flag and the Antlers. The arrangement of these symbols upon an Elks altar is both reverent and patriotic in concept of ascending inspirational power, and possesses sublime beauty and deep import. It is in full accord with the religious and civic traditions of the American people and the customs and laws of their government.

"Upon the altar erected to this triune love, the Order reverently spreads the Flag of our country so that it always looks upward to the

Holy Bible as the eternal source of the people's inalienable rights and moral duties; and upon the opened pages of this Sacred Book it places the Spreading Antlers of Protection, symbolic of its all-embracing brotherhood. Thus our altar is a manifestation of devotion to God, country and countrymen."

——1956——

At the 1956 Grand Lodge Convention, Past Grand Exalted Ruler Malley, Chairman of the Special Ritual Committee, reported that "the present treatment of the American Flag in the Rituals of our Order is contrary to Section 176 of Title 36 U.S. Code Annotated". The Special Ritual Committee composed of Past Grand Exalted Rulers Malley, McClelland and Sullivan, then recommended certain changes in procedure, instructions and Ritual necessary to bring our Ritual in conformity with the law as interpreted by the Committee on Judiciary. The changes provided for the removal of the Flag from the altar and the use of an altar cover, with the Flag to be placed in position at the right of the altar. The recommendations were unanimously adopted.

Spanish-American War

Following the outbreak of the Spanish-American War in 1898, Grand Exalted Ruler Meade D. Detweiler issued an official circular to all subordinate lodges suggesting that each lodge adopt a resolution reading as follows:

"The Benevolent and Protective Order of Elks, emphatically and exclusively an American Order, in this hour of the nation's appeal to patriotism in defense of its rights and the rights of humanity, responds to its sense of duty, its love of country and its devotion to the great American ideas which gave it birth.

"Resolved: That all members of subordinate lodges, who at their country's call have enlisted in the service of the United States Government, at the sacrifice of their business and private interests, shall be protected during the term of their service.

"First: That all dues incurred during the period of their enlistment shall be remitted and not charged against them.

"Second: That during their absence a special committee of three shall be appointed to ascertain the circumstances of those dependent upon them for a livelihood, to provide them with such livelihood, if necessary, during the term of the enlistment of our Brothers."

At the Grand Lodge Session in New Orleans, Louisiana, in May, 1898, Past Grand Exalted Ruler Edwin B. Hay offered the following resolution:

"Whereas, the Benevolent and Protective Order of Elks, being an American institution, and the country today is unhappily engaged in war with a foreign power, be it

"Resolved: That the Grand Lodge now in session in the City of New Orleans, Louisiana, representing as it does 48,000 Elks, tenders to the President of the United States its sympathy in these trying moments and its hearty interest in his every act pertaining to the welfare of the country, assuring him of loyalty and devotion to the Flag and all it symbolizes, and an indulgence in the hope that a speedy restoration of peace may follow a victorious arbitrament of arms.

"Resolved: That a copy of these resolutions, signed by the Grand Exalted Ruler and attested by the Grand Secretary, under seal, be forwarded at once to the President of the United States."

This resolution was adopted by a rising vote.

JOHN GALVIN
1898-99

BASIL M. ALLEN
1899-1900

JEROME B. FISHER
1900-01

CHARLES E. PICKETT
1901-02

GEORGE P. CRONK
1902-03

Grand Exalted Rulers

FOURTH DECADE

1898-1908

JOSEPH T. FANNING
1903-04

WILLIAM J. O'BRIEN, JR.
1904-05

ROBERT W. BROWN
1905-06

HENRY A. MELVIN
1906-07

JOHN K. TENER
1907-08

S E C T I O N

Fourth Decade

At the 1899 Session of the Grand Lodge, Arthur Moreland explained why New York Lodge had opposed the endorsement of the new Constitution passed by the Grand Lodge in 1898 and he and Thomas F. Brogan, of New York Lodge, were added to the Committee on Constitution and a compromise Constitution was adopted by the Grand Lodge and approved by the subordinate lodges. In 1902, President Theodore Roosevelt appealed to Congress for legislation providing for the protection of the game and wild creatures of the forest reserves and said:

> "It is, for instance, a serious count against our national good sense to permit the present practice of butchering such a stately and beautiful creature as the elk for its antlers and its tusks."

For the following fifteen years the Grand Lodge and the subordinate lodges cooperated in every possible way to preserve the herds of elk.

The gradual reduction of the herds, however, was not due to the slaughter of the elk for their teeth, but to the lack of winter protection and food supplies.

One of the strongest efforts of the Order to correct this situation was devoted to pressing upon Congress the necessity of the creation of additional winter reserves for the animals.

A representative of the United States Forest Service, speaking at the Grand Lodge Session in 1919, said that the Order had been of great assistance in investigating conditions on elk ranges, memorializing Congress to provide for the purchase of feeding stations and in refuting the idea that the elk tooth was an emblem of the Order.

Today the herds are so great, Federal park officials are seeking aid from hunters in reducing their numbers.

In the matter of requirements for membership in the Order it was provided in 1903 that the applicant be "in possession of the five human senses."

However, before this period came to an end some of the most important changes in the Constitution and Statutes took place as the result of the recommendations of the Special Committee on Revision of the Constitution appointed in 1906.

It is true that a few of the important changes recommended by this Special Committee were repealed in the next two Grand Lodge Sessions but most of them have continued to the present day.

One of the outstanding recommendations of the Committee was a complete change in the judicial system of the Order and the creation of Subordinate Forums and the Grand Forum, a system that has been practically unchanged since its adoption.

The growth of the Order in membership continued each year in this Decade, the percentage of such growth being 540.

The Order was just 30 years of age when sentiment developed for the establishment of a National Home for the aged and needy members of the Order.

Five years later the first Home was established in Bedford, Virginia, to be succeeded in another eight years by the magnificent structure now nestling in the foothills of the Peaks of Otter in the Blue Ridge Mountains of Virginia.

In the 36 years of its existence it has housed over 2,400 members of the Order. As this History is written there are about 300 residents at the Home, each occupying a single outside room with running hot and cold water, and attractively decorated and comfortably furnished.

Fourth Decade—1898-1908

The Grand Exalted Rulers during this period were:

JOHN GALVIN, Cincinnati, Ohio, Lodge, No. 5 1898-1899

BASIL M. ALLEN, Birmingham, Alabama, Lodge, No. 79 1899-1900

JEROME B. FISHER, Jamestown, New York, Lodge, No. 263 1900-1901

CHARLES E. PICKETT, Waterloo, Iowa, Lodge, No. 290 1901-1902

GEORGE P. CRONK, Omaha, Nebraska, Lodge, No. 39 1902-1903

JOSEPH T. FANNING, Indianapolis, Indiana, Lodge, No. 13 1903-1904

WILLIAM J. O'BRIEN, JR., Baltimore, Maryland, Lodge, No. 7 ...1904-1905

ROBERT W. BROWN, Louisville, Kentucky, Lodge, No. 8 1905-1906

HENRY A. MELVIN, Oakland, California, Lodge, No. 171 1906-1907

JOHN K. TENER, Charleroi, Pennsylvania, Lodge, No. 494 1907-1908

GRAND SECRETARIES

At the beginning of the Fourth Decade George A. Reynolds of Saginaw, Michigan, Lodge, No. 47, was serving as Grand Secretary.

He continued in that office until the Grand Lodge Session in Cincinnati, Ohio, in July, 1904.

At that Session Fred C. Robinson of Dubuque, Iowa, Lodge, No. 297, was elected Grand Secretary.

He served until September, 1927, when he resigned.

MEMBERSHIP AND CHARITABLE EXPENDITURES

YEAR	MEMBERSHIP	CHARITABLE EXPENDITURES
1898-1899	60,129	$ 46,774.47
1899-1900	77,351	53,075.43
1900-1901	99,827	80,683.73
1901-1902	128,679	225,867.34
1902-1903	155,434	189,918.19
1903-1904	177,527	143,072.26
1904-1905	199,370	237,021.29
1905-1906	225,016	244,654.97
1906-1907	254,532	276,613.92
1907-1908	284,321	376,491.37

In this Decade the Grand Lodge Sessions were held in the following cities:

1899	St. Louis, Missouri	1904	Cincinnati, Ohio
1900	Atlantic City, New Jersey	1905	Buffalo, New York
1901	Milwaukee, Wisconsin	1906	Denver, Colorado
1902	Salt Lake City, Utah	1907	Philadelphia, Pennsylvania
1903	Baltimore, Maryland	1908	Dallas, Texas

At the end of this Decade the assets of the 1,119 lodges amounted to $15,267,323.51.

Preservation of the Elk

————1903————

In the report of Grand Exalted Ruler George P. Cronk, at the Grand Lodge Session in Baltimore, Maryland, in 1903, he referred to the past efforts put forth by many individuals looking to the prevention of the wanton slaughter of the elk.

He then stated that President Theodore Roosevelt, in his address to Congress, on December 2, 1902, said:

> "Legislation should be provided for the protection of the game and wild creatures in the forest reserves. Senseless slaughter of game, which can, by judicious protection, be permanently preserved on the National Reserves for the people as a whole should be stopped at once.

> "It is, for instance, a serious count against our national good sense to permit the present practice of butchering such a stately and beautiful creature as the elk for its antlers and its tusks."

After reading the President's address, the Grand Exalted Ruler promptly wired him as follows:

> "December 3, 1902
> Honorable Theodore Roosevelt,
> President of the United States,
> Washington, D. C.

> "In behalf of the Benevolent and Protective Order of Elks, I thank you for your recommendation to Congress looking to the preservation of the elk.
> > George P. Cronk
> > Grand Exalted Ruler"

There was the following reply:

> "My dear Sir:

> "The President requests me to thank you cordially for your telegram of the 3rd instant, and to state that few things have pleased him more

than your message; that he was very anxious to secure the aid and influence of the Beneficent Order of Elks in order to protect those beautiful animals.

> Very truly yours,
> George B. Cortelyou,
> Secretary to the President"

Grand Exalted Ruler Cronk recommended that the matter be referred to the Committee on Good of the Order, to be reported on fully at the next Session.

At the same Session a resolution was presented by Cheyenne Lodge No. 660, referring to the fact that members of the Order like to wear an elk's tooth, thereby increasing the incentive of the hunter to slaughter the elk against the laws of the state.

At this 1903 Grand Lodge Session, the Committee on Good of the Order recommended that a memorial be sent to Congress to the effect that suitable provisions be made by the Government for the proper care, protection and maintenance of the elk, especially those that are driven, by heavy snows during the winter months, from the mountain ranges to seek shelter in the valleys below.

The Committee further recommended that all lodges of the Order in the northern and western States give this subject their special attention, and make the utmost endeavor at all times to stop the destruction of the elk.

These recommendations were adopted.

1904

In 1904, Seattle Lodge No. 92 offered a resolution that the Grand Lodge take active steps toward the enactment of a law prohibiting the killing of the elk for a period of ten years.

The Committee on Good of the Order, which presented the resolution, thought it best that the subordinate lodges request their representatives in Congress to act in this matter, and to urge them to support appropriate legislation.

This recommendation was adopted.

1906

At the Grand Lodge Session of 1906, Past Grand Exalted Ruler Allen offered the following recommendation for the Good of the Order Committee:

> "The Committee on Good of the Order, to whom was referred the suggestion of J. P. Thompson touching the protection and preservation of the noble animal whose name we have adopted, begs leave to report

that at the Baltimore Session of the Grand Lodge, held July, 1903, the matter under consideration was made the subject of a resolution of this Committee; that at the Cincinnati Session of the Grand Lodge, held July, 1904, the matter was again brought to the attention of the Order and a resolution was adopted that action be taken by subordinate lodges to influence their representatives in Congress with a view to the enactment of the desired legislation.

"Your Committee recommends that the matter be referred to the incoming Grand Exalted Ruler, with a request to investigate and ascertain the exact status of the laws on this subject, both State and Federal, and to take such steps as he may deem necessary for the enactment of necessary laws for the protection of the elk and its preservation."

This recommendation was adopted.

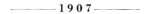

1907

In 1907, Grand Exalted Ruler Henry A. Melvin reported the exact laws of the States regarding this matter. He concluded that the States do everything in their power but they cannot, because of the terrain and such, halt the useless killing.

He said that much of the killing of the elk was being done because of the high price of their tusks.

He reported the receipt of a letter from President Theodore Roosevelt, referring to his understanding that there was great slaughter of elk because of the wearing of elk's teeth by the members of the Order, and then saying:

"Is it not possible that your Order, which has done so much for uplifting our American citizenship and for rendering life among so many of our people both easier and happier, may now come to the front again in rendering the service to our whole people that would be rendered by the abolition of this destructive custom?"

The Grand Exalted Ruler stated that the Legislature of the State of Wyoming had passed a resolution asking

"the Order's discontinuance, and decrying of, the wearing of elk's teeth as emblems, to the end that we may see these animals thrive and multiply in further peace than is now enjoyed by them."

He then suggested that the Grand Lodge forbid the wearing of elk's teeth by any member of the Order in connection with any words, insignia or devices referring to the Order.

This suggestion was referred to the Committee on Good of the Order. The Committee reviewed the matter quite fully and after stating that its members did not

"in any way admit that wearing the teeth of the elk in articles of adornment by members of the Benevolent and Protective Order of Elks is responsible to any considerable extent for the destruction and gradual extermination of the noble animal whose name our Order bears"

and made the following recommendations:

1. The appointment by the incoming Grand Exalted Ruler of a special commission to investigate and consider this entire subject thoroughly.

2. The adoption of a resolution requesting the membership of the Order to dispense with the use of the elk tooth as an article of personal adornment.

This Committee was composed of Past Grand Exalted Rulers Galvin, Fanning, Allen, Meyers, Apperly, Fisher, O'Brien and Brown.

Its recommendations were adopted.

——— 1 9 0 8 ———

In 1908, the Special Commission on the Preservation of the Elk made an 8,000-word report on its findings, based on a two-week trip into the heart of what might properly be regarded as the animal elk territory, where they made contact with settlers, game wardens, guides and hunters, and on a campaign of correspondence which embraced letters to and from over three hundred individuals possessing special knowledge of the subject.

This Commission was composed of:

Perry A. Clay, Denver, Colorado, Lodge, No. 17
D. A. Preston, Rock Springs, Wyoming, Lodge, No. 624
Frank E. Herring, South Bend, Indiana, Lodge, No. 235

The report was exhaustive, detailed and interesting.

It was the considered conclusion of the Commission that the animal elk was dying out, not so much from illegal killing for the sale of the teeth (which was responsible for what amounted to the smallest percentage of death among the animals), but to the impossibility of the animals finding food because, particularly in winter, it had been shut off by the advance of civilization from its natural grazing grounds.

Of the first factor, the Commission said in its report:

"There is no question that the widespread report to the effect that the elk is being exterminated in order to get their tusks for commercial purposes is without foundation in reason or in fact."

As to the other factor, the Commission reported that, as the result of its exhaustive studies, its members had arrived definitely at the conclusion that the preservation of the animal elk was absolutely dependent upon steps being taken by which they would be provided sustenance in the winter by the establishment of ranges for this purpose.

The Commission made the following recommendations:

"Your Commission believes that it lies within the power of this grand organization to determine the fate of the elk. By concerted action we may so secure the enactment of national and state legislation as will preserve to posterity this creature of unequalled beauty, so that our children's children may see him, as we do, in all of his primitive grandeur and glory.

"Your Commission therefore recommends that this Grand Lodge on behalf of the Order prepare and transmit to the National Congress a memorial setting forth our findings and praying that body to enact such a law as will preserve our elk from the present danger of extinction by severe winters."

The report of the Commission was adopted.

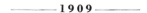

——— 1909 ———

The report of the Commission at the 1909 Grand Lodge Session stated that a joint resolution had been introduced by Senator Warren of Wyoming in the United States Senate, designed to establish a winter game preserve in Wyoming for the elk, and that by reason of the interest on the part of the Order, the Legislature of Wyoming had sent a joint memorial to Congress, asking that body to take the legislative steps asked by the Order.

The Commission recommended that a committee of three members of the Grand Lodge be appointed to continue this work, and that each lodge be asked to pass a resolution appealing to members of Congress to give this matter their attention.

——— 1910 ———

In 1910, Grand Exalted Ruler Sammis reported that no legislation on the subject was enacted because those members of Congress who represented districts where elk abound deemed it wholly unnecessary.

He stated that in Wyoming it was estimated that the elk had increased from 10,000 to nearly 50,000, as a result of the laws that had been enacted by that State.

He suggested the discontinuance of the Committee.

The Committee: R. E. Brown, Bozeman, Montana, Lodge, No. 463, Chairman; John M. Kohler, Kenosha, Wisconsin, Lodge, No. 750, and C. H. Dill, Fargo, North Dakota, Lodge, No. 260—closed its report with the following statement:

"Having reached the conclusion, as we have, that conditions are favorable to the continued welfare of the elk, and that its preservation and protection may safely be left to the governments and people of the states where it is chiefly found, and that, for the present at least, no further attention to this subject is necessary on the part of our Order, we respectfully recommend that this Committee be abolished."

This recommendation was adopted.

————1911————

In the Grand Lodge year of 1910-11, however, after a national magazine published an article which reflected on the Order in connection with this subject, it once more became alive.

Grand Exalted Ruler Herrmann, in his report to the Grand Lodge Session in 1911, stated that he had attempted to get the magazine referred to, to publish a story of what the Order of Elks had done on behalf of the preservation of the elk animal.

He was not successful in this, but the editor of the magazine did write to him saying that he deeply appreciated the part the Order had played in the preservation of the species.

The Grand Exalted Ruler also reported that he had received a copy of a Salt Lake City paper in which the story of the death by starvation of the American elk was enlarged upon, and that under the circumstances he had felt it necessary to bring the matter of the preservation of the animal once more to the attention of the Grand Lodge.

He said:

"I do not doubt that, with the proper and persistent effort, both the Congress and Legislatures will appreciate the necessity of the situation and take steps to avoid a condition which would be regretted by all Elks and also by all intelligent and progressive citizens."

He said that he did not wish to imply that the condition of the American elk was as serious as had been charged and added that the report of the Clay Commission was too full and complete to permit a doubt of the correctness of the facts produced by it or of the soundness of its conclusions.

At the same Grand Lodge Session there was presented a resolution of Sheridan, Wyoming, Lodge, No. 520, petitioning the Grand Lodge to take suitable action toward the protection of the elk, as outlined in a statement of facts presented in the resolution, and do all things necessary to the end that the elk herd may be preserved and increased for the benefit of posterity.

The resolution called for "the appointment of a special committee of the Grand Lodge to confer with the Federal Government looking to the withdrawal of all open land in the Jackson Hole, to the cession of the following territory, and abolition of grazing permits therein." (Description of the territory followed.)

As a result, a motion was adopted to appoint a committee of five to study the situation, and $2,500 was appropriated for the expense thereof.

The following committee was appointed:

Rush L. Holland, Colorado Springs, Colorado, Lodge, No. 309

Joseph T. Fanning, Indianapolis, Indiana, Lodge, No. 13

William J. O'Brien, Jr., Baltimore, Maryland, Lodge, No. 7

George E. Chamberlain, Portland, Oregon, Lodge, No. 142

Edward J. Kelly, Cheyenne, Wyoming, Lodge, No. 660

The name of B. C. Casanas, New Orleans Lodge No. 30, was substituted for that of Wm. J. O'Brien, Jr.

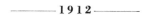

1912

In making its report in 1912 this Commission reported that its members had directed its activities mainly toward securing protection for elk from the Federal Government directly, and also indirectly through its assistance in the several states where the elk abound.

The Commission recommended that the Grand Lodge continue this work in order that the succeeding committee might be able to urge further legislation from the Federal Government for the preservation of the elk, and additional protection in several states where there are elk.

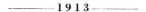

1913

In 1913, the Committee, composed of Edward J. Kelly, Cheyenne, Wyoming, Lodge, No. 660, Chairman; Ralph Hagan, Los Angeles, California, Lodge, No. 99; Thomas M. Hunter, Denver, Colorado, Lodge, No. 17, and John M. Kohler, Kenosha, Wisconsin, Lodge, No. 750, having made another exhaustive study of the condition of the elk, closed its report as follows:

"From figures compiled by the Committee on Preservation of the Elk, we find that the total number of elk in the United States has increased from 52,918 to 70,913."

The Committee stated that it believed this was at least in part due to the work of the Order.

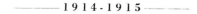

1914-1915

The matter of the preservation of the elk did not come up in any form for consideration at the Grand Lodge Session of either 1914 or 1915.

At the Grand Lodge Session in 1916, the Committee on Judiciary offered the following resolution:

"*Whereas,* this Order and its membership is deeply concerned at the prospective danger of the extinction of the American elk, and

"*Whereas,* the Grand Lodge and all thoughtful members of the Order deprecate the slaughter of this beautiful animal by unscrupulous hunters, and the tacit encouragement thereof in the wearing of elk's teeth or tusks by some members of the Order,

"Be it resolved by the Grand Lodge of the Benevolent and Protective Order of Elks, that the Chamberlain-Hayden Game Refuge Bill now pending in the Congress of the United States of America be, and the same is, endorsed and approved by the Grand Lodge, and that the incoming Grand Exalted Ruler appoint a committee of three members to urge its passage, and the subordinate lodges and members of the Order be, and are hereby, requested to urge upon their Senators and Representatives in Congress the immediate passage of this measure to the end that the existing herds of elk may be properly protected and permitted to multiply unmolested in federal game refuges.

"And, be it further resolved that members of the Order so far as possible discourage the wearing of elk's teeth or tusks, and thereby eliminate one of the possible incentives for the indiscriminate killing of this beautiful animal from which our Order derives its name."

This resolution was adopted, and as a result, the following committee on the preservation of the elk was appointed:

Past Grand Exalted Ruler John K. Tener, Charleroi, Pennsylvania, Lodge, No. 494, Chairman; Past Grand Exalted Ruler Joseph T. Fanning, Indianapolis, Indiana, Lodge, No. 13, and Past Grand Exalted Ruler Jerome B. Fisher, Jamestown, New York, Lodge, No. 263.

————1917————

At the Grand Lodge Session in 1917, Past Grand Exalted Ruler John K. Tener, Chairman of the special committee to urge the passage of the game refuge bill, reported that the Committee endeavored, by personal appeal to the members of both branches of Congress, to secure favorable and final action on the bill in question.

While the House Committee to which this bill was referred reported favorably on it, because of the necessity of immediate consideration of legislation in preparation for war it was impossible to advance the bill further.

The Committee stated that the bill had been again introduced in the current session of Congress, and would come up in due time.

At the Grand Lodge Session in 1919, Mr. J. W. Nelson of the United States Forest Service read a paper on "The Preservation of Our American Elk."

This dealt largely with the studies that had been made by the Federal Government of the needs of the elk which had resulted in the issuance of a circular entitled "Our National Elk Herds," which gave the early history of the elk and presented a "Program" for their future management.

This "Program" embraced many objectives, the most important of which were the following:

The extension of two of the national forests to provide increased winter range for the elk.

The acquirement by purchase, if necessary, of needed private lands within the winter elk range estimated to cost approximately $900,000.

Statements by Mr. Nelson of particular interest to the members of the Order were the following:

"The Benevolent and Protective Order of Elks has been of great assistance in investigating conditions on elk ranges, in memorializing Congress to provide for the purchase of feeding stations and in refuting the idea that the elk tooth was an emblem of the Order.

"I want to call your attention at this time to the similarity in the conclusions reached in this Program to the findings of your Commissions after personal investigation of the elk ranges as shown by their reports for 1908, 1912 and 1913."

Since that time the question of the preservation of the elk animal has not been a matter of Grand Lodge action or consideration.

A memorandum of the Fish and Wildlife Service of the Department of the Interior in 1952 carried the following information relative to the Jackson Hole region:

An executive order, dated April 21, 1915, reserved for use as a refuge 1,240 acres acquired by purchase and 840 acres of government land.

A second order, on July 8, 1916, added 520 acres of land acquired by purchase and 160 acres of public land. The refuge thus comprised 2,760 acres.

Later, the Izaak Walton League of America, through popular subscription, raised sufficient funds to purchase 1,760 acres as an addition to the refuge, the gift being accepted by Congress in 1927

In 1936 there were added 3,165 acres of public land to the refuge; in 1937 there were added 658 acres. Under an Act of Congress in 1935, 10,800 acres of land were purchased and made part of the refuge and another 3,082 acres are under lease.

A. P. Nelson photo, courtesy of Fish and Wildlife Service.

Elk on feed ground on lower lands of the Izaak Walton League addition to the Jackson Hole elk refuge in Wyoming.

That these steps have been effective is evidenced by an Associated Press news item of November, 1951, which bore the heading:

"Yellowstone Traps Elk
to Reduce Herd
Park Officials Ship Them
Out for Hunters to Shoot"

Further evidence that steps for protecting elk life have been very successful is found in the fact that, in 1913, Edward J. Kelly of Cheyenne Lodge No. 660, Chairman of the Grand Lodge Committee on the Preservation of the Elk estimated the total elk population of California, Oregon, Washington, Utah, Colorado, Montana, Idaho and Wyoming as 73,425, while U. S. Government reports for 1939 reported a total elk population of 205,900 in those States.

Elks National Home

The First Move

At the Grand Lodge Session which was held in New Orleans in 1898, a resolution was adopted setting forth the desirability of establishing a national home for aged and needy members of the Order

A Committee composed of A. C. Smith of Boston, Mass., Lodge, No. 10; Past Grand Exalted Rulers Edwin B. Hay, Washington, D. C., Lodge, No. 15, and William G. Meyers, Philadelphia, Pa., Lodge, No. 2, was appointed by Grand Exalted Ruler Meade D. Detweiler to consider the feasibility of such a project.

At the Annual Grand Lodge Session, held at St. Louis in 1899, the Committee reported favorably on the project.

From among the members present at the Grand Lodge Session, there were obtained subscriptions of $20,000 toward this work.

The Committee was reappointed and authorized to work in conjunction with Grand Exalted Ruler B. M. Allen, of Birmingham, Alabama, Lodge, No. 79, and the Board of Grand Trustees, consisting of Joseph T. Fanning, Indianapolis, Indiana, Lodge, No. 13; Henry W. Mears, Baltimore, Maryland, Lodge, No. 7, and John D. O'Shea, Lynn, Massachusetts, Lodge No. 117, in negotiating for, and securing, a site suitable for a home.

The Committee reported to the Grand Lodge in Atlantic City in 1900 that its members had examined numerous sites offered, but that time was too short to visit all of those suggested, and no decision had been reached.

A new special committee, composed of Past Grand Exalted Ruler Detweiler; George P. Cronk, Omaha, Nebraska, Lodge, No. 39, and W. Mell Drennan, Birmingham, Alabama, Lodge, No. 79, was appointed to prosecute the work, acting as a joint committee with Past Grand Exalted Ruler Jerome B. Fisher and the Board of Grand Trustees, consisting of Fanning, Mears and O'Shea.

Past Grand Exalted Ruler Meade D. Detweiler was chosen as Chairman of the Joint Committee.

A report was made at the Grand Lodge Session in Milwaukee in 1901, but a selection was not made.

The Home Committee was continued, as was the Joint Committee, with the addition of Grand Exalted Ruler Charles E. Pickett and the continuation of retiring Grand Exalted Ruler Jerome B. Fisher.

Shortly afterwards the availability of the Hotel Bedford property in the town of Bedford City, Virginia, was brought to the attention of the Committee.

Property Purchased

The property was finally bought, and the purchase reported to the Grand Lodge Session at Salt Lake City in 1902.

The Committee was amended by the substitution of Past Grand Exalted Ruler Pickett for George P. Cronk, who, by his election as Grand Exalted Ruler, became, ex officio, a member of the Joint Committee.

THE FIRST ELKS NATIONAL HOME

This was previously the Hotel Bedford, purchased by the Grand Lodge Committee serving in the Grand Lodge year of 1901-1902.

The total purchase cost of this property acquired from the Receiver in Bankruptcy was $12,500, but it provided a commodious home of ample size, fairly well-equipped throughout. It had previously been a failure as a hotel project.

Dedication of Home

This Home was dedicated May 21, 1903.

At the dedicatory ceremony, addresses were delivered by Grand Exalted Ruler George P. Cronk, Past Grand Exalted Ruler Meade D. Detweiler, Grand Trustee Joseph T. Fanning, U. S. Senator John W. Daniel, a member of Lynchburg, Va., Lodge, No. 321, Governor Montague of Virginia, Mayor Campbell of Bedford City and Frederick Warde, St. Louis, Mo., Lodge, No. 9.

Thirty thousand dollars was spent on the furnishings and equipment of the Home.

The management of the Home was placed in the hands of three Governors appointed by the Grand Exalted Ruler.

The first board was composed of Past Grand Exalted Ruler Meade D. Detweiler, Thomas F. McNulty, Baltimore, Maryland, Lodge, No. 7, and Louis Lazarus, Lynchburg, Virginia, Lodge, No. 321.

Upon Detweiler's death in 1904, Champe S. Andrews, Past Exalted Ruler of New York Lodge No. 1, was appointed to fill his unexpired term, and at the expiration of Lazarus' term, Eugene L. Lewis, Cincinnati Lodge No. 5, became a member of the board.

Thomas F. McNulty, whose term expired in 1905, was reappointed.

Grand Trustees Given Jurisdiction

At the Grand Lodge Session held in Denver, Colorado, in 1906, the Committee on Constitutional Revision recommended that the Board of Governors of the Elks National Home be abolished; the number of Grand Trustees be increased from three to five, and the Board of Grand Trustees given jurisdiction over the Home.

This recommendation was adopted by the Grand Lodge, and the supervision of the Home passed to a Board of Grand Trustees consisting of John D. O'Shea, Chairman, Lynn, Massachusetts Lodge, No. 117; Benjamin F. McNulty, San Antonio, Texas Lodge, No. 216, and W. H. Haviland, Butte, Montana, Lodge, No. 240.

At the same Session of the Grand Lodge a new Constitution was adopted which provided that the number of Grand Trustees be increased from three to five.

At the Grand Lodge Session in Philadelphia in 1907, the following Brothers were elected to the Board of Grand Trustees: Alfred T. Holley, Hackensack, New Jersey, Lodge, No. 658; Charles C. Schmidt, Wheeling, West Virginia, Lodge, No. 28; Thomas F. McNulty, Baltimore, Maryland, Lodge, No. 7, and Thomas B. Mills, Superior, Wisconsin, Lodge, No. 403. W. H. Haviland, Butte, Montana, Lodge, No. 240, was continued as a member of the Board of Grand Trustees and became Chairman.

The same membership on the Board continued for the Grand Lodge year of 1908-1909.

The Home Is Criticized

Grand Exalted Ruler Rush L. Holland, in his report to the Grand Lodge at its Session held in Los Angeles in 1909, severely criticized the Elks National Home as it existed at that time.

He commended the purpose of the institution and its management, and his criticism was directed to the location, and to the character and condition, of the building.

Toward the close of his report he said:

"It is generally not difficult to find fault, but a very different proposition to suggest the remedy. In this instance, however, the remedy is as easy to suggest as the fault is to discover. To say that the National Home as now maintained is an institution of which the Order justly may be proud is to confess ourselves blind to actual conditions. To sit idly down and say that these conditions cannot be remedied is to confess that our boast is vain that the Order is composed of men of a high order of intelligence and business sagacity and forethought. Obviously, the only thing to do is to abandon the present institution and erect or acquire another properly located. This statement may reverse the logical and best order of procedure, although it is open to some question. In the opinion of your Grand Exalted Ruler this matter is of supreme importance and this Session of the Grand Lodge should not be closed until a plan of procedure has been agreed upon and put into active operation."

The Grand Exalted Ruler recommended that the matter be referred to a special committee to report to the Grand Lodge before the close of the Session, together with such recommendations as might be considered advisable.

When that subject was brought before the Grand Lodge, that body adopted a recommendation which read as follows:

"That this whole matter be referred to a committee of five to be appointed by the incoming Grand Exalted Ruler to report in detail at the next meeting of the Grand Lodge."

A New Committee Appointed

Grand Exalted Ruler J. U. Sammis appointed the Committee on Elks National Home—a group that became known as the Kingsley Committee—composed of the following members: Calvin L. Kingsley, Waterloo, Iowa, Lodge, No. 290, Chairman; Charles A. Betzler, Chicago, Illinois, Lodge, No. 4; Emil Ferrant, Minneapolis, Minnesota, Lodge, No. 44; Wiley L. Morgan, Knoxville, Tennessee, Lodge, No. 160, and D. M. Hailey, McAlester, Oklahoma, Lodge, No. 533.

At the Grand Lodge Convention, held in Detroit in 1910, the Committee reported and recommended:

1. That Bedford City, Virginia, be abandoned as the location of the Elks National Home and a new and thoroughly modern institution be established elsewhere.

2. Or, that the Home be retained at Bedford City, Virginia, the present building to be razed and new and modern structures erected upon its site.

3. Or, that the present Home at Bedford City, Virginia, be remodeled extensively.

The following resolution was offered by Fred Harper of Lynchburg, Virginia, Lodge, No. 321:

"*Resolved:* That the Board of Grand Trustees be, and are hereby, directed to prepare and submit to the next session of the Grand Lodge a specific and definite plan for the repair, alteration and improvement of the National Home building at Bedford City, Virginia, and for the beautification of the grounds and approaches thereto, together with an estimate in detail of the cost thereof."

This resolution was amended to read as follows:

"That the Grand Trustees be authorized to make such expenditures as may be necessary during the coming year to keep the buildings in order and put the house in order at Bedford City."

It was further amended as follows:

"Pending the report on the resolution that the matter be referred to the next Grand Lodge meeting in Atlantic City next year, this Grand Lodge limit the amount to be spent on repairs for the Elks National Home at Bedford City to the sum of $7,500."

It was further resolved:

"That the Board of Grand Trustees be instructed to prepare their report and send it to the subordinate lodges at least sixty days before the next Grand Lodge meeting to the end that every member attending may have digested the report and be ready to proceed with the business understandingly."

A New Home Recommended

At the Session of the Grand Lodge held in Atlantic City in 1911, the Board of Grand Trustees made an extremely comprehensive report on the whole situation.

They paid tribute to the thoroughness of the work done by the so-called Kingsley Committee.

This Board of Grand Trustees consisted of: Thomas F. Mc-Nulty, Baltimore, Maryland, Lodge, No. 7, Chairman; Thomas B. Mills, Superior, Wisconsin, Lodge, No. 403; Alfred T. Holley, Hackensack, New Jersey, Lodge, No. 658; Perry A. Clay, Denver, Colorado, Lodge, No. 17, and Charles C. Schmidt, Wheeling, West Virginia, Lodge, No. 28.

The Board made the following recommendation:

"That no plan looking toward any repair or exclusive remodeling, or in fact any kind of remodeling of the present Home, be considered by the Grand Lodge."

and stated:

"We favor the building of an entirely new Home—one in keeping with the standing and dignity of the Order.

"There should not be, in our judgment, any further delay from any cause whatsoever.

"The building of a new Elks National Home should be commenced at once; and any question as to change of location or plans, or any further suggestion that might cause delay, should be referred, with full power to act, to those whom the Grand Lodge may clothe with authority to proceed with the work, including the right to acquire additional property, if necessary, at the present location of the Home or elsewhere."

A New Home Authorized

The following resolution was adopted by the Grand Lodge:

"*Resolved:* That the report of the Board of Grand Trustees relating to the Elks National Home, as approved by Grand Exalted Ruler Herrmann, be and at the same time is hereby approved, ratified and concurred in, and

"*Resolved:* That as recommended by said report, an entirely new Home (in keeping with the standing and dignity of the Order), be forthwith proceeded with at Bedford City, Virginia.

"*Resolved:* That the plans and drawings submitted with the said report be and the same are hereby accepted and approved, and

"*Resolved:* That a Commission for the purpose of constructing such new Home be and the same is hereby created, consisting of Grand Exalted Ruler Herrmann, Grand Exalted Ruler-elect Sullivan, the Board of Grand Trustees, and three members to be appointed by the incoming Grand Exalted Ruler; that said Commission shall select its own Chairman and Secretary and shall have full power and authority to proceed at once to carry into execution said plans, and

"*Resolved:* That to provide the funds necessary to carry out the purposes of said Commission hereby created, there be levied a per capita tax of twenty-five cents upon each subordinate lodge for each member upon its rolls on the first day of September, 1911, payable by each subordinate lodge through the office of the Grand Secretary not later than October 10, 1911, and

"*Resolved:* That the said Commission is also hereby authorized to make provision for the care and maintenance of the residents of the Home during the process of construction as the same may be found necessary."

The New Elks National Home Commission

Grand Exalted Ruler Sullivan appointed Patrick T. Powers, Jersey City, New Jersey, Lodge, No. 211; Calvin L. Kingsley, Waterloo, Iowa, Lodge, No. 290, and Samuel V. Perrott, Indianapolis, Indiana, Lodge, No. 13, as the additional members. Past Grand Exalted Ruler August Herrmann was chosen as Chairman.

Thus, the New Elks National Home Commission consisted of the following:

August Herrmann, Cincinnati, Ohio, Lodge, No. 5, Chairman

Thomas B. Mills, Superior, Wisconsin, Lodge, No. 403

Alfred T. Holley, Hackensack, New Jersey, Lodge, No. 658

ELKS NATIONAL HOME, BEDFORD, VIRGINIA

Perry A. Clay, Denver, Colorado, Lodge, No. 17
Charles C. Schmidt, Wheeling, West Virginia, Lodge, No. 28
Cary L. Applegate, Salt Lake City, Utah, Lodge, No. 85
Patrick T. Powers, Jersey City, New Jersey, Lodge, No. 211
Calvin L. Kingsley, Waterloo, Iowa, Lodge, No. 290
Samuel V. Perrott, Indianapolis, Indiana, Lodge, No. 13
John P. Sullivan, New Orleans, Louisiana, Lodge, No. 30

At the Grand Lodge Session held in Portland, Oregon, in 1912, an additional assessment of twenty-five cents per capita was made for the purpose of raising the fund for building the Elks National Home.

At that Session Thomas B. Mills was elected Grand Exalted Ruler and was succeeded on the Board of Grand Trustees and the New Elks National Home Commission by John J. Faulknei of East St. Louis, Illinois, Lodge, No. 664.

Also during that year, Charles C. Schmidt died and was succeeded on the Board of Grand Trustees and the New Elks National Home Commission by James R. Nicholson, Springfield, Massachusetts, Lodge, No. 61.

At the Grand Lodge Convention in Rochester, New York, in 1913, the New Elks National Home Commission submitted its report and the following recommendations were adopted by the Grand Lodge:

"That the plans and specifications as revised by the architect, Otten heimer, Stern & Reichert, of Chicago, and approved by the Commission, be approved by the Grand Lodge.

"That the bid of Mr. P. J. Moran of Salt Lake City, referred to in its report, should be accepted, and that the Commission be authorized to enter into a contract with said contractor for the work, and that the same be commenced at once.

"That another per capita tax of twenty-five cents upon each subordinate lodge for each member upon its rolls on the first day of September, 1913, payable by each subordinate lodge to the office of the Grand Secretary not later than October 10, 1913, be levied for the purpose of providing additional funds necessary to carry out the proposed improvements."

Past Grand Exalted Ruler Thomas B. Mills was added to the new Elks National Home Commission, and Samuel V. Perrott, Indianapolis, Indiana, Lodge, No. 13, succeeded Alfred T. Holley, Hackensack, New Jersey, Lodge, No. 658, on the Board of Grand Trustees, Fred Harper, Lynchburg, Virginia, Lodge, No. 321, was also made a member of the Commission.

1914

At the Grand Lodge Session in Denver in 1914 the Commission reported that it had entered into a contract with P. J. Moran of Salt Lake City for the erection of the New Elks National Home, at Bedford City, Virginia, as directed by the Grand Lodge Session in Rochester, New York, in 1913.

That year Past Grand Exalted Ruler Leach became a member of the Commission.

In 1915, Past Grand Exalted Ruler Raymond Benjamin was added to the Commission and J. Edgar Masters, Charleroi, Pa., Lodge, No. 494, succeeding James R. Nicholson, elected Grand Exalted Ruler that year, as Grand Trustee, became a member of the Commission.

At the Grand Lodge Session in Los Angeles in 1915 the Commission reported its progress in construction and was authorized to provide a suitable cornerstone, with appropriate ceremonies incident thereto, and also to provide dedicatory services upon the completion of the Home.

The cornerstone was laid on September 25, 1915.

Dedication

The Home was dedicated July 8, 1916.

The dedicatory services were conducted by the Grand Lodge Officers, Grand Exalted Ruler James R. Nicholson presiding. Addresses were delivered by Governor Henry C. Stuart of Virginia, Past Grand Exalted Rulers Jerome B. Fisher and Fred Harper.

The Commission reported costs as follows:

The excavation and grading and erection of the buildings proper about $340,000.00

The furniture, carpets, draperies and lighting fixtures represented an outlay of about 35,000.00

The laundry equipment, refrigerating plant, cleaning system and fire protection equipment cost 8,000.00

Landscaping, sewerage, building and out-buildings.... 35,000.00

Architects' fees, superintendence and other incidentals brought the costs to a total of $450,000.00

The Elks National Home, very properly, is regarded with pride by the members of the Order who know of the splendid fraternal service which is being performed there, in which service all Elks share.

The Home is a beautiful structure most effectively combining classic and mission features of architecture.

In its most appropriate setting, the first view compels an admiration which grows as the details of its arrangement and its furnishings, and the completeness of its equipment to fulfill its purposes, are more carefully noted.

Home Expansion

From time to time substantial additions have been made, increasing its capacity sufficiently to care for more than four hundred members.

The initial cost of the Home was provided by assessments upon every member of the Order. The cost of some of the additions has been provided in part from the net earnings of *The Elks Magazine*.

The Main Building

In the main building are located the administrative offices, the quarters of the superintendent's family, dining room, kitchen, laundry, bakery, barbershop, a well-stocked library and a recreation room with tables for pool, billiards, checkers, cards and chess.

View of a resident's room.

View of portion of farm area.

In the attractive dining room well-selected meals are served under the direction of competent dieticians.

The Cottages

Adjoining the main building are eight cottages capable of accom modating more than four hundred residents.

Each resident has his own outside room with hot and cold run ning water. Each room is comfortably and attractively furnished

The average number of residents during the year ending May 31, 1967, was 237. Since the Home was dedicated 3,342 members of the Order have taken advantage of the facilities and comforts it provides.

The Hospital

In one of the wings there is a thoroughly equipped, forty-room modern hospital which has passed out of the infirmary class ana has been welcomed into membership in the Virginia Hospital Association.

Management Policy

The Order has maintained a distinctive policy in the administration of this haven for its aged and indigent members. It has never been regarded as an ordinary charitable institution, to be peopled by inmates who might there receive merely shelter and food; whose conduct and movements would be rigidly prescribed, hampered by irksome institutional rules and regulations.

A Real Home

On the contrary, it has been conducted consistently as a real home, in which each resident Brother has the fullest possible freedom of action, with every consideration for his right of personal privacy and where every effort is made to insure his comfort, well-being and happiness as a worthy and esteemed Brother Elk.

The Grand Lodge is responsible for the cost of providing, erecting, maintaining and equipping the necessary buildings of the Home and for the upkeep of the grounds and insurance on the buildings.

Grand Lodge Statutes also provide that Grand Lodge pay one-half of maintenance cost of residents at the home with the subordinate lodge of which the guest is a member paying the other half, provided the Brother has no other means of support. Guests receiving pensions of any kind are permitted to retain a reasonable amount for spending-money, with the balance applied against maintenance costs thus reducing the monthly amount paid by both the Grand Lodge and subordinate lodges.

The cost for the year 1966–'67 was $1,293.65 per resident.

Area

The total area of the Home is 167 acres. Of this, 100 acres is farm land.

There are the farm buildings, necessary for the maintenance of a farm, and they accommodate a herd of 40 cows.

Outdoor Diversions

A nine-hole golf course is provided for those residents interested in that sport, and the necessary space is set aside for those who are interested in doing a little gardening.

Fred Harper Memorial Auditorium

In the rear of the main building is the Fred Harper Memorial Auditorium, a gift of Past Grand Exalted Ruler Robert S. Barrett. This has sound and projection equipment, air-conditioning and is equipped with comfortable chairs.

Twice a week motion pictures are shown, each showing embracing a full-length feature, a short and the latest news.

"Home Again"

The Board of Grand Trustees produced a 28 minute film in sound and color, entitled "Home Again," which tells the story of the Home. The film had its premier showing at the Grand Lodge Convention of 1958 in New York City. Lodges may obtain the loan of prints from the Grand Secretary.

The Home Lodge

The residents of the Home have an Elks Home Lodge. It hasn't a charter like other lodges and it hasn't any initiation fees or dues. However, it exists as a lodge: regular meetings are held, officers are elected and, like the chartered Elks lodges, it observes those special days designated for observance by the Grand Lodge, such as Flag Day and Memorial Sunday.

On the second floor of the main building there is a well-equipped lodge room where its meetings are held.

The Home—Its Operation

In 1967 the Grand Trustees said in their report:

"The Home is a credit to the Fraternal Order of Elks; it is well maintained and well managed.

"This glowing statement was offered recently following an inspection by John P. Pate, consultant, Homes for Aged—Bureau of Hospitalization and Homes for Aged, Commonwealth of Virginia.

"We must concur wholeheartedly with Mr. Pate's report, even though we are not surprised at his findings. We all know that the Elks National Home at Bedford, Virginia, is an ideal home for our senior Elks. It was planned that way, and Superintendent Irvin is carrying on the tradition of providing for the 'home sweet home' atmosphere."

A TRIBUTE
by
Fred Harper, Past Grand Exalted Ruler

Not far from the Blue Ridge Mountains—almost in the shadow of the mighty Peaks of Otter—there stands a magnificent structure, dedicated to a most glorious service. It is the Elks National Home, provided by the Order of Elks for those members who may have been overtaken by adversity, and whose whitening heads have become bowed by the hostile winds of adversity.

It is not an asylum filled with inmates as a matter of charity or of public policy. It is not an institution for members who may have become destitute to receive mere shelter and alms, but it is a Home, a house prepared by the stalwart and vigorous members of a great Family for the occupancy of their less fortunate Brothers.

How sweet it is to know that whenever or wherever a Brother may be broken in health, his fortune shattered, and he is no longer able to withstand the rough seas of Life, he may know that, as in his Father's home there are many mansions, so in Brothers' Home there is room for all and a room he may call his own.

Though he may come from the rocky coast of Maine or from the blue waters of the far-off Pacific, he is no stranger. Like a son who becomes heir to his father, so he claims what is his. Outstretched hands welcome him and loving hearts administer to his every want and need.

From the broad verandas the green fields of Virginia stretch out before him, smiling in the sunshine. The towering mountains, whose majestic peaks pierce the clouds, stand on eternal guard. Beneath the blue skies—across whose depths float fleecy clouds like ships of pearl on a turquoise sea; there he may take his ease—in peace with the world and with his God—and at nightfall when he has become weary of the lengthening of the day, he may seek his couch for a night of rest, and well may he bend his head in reverence and ask God's richest blessing on such a Home—a Home prepared by faithful Brothers for Brothers who are faithful—a Beautiful Temple of Fidelity.

Flag Day

Grand Exalted Ruler Henry A. Melvin, in his report to the Grand Lodge in 1907, recommended the celebration of Flag Day by the Benevolent and Protective Order of Elks.

The Grand Lodge, at Philadelphia, in 1907, adopted this suggestion of the Grand Exalted Ruler and by resolution designated June 14 as Flag Day. The Committee on Work and Ritual was instructed to prepare a Flag Day Ritual at the next Session of the Grand Lodge.

That Committee consisted of James L. King, of Topeka Lodge No. 204; Charles B. Lahan, Chicago Lodge No. 4, and William M. Hargest of Harrisburg Lodge No. 12. They presented and exemplified to the Grand Lodge Session in Dallas, Texas, in 1908, a Flag Day Ritual.

The Grand Lodge at that time unanimously adopted the Ritual prepared by the Committee.

The Grand Lodge in Session in Atlantic City in 1911 passed a resolution making obligatory on all subordinate lodges the observance of Flag Day and the use of the Ritual adopted at Dallas in 1908.

The Benevolent and Protective Order of Elks was the first fraternal organization to require by positive mandate that subordinate lodges should observe Flag Day with appropriate ceremonies.

It is to be expected that an organization dedicated to patriotic service should seek to promote a proper knowledge of, and respect for, the American Flag, and all that it represents. The Order of Elks has done this in many ways. Perhaps the most effective of its prescribed activities is the Flag Day Service.

The Ritual for the occasion is an elaborate one and it is quite generally conducted as a public ceremonial. It is designed to be informative as well as inspirational; and the colorful pageantry provided lends itself admirably to the achievement of these objectives.

Grand Secretary Masters calls our attention to a letter dated June 14, 1917, and signed by Robert C. Jones as Secretary of San Diego, California, Lodge No. 168, addressed to the *Elks-Antler* and appearing in the July, 1917, issue of that publication.

The letter includes a statement that at a meeting of San Diego

Lodge held on June 9, 1904, C. Fred Henking moved that a Flag Program be carried out at the next meeting and as a result, on June 16, 1904, there was a program very much like the present Flag Day program of the Order.

It is further stated in the letter that C. Fred Henking took up the matter of Flag observance with a number of Grand Lodge members, "with the result that Brother Henry A. Melvin, Grand Exalted Ruler 1906-07, in his annual report to the Grand Lodge, advocated the observance of Flag Day."

At the Grand Lodge Session of 1916 Chairman John C. Futrall of the Ritual Commission offered the following resolution:

"*Whereas,* Grand Exalted Ruler Henry A. Melvin in his report to the Grand Lodge in 1907 recommended the celebration of Flag Day by the Benevolent and Protective Order of Elks, as recorded on page 46 of the Grand Lodge Proceedings for 1907, and

"*Whereas,* the Grand Lodge at Philadelphia in 1907 adopted the suggestion of the Grand Exalted Ruler and instructed the Committee on Work and Ritual to present a Flag Day Ritual at the next Session of the Grand Lodge, and

"*Whereas,* this Committee, consisting of James L. King, of Topeka Lodge No. 204; Charles Beecher Lahan, Chicago Lodge No. 4, and William M. Hargest of Harrisburg Lodge No. 12, did present and exemplify to the Grand Lodge in session at Dallas, Texas, in 1908 a Flag Day Ritual, and

"*Whereas,* the Grand Lodge at that time unanimously adopted the Ritual prepared by the Committee, as recorded on page 183 of the Grand Lodge Proceedings of 1908, which Ritual was, in 1908, copyrighted by the Chairman of the Committee, and the copyright assigned to the Grand Lodge, and

"*Whereas,* the Grand Lodge in session at Atlantic City in 1911, passed a resolution making obligatory on all subordinate lodges the observance of Flag Day and the use of the Flag Day Service adopted at Dallas in 1908, as recorded in the Grand Lodge Proceedings for 1911, on pages 254 and 255, and

"*Whereas,* there have been recently circulated printed letters and statements to the effect that the celebration of Flag Day was 'instituted' and 'inaugurated' by another member of the Order who was in no wise connected with the institution or inauguration of this custom, and

"*Whereas,* such statements, if allowed to go unchallenged, might in course of time obscure the fact that the observance of Flag Day was recommended to the Grand Lodge by Grand Exalted Ruler Melvin and that the Flag Day Service was written and prepared by the Committee consisting of Brothers King, Lahan and Hargest, now therefore be it

"*Resolved:* That the facts as above stated be inserted in the minutes of the Grand Lodge, and be it further

"*Resolved:* That all Elk publications which have published letters or statements calculated to give rise to a false impression concerning the authorship of the Flag Day Service be requested to publish a copy of these resolutions.

WILLIAM T. PHILLIPS
JOHN C. FUTRALL
Members Ritual Commission"

In 1965, Section 229 prescribing the Flag Day Services, was amended to read as follows:

"It shall be the duty of each Subordinate Lodge to hold the service known as 'Flag Day Services' at the time and in the manner prescribed by the Ritual of the Order. The Grand Exalted Ruler or the District Deputy Grand Exalted Ruler may, in exceptional cases and for good cause, grant a dispensation for a different day or to any two or more Lodges to hold such services jointly, provided further, that the Grand Exalted Ruler or his area District Deputy may grant permission to a Lodge or Lodges to sponsor or conduct public programs or exercises substantially consisting of that portion of the Flag Day Ritual relating to the parade of the flags and the narrated History of the Flag, with appropriate music or other setting in keeping with the occasion. It is specifically understood, however, that such programs or exercises shall not eliminate or limit the required observance of the Annual 'Flag Day Services' prescribed in this Section and by the Ritual of the Order."

RUSH L. HOLLAND
1908-09

AUGUST HERRMANN
1910-11

J. U. SAMMIS
1909-10

JOHN P. SULLIVAN
1911-12

Grand Exalted Rulers

F I F T H   D E C A D E

1908-1918

THOMAS B. MILLS
1912-13

EDWARD LEACH
1913-14

JAMES R. NICHOLSON
1915-16

RAYMOND BENJAMIN
1914-15

EDWARD RIGHTOR
1916-17

FRED HARPER
1917-18

216

S E C T I O N

Fifth Decade

In 1908, a Committee on Protection of Name and Emblem recommended the adoption of an official emblem, the recommendation being accompanied by a suggested design, which the Grand Lodge adopted.

In 1912, the provision that an applicant for membership must believe in the existence of a Supreme Being was adopted.

Each year showed a growth of membership and although the increase was somewhat lessened there still was an increase of 80 per cent.

While the subordinate lodges had been active in assisting the youth of America, the Grand Lodge did not adopt a national program of such activity until 1913.

At that time there was created a Grand Lodge Committee known as the Committee on the Big Brother Movement.

This Committee served effectively (the definite number of lodges cooperating reaching nearly 1,200) until 1919 when its work was taken over by a new committee of broader powers and responsibility—the Social and Community Welfare Committee.

For many years there was agitation in the Grand Lodge for legalizing State Associations. It was not until 1914, however, that the Grand Lodge created a committee to study the advisability of a plan for the organization and official recognition of State Associations, and not until 1915 that they were given such recognition.

This Decade was nearly at its end when our country was drawn into the vortex of the first World War.

That was in April, 1917.

In July of that year nearly 2,000 members of the Grand Lodge in Boston arose as one man and unanimously adopted a resolution appropriating $1,000,000.00 for war relief and created the Elks War Relief Commission.

The record of this first great patriotic service of the Order, covering the field hospitals sent overseas, the Reconstruction Hospital erected in Boston and turned over to the United States Army, the financial support of the Salvation Army and the educational loans to returning servicemen, is a record of which every member of the Order may justly be proud.

It was in this Decade that the practice of observing Mother's Day was adopted.

Fifth Decade——1908-1918

GRAND EXALTED RULERS

During this Decade the Grand Exalted Rulers were:

RUSH L. HOLLAND, Colorado Springs, Colorado, Lodge, No. 309	1908-1909
J. U. SAMMIS, Le Mars, Iowa, Lodge, No. 428	1909-1910
AUGUST HERRMANN, Cincinnati, Ohio, Lodge, No. 5	1910-1911
JOHN P. SULLIVAN, New Orleans, Louisiana, Lodge, No. 30	1911-1912
THOMAS B. MILLS, Superior, Wisconsin, Lodge, No. 403	1912-1913
EDWARD LEACH, New York, New York, Lodge, No. 1	1913-1914
RAYMOND BENJAMIN, Napa, California, Lodge, No. 832	1914-1915
JAMES R. NICHOLSON, Springfield, Massachusetts, Lodge, No. 61	1915-1916
EDWARD RIGHTOR, New Orleans, Louisiana, Lodge, No. 30	1916-1917
FRED HARPER, Lynchburg, Virginia, Lodge, No. 321	1917-1918

Fred C. Robinson, who was elected Grand Secretary in 1904, continued in that office throughout the Decade and until 1927.

MEMBERSHIP AND CHARITABLE EXPENDITURES

The membership of the Order in this Decade increased from 284,321 to 493,733. The number of lodges increased from 1,119 lodges to 1,280.

YEAR	MEMBERSHIP	CHARITABLE EXPENDITURES
1908-1909	304,899	$351,670.09
1909-1910	331,228	365,404.90
1910-1911	359,677	401,091.25
1911-1912	384,026	458,301.86
1912-1913	408,281	467,698.53
1913-1914	428,479	592,404.35
1914-1915	442,658	625,633.14
1915-1916	453,516	656,245.97
1916-1917	474,690	714,611.81
1917-1918	493,733	925,532.41

The Grand Lodge Sessions for this period were held in the following cities:

1909	Los Angeles, California	1914	Denver, Colorado
1910	Detroit, Michigan	1915	Los Angeles, California
1911	Atlantic City, New Jersey	1916	Baltimore, Maryland
1912	Portland, Oregon	1917	Boston, Massachusetts
1913	Rochester, New York	1918	Atlantic City, New Jersey

At the end of this Decade the assets of the 1,280 lodges amounted to $32,045,765.65.

Protection of the Name and Emblem

At the Grand Lodge Session in Philadelphia, in 1907, the following resolution was adopted:

"*Resolved:* That the incoming Grand Exalted Ruler appoint a Commission of three for the purpose of acting with the Grand Exalted Ruler to secure legislation in the various states to protect our name and emblem from abuse by imitation and to prosecute any per-

Official Emblem of the Benevolent and Protective Order of Elks

sons or organizations so imitating our name and emblem and to make such recommendations concerning an official emblem as may be deemed necessary."

Grand Exalted Ruler Tener appointed a Commission on Protection of Name and Emblem composed of James M. Challiss, Atkinson, Kan., Lodge, No. 647, Chairman; Frederick Hughes, White Plains, N. Y., Lodge, No. 535, and John P. Ross, Macon, Ga., Lodge, No. 230.

———— 1908 ————

At the Grand Lodge Session of 1908 that Commission made a report of which the following is a brief digest.

There were few states where there were proper laws for the protection of the name and emblem of a secret society.

The Commission thought that the District Deputies should be enlisted in the cause and it should be made one of their designated duties, cooperating with the Commission, to secure the help of all local lodges in the formation of favorable opinion and for interviewing, and interesting, members of the Legislatures to the end that the legislative bodies might be impressed with the fact that the protection sought was desired by a considerable portion of their constituents.

The Commission did secure some legislation in a few states.

The House of Representatives of the 59th Congress passed a special bill making it a misdemeanor for a person to wear fraudulently in the District of Columbia the badge insignia or letters of the Benevolent and Protective Order of Elks of the United States of America.

That bill failed in the Senate but was reintroduced in the next session.

A letter over the signature of the Grand Exalted Ruler was sent to the Secretaries of State of all the states in the Union protesting against the issuance of Charters to any who assumed the use of the name of the Order, or any name bearing resemblance thereto, and calling attention to the objects, aims and purposes of the Order, and the fact that it had for over forty years appropriated and used its present title, that for more than twenty-five years it had been a corporation incorporated under that name and was subsequently incorporated under the laws of the United States for the District of Columbia.

Proceedings were instituted in several states and a permanent injunction was obtained in Georgia against any society using a name in close resemblance to the name of the Order.

The Emblem

As to the emblem the Commission report, condensed, was along the following lines:

The Commission was somewhat at a loss to advise what form of legislation to suggest, by reason of the fact that the Order had no particular emblem to protect.

The elk's head and antlers had been used by the Order on its stationery, stamped on the cover of its Constitution and printed reports and proceedings, and incorporated in the seal of the Grand Lodge for upwards of forty years, thus constituting the elk's head and antlers as the recognized emblem of the Order. This combination had also been nationally worn as a badge or lapel button for a considerable length of time.

Neither this emblem, however, nor any other, had been officially adopted by the Grand Lodge and protected under the Federal laws.

At the Grand Lodge Session at Baltimore in 1903, a Committee, appointed for the selection of a design for an emblem and the protection of the same, had recommended "that the official emblem of the Order shall be the combination of the antlers, the letters B.P.O.E., and the dial showing the hour eleven o'clock," but that the matter of the arrangement and the legal protection of the same be left to the Grand Exalted Ruler and the Board of Grand Trustees and that the District Deputies should be instructed to secure legislation for such protection in states where statutes had not already been enacted.

The Challiss Committee reported that legislation had been secured in a number of states making the wearing of the emblem of the Order by other than members a misdemeanor but that these statutes could only be made absolutely effective by the adoption of an official emblem by the Grand Lodge and offered the following recommendations, which were adopted:

"1. That the work of this Commission be continued and that the legal proceedings instituted in the State of New York be protected or prosecuted as may be necessary to the Court of Appeals in said State by a Commission to be appointed for the ensuing year.

"2. That the labors of the present Commission be continued by the incoming Commission in the securing of legislation in the states where there are no statutes or adequate legislation for the protection of our name and emblem.

"3. That the District Deputy Grand Exalted Rulers, upon request of the Grand Exalted Ruler, be required to cooperate with and assist the Commission in every way practicable in the performance of its duties.

"4. That the combination of a dial showing the hour of eleven with a white face and red Roman numerals circumscribed by a blue circle containing the initials B.P.O.E. on which dial and circle shall rest an elk's head and antlers which shall be surmounted by a red star, be adopted as the official emblem of the Benevolent and Protective Order of Elks of the United States of America and that the same be patented. Such action in no manner to be deemed or held to be a waiver of any rights the B.P.O.E. of the United States of America may have acquired by user, any prior appropriation of any other emblem."

———— 1909 ————

There follows a digest of the report of the Commission at the Grand Lodge Session in 1909.

Litigation which had been pending in the State of New York to restrain the use of the Order's name and emblem by imitators was decided favorably to the Order and a perpetual injunction was issued.

Among the other duties imposed upon the Commission was the attempt to secure the enactment into law of the form of bill which the Commission had proposed and which had been adopted at the last Grand Lodge Session. In carrying out this obligation the

Commission had been in constant communication with the District Deputies of the Grand Exalted Ruler who in a special circular called upon the District Deputies to assist and cooperate with the Commission in every way possible.

There remained at the beginning of the Grand Lodge year twenty-one states in the Union which were without adequate legislation on the subject of the protection of names and emblems of benevolent and charitable organizations.

Adequate legislation and in several instances the passage of the Commission bill without the slightest change had been secured in the states of Maine, Michigan, New Hampshire, New Mexico, Oklahoma, Wyoming and Texas.

In the states of Missouri and New Jersey, such bills had been passed by the Legislature but were vetoed by the Governors. The Commission was of the opinion that while there was much that remained to be done it could be successfully carried on through the office of the Grand Exalted Ruler and the Commission recommended that after the payment of indebtedness incurred in pending litigation the unexpended balance of the fund appropriated for the use of the Commission be returned to the General Fund.

One of the designated duties of the Commission being the securing of a patent upon the design of the official emblem adopted at the Grand Lodge Session, it took steps to secure a patent upon the design as the official emblem in the name of Frederick Hughes, original designer, for the benefit of the Grand Lodge.

When application was made for such a patent it was ascertained that a manufacturing jeweler in Cincinnati had filed a claim for a design patent upon the identical emblem which had been adopted at Dallas and secured his design from newspaper reports of the emblem as adopted there.

Immediately following his application for patent upon the design adopted by the Grand Lodge, the Elk press was unwittingly placed in an unenviable position by carrying the advertisements of this manufacturer who, the Commission stated, originally claimed he was the designer and patentee of this emblem and was the sole manufacturer authorized to manufacture such emblem.

He went so far as to threaten and intimidate potential purchasers of emblems, by his claim that he was the sole patentee and that parties procuring emblems from any other source did so at their peril.

The Commission prepared and forwarded to all Elk publications whose addresses were procurable a notice warning the Brotherhood at large of the attempted imposition and stating that no one had been so far authorized to manufacture the official emblem.

The Elk press cooperated and every one of the publications gave this notice due prominence and many made editorial comments on it.

Through vigorous efforts on the part of the Commission the objectionable advertising was amended.

After considerable negotiation, the Commission, through its attorney at Washington compromised, possibly somewhat in principle, in the interests of expediency and secured the withdrawal of the application for a patent filed by the manufacturer in question by reimbursing him for the amount of expense he had been put to in attempting to secure a patent to himself upon the official emblem.

The amount paid was a trifling sum but it resulted in the applicant for a patent upon the Order's design withdrawing his application. A patent then was issued upon the design as originally adopted by Frederick Hughes, the patentee, and was by Frederick Hughes immediately without compensation assigned to the Grand Lodge.

One of the chief obstacles to the successful prosecution of parties who unlawfully wore the emblems of the Order had been the fact that until the last Session of the Grand Lodge there had been no regularly adopted official emblem.

By the action taken in adopting an emblem and securing a patent on the same this obstacle had been in a great part removed but it should be borne in mind that the adoption of this official emblem was not to the exclusion of emblems which may have heretofore been worn and generally recognized for years as being emblems of the Order.

The Commission had prepared a Statute which it submitted prescribing how and for what purpose the official emblem might be used in certain instances.

The report of the Commission was adopted and the proposed Statute referred to the Judiciary Committee.

This recommended Statute was adopted and still remains in the Statutes of the Order.

It provides as follows:

"Sec. 61. The official emblem, as distinguished from the other emblems of the Order, shall be manufactured and sold under a license to be issued by the Grand Exalted Ruler and Grand Secretary, which license may be revoked at the discretion of the Grand Exalted Ruler, or at the pleasure of the Grand Lodge.

"Subordinate Lodges may use the official emblem without special permission, upon Lodge stationery, special life membership cards, and window decorations, and murals and other monuments, and in any other manner strictly connected with Lodge purposes.

"Nothing herein contained shall be held or deemed to in any manner limit the unrestricted use of our ancient and commonly accepted emblems by Elks in good standing."

Notwithstanding the optimism of the Commission on Protection of the Name and Emblem in respect to securing the enactment of state legislation providing such protection, they were to have only scattered results in that direction in the years immediately following their report.

However, there appeared to be little difficulty in respect to the protection of the emblem.

As to the name, the principal problem related thereto was the organization of negroes under the name of The Improved Benevolent and Protective Order of Elks of the World.

It was against that organization that injunctions were secured in some states but the change in the name appeared to make it impossible to secure a complete coverage of protection throughout the country.

———— 1918 ————

Attempts along that line practically ceased after Grand Exalted Ruler Fred Harper, Lynchburg, Va., Lodge, No. 321, said in his annual report:

"In my opinion, the most dignified and effective course for our Order to pursue in the premises is to refrain from further litigation, and to pay no further attention to the negro Elks, except to show them such consideration as may properly be due an organization which claims to be engaged in benevolent and charitable work among a race which both needs and deserves such service."

Tuberculosis Sanitarium

Grand Exalted Ruler Sammis in his report to the Grand Lodge in 1910 said that during his travels his attention had frequently been called to the fact that many scores of members of the Order were victims of tuberculosis and that facilities available for their treatment were most meager even when the question of expense was not a consideration.

He spoke about an investigation he made in Denver. He found that the Sick Committee of Denver Lodge had a list of about twenty tuberculosis patients upon which it was calling, all of whom were Elks from other lodges.

He stated that they were living and boarding in private houses, wherever, in fact, they could procure a roof under which to sleep and in most instances were without the care, attention and surroundings which alone could furnish relief in such cases.

The Grand Exalted Ruler covered this subject at considerable length. He concluded by recommending that if the Committee on Elks National Home was going to be continued for any purpose it might properly be authorized to investigate the subject and if the Committee was discontinued, or it was thought that this additional duty would make its work too onerous, he recommended that a special committee be appointed whose particular duty it should be to make investigation and report some method of reaching the situation so that the expense involved in caring for the afflicted Brothers from every section should be equitably distributed among all the members of the Order.

Tuberculosis Sanitarium Committee

As a result, a resolution was adopted by the Grand Lodge providing for the appointment of a Committee of five by the Grand Exalted Ruler for the purpose of investigating this subject and that such Committee proceed forthwith with such investigation and report to the Grand Lodge at the next Session.

That resolution was taken up at a later meeting at the same Grand Lodge Session and in its stead there was adopted, according to the printed Proceedings, the following:

"Be it resolved by the Grand Lodge of the B.P.O. Elks in annual convention assembled that the Grand Exalted Ruler-elect be and is hereby authorized and instructed to appoint a Committee of five to make thorough investigation as to the advisability of the establishment of a national hospital for the care and treatment of the members of this Order who may be afflicted with the dreadful disease commonly designated as the 'White Plague' and that such Committee be instructed to make full report of their investigation and conclusion at our next regular Session to be held at Atlantic City.

"Be it further resolved that the sum of $5,000 be and is hereby appropriated to meet the expenses necessarily incurred by the said Committee in its work."

Grand Exalted Ruler Herrmann appointed the following Committee:

Joseph A. Burkart, Washington, D. C., Lodge, No. 15
Harry Lowenthal, Evansville, Ind., Lodge, No. 116
R. E. O'Malley, Kansas City, Mo., Lodge, No. 26
Charles D. Wolfe, Williamsport, Pa., Lodge, No. 173
George W. Benham, Auburn, N. Y., Lodge, No. 474

In its report to the Grand Lodge Session in 1911 the Committee stated it had received a communication from E. F. Arthur of Denver, Colo., Lodge, No. 17, directing attention to an error in the minutes of the Grand Lodge Session in Detroit and stating that the resolution which was actually adopted was his own, which did not provide for any appropriation for the purpose of investigation and that he would protest against expenditure of any moneys to meet the expenses of the Committee.

Investigation disclosed that the error complained of by Mr. Arthur had actually occurred, the resolution providing simply for the appointment of a Committee of five for the purpose of investigating this subject and reporting to the Grand Lodge at its next Session and making no provision for the expenses necessarily incidental to a comprehensive investigation.

Grand Exalted Ruler Herrmann, desirous of adhering as closely as possible to the resolution of the Grand Lodge, without violating Grand Lodge law, referred to the Chairman of the Judiciary Committee for an opinion on the entire unfortunate situation; the Chairman held that the Committee was without authority to spend any money upon its investigation but that the Chairman might under the law, and should be, reimbursed for his expense for printing, postage, telegrams and clerical assistance.

The Committee sent a communication, however, to the Secretary of each lodge of the Order, as well as to each Grand Lodge Officer and District Deputy, in the form of a questionnaire about conditions in their respective lodges in this matter, suggesting that the Grand Lodge would reimburse them for the expense involved in that.

They also sent a letter to the Secretaries of the lodges in those communities, such as Colorado, New Mexico and Arizona, where tubercular residents from other states had become residents and charges upon the local lodges, to learn more about that situation.

COMMITTEE REPORT

The Committee made an extensive report on the replies they received and offered the following recommendations:

"1. We recommend that a Committee on Tuberculosis Sanitarium be appointed for the coming Grand Lodge year and that it be directed and empowered to make such additional investigation of the subject as may be possible.

"2. That the sum of $5,000, or so much thereof as may be necessary, not otherwise appropriated from Grand Lodge funds, be appropriated for the use of such Committee.

"3. That the report of said Committee be printed and distributed among the members of the Grand Lodge attending the annual Session thereof in the year 1912 to enable intelligent discussion and action on the important subject in hand."

The Committee also asked for reimbursement to its Chairman of the sum of $118.40 expended by him in connection with the work of the Committee for printing, postage, telegrams and clerical assistance.

The report was unanimously adopted.

A New Committee

In 1911 a new Committee of five was appointed to carry on this investigation.

Among the methods suggested to the Committee for caring for tuberculosis sufferers, and to follow the practical suggestions as to the best plans under existing circumstances for carrying these out effectively, were the following:

"The best medical judgment is that the present method of handling the disease is unsatisfactory.

"The vital factors in the treatment consist of rest, pure air and food.

"The matter of climate is not held to be one of primary importance as a fair percentage of cases in all stages will recover or improve under careful treatment in any locality where pure air and food can be found."

The Committee reached the conclusion that existing conditions did not justify the undertaking by the Grand Lodge of the establishment of a central institution for the care, maintenance and treatment of tubercular Elks.

Aside from this being unwarranted, the Committee was of the opinion that it was inadvisable to recommend the establishment of a sanitarium of any kind during the erection, or before the completion, of the National Home at Bedford City, Virginia.

They had been supplied with figures by recognized authorities, showing that a sanitarium of 100 beds would cost $100,000, and that the yearly cost of maintenance would amount to $75,000.

Not only upon grounds of economy, but in an effort to be more effective in its results, the Committee said it had been maintained that the proper procedure would be to effect arrangements with such institutions as were already in operation for the treatment and care of the Order's cases.

The Committee stated that it had learned from some of the leading sanitariums of the country that they could accommodate from one to twenty-five patients each at a cost ranging from $7.50 to $18 a week.

They stated that one of the most difficult propositions encountered in the fight being waged to cure and prevent the spread of this affliction was to get the incipient case to submit to proper examination and treatment, stating that it was desirable that cases be taken in the early stages.

The Committee revealed that it was firmly of the opinion that there was only one other plan to be adopted to meet and solve the great problem successfully, and that was for the Grand Lodge to provide an appropriation of not less than $20,000 for the ensuing year to be used for the aid and relief of our Brothers who were suffering from tuberculosis. The Committee stated that it recommended the continuation of a Committee on Tuberculosis and that that Committee be empowered and directed to manage and disburse the fund provided.

The Committee also recommended that all cases properly entitled to, or seeking, aid must be reported to the Committee for consideration and investigation, and upon the Committee's becoming fully satisfied of the merits of a particular case, the applicant be assigned by them to the nearest and best suited place for the treatment required. It was the opinion of the Committee that the Continuing Committee should be authorized and directed to conduct a systematic campaign of education and instruction on this subject among the members of the Order.

COMMITTEE RECOMMENDATION

As a result, the Chairman of the Committee offered the following resolution:

> "*Resolved:* That the report of the Committee be approved and it recommendation be concurred in, and

> "*Resolved:* Further that there be and now is appropriated from the Emergency Charity Fund the sum of $20,000 to be used for the aid and relief of the Brothers suffering from the great 'White Plague' as recommended in said report, and

> "*Resolved:* That a Committee on Tuberculosis consisting of five members be appointed with full power on this subject matter and with power to manage and disburse the funds herein appropriated in the manner recommended by the said report and to employ such clerical and other aid as they may find necessary."

The resolution was unanimously adopted.

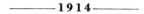

———— 1913 ————

The Committee on Tuberculosis Sanitarium reporting in 1913 held that it had received requests, and had filled such requests, amounting to only $1,630. They stated that while the requests had not been notably large, the Committee was convinced that many cases existed throughout the Order that should be receiving attention, and would be, were they not kept from our notice either by absence of the knowledge that had been available, or by the reluctance of deserving Brothers to ask for or receive assistance from the funds set aside for that purpose.

The Committee recommended a continuance of a Committee, the same to be known thereafter as the Committee on Tuberculosis, and that that Committee be fully empowered and directed to manage and disburse the unexpended balance of the fund appropriated the previous year. The report and recommendation were adopted.

———— 1914 ————

The Committee this year reported they found eleven beneficiaries on the list when they took up the work and that they had added eleven names, making a total of twenty-two members of the Order who had received benefits during the year the Committee served.

Of these, two had died and one had been reported as fully recovered, leaving a total of nineteen afflicted Brothers, 18 of whom were receiving $10 a week, and one $7.50.

The Committee stated that out of the $20,000 that had been appropriated in 1912 there had been a total expenditure of $9,472.50.

The Committee recommended that the sum of $5,000, in addition to the $10,528.50 then on hand, be appropriated by the Grand Lodge to continue the work during the ensuing year.

It was further recommended that the Tuberculosis Committee be discontinued and its powers be transferred to the Grand Exalted Ruler and Chair Officers for the ensuing year and that the said Grand Exalted Ruler and Chair Officers be requested to make a special investigation and report to the Grand Lodge at its next meeting as to the advisability or inadvisability of continuing the work.

The report was adopted.

———— 1915 ————

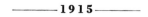

In his report to the Grand Lodge in 1915, Grand Exalted Ruler Benjamin recommended the discontinuance of the fund but not the immediate cessation of the work of relieving the suffering Brothers then dependent on the Order.

He gave his opinion that, in appropriating money for the relief of members suffering from one incurable disease and making no provision to assist others who were equal sufferers from other incurable afflictions, there was unfair discrimination against many worthy and needy Brothers.

He recommended therefore the establishment of a General Assistance Fund and that the sum of $15,000 be appropriated thereto.

The following resolution was adopted by the Grand Lodge:

"1. That the Tuberculosis Fund, as such, be discontinued, and the balance remaining be returned to the General Fund.

"2. That a fund to be known as 'General Assistance Fund' be created, and that the sum of $15,000 be appropriated thereto.

"3. That the 'General Assistance Fund' be administered and disbursed by the Grand Exalted Ruler in the following manner:

"First: To assist members now upon our rolls as sufferers from tuberculosis until such time as other adequate assistance is arranged for them.

"Second: To assist any worthy and needy member of the Order who is a sufferer from disease of any incurable character, or from injuries causing total disability.

"4. That said fund be administered under the following conditions:
   "(a) That the assisted member is without funds or property and without relatives able or willing to care for him.
   "(b) That the lodge to which such assisted member belongs contribute to his support at least one-third of the amount contributed by the Grand Lodge."

The Order and the American Youth

Since the early days of the Order the subordinate lodges have been active in various ways in the development of the American youth and the broadening of his opportunities.

It was not, however, until 1911 that there was given in the Grand Lodge consideration to a national campaign designed to inspire and direct the subordinate lodges of the Order in this most commendable activity.

The Big Brother Movement

At that Grand Lodge Session in Atlantic City, N. J., Grand Exalted

Ruler Herrmann furnished the Grand Lodge with an elaborate report concerning a matter which he regarded as considerably agitating the country at the time—the Big Brother Movement.

He referred to the Big Brother Movement as follows:

"It is a movement which involves the exercise of that charity which leads the boy—the little brother—who, possibly, for lack of right home influences, or because of evil associations, or because of what is called incorrigibility, has fallen, and has bitterness in his heart, to the knowledge of the fact that he is an integral part of humanity and that it depends, in the largest degree, upon himself whether his future is one of rectitude, making him a valuable element of society, or otherwise.

"The work is not done by severity, nor by distrust of his sincerity, but by kindness shown to him and continued to him by his Big Brothers —that is to say, by you, my Brothers, and by me, and by all whose hearts are not callous but who once were boys and know the temptations and the dangers to which the boy is exposed."

At the Grand Lodge Session of 1913 Past Exalted Ruler John F. Reilly, Hammond, Indiana, Lodge, No. 485, presented for the consideration of the members of the Grand Lodge the Hammond Plan of animating the Big Brother Movement.

The plan was outlined as follows:

"To work in conjunction with the Judge of the Juvenile Court.

"The lodge to furnish the names of its members who are willing to act as Big Brothers, to the Judge of the Juvenile Court. The Judge, instead of committing or paroling a boy to the custody of a Probation or other officer, asks a Big Brother to look after the boy.

"Under this plan of work the little fellow who has been brought into Court for the first time is not obliged to report to the Court or Probation Officer but the report of the boy's conduct of progress is made by the Big Brother, thus eliminating the one objectionable feature of the Juvenile Court System—visibly, the rule requiring a boy to report at stated intervals to the officer attached to the Court.

"The Big Brother, in looking after the little brother, must necessarily come in contact with the parent or parents of the boy and he is in a position to acquaint himself with the causes which are responsible for the boy's delinquency.

"The Big Brother also has the opportunity to help the parents of the boy to live along right lines and to help the parents by advice and example to make it easier for the little fellow, with the aid of the Big Brother, to become a better boy."

There was created by the Grand Lodge a Committee of three, to be known as the Committee on the Big Brother Movement, whose duty it would be "to promulgate and advance the plan of Hammond Lodge in this movement, to the end that the plan be adopted and put into practical operation in every lodge of this Order."

Of this Committee John F. Reilly was made Chairman. He continued to serve in that capacity with all succeeding committees of the original one until 1918.

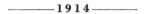

————1914————

At the Grand Lodge Session in 1914 the Committee reported having sent out more than 7,000 communications to subordinate lodges and committees thereof and 20,000 booklets to the same groups containing the Hammond Plan.

The Chairman stated that 901 lodges, with a membership of over 308,000, were then actively engaged in the Big Brother Movement.

He estimated that over 5,000 boys were then being looked after by Big Brother Elks.

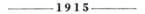

————1915————

By the time of the Grand Lodge Session in 1915 the Committee was able to report that 1,011 lodges, with a membership of 368,192, were active in the movement.

————1916————

In the following year Chairman Reilly reported that the Big Brother Movement was sponsored by 1,107 lodges with a membership of 405,584.

(At that time the Order had 1,284 lodges with a membership of 453,516.)

The Chairman stated that reports from 700 of the active lodges indicated that approximately 20,000 little brothers were being looked after by Big Brother Elks, making a total of 25,000 since the beginning of the movement three years before.

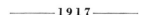

————1917————

At the Grand Lodge Session in 1917, Chairman Reilly stated that reports from the lodges indicated that approximately 30,000 little brothers were being looked after by members of the Order at that time. He said:

"The past year has been one of expectancy and fruitful accomplishment, and we believe that our efforts to extend the work of the Big Brother Movement have not been in vain. This Movement in Elkdom has passed the experimental period and has assumed such proportions as to command the attention of all persons interested in the proper development of the little brothers. It is an unselfish work and one that appeals particularly to the members of our great Order.

"Let every Elk, then, take upon himself the duty of looking after some unfortunate little brother."

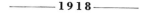

—————1918—————

At this Session of the Grand Lodge the number of lodges reported as active in the movement was 1,152, having a combined membership of 425,000.

For the Grand Lodge's year 1918-1919, Past Exalted Ruler John C. Karel, Milwaukee, Wis., Lodge, No. 46, was appointed Chairman of the Big Brother Committee.

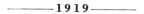

—————1919—————

Chairman Karel, in making his report at the Grand Lodge Session of 1919, expressed the feeling that there was no undertaking of the Order which had reflected more credit upon it or given more merit and satisfaction than the Big Brother Movement. He said:

"In the hands of the Big Brothers lies a large and nobly constructed share in making the America of tomorrow, and our Order should take the initiative in entering the broader field of endeavor for the uplift of humanity and the conservation of American boyhood.

"It is in keeping with the spirit of the recent Americanization conference held under the auspices of the Department of the Interior in Washington, that your Committee recommends the discontinuance of the Big Brother Committee and that its work be merged in that of a new committee to be instituted in its stead with broader powers and to be known as 'The Social and Community Welfare Committee of the Benevolent and Protective Order of Elks.' "

The discontinuance of the Big Brother Committee of the Grand Lodge did not mean a discontinuance of the Order's support of the Big Brother Movement. That splendid activity contributing to the proper development of the youth of our country continued to receive the support of the subordinate lodges under the direction of the Social and Community Welfare Committee.

In his report to the Grand Lodge in 1921, Chairman Masters of the Social and Community Welfare Committee, stated that 90 per cent of the lodges reporting to his Committee were engaged in Big Brother work.

He emphasized the fact that when the Big Brother Committee was merged with the Social and Community Welfare Committee there was no thought of giving up this important service.

The Chairman referred to the fact that the National Federation of Big Brothers had always given due credit to the Elks for their splendid Big Brother work.

The Elks-Antlers

The story of the Order's support of the *Elks-Antlers* appears under that title in this History.

Boy Scouts

Organized in 1910, the Boy Scouts of America had been in existence only a very short time before subordinate lodges of the Order began to give the movement their support.

At the end of its first ten years, fourteen Elk lodges were sponsoring Boy Scout troops.

This cooperation developed steadily year by year until, by 1946, there were 287 lodges supporting Boy Scout troops.

It was then that the Grand Lodge participated directly in the movement. In that year Grand Exalted Ruler Broughton appointed Past Grand Exalted Ruler Hart to represent the Order on the Boy Scouts of America National Civic Relationship Committee.

In the report that Past Grand Exalted Ruler Hart made at the Grand Lodge Session in 1947 he referred to the fact that many lodges had been most generous in their support of the Boy Scouts during the years but he urged that the Order get more strongly behind that movement.

At the conclusion of his address Past Grand Exalted Ruler E. Mark Sullivan offered the following resolution:

"Be it resolved by the Grand Lodge of the Benevolent and Protective Order of Elks, acting in accordance with the recommendations of this Session, contained in the report of Past Grand Exalted Ruler Hart and in the address of acceptance by Brother L. A. Lewis, Grand Exalted Ruler-elect, that the Grand Lodge earnestly recommend to the subordinate lodges of the Order that they enthusiastically participate in and support the program of sponsoring and leading Boy Scout Troops within their respective jurisdictions and urge them to give special consideration to the needs of Scout work in less-privileged neighborhoods and districts."

This resolution was adopted.

Past Grand Exalted Ruler Hart continued to represent the Order on the Boy Scouts of America National Civic Relationship Committee until his death in 1951.

In the 20 years intervening between 1947 and the date of

this History, the number of Scout units sponsored by subordinate lodges has increased from 287 to 990.

Elk support of the Scouts has not been by any means limited to sponsorship of units, for a survey covering the years 1947-1949 shows that Elk lodges contributed cash and office equipment to Scout agencies in the total amount of $168,000.

Hundreds of individual Elks contribute what is even more important—leadership—by serving on Scout councils, district committees, such as Scoutmasters and advisers.

State Associations

Prior to 1915, the Constitution of the Order provided that there should be no "branches, adjuncts, or auxiliaries in the Order." But as far back as the early '90's, the question of state organizations was a matter of vociferous, if not widespread, discussion among the members of the Grand Lodge, although at that time its advocates were not aiming at state organizations as known today. The objective then was State Grand Lodges which would legislate for their own states under the directives of a Supreme Lodge.

The proponents of this drastic change in the government of the Order advanced the theory that membership was increasing at so rapid a rate that the Grand Lodge eventually must become too large and unwieldy to function effectively as a national legislative body. The fallacy of this argument which seemed so reasonable at the time was demonstrated at the Grand Lodge Session in 1946 when the attendance of members reached an all-time high of 3,313.

The agitation for State Grand Lodges during the 1890's never reached the floor of the Grand Lodge but was confined mainly to sidewalk and hotel lobby conversation. At that time it was evident to even the most violent proponents that subordinate lodges never would sell their birthright, granted by the men who drafted the Constitution of the Order of Elks, for a form of government that would rob them of their power of participating in legislative activities in a national body; that, in brief, was the earliest thinking about the need for State Associations.

After the agitation for State Grand Lodges had been silenced effectively by the indifference of the rank and file and the good sense of the members of the Grand Lodge, many members began to discuss state organizations of a far different kind—a kind that might be brought within the scope of the Constitution and become beneficial to the Order as a whole. As a result, about the beginning of this century, regardless of the Constitutional prohibition against auxiliary organizations of any kind, states began to organize and carry on without benefit of recognition.

According to available records the oldest of these organizations are the Ohio Elks Association and the West Virginia State Elks Association. The former had its inception in 1898 and the latter was founded in 1908.

Denver, 1906

By 1906, the movement toward the organization of State Associations had developed to a point where Grand Lodge action was imperative and at the Convention in Denver that year Grand Exalted Ruler Robert W. Brown said:

> "While no ban has been placed upon State Associations, it is probable that if they were to be continued the Grand Lodge should describe their sphere. If judgment be to the contrary, it should be so declared and the quicker it is known the better."

Philadelphia, 1907

Continuing the discussion at the Grand Lodge Session in Philadelphia the following year, Grand Exalted Ruler Henry A. Melvin said he felt it was his duty to bring the matter of State Associations again to the attention of the Grand Lodge. Recognizing that State Associations "may, perhaps, be conducive to good fellowship," Brother Melvin reminded the Grand Lodge that nothing must detract from the national character of the Order. Grand Exalted Ruler Melvin then stressed the fact that the growth and solidarity of the national fraternal sentiment had depended on there not being numerous jurisdictional divisions, each having independent functions and policies.

At that Grand Lodge Session, the Committee on Revision of the Statutes of the Order, headed by Past Grand Exalted Ruler Charles E. Pickett as Chairman, recommended the amendment of Section 215 of the Statutes by adding the following clause:

> "Nothing herein contained to prevent the members of the lodges in the various states from holding reunions, which shall be open to all Elks in good standing, provided, however, that they shall not in any manner assume any of the functions of the powers of government, or in any manner attempt to influence or control by indorsement or otherwise the legislation of the Grand Lodge, or the election of its officers, or any other matter involving the policy of the Order."

The Grand Lodge accepted the report of the Committee and amended the Statutes as recommended, although the constitutionality of this action was open to question. With the definition of policy and position provided by the amendment as a guide, several states organized associations which functioned with varying degrees of success, but without any authorization beyond that accorded by the amended clause in the Statutes. Affairs of the Associations were conducted so as not to interfere with the functions of the Grand Lodge, or in any way usurp its constitutional status as a national body. As a result, many members were won over to the utility of state organizations and while there was considerable opposition, the opponents were disturbed, not by the methods of existing associations, but by the fear that they might lead to a change in the Order's fundamental principles of government. Weight was added to this thought by the fact that by 1914 there were twenty-three associations in existence.

Denver, 1914

In the interim between 1907 and 1914 there was much talk about State Associations having increased latitude, but, as Mark Twain said about the weather, "nobody did anything about it." In 1914, when the Grand Lodge met again in Denver, the Associations decided to take action and called a meeting of representatives of the various state bodies. On their behalf, the following resolution was presented to the Grand Lodge and was adopted unanimously:

> "*Resolved:* That the incoming Grand Exalted Ruler appoint a committee of five (the number subsequently was changed to three) to devise and report to the next Grand Lodge (1915 Session) a plan for the organization and official recognition of State Associations of Elks."

The action by which this Committee was appointed was the result of a compromise. In fact, there seemed to be such a divergence of opinion that up to the Monday evening preceding the Convention it was not felt that battle on the Grand Lodge floor on this subject could be avoided. However, the Committee created by the resolution was duly appointed and Bruce A. Campbell, East St. Louis, Illinois, Lodge, No. 644, later Grand Exalted Ruler, was named Chairman. The other members were Carl S. Bucher of Muskogee, Oklahoma, Lodge, No. 517, and Richard P. Rooney of Newark, New Jersey, Lodge, No. 21.

Los Angeles, 1915

At the Grand Lodge Session, in Los Angeles, 1915, Chairman Campbell submitted one of the most complete and comprehensive reports ever presented to the delegates in convention. The report was the result of a minute survey and study of every phase of the problem. The attitude of the rank-and-file toward State Associations, their possible effect upon the future of the Order and its

fundamental principles, and the desires of Associations themselves as then existing, were thoroughly analyzed and given deep
consideration.

The report recommended the recognition of State Elks Associations and presented a plan of organization which, while retaining
the sovereignty of the Grand Lodge, accorded State Associations
complete autonomy within the limits of the Constitution. It also
recommended the enactment of the Constitutional amendment
and statutory changes necessary to legalize the recognition of State
Associations. The recommendation of the Committee contained
eight salient provisions:

1. Subordinate lodges join State Associations on a voluntary
   basis.
2. State Associations be empowered to propose new Statutes or
   amendments to the Constitution.
3. Each State Association be allowed to draft its own Constitution and By-Laws, subject to review by Grand Lodge authorities.
4. Applications for dispensation for a new lodge be referred to
   the State Association for approval.
5. Officers of the State Associations be subject to call by the
   Grand Exalted Ruler for advice, recommendations or information.
6. The secret work of the Order not be subject to State Association conference.
7. Separate State Association delegates to the Grand Lodge not
   be permitted.
8. Public displays, parades and similar festivities be permitted
   at State Association meetings or reunions.

To incorporate the recommendation of the Committee into the
Constitution in the form of amendments, it was first necessary to
amend Article 3, Sections 19 and 21, of the Constitution. This was
done by the Grand Lodge and by the subordinate lodges by ref-
erendum vote. Then a resolution was adopted authorizing the incoming Grand Exalted Ruler to appoint a special committee of
three for State Associations, the duty of this committee being to
prepare and recommend appropriate statutes and amendments
of existing statutes to carry out the purposes and objects of the
Constitutional amendments previously adopted by the Grand
Lodge as a result of the recommendations of the Committee of
Messrs. Campbell, Bucher and Rooney. This resolution was
adopted and Bruce A. Campbell again was appointed Chairman
of the Committee, the other members being Jerry F. Holloran of
Victor, Colorado, Lodge, No. 367, and Edward Sceery of Paterson,
New Jersey, Lodge, No. 60.

This Committee reported to the Grand Lodge Session in Baltimore in Maryland in 1916. The Constitutional amendment of Article 3, Sections 19 and 21, having been approved by the subordinate lodges, the new statutes recommended by the Committee were adopted by the Grand Lodge. These statutes were written in their original forms substantially as they exist today.

An amendment to the Grand Lodge Statutes also provided for the appointment of a standing Committee on State Associations. For this Committee the Grand Exalted Ruler appointed Bruce A. Campbell as Chairman, and Ralph Hagan of Los Angeles, California, Lodge, No. 99, and R. A. Gordon of Atlanta, Georgia, Lodge, No. 78.

This Committee was authorized and directed by the Grand Lodge to call a conference of representatives of State Associations to endeavor to frame a Constitution and By-Laws for State Associations that would be uniform insofar as local conditions would permit.

On November 15, 1916, the Committee issued a letter to officers and members of State Associations, calling attention to the new Statutes relative to their government and also calling a conference, as directed, to meet at St. Louis, Missouri, on January 5 and 6, 1917. The St. Louis conference was attended by 135 representatives from 35 State Associations, indicating the further growth of the State Association movement. The conference drafted a recommended uniform Constitution and By-Laws and also a ritual for the installation of officers of State Associations.

Prior to this legislation, the chief functions of State Associations had been to bring the Brothers together in state reunions for a few days of fun, discuss Elk problems in the abstract and then go home.

However, when State Associations assumed legal status their members realized that if they were to justify the hopes of their advocates and friends, they must do more than act as vehicles for state reunions, much as these functions promoted good-fellowship and brought the neighbors of the state together. Under the Grand Lodge laws the state organizations were given full freedom to select the activities best suited to state conditions and to carry them on in their own way. Today, these organizations are following many paths of human welfare, aiding the underprivileged, serving the sick and handicapped, doing fine work in the field of education, and carrying on in the real spirit of Elkdom on a state-wide cooperative basis.

Some State Associations sponsor hospitals for crippled children or adults. Others maintain clinics and camps for underprivileged and crippled children and are engaged in child welfare activities, as well as many other forms of social work. Juvenile delinquency is receiving a good share of attention. In a growing number of states Mobile home therapy programs for the rehabilitation of physically handicapped children are the major projects. One Association has done outstanding work in

Group attending State Association Conference at St. Louis in 1917

Group of prominent members of the Grand Lodge in 1917 who attended the State Association Conference in St. Louis in January of that year. Purpose of the Conference was to frame the Constitution and By-Laws of the State Associations and 135 representatives from 35 State Associations were in attendance.

Top Row (left to right): F. J. Schrader, P.E.R., Allegheny, Pa., Lodge, No. 339; O. K. Cowell, P.E.R., Sunbury, Pa., Lodge, No. 267; Edwin G. Slough, P.E.R., Mansfield, Ohio, Lodge, No. 56; Dr. Ralph Hagan, Los Angeles, Calif., Lodge, No. 99; Joseph Brand, P.E.R., Bronx, N. Y., Lodge, No. 871, and Frank L. Rain, Fairbury, Neb., Lodge, No. 1203, Grand Exalted Ruler, 1919-1920.

Bottom Row (left to right): Fred A. Pope, P.E.R., Somerville, N. J., Lodge, No. 1068; Edward Rightor, New Orleans, La., Lodge, No. 30, Grand Exalted Ruler, 1916-1917; Robert A. Gordon, Atlanta, Ga., Lodge, No. 78; John H. Mitchell, St. Paul, Minn., Lodge, No. 59, Justice of Grand Forum; Fred Harper, Lynchburg, Va., Lodge, No. 321, Grand Exalted Ruler, 1917-1918, and Bruce A. Campbell, East St. Louis, Ill., Lodge, No. 664, Grand Exalted Ruler, 1918-1919.

Chairman Campbell, Dr. Hagan and Robert Gordon constituted the standing Committee on State Associations which called the Conference at St. Louis.

the rehabilitation of veterans through occupational therapy. Hundreds of scholarships have been issued each year throughout the nation. State Associations have cooperated with Elks War Commission, the Elks National Foundation and the Elks National Service Commission.

State Associations are voluntary organizations. They are dependent for existence upon the subordinate lodges of their state. Membership is not compulsory. The work they are doing is an outlet on a state-wide scale for the rank and file.

It is remarkable that such organizations have come so far since the days when their time was occupied in fighting for recognition. They are organizations of the laity; mediums of greater expression for the men who do not attain membership in the Grand Lodge. Their works demonstrate that the "great heart of Elkdom" always strives for greater expression and larger fields.

State Elks Associations are marching on, obeying the Order's admonition to "do the duty that lies nearest thee," and reaching out into almost every path of human welfare, actuated only by a desire "to do good unto all men." State Associations, left upon their own, have found a secure place in the economy of the Order and in the hearts of humankind.

Years before State Associations were recognized by the Grand Lodge, they were engaged in charitable, humanitarian and community welfare work.

Since such recognition and the resulting increase in the number of Associations and the broadening of their interests and programs, these activities have been developing and expanding year by year.

At the time of the writing of this History, the major services of that character of the 48 State Associations (Delaware and Maryland being united with the District of Columbia in one Association and California and Hawaii in another) are as follows:

ALASKA	Cerebral Palsy Mobile Treatment Units
ALABAMA	Elks Memorial Center—50 bed Vocational rehabilitation facility.
ARIZONA	Arizona Elks Association Hospital
ARKANSAS	Retarded Children Program
CALIFORNIA and HAWAII	Aid to handicapped children through mobile cerebral palsy therapy units, grants to teaching hospitals for care of children with eye problems, scholarships for technicians.

COLORADO	Laradon Hall training and rehabilitation of mentally retarded children.
CONNECTICUT	Crippled Children.
FLORIDA	Harry-Anna Crippled Children's Hospital and mobile therapy units.
GEORGIA	Aidmore Crippled Children's Hospital.
IDAHO	Elks Rehabilitation center.
ILLINOIS	Crippled Children—Mobile units for home treatment of Cerebral Palsy.
INDIANA	Cancer Research Program.
IOWA	Hospitalized Veteran Program.
KANSAS	Contributions to Institute of Logapedics, Scholarship and Youth Programs.
KENTUCKY	Aid to assist mentally retarded youngsters.
LOUISIANA	Eye Banks and Scholarship Programs.
MAINE	Crippled Children—Nurses scholarships.
MARYLAND DELAWARE and D. of C.	Operates Boy Camps.
MASSACHUSETTS	Scholarships—Contribution to various hospitals, schools and institutions.
MICHIGAN	Crippled and Handicapped Children.
MINNESOTA	Youth Camp for Underprivileged Boys.
MISSISSIPPI	Crippled Children.
MISSOURI	Mobile Dental Units.
MONTANA	Mobile Speech and Hearing Clinics.
NEBRASKA	Rehabilitation of Crippled Children.
NEVADA	Mobile Speech Therapy Programs.
NEW HAMPSHIRE	Contributes to Crotched Mountain Hospital.
NEW JERSEY	Crippled Children's Programs, Scholarship for handicapped youngsters.
NEW MEXICO	Mobile Units Cerebral Palsy Treatment.
NEW YORK	Scholarships—Mobile Cerebral Palsey Treatment units.

NORTH CAROLINA	Elks Boys Camp.
NORTH DAKOTA	Youth Camp for physically handicapped children.
OHIO	Cerebral Palsey Service Centers with two fully equipped traveling centers.
OKLAHOMA	Youth Center, available to lodges, Youth groups, schools and other organizations.
OREGON	Visually Handicapped Children Program and mobile therapy units.
PENNSYLVANIA	Scholarships—Home treatment of Cerebral Palsy.
RHODE ISLAND	Crippled Children, Scholarships.
SOUTH CAROLINA	Scholarships—Student Aid.
SOUTH DAKOTA	Aid to Handicapped Children.
TENNESSEE	Nurses Scholarship Program.
TEXAS	Owns and operates Crippled Children's Hospital.
UTAH	Crippled and Handicapped Persons Program.
VERMONT	Operates Summer Camp for retarded children.
VIRGINIA	Maintains Boys Camp.
WASHINGTON	Mobile Physical Therapy Program.
WEST VIRGINIA	Operates three Crippled and Handicapped Children's Camps.
WISCONSIN	Scholarships
WYOMING	Scholarships—Crippled Children.

Every State Association in the Order is sponsoring Veterans Hospital Service.

Elks War Relief Commission, World War I

On the opening of the July, 1917, Grand Lodge Session in Boston, Mass., a resolution which had a two-fold purpose was offered.

It proposed, first, an expression of approval and endorsement of the actions of President Wilson in endeavoring to preserve peace and in meeting the situation of war when it was thrust upon us, and, second, a pledge of "the best that we have to offer in service at the front and in resource and fealty at home, today and always." Its sponsor was James L. McGovern, Bridgeport, Conn., Lodge, No. 36.

The resolution was unanimously adopted.

Following the declaration of war against Germany the preceding April, Grand Exalted Ruler Edward Rightor had appointed a Committee to study what the Order should do in the international crisis, such Committee to report to the Grand Lodge Session to be held that year.

The Committee consisted of Past Grand Exalted Ruler John K. Tener, Charleroi, Pa., Lodge, No. 494, Chairman; Past Grand Exalted Ruler Joseph T. Fanning, Indianapolis, Ind., Lodge, No. 13; Past Grand Exalted Ruler Jerome B. Fisher, Jamestown, N. Y., Lodge, No. 263; Senator George E. Chamberlain, Past Exalted Ruler, Portland, Ore., Lodge, No. 142; Governor C. H. Brough, Fayetteville, Ark., Lodge, No. 1104; Past Grand Exalted Ruler James R. Nicholson, Springfield, Mass., Lodge, No. 61.

After exhaustive study, the Committee filed its report including these recommendations: That the Elks give first consideration to the sick and wounded on the battlefields of France and equip base hospitals for their care; that the Order create a fund for war relief work.

The following resolution offered by R. E. Umbel, Uniontown, Pa., Lodge, No. 370, was unanimously and with great enthusiasm adopted by a rising vote and that action was followed by the singing of "America":

"RESOLVED: That the sum of one million dollars be appropriated by the Grand Lodge of the Benevolent and Protective Order of Elks of the United States of America, to be known as 'The War Relief Fund,' such fund to be contributed by our subordinate lodges."

The first act of Grand Exalted Ruler Fred Harper, elected at the Boston Convention, was to appoint an Elks War Relief Commission composed of the following Past Grand Exalted Rulers:

John K. Tener, Charleroi, Pa., Lodge, No. 494, Chairman
Joseph T. Fanning, Indianapolis, Ind., Lodge, No. 13, Secretary
Jerome B. Fisher, Jamestown, N. Y., Lodge, No. 263
James R. Nicholson, Springfield, Mass., Lodge, No. 61
Edward Rightor, New Orleans, La., Lodge, No. 30

Base Hospitals

The first activity of the Commission was to finance and provide the necessary equipment for two base hospitals: No. 41, organized from the faculty and alumni of the University of Virginia, and No. 46, organized from the faculty and alumni of the University of Oregon.

These were the first base hospital units to reach the battle area in France, where they rendered distinguished service throughout the war.

Reconstruction Hospital

The ever-increasing number of maimed and wounded members of our Forces who were brought home soon overtaxed the then available hospitals and created an exigent need for additional facilities.

After securing the grateful approval of the Government, the Commission promptly constructed and equipped a Reconstruction Hospital, of 700-bed capacity, in Boston. Dedicated and turned over to the Government on November 16, 1918, it was the first such hospital to be established in the United States. It was continuously operated to its full capacity for several years, until the need for it passed in 1921.

Community House — Camp Sherman

In the summer of 1918, it became apparent that Camp Sherman, Ohio, would need a Community House to take care of the families visiting the 40,000 soldiers stationed there. The Commission met this need by the erection of a 72-room structure which so effectively served its purpose, particularly during the great flu epidemic, as to merit the grateful acknowledgment of the military Commandant of the Camp.

At the Grand Lodge Session in Boston on July 12, 1917, in response to a request from Food Commissioner Herbert Hoover that a representative of the Order of Elks attend a conference he had planned with representatives of fraternal organizations, Grand Exalted Ruler Fred Harper appointed Bruce A. Campbell, retiring Chairman of the State Associations Committee, to represent the Order at this conference.

Following that conference, the Food Commissioner decided to hold conferences of accredited representatives of a number of fraternal organizations.

The first fraternal organization to be invited to such a conference was the Benevolent and Protective Order of Elks and that meeting was held on August 2, 1917.

President Wilson and members of Elks Conference, August 2, 1917

The photograph above shows the members of that conference as they were received at the White House by President Wilson following the meeting with the Food Commissioner.

The group from left to right comprises the following: John Reilly, Chairman of the Big Brother Committee; Albert L. Dunn, Past Exalted Ruler of Atlanta, Georgia, Lodge, No. 78; Harry Houston of the Grand Lodge Auditing Committee; Calvin L. Kingsley, Grand Trustee; E. R. Ingersoll, Grand Esteemed Loyal Knight; Patrick T. Powers, Grand Trustee; Thomas L. Reilly, Grand Esteemed Leading Knight; Past Grand Exalted Ruler Joseph T. Fanning, Secretary of the Elks War Relief Commission; Grand Exalted Ruler Fred Harper; Past Grand Exalted Ruler John K. Tener, Chairman of the Elks War Relief Commission; President Woodrow Wilson; Past Grand Exalted Ruler James R. Nicholson; Senator George Chamberlain of Oregon; Joseph A. Burkart, Past Exalted Ruler of Washington, D. C., Lodge, No. 15; Fred C. Robinson, Grand Secretary; Charles White, Grand Treasurer; Past Grand Exalted Ruler Edward Leach; Bruce A. Campbell, Past Exalted Ruler of East St. Louis, Illinois, Lodge, No. 664; J. Edgar Masters, Grand Trustee; Samuel C. Todd of Charleroi, Pennsylvania, Lodge, No. 494, and Fred J. Mersheimer, Exalted Ruler of Washington, Lodge, No. 15.

New Orleans Hospital Proposal

In 1918 the Commission offered to build a Reconstruction Hospital for the Government at New Orleans, similar to the one in Boston.

The Surgeon-General of the War Department accepted the proposition. However, the War Industries Board ruled that it would not approve any further construction work by the Department for hospitals or other purposes until a survey be made dis-

247

Members of the Elks War Relief Commission (1917). From left to right: Past Grand Exalted Rulers Fred Harper, Jerome B. Fisher, John K. Tener, Joseph T. Fanning, Edward Rightor and James R. Nicholson.

closing that there were no available structures already erected that could be used.

A War Department Commission reported that there were available buildings in New Orleans and the War Relief Commission withdrew its offer.

Salvation Army

In the meantime the Salvation Army was performing a wonderful service among our soldiers in France; but it was severely handicapped by lack of funds. To assist in meeting this exigency and to insure the continuance of this service, the War Relief Commission and the subordinate lodges all over the country fostered the campaigns of the Army for the needed funds, in many instances assuming the entire cost of such campaigns.

In addition to this service the Commission at Christmas time in 1918 presented the Army with a check for $60,000 for assistance in its post-war relief.

Because of this nationwide cooperation, characterized by a most gratifying success, and because of the large cash donation referred to, the Commander of the Salvation Army requested the privilege of addressing the Grand Lodge in session at Atlantic City in 1919. In that wonderful speech, which touched the heart of every hearer, Commander Evangeline Booth said:

"When the war came, some of those who knew us well, knew our teachings, and the nature of our activities; even they said 'you are not wanted in the War; there is no place for you on the battlefield; stay at home and go on with your street preaching.' But again at this

Commander Evangeline Booth of the Salvation Army, who addressed the Grand Lodge Convention in Atlantic City in 1919 for the purpose of paying tribute to the Order of Elks for the support given the Salvation Army in its successful relief work on the battlefields of France.

crucial hour, when we were in dire want of money and friends, all over the country from sea to sea, the Order of Elks rushed to our aid. They very largely furnished the funds; they pleaded our cause; they saw to it that we had the opportunity, proving not only the strength and loyalty of the friendship of their Order, but its confidence in the Salvation Army, to meet a great and deep need upon the battlefields of France.

"The Salvation Army can never forget or get away from its deep sense of indebtedness and gratitude to the grand body of men that is before me this morning. . . . I say without hesitancy that our organization could not have achieved its exceptional success in this war, but for the splendid, practical, tangible aid that was rendered to us by the Elks."

Food Conservation

The Government's recognition of the Order of Elks as an effective agency for a nationwide service is worthy of note. This Order was the first fraternal organization whose aid was sought in the movement for food conservation during the war. The splendid results accomplished by the Elks in this service thoroughly justified the confidence thus imposed.

Additional Million-Dollar Appropriation

Following the presentation and acceptance of the Commission's report at the Grand Lodge Session in 1918, there was unanimously adopted a resolution appropriating an additional million dollars.

At a later Session, the Commission members were gratified to report that it had not been found necessary to call for the additional funds.

Motion Pictures

In the year 1919 the War Relief Commission completed the production of two motion pictures, "The Way Back" and "The Spirit of Elkdom," and by the time the report of the Commission was made in July of 1920, these films had been shown in 200 subordinate lodges.

"The Way Back" was a five-reel special feature intended to arouse interest throughout the country in the Government's vocational training program and the Commission felt that much had been accomplished by it in that direction.

"The Spirit of Elkdom" was a three-reel picture, somewhat historical in character, dealing especially with the war work activities of the Order, as well as the vocational training work in which the Order was cooperating, through the Elks War Relief Commission, with the Federal Board for Vocational Education.

The pictures received much praise and aroused a full measure of enthusiasm in the various communities where they were shown.

Vocational Training

Among the most distinctive and most helpful services by the Order in war relief work was the vocational training of our disabled soldiers, a field it had entirely to itself, in accredited association with the Federal Board of Vocational Education.

Unfortunately, the restricted terms of the Congressional enactments had left many disabled veterans unprovided for as to vocational training. The Elks War Relief Commission undertook to care for these exceptional cases, as well as to aid in the publicity campaign necessary to ascertain and locate many entitled to receive such training, and to provide for them until they could avail themselves of such Federal aid.

During this period of training, and in preparation therefor, many of the veterans were in dire need of financial assistance. Realizing that loans to them would be preferable to charitable gifts, the Commission created a revolving fund from which loans could be made, repayments becoming available for other similar loans. Nearly 40,000 such loans were made, and it is interesting to note that every dollar was repaid, except in a few cases where death, or other intervening causes, made it impossible.

This unique service, thus performed by the Order, was so conspicuously effective that the Government eventually followed the Order's example and created a similar revolving fund, taking over this particular activity.

Recognition of the part taken by the Elks in this great work was given in the United States Congress in a speech on vocational training made by John F. Miller, a member of the House of Representatives from the State of Washington, who said:

> "Realizing the above program and desiring to participate directly in it, the Benevolent and Protective Order of Elks, through the National Elks War Relief Commission, has placed at the disposal of the Federal Board a quarter of a million dollars to be used in this humane and practical work, enabling the Federal Board to carry on much of its work, without being subjected to the delay of technical rules and regulations which, in many cases, would defeat the object of the vocational education law.

> "The Elks Fund thus provided us the first instance of the kind in the history of the country where a great, patriotic, fraternal organization has come to the aid of the Government in so timely, helpful and substantial a manner."

Appreciation of the assistance received from the Benevolent and Protective Order of Elks was further expressed by Dr. C. E. Prosser, Director of the Federal Board for Vocational Education, as follows:

> "No one action taken by any public or private agency will do so much to bring about prompt and effective care of disabled soldiers, sailors and marines, resulting from the war, as the action taken by the Elks War Relief Commission. As a result, instead of waiting for weeks or months, under privation and humiliation such as no soldier of the Republic should undergo, because of official delays, many of which are unavoidable, they will now find themselves properly taken care of at once and placed in the line of reeducation which will enable them to make the future safe for themselves and their dependents."

Speech by Congressman Reed

Just preceding the adjournment of Congress on June 3, 1920, Representative Daniel A. Reed of New York, a member of Dunkirk, N. Y., Lodge, No. 922, addressed the House on the subject of the "war relief activities and rehabilitation work of the Benevolent and Protective Order of Elks of the United States of America," his speech being devoted largely to the cooperation of the Elks War Relief Commission and the Federal Board for Vocational Education. Congressman Reed was a member of the Committee on Education of the House of Representatives, which investigated the Government's vocational training work.

Speaking of various volunteer agencies which had cooperated with or assisted the Government in the many problems incident to and following the war, Congressman Reed said:

> "I would say that foremost among such volunteer agencies, acting both as a whole and individually, came the Benevolent and Protective Order of Elks, with their more than 500,000 patriotic American citizens making up the membership of the Order.

> "This great Order seemed to sense with prophetic vision the frightful consequences of war and proceeded to set in motion and bring to successful fruition or achievement through its Elks War Relief Commission, a service most essential and timely which had not been anticipated or performed by any other agency."

After enumerating the activities of the Elks in connection with the war problems, Congressman Reed said:

> "In all these matters undertaken and so successfully carried out by the Elks there have been no public drives, no street canvassing for funds, and no money has been solicited or received by them from any source outside the individual Elks of the subordinate Elk lodges.

> "As was stated on the floor of the House by the gentleman from Washington (Mr. Miller) at the time this generous offer was accepted on behalf of the representatives of the Government: 'The Elks Fund thus provided is the first instance of the kind in the history of the country where a great patriotic fraternal organization has come to the aid of the Government in so timely, helpful and substantial a manner.'"

> "And greater than all this giving of money, greater than the erection of the magnificent Reconstruction Hospital at Boston or the equipping of the two large base hospitals in France, or the donations and assistance to the Salvation Army, has been the spirit of sympathy and helpfulness reflecting the fraternal fellowship in which the membership of the splendid Benevolent and Protective Order of Elks has by personal contact encouraged so many thousands of our wounded and disabled heroes to carry on successfully in refitting or reeducating themselves for the future."

European Relief

The Commission made a donation of $10,000 to the European Relief Council through the Chairman, Herbert Hoover, for the relief of starving and destitute children of Europe.

In acknowledging this gift, Chairman Hoover said:

"On behalf of the European Relief Council I beg to acknowledge receipt of the generous gift from your organization.

"You represent an enormous body of the able and competent men of this country who have now become the hosts of 1,000 children of eastern and central Europe until next harvest. I am sure you will all feel some of the glow that comes from making these children smile, and I beg that you will go as far as you can in bringing your great strength toward further support of this cause.

"There are 3,500,000 of these waif and undernourished children who during the coming winter will suffer the miseries of cold and hunger if the United States, which has so far brought them through, should fail now. They are a charge upon our civilization and a test of our national character."

Elks in Service

More than 70,000 Elks saw service under the Stars and Stripes in every part of the vast war machine and when peace finally came more than 1,000 Elks had made the supreme sacrifice and joined the ranks of Absent Brothers. But while the boys were fighting "Over There," Elkdom at home was functioning in the grand traditions of the Order.

General John J. Pershing, Commander of the American Expeditionary Forces, whose first public statement following his return from France was made at a reception tendered him by Grand Lodge Officers at the home of New York Lodge No. 1.

In his first public address following the return to this country, which was made at a reception tendered him at the home of New York Lodge No. 1, General John J. Pershing, Commander, American Expeditionary Forces, said:

> "No one knows better than an Elk what the Order stands for; and realizing, as I do, just what the vows of an Elk require him to do, prescribing in many ways the conduct of his life, I can readily appreciate, and do appreciate, the great work that has been accomplished by this Order.

> "We who were fortunate enough to be sent to the battlefields of Europe to represent our people, felt that we had a united nation behind us; and I know of no organization or body of men whose patriotism, whose loyalty and whose benevolence have contributed in a greater degree to making that a possibility.

> "We have felt not only the spirit of your patriotism, but we have felt the national benefits of your efforts to carry forward the principles for which America has stood in this war."

Personnel

During the life of the Commission, Past Grand Exalted Rulers Fred Harper and Bruce A. Campbell became members of the Commission.

Past Grand Exalted Ruler Fisher died during his service on the Commission.

Receipts and Expenditures

A statement of the receipts and expenditures of the Elks War Relief Commission will be found in the Appendix of this History.

Mother's Day

At the Session of the Grand Lodge in Boston in 1917 a resolution was unanimously adopted recommending that each subordinate lodge, on its nearest meeting night to the second Sunday in May of each year, hold a special service to commemorate Mother's Day.

The following year, at the Grand Lodge Session in Atlantic City, J. E. McCormick of Modesto, California, Lodge, No. 1282, submitted a form of Ritual for Mother's Day.

It was voted that this Ritual be adopted as an optional ceremonial for subordinate lodges.

At the Grand Lodge Session of 1925, held in Portland, Oregon, the Committee on Social and Community Welfare, which, at that time, had charge of matters of ritual, offered a new Mother's Day Ritual.

William Sinek, Chicago Lodge No. 4, who presented this new Mother's Day Ritual to the Grand Lodge for that Committee, of which Past Grand Exalted Ruler John P. Sullivan was Chairman, stated that the entire Ritual was new, with the exception of the tribute which had been incorporated in the Ritual of Brother McCormick and said that the tribute, "being very beautiful, remained the same."

He then explained that in bringing "Mother" into the Ritual the one thought that was in the minds of the members of the Committee was that the Mother who is with us, as well as the Mother who has passed away, should be considered.

At that Grand Lodge Session a motion was offered that the observance of Mother's Day by each subordinate lodge be made mandatory. That motion was adopted.

In 1930, the Ritualistic Committee reported that in 1929 there had been submitted to it a communication by a committee representing the California State Elks Association, requesting that the Mother's Day Ritual adopted in 1925 be discontinued and that the one written by Brother McCormick be again adopted as the official Mother's Day Ritual.

The Committee stated that the Ritual then in use was still very largely the handiwork of Brother McCormick and differed very little from the former Ritual except that the ceremony of building the word "Mother" in a floral setting had been omitted from the new Ritual.

The Committee recommended that, until a new Ritual of Special Services was printed, subordinate lodges be permitted to interpolate in the new Ritual the ceremony of building the word "Mother," or use the former Ritual in its entirety if they so desired.

Mother's Day Address
delivered by
Past Grand Exalted Ruler E. Mark Sullivan
at Medford, Mass., Lodge, No. 915—May 11, 1944

"This week is National Family Week throughout the United States, and on Monday evening last over a national broadcast were heard leaders of three faiths—Catholic, Jewish and Protestant—in a program emphasizing 'the spiritual foundations and resources of the family.'

"Approving the observance of National Family Week, the President of our country said he hoped the result would be 'an increased reverence and respect for the American home' and 'may it invite

255

God's blessing in a special manner on the American family.'

"In the spirit of this week and of this evening's service it may be asked: 'What of the nest and its nestlings, if the mother-bird is gone?'

"Medford Lodge of Elks has long and faithfully held Annual Mother's Day ceremonies. And in this, America's third year of this World War, we are met tonight:

> 'Not for the star-crowned heroes,
>> the men that conquer and slay,
> But a song for those that bore them,
>> the mothers braver than they.'

"Apples seldom fall far from the tree they grow on, and a worthy son springs only from a worthy mother. She is now your constant inspiration as she was the sanctifying spirit of the roof beneath which you were reared. Her breast was the pillow of your infancy. From her sweet lips your lips caught their first soft utterances. Those lips pressed yours when fever burned your infant brow. Oft were her midnight watches by your restless cot, prolonged till the last pale star had set and dazzling morn broke on her weary eyes. And still her dear face, faded through fond care, hung over your sleep and was there to greet your wakening.

"With your little palms folded between her warm hands, often she taught you to lift your eyes unto the hills whence cometh our strength, and her faith will ever abide with you, and no man shall take it from you.

"Such were our Mothers' tasks. And when she passed from us it seemed 'like the ceasing of exquisite music.'

" 'The song of devoted motherhood is ceaseless, the whole world round.' We were lulled to sleep by that song in our infancy; and now we hear it again. The wife of our manhood, yes, the mother of our children's children are our own fond mother reincarnate. With equal tenderness and patient care they cradle God's blessed gift to our households. The miracle of Motherhood is unending.

"True Motherhood is a partnership with God. What strength, what purity, what love, what wisdom, should be hers who would help God to fashion an immortal soul! How august is her place in God's divine plan!

"In all the ages woman has been man's greatest inspiration to deeds of valor and to nobility. When the Christian Church sought to convert the pagan she first implanted in him the human ideal of chivalry— respect for woman. From this seed budded the Christian ideal that makes chastity perfect chivalry in a boy and truest womanhood in a girl.

"The progress of a nation's culture is best measured by the estimation in which it holds its women.

"The ancient pagans held women as chattels and toys. Their women had no personal rights. They were the absolute subjects of the male masters of the household.

"This was not so with the women of the Old Testament. But not until Christ made Mary the tabernacle of His entrance into this earth did woman achieve her rightful place among men. In that act was set the divine seal upon the personal dignity of womanhood and motherhood. In that act was proclaimed unto all ages woman's inalienable rights as man's equal. And in all history no nation has ever ignored, or for long disregarded, the inalienable rights of womanhood and holy state of motherhood and survived. This is fundamental. It applies with as much force to the present as to the ancient past; to the fast-expanding feminism of the divorce mill as to the luxury of the brothels of Pompeii, now long buried beneath ancient ashes of a still rumbling Vesuvius. This same pagan view of motherhood, manifested by both Nazis and Communists, would have resulted in their mutual slaughter had not the perfidy of their unholy alliance against weaker Christian neighbors at last made them mutual antagonists and in that event military exigency of national defense made the United States and Great Britain the saving allies of Russia.

"A degraded womanhood makes for a degraded people. Womanhood is degraded when by edict her principal function is to breed men to bear arms for unrighteous enrichment of a proud, imperious government. The stream of human life can never rise higher than its source.

"A truly great nation is a nation of exalted mothers of righteous men.

"Our nation is something more than the United States of America. It is the united homes of America, in every one of which Mother is enthroned and directs the destiny of her obedient subjects with a divine love. The family, not the state, is the primary unit of our nation, politically, socially and religiously. If there is not unity in the family, then there is none in the nation. Here is the source of love and thought for others that makes all people of our land kin.

"On one occasion abroad an English lady said to an American, 'You have no queen in your country.' He replied, 'In your country you boast of only one queen. In my country every good mother is a queen, and we boast of millions of them.'

"In such a reverent hour as this, I like to recall the familiar prayer, 'God Bless the Mother that Bore Him,' she who first gathered him in her own flesh; she who endowed him with her mind and blessed him with her love and in whose prayers he is ever foremost. Evil companions and unhappy circumstances may turn him from the path she set before him. But the true son of a good mother, errant though he be, will one day surely turn to the altar of her blest memory, reclaimed by her unceasing love.

> "Mother o' Mine,
>   If I were hanged on the highest hill,
>   I know whose love would follow me still,
>   Mother o'Mine.
>   If I were drowned in the deepest sea,
>   I know whose tears would come down to me,
>   Mother o'Mine.

If I were damned, both body and soul,
I know whose prayers would make me whole,
Mother o'Mine."

Community Welfare, Charitable and Patriotic Activities

At the Grand Lodge Session of 1919 there was created the Social and Community Welfare Committee.

In the motion recommending its creation it was stated:

"This new Committee should absorb and embrace all the work hitherto dealt with by the Big Brothers of our Order, and should, as the title indicates, be empowered to interest itself further in every phase of humanitarian effort for the uplift, not only of the individual, but of the community of which that individual is an integral part."

W. W. Mountain, Flint, Michigan, Lodge, No. 222, was named Chairman of the Committee.

1920

At the 1920 Convention the Committee on Social and Community Welfare reported that it had sent a communication to the subordinate lodges telling about its appointment and purposes and offering to cooperate in every way it could.

The report stated that replies were received from about 50 per cent of the subordinate lodges and that with very few exceptions replies indicated that spendid war relief work had been done, that they had given up their homes to Red Cross work, made hospitals of them during influenza epidemics and were working with the civic authorities with splendid results.

The Committee felt that it had not accomplished much in the year but still thought that the movement was so important that the special Committee should be continued and its membership increased from three to five members.

The Committee was continued and for the year from July, 1920, to July, 1921, the Chairman was J. E. Masters, Charleroi, Pa., Lodge, No. 494.

1921

Chairman Masters in his report to the Grand Lodge in 1921 stated that fairly complete returns from more than 700 lodges showed that the first concern of Elkdom is charity. He stated that a study of these replies brought out the thought that Elk charity is not confined to the Order but finds its way into all conditions of society.

Distributing Christmas baskets, furnishing food, fuel and clothing, cash donations to relief funds, subscriptions to charitable institutions, and ministry to misfortune are but a few of the countless ways in which the hand of Elk charity has been raised to the help of mankind, Chairman Masters stated. He referred to the fact that in the preceding year more than $1,600,000 had been given by the Order to relieve want and distress.

The Chairman said:

> "It is most gratifying to state that the report submitted to our Committee evidenced a keen desire on the part of our lodges to participate in general welfare work. Hitherto most lodges have supported in a perfunctory way this movement. The relations have been cordial rather than vital. But this has been changed and we find Elk lodges everywhere joining enthusiastically in plans for the betterment of social conditions in their communities. Many important matters for public good have been taken up by our lodges. We find them giving attention to public health, child welfare, city playgrounds, wholesale amusements and recreation, better housing conditions, elimination of the slums, education and art, law enforcement, employment, the Red Cross, the Salvation Army, and so forth."

Among the activities shown by the various lodges the Committee listed the following: Christmas baskets distributed, picnics for boys, public band concerts, prison reform, employment assistance, maintenance of rooms in hospitals, paying expenses of community nurses, Americanization work, development of the patriotic spirit among children of the schools.

—————1922—————

William T. Byrne, Albany, New York, Lodge, No. 49, was named Chairman from July, 1921, to July, 1922.

The Committee reported that in a communication sent to the lodges they urged the appointment of a local Elks' Social and Community Welfare Committee, and in a letter to the District Deputies they suggested that when they visited their lodges the work of these Committees should be discussed, and that they should be able to find plenty of subject matter in that work, which would include the following:

> "All-year charities, relief of cold and hunger suffering, Thanksgiving and Christmas cheer, little brothers on the street, fallen boys in detention homes, parole boys in juvenile courts, public health and schools, child welfare, Boy Scouts, Flag Day and teaching allegiance to our Flag, advocating an Elk Field in every town, athletics, play-

grounds, crippled children, all worthy charities, raising up of the fallen, American work above all else."

----------1923----------

Past Grand Exalted Ruler John P. Sullivan, reporting to the Grand Lodge as Chairman of the Social and Community Welfare Committee in 1923, set forth the objects of that Committee in the following words:

> "The Grand Lodge, in convention assembled in Atlantic City in 1922, upon the recommendation of the New Membership Committee, consolidated that Committee with the Committee on Social and Community Welfare.

> "The consolidation was perfected to permit Elkdom to meet the greater opportunities for useful service to humanity, and to communities, through the creation of a central body, devoting its time to helping solve the innumerable problems that arise among the subordinate lodges."

He stated that during the preceding year the reports of subordinate lodges showed that glorious results had been attained in the following activities:

Carrying on the great work of Americanization.
Substantial support and encouragement in the field of education.
Bringing sunshine and happiness into the lives of the unfortunate.
Helping the Boy Scout organization.
Aiding the Red Cross and Salvation Army.
The Big Brother Movement.
Child Welfare.
Establishment of free clinics and other medical relief to conserve and protect the health of communities.

Up to that time 849 lodges had reported the formation of Social and Community Welfare Committees.

----------1924----------

At the Grand Lodge Session of 1924 the Committee stated that reports from the subordinate lodges showed the number of community service activities engaged in by the lodges as follows:
1,088 lodges—one or more activities
1,042 lodges—two or more activities
  980 lodges—three or more activities

902 lodges—four or more activities
790 lodges—five or more activities
637 lodges—six or more activities
467 lodges—seven or more activities
296 lodges—eight or more activities
138 lodges—nine or more activities
 64 lodges—ten or more activities
 30 lodges—eleven or more activities
 12 lodges—twelve or more activities
  4 lodges—thirteen or more activities
  2 lodges—fourteen or more activities

——————1925——————

The Committee reported that the Order had expended during the previous year in Social and Community Welfare work $2,370,193.38, an increase of $396,477.30 over the preceding year.

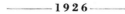

——————1926——————

At the Grand Lodge Session this year, Chairman Sullivan stated that the year had been the best, in point of general activity of the lodges of the Order in doing Social and Community Welfare work, that the Order had ever had.

He reported that the Order had spent in that work during the year, $2,370,199.44 and enumerated the items as follows:

For summer community entertainments—outings, picnics and the like	$ 102,163.92
Maintenance of, or contributions toward the maintenance of, summer camps, at which, all-told, 16,595 persons were kept last year	45,701.78
Contributions and donations toward public playgrounds	20,841.09
Encouragement of junior and juvenile athletics	13,355.52
Rent payments for 1,021 needy families	31,458.99
Fuel furnished to 3,735 needy families	39,377.06
Food furnished (other than at holidays) to 8,010 needy families	94,078.24
Clothing furnished (other than at holidays) to 13,992 needy individuals	74,482.54
Thanksgiving baskets furnished to 12,355 families	48,700.48
Christmas baskets and Christmas tree parties for 95,897 families and 413,238 children	804,960.95
Contributions to Boy Scouts and Girl Scouts	36,378.16
Aid extended to 4,773 cases through Big Brother work	27,147.87

Donations to hospitals, hospital rooms maintained, wards equipped, public health donations, etc. .... $ 123,476.35

Medical aid extended to 4,640 cases (including Crippled Children's work) 127,556.99

Cost of giving 181 hospital entertainments 15,230.11

Prizes awarded in patriotic essay contests 7,790.22

Relief extended to 1,307 veterans 10,209.46

Educational work (children kept in school) including 107 college scholarships maintained by Elks 37,487.36

Amount raised by Elks through benefit or subscription entertainments for other and existing social agencies 42,601.25

Miscellaneous activities, too varied to classify (this figure including also total from those lodges which did not submit itemized reports) 663,561.00

Total $2,370,199.44

———— 1 9 2 7 ————

Past Grand Exalted Ruler Sullivan presented the report for the Committee. He reported that there were 1,414 lodges at that time engaging in community service activities.

He stated that in the preceding ten years his own lodge, New Orleans Lodge, had raised and spent nearly a million dollars in charitable activities.

Reporting on the benefactions of the subordinate lodges in the preceding five years he stated the increased expenditures of community welfare activities were as follows:

1922-1923	$1,456,501.69	1924-1925	$2,370,193.38
1923-1924	$1,973,716.08	1925-1926	$2,370,199.44
	1926-1927	$2,881,318.93	

It was at the conclusion of this report of Past Grand Exalted Ruler Sullivan that the resolution was offered for the organization and control of Junior Elks, which was finally consummated under the name of the Antlers, to which a section of this History is devoted.

After he submitted the detailed figures of expenditures for community welfare by the subordinate lodges, the Chairman in his report to the Committee said:

"In short, the result is a big, round, mouth-filling set of figures which reads like a census report, even though it represents the bringing of light into the dark places of the heart, the alleviation of suffering, the rekindling of hope in the night of despair, the banishment of pain, the feeding of the hungry, the healing of the sick, the gladdening of those burdened with sorrow and with grief—even though it represents the welfare work that the Elks of this country have done from year's end to year's end throughout the nation whose banner is first in their hearts as it is first upon their altars.

"Those lodges and the splendid men who make them up have left their mark on no set of ledger sheets but on the hearts of communities— of states—of a nation.

"Instances? The difficulty is not to give instances but to keep from giving them endlessly."

Then, after naming a vast number of examples of the charitable and community service work done by the individual lodges, the Chairman said:

"What shall the accountant and the statistician make of these? Wherever disaster has struck, there have the Elks of this nation been ready with their hands, their hearts and their purses to aid those afflicted and sorely distressed."

—————1928—————

Grand Exalted Ruler Malley in his report to the Grand Lodge in 1928 paid a tribute to the work of the Social and Welfare Committee and particularly to his Chairman, Past Grand Exalted Ruler John P. Sullivan, stating that the Committee under Past Grand Exalted Ruler Sullivan's leadership had a record of achievement during the years of existence which was most commendable, and he credited this largely to the enthusiasm and the initiative of Chairman Sullivan.

He stated, however, that he felt that the Order had reached a stage of development which required a reorganization of its committee structure and reassignment of duties. He referred to the fact that the primary duty of the Elks National Foundation Trustees, just created, would be to accumulate and administer their fund, but that since the fund was to be used to foster the humanitarian works taken up by groups of subordinate lodges, the Foundation Trustees must require intimate knowledge of Elk activities of civic, social and community interest, and guide the group movements of lodges in these fields.

He felt, under those circumstances, that conflict with the Social and Community Welfare Committee would be unavoidable and would handicap both agencies.

He therefore recommended that the Social and Community Welfare Committee be discontinued and that the guidance of welfare work conducted by individual subordinate lodges with subordinate lodge funds be exercised by the Good of the Order Committee, and that the ritual work which had also been directed by the Social and Community Welfare Committee be entrusted to a Committee created for the purpose.

This recommendation of the Grand Exalted Ruler was adopted.

At this Convention W. C. Robertson, reporting for the Committee on Social and Community Welfare as acting Chairman, referred to the fact that during the six years the Committee had been in operation the interest in Social and Community Welfare had been more than doubled.

He stated that in 1922-1923, $1,456,501.69 was expended by subordinate lodges in the interest of this work and that in the year just closed there had been similarly expended $2,890,288.65.

He detailed these expenses as follows:

Amount spent on summer outings for the underprivileged $	135,492.13
Amount contributed toward the maintenance of 22,539 persons in camps and health resorts during the past summer	40,548.65
Amount spent for playground donations, athletics, etc.	20,820.71
Rent paid for 912 needy families during winter	37,211.97
Food relief brought to 10,311 needy families at times other than Christmas, Thanksgiving, etc.	112,443.40
Gifts of clothing (at times other than Christmas or holidays) to 15,459 needy individuals	72,992.95
Thanksgiving baskets sent to 11,316 needy families	48,863.28
Christmas benefactions extended to 99,221 needy families and 426,662 children through baskets, tree parties, shows, gift distributions, entertainments and donations to Christmas community funds	898,006.55
Donations to Boy Scouts, Girl Scouts, Girl Reserves, Camp Fire Girls, Sea Scouts, etc.	45,760.87
Aid extended to 2,578 youngsters through Big Brother work	11,628.82
Special Medical Aid extended to 2,862 needy cases	64,917.18
Amount spent for entertainments in hospitals (exclusive of donations of sweetmeats, fruits, talent, music)	18,008.98
Special Aid extended to 4,627 crippled children	138,880.85
Amount spent for donations to hospitals, upkeep of wards, flowers to sick and bereaved, funeral expenses	529,184.90
Various forms of Veterans' relief	7,118.87
Amount spent for public observance of Flag Day	61,595.27
Educational Activities of all kinds, ranging from furnishing books or clothing, glasses or dentistry to needy school children, and the support of milk funds, to college endowments and scholarship maintenance	77,020.53
Amount raised by benefits, tag days, etc., for other agencies of welfare work, and donated to them	27,775.71

Fuel furnished to 3,727 needy families during winter............ $ 40,776.24
Flood Relief (to Grand Exalted Ruler's Fund or Red Cross)   128,730.70
Other donations, too miscellaneous in their nature to be
    classified individually (local disaster relief, traveling ex-
    penses, cost of band concert, moving a piano to the next
    county, providing a duck dinner in almshouse, etc.)........   372,510.09
                                                                ─────────────
    Total reported cash expenditure for welfare work.... $2,890,288.65

It should be remembered that these figures cover the expenditures
of the subordinate lodges only, and do not include similar expenditures by the State Associations and the Grand Lodge.

Although the Grand Lodge Committee on Social and Community Welfare was eliminated in 1928, a very large percentage
of the lodges of the Order continued Social and Community Welfare Committees and many have such committees at the present
time.

However, whether or not that term was used for a subordinate
lodge committee dealing with matters of community assistance, it
is true that the subordinate lodges, practically without any exceptions, continued to carry on and extend their social and community welfare work.

While dollars-and-cents figures do not indicate the real community activities and the results, they are, at least, a partial guide
to what the lodges have been doing.

In 1950-51, Grand Exalted Ruler Kyle emphasized community
service as an opportunity for subordinate lodges to play an important, if not vital, role in strengthening the country's social
fabric in the mounting struggle against communism. This program for developing Elks lodges' relations with their home communities was a major reason for the establishment of District
Deputy Clinics, which were held for the first time in Grand Exalted
Ruler Kyle's administration.

For the year 1966–1967 the subordinate lodges expended a
total of $8,119,745.95.

The details by items were as follows:

Relief of Members, Widows, Orphans,
    Dependents, Burials, etc. ....$ 630,482.37
Summer Outings, Camps and Health Resorts 371,820.55
Cerebral Palsy 905,474.96
Crippled Children 973,087.51
Medical Aid and Hospitals 470,102.16

Care of Needy Families, including
Thanksgiving & Christmas Baskets 1,095,566.14
Elks National Foundation 376,451.39
Youth Work (except for scholarships,
free textbooks, etc.) 1,341,574.97
Scholarships, Free Textbooks, etc. 570,487.49
Red Cross, Salvation Army, etc. 241,474.43
Veterans' Relief 184,559.59
Miscellaneous 705,846.75
Flag Day, Constitution Day, Fourth of July, etc. ... 252,817.64
Total.................... $8,119,745.95

S E C T I O N

Sixth Decade

In this Decade there was recorded the first drop in membership during the Order's existence, although for the entire Decade there was an increase of 63 per cent.

From 1918 to 1924 there was an increase in membership of 70 per cent. The following year there was the first decrease of any year since the Order was founded and that was a decrease of 9 per cent.

From 1924 to 1928 there was a drop of a little less than 4 per cent.

It was in this Decade that the Order took its first stand as a vigorous opponent of Communism (then called Bolshevism) which it has retained to the present day.

It is interesting to note, at the time this History is being written, when the evils of Communism are so generally understood and opposed throughout the country, that over thirty years ago, at the beginning of the Sixth Decade in the life of the Order, it was even then fighting that evil ideology.

BRUCE A. CAMPBELL
1918-19

WILLIAM M. ABBOTT
1920-21

FRANK L. RAIN
1919-20

W. W. MOUNTAIN
1921-22

J. EDGAR MASTERS
1922-23

Grand Exalted Rulers

SIXTH DECADE

1918-1928

JAMES G. McFARLAND
1923-24

WILLIAM H. ATWELL
1925-26

JOHN G. PRICE
1924-25

CHARLES H. GRAKELOW
1926-27

JOHN F. MALLEY
1927-28

The close of World War I coming in this Decade, there was authorized and erected the Elks National Memorial Building in Chicago as "A suitable Memorial to the valor and sacrifice of those heroes who have shed a radiance of glory over the whole Order."

The result is a Memorial Building recognized by the well informed as one of the most magnificent buildings of its character in the world.

It should be visited by every member of the Order.

Under the direction of the Grand Lodge Commission entrusted with the responsibility of erecting the Memorial Building was placed the creation of a "National Journal"—*The Elks Magazine*, with which every Elk is thoroughly familiar.

Probably the first request for assistance coming to the Order from an important branch of the United States Government was made by the Secretary of the Navy to assist in raising the money for the restoration of "Old Ironsides," the historic frigate "The Constitution," which request was made and executed in this Decade.

As this Decade drew to a close there was established the greatest benevolent agency ever created by the Order, the Elks National Foundation.

It is a source of pride to all Elks that in the first twenty-four years of its existence the Foundation has accumulated a fund of around $3,000,000 and has expended out of its interest income for educational, charitable and humanitarian purposes three quarters of a million dollars.

Sixth Decade——1918-1928

In this Decade those who served the Order as Grand Exalted Rulers were:

Bruce A. Campbell, East St. Louis, Ill., Lodge No. 664	1918-1919
Frank L. Rain, Fairbury, Nebr., Lodge No. 1203	1919-1920
William M. Abbott, San Francisco, Cal., Lodge No. 3	1920-1921
W. W. Mountain, Flint, Mich., Lodge No. 222	1921-1922
J. Edgar Masters, Charleroi, Pa., Lodge No. 494	1922-1923
James G. McFarland, Watertown, S. D., Lodge No. 838	1923-1924
John G. Price, Columbus, Ohio, Lodge No. 37	1924-1925
William H. Atwell, Dallas, Texas, Lodge No. 71	1925-1926
Charles H. Grakelow, Philadelphia, Pa., Lodge No. 2	1926-1927
John F. Malley, Springfield, Mass., Lodge No. 61	1927-1928

Fred C. Robinson, who had served as Grand Secretary for fourteen years prior to the beginning of the Sixth Decade, continued in that office until September, 1927, when he resigned.

The then Grand Exalted Ruler, John F. Malley, appointed Past Grand Exalted Ruler J. Edgar Masters to fill out the unexpired term.

MEMBERSHIP AND CHARITABLE EXPENDITURES

In these ten years the Order grew in membership from 493,733 to 808,241.

The number of lodges increased from 1,280 to 1,420.

YEAR	MEMBERSHIP	CHARITABLE EXPENDITURES
1918-1919	527,522	$1,049,206.73
1919-1920	645,678	1,285,560.16
1920-1921	767,661	1,566,234.63
1921-1922	812,657	2,044,218.97
1922-1923	826,825	2,017,561.11
1923-1924	839,429	2,432,641.50
1924-1925	832,083	2,484,250.18
1925-1926	825,960	2,407,008.10
1926-1927	816,000	2,497,923.97
1927-1928	808,658	2,556,634.44

During these years, the cities in which the Grand Lodge Sessions were held were:

1919	Atlantic City, New Jersey	1924	Boston, Massachusetts
1920	Chicago, Illinois	1925	Portland, Oregon
1921	Los Angeles, California	1926	Chicago, Illinois
1922	Atlantic City, New Jersey	1927	Cincinnati, Ohio
1923	Atlanta, Georgia	1928	Miami, Florida

At the end of this Decade the assets of the 1,420 lodges amounted to $96,529,453.10.

Communism

Bolshevism

Grand Exalted Ruler Campbell, in his report to the Grand Lodge Session at Atlantic City in 1919, advised that Seattle, Washington, Lodge had communicated with him saying that a member of the

Order had expressed his sympathy with Bolshevism and stating that he was for the Bolshevists. The lodge wanted to know whether or not charges could be preferred against him and he be expelled from the Order for his stand.

Grand Exalted Ruler Campbell referred this matter to the Judiciary Committee, and at the same Grand Lodge Session Chairman William M. Abbott submitted a very comprehensive reply on the subject.

The Abbott Report

From that report the following are extracts:

"The determination of this question necessarily involves a correct understanding of what the term 'Bolshevism' means. According to a very late authority, 'Bolsheviki' is defined as a Russian party of extreme radicals having as its aim a complete realization of the Socialist community.

"Bolshevism is no new thing even in Russia. Formerly its predecessors called themselves 'Nihilists' or 'Terrorists' or 'Anarchists.' By whatever name they went, their methods were and are identical. The Bolsheviki stand for the theory of a permanent revolution and the overthrow of existing governments by force and not by peaceful means. They put forth their faith in but one kind of movement—an armed insurrection of workmen and peasants.

"In his final analysis, a Bolshevist is one who believes that the will of the people unhampered by any constitutional guarantees or legal provision previously enacted for the protection of life, liberty or property shall be controlling, and that the rights of liberty and property be subject to the unbridled will of a Soviet or legislature.

"In its present form, it is a menace to our American ideals and constitutional government. It is the antithesis of Americanism, for whatever shall undermine our institutions and make prejudice or fancy superior to our constitutional laws is an attack upon our flag and a blow to our Order.

"Every Elk has taken a solemn obligation to support the Constitution and laws of the United States of America, and we have been taught as one of the fundamental principles of the Order that the American flag, typical as it is of our form of government, should be first in our hearts as loyal Elks.

"No man can be a Bolshevist and remain a loyal American citizen.

"Among the things defined in Section 83A of the Grand Lodge Statutes is a violation of obligation. Clearly, any member of the Order who publicly proclaims that he is a Bolshevist or that his sympathy is with the Bolshevists or that 'he is for them' and other sentiments of similar character is not worthy to remain a member of our great American Order, because if he is sincere, he is lending aid and support to the undermining of the Constitution and Statutes of the United States and is directly aiding in and sympathizing with an attempt to overthrow by force the government under which we live, and substitute in its place a form of government which is foreign to our ideals and to the principles which were set up in this country and expressed in and protected by the Constitution of the United States, and this is a violation of his obligation.

"We are therefore of the opinion that if you believe that the statements of the member were uttered in all sincerity and expressed his views upon the subject of Bolshevism, you should prefer charges against him."

Grand Exalted Ruler Campbell stated that he heartily concurred in this opinion, and recommended that at that Session of the Grand Lodge strong and vigorous resolutions be passed, pledging our Order to do everything in its power to drive from our country all organizations and individuals who are not in sympathy with our form of government, who do not give undivided allegiance to its flag, and who seek to disorganize and disrupt the great principles upon which America is founded, and that we pledge ourselves to be steadfastly opposed to, and pledge by lawful means to drive from the nation, the Bolsheviki, the Anarchists, the I.W.W., and all other organizations and individuals who do not believe in America, and in America alone.

At that Session the following resolution was adopted:

"Let it therefore be resolved that the Grand Lodge of the Benevolent and Protective Order of Elks, in annual session assembled, hereby pledges this Order to use all lawful means to check and prevent the extension of the dangerous doctrines which threaten our free institutions and our flag, and that no person should be permitted to join or remain in our Order who openly or covertly, indirectly or directly gives aid or support to the doctrines and practices and purposes of the Bolsheviki, Anarchists, I.W.W. or similar organizations, or who does not give undivided allegiance to our flag and the great principles which constitute a free government of which it is the emblem."

No Grand Exalted Ruler between Campbell and Shannon made any reference to Communism in his report to the Grand Lodge.

Grand Exalted Ruler Michael F. Shannon, in his speech of acceptance in 1934, said:

"This year there stands before the Order of Elks, an objective more important than all others. While the President of the United States and all other duly appointed officers of our government and the legitimate organizations of industry and labor are struggling to restore order out of economic chaos, forces that have nothing in common with these duly constituted officials; forces that have nothing to do with these industrial organizations, that have no sympathy with the accredited leaders of labor, who refer to the great mass of our people—the small home owner, the ordinary businessman, the men of the sciences and the professions as the 'bourgeois'—contend that in this country there is a class apart whom they pretend to love called 'the worker and the farmer.'

"These may rank with the lowest grade of workers and the most poorly educated farmers of the most backward of all foreign countries. To exalt this imaginary class, a separate class that does not exist in America, they would destroy the business of the country, disrupt forever the family relations, abolish religion, liquidate American institutions and tear down the Flag."

He then quoted Governor Alfred Ritchie of Maryland as saying:

"The next trouble will not only be against depression, but against Communist forces far more destructive."

He quoted, also, Bainbridge Colby, Secretary of State under President Wilson, as follows:

"The Russian revolution is looked upon as a prelude to the overthrow of democratic civilization throughout the world."

He also referred to a statement of Josef V. Stalin which appeared in "Pravda," the official paper of the Communists in Russia, as follows:

"The Communist Internationale has created possibilities for the Communist Party of the United States to reach the stage where it is able to prepare the masses for the coming revolution."

He told his audience that the time had come when the issue is "Shall it be the Stars and Stripes of the United States of America or shall it be the Red Flag of the Communist Internationale?"

He stated that the people of the country were divided into three groups: those who would destroy the churches, degrade the family relations and salute the Red Flag of Revolution. He said there is a second group of people who are apathetic and will not do anything.

In the third group is the Benevolent and Protective Order of Elks of the U. S. A. He called upon them to be alert and watchful against the Communists, to investigate the school teachers, to close public schools against Communists' meetings, to support the public officials and encourage them and to support and encourage the Police Department.

Finally he said:

"When the 1,400 Elk Lodges move forward like well-trained sharpshooters at the zero hour, we will have made a substantial contribution to the well being of our great country.

"The watchword of the Benevolent and Protective Order of Elks is 'pro-America.' I give you this as a cornerstone of the program of 1934."

The Pro-America Petitions Are Presented

Grand Exalted Ruler Michael F. Shannon addressing the 299 Elk members of the Senate and House of Representatives as he presented the petition, bearing hundreds of thousands of signatures, advocating his eight-point anti-communist legislative program.

Vice-President John N. Garner, who responded for the Senate, and Speaker Joseph W. Byrnes, who replied for the House, may be seen behind the petitions. This impressive ceremony was held on the steps of the Capitol on March 26, 1935.

The following March 26th, Grand Exalted Ruler Shannon addressed the 299 Elk members of the Senate and House of Representatives of the United States as he presented a petition bearing hundreds of thousands of signatures advocating an anti-communist legislative program.

Vice President John N. Garner responded for the Senate and Speaker Joseph W. Byrnes replied for the House of Representatives.

July 1938——July 1939

Grand Exalted Ruler McCormick

In his talk at the opening ceremonies in 1939 Grand Exalted Ruler McCormick said:

"Communism is diametrically opposed to Democracy and Americanism: And, as Elks, we dedicate our monies and our manpower to an attempt to rid our country of every person who is in any way, shape or form connected with it.

"Without God there can be no Democracy; without religion there can be no government by the people and for the people.

"So I commend to my Brother Elks and to the friends of the Order, continuation of all humanitarian, civic and community welfare endeavors and a militant Americanism, to the end that we may give this great country of ours to our successors as it was given to us by our fathers and mothers, grandfathers and grandmothers, a country with a government of, for and by the people, where all of God's creatures may be accorded happiness and opportunity.

"My Brother Elks—Democracy cannot, must not, shall not fail!"

In his report to the Grand Lodge in Session in St. Louis in 1939 Grand Exalted Ruler Edward J. McCormick said:

"Realizing that our country was in greater danger at this time than ever before in its history because of the widespread existence of subversive activities and because of the 'boring from within' program of un-American organizations, I called upon the subordinate lodges of Elkdom to dedicate a considerable part of the lodge year to the promulgation of Americanism. The first week in March was designated by me as 'Americanism' week and all lodges were asked to participate. A program of activity was formulated and sent to all Grand Lodge Officers, State Presidents and Exalted Rulers."

The Grand Exalted Ruler stated that the response had been most outstanding and he expressed his gratitude to all the churches and fraternal and patriotic organizations who extended encouragement and help during Americanism Week, to the governors of many States and to the mayors of hundreds of cities and to the many statesmen who, by pronouncement and letter, gave active and moral support. He said:

"As a result of our efforts, other organizations have been inoculated to greater activity and legislators and public servants have searched with greater tenacity for ways and means to check the activities of those who would take from us 'liberty and freedom.' "

July 1939——July 1940

Grand Exalted Ruler Warner

Grand Exalted Ruler Henry C. Warner in his Speech of Acceptance at the St. Louis Session in 1939 also emphasized the great danger of Communism and totalitarianism and said:

"We must have freedom to enable us to progress and we can only develop to the utmost in a free country. When one man becomes so powerful that he restricts his fellow men, danger follows. If the creative mind of the individual is crushed, only sterility remains, from which no good is likely to develop.

"Those engaged in many forms of endeavor frequently feel that all of the progress of the nation is dependent upon the effort in which they are engaged, but the members of the Order of Elks know that industry and thrift and the principles in the Bill of Rights, in the Constitution of the United States, and in the long line of decisions of the courts upholding freedom and liberty are the foundations upon which the future of this Government must depend. They know, too, that the teachings of religion must be followed to insure good citizenship.

"Stern duties will continue to confront every American citizen and every member of our Order during the coming year, and those duties must not be neglected. Our members must meet those duties with intelligence, courage and unquestioned patriotism. Our problem is to determine how our efforts should be directed in order safely to insure the perpetuation of our governmental institutions.

"A Grand Lodge effort for several years has been devoted to combatting un-American activities with excellent results. Those who know history will realize the fallacy of Communism. Communistic plans have been tried under the most favorable circumstances, and have always failed. The educated person realizes the innate desire of man for prosperity and well-being, for liberty of conscience, for freedom to earn and to spend, for equality before the law, for the right of property and equal opportunities for youth. History teaches that social changes must come in a slow and orderly, well regulated manner.

"If we hasten, as did Germany and Spain, there is revolution and reaction. Civilization progresses by evolution not revolution.

"The best way to combat Communism is to educate against it. It is fortunate that the children of this country have an opportunity for education, but we must teach them the true meaning of a republican form of government.

"Communism flourishes where the souls of the people are dead, where they have lost their true conception of the value of liberty. Dictators do not exist where there is a dominant, active, liberty-loving people.

"The United States is the last great stronghold of an undefeated republican form of government. It will remain such a stronghold only so long as we have the determination to defend it.

"The most precious possession in the world today is the American Bill of Rights. It was obtained at great cost and sacrifice and it must be retained, even at a greater cost. The right of free speech, free press and free religion, yes, even the right to a republican form of government is now being challenged. It is our duty to defend it.

"In that we will not fail."

July 1940——July 1941

Grand Exalted Ruler Joseph G. Buch

During the administration of Grand Exalted Ruler Buch the war clouds began to gather and the patriotic efforts of the Grand Exalted Ruler and the members of the Order were divided between participation in movements designed to protect our country against subversive activities and to strengthen its preparedness for war.

Before that Grand Lodge year had ended, war had come and the thoughts and activities of all patriotic citizens were concentrated on contributing to the success of our country in the war into which it had been forced.

July 1941——July 1945

During all this period our country was engaged in the great World War II.

Not only were the thoughts and efforts of all loyal Americans devoted to the winning in that war fought on foreign soil but at the same time subversive activities here in our country were materially lessened.

On June 10, 1943, the Communist International (Comintern) was dissolved and Communist Information Bureau (Cominform) was set up.

Whether this move was merely a gesture or a genuine move in lessening the subversive activities of the Communists, it was generally thought that from the time this move was taken until the end of World War II, during which period our country and the Soviet Republic were partners in arms, there was indeed such a lessening.

However, the fighting phase of World War II was hardly over before those activities were renewed.

July 1945——July 1946

It was during the term of Grand Exalted Ruler Wade H. Kepner that the renewed subversive activities of the Communists began to be evident.

In his address at the Grand Lodge Session in 1946, Grand Exalted Ruler Kepner said:

"As I have traveled around the country I couldn't help seeing and feeling the danger of another sneak attack—one which can be far more formidable and may be far closer upon us, more real than any of us realize.

"I have been asked all over the country from time to time, 'What is the standing of the Elks in regard to Communists?' I think you have heard me express my stand.

"You know that the Order of Elks is going to fight the 'ism' of any foreign nation that attempts to invade our shores, even though it is one who is supposed to have been our ally in the war.

"We are going to fight it and be on our guard in fifteen hundred communities. There are people who hide behind the protection of the American flag and tear down the things in this country that have come to be so dear to us.

"There are enemies from without and there are enemies from within.

"We are going to stand by America. We are going to stand by those principles that we believe in with our fists clenched.

"We are going to face people looking at us. We will stand by our colors.

"We will not compromise to anybody no matter who he may be if we do not believe the principles he preaches or teaches."

July 1946——July 1947

In his Speech of Acceptance at the same Grand Lodge Session, Grand Exalted Ruler Broughton indicated his recognition of the growing threat of subversive activities in the following words:

"The Benevolent and Protective Order of Elks has thrived because it is truly American and in these trying times that lie ahead when peace is in the making, we can give this as a lesson to nations that want freedom and are willing to subscribe to a doctrine of liberty. You cannot have liberty where tyrants exist or where the people have little choice or voice in their government. To preserve our liberty we have a job ahead. We cannot allow the voice of an enemy, whether within or without to preach against the principles we have so valiantly fought for and be true to those who gave their lives in World Wars I and II.

"We are willing and stand ready to aid suffering humanity the world over; but, when some foreign group attempts to spread un-American propaganda to undermine our government, we rebel. That is our fight and to a finish. This sort of seed is foreign to our teachings and patriotic duty. Let us keep it foreign.

"I, here and now, promise you my sponsors, to defend our system of government, with all the strength I have. This I owe to you and to the greatest of all American Orders. Our Order did not grow or prosper from inactivity. It grew because we stood for certain principles and we have implanted those principles in the hearts and minds of individuals. We stand for the four essential freedoms. We believe in the brotherhood of man and down through the ages we have kept the faith."

July 1947——July 1952

Grand Exalted Ruler Lewis, during his period of service, 1947-1948, vigorously denounced Communism and the subversive activities of Communists and strongly urged all Elks to be constantly on guard against this menace.

Freedom Train

During that year there was created by the American Heritage Foundation and the Attorney-General of the United States the Freedom Train.

The Freedom Train, designed to help "raise the level of active citizenship," carried originals or reproductions of many of the

Grand Exalted Ruler L. A. Lewis directs attention to the "Freedom Train" which he visited during its stay in New York City in September, 1948.

most important documents in the history of the United States, such as Jefferson's draft of the Declaration of Independence, Orders of the Continental Congress, Lincoln letters and papers and scores of others to the people of three hundred communities across the country.

On the editorial page of *The Elks Magazine* of December 1947, there appeared the following:

"Grand Exalted Ruler L. A. Lewis, in the line of official business, was in New York City at the time the Freedom Train set out upon its journey. He thus became a first hand witness to the efforts of Communists to sabotage the train's objective by the establishment of a picket line for the distribution of literature calculated to belittle its patriotic motives. Incensed at what he termed the effrontery of this move, the Grand Exalted Ruler called upon every lodge of the Order to reply to this Communist affront by redoubling support of the Train.

"The Grand Exalted Ruler's indignation at this Communistic maneuver was well taken for it evidenced the fact that Communism was again on the loose. Its action toward the Freedom Train was undoubtedly for the purpose of taking soundings as to just how far preliminary subversive activities could be carried on.

"The insult to the Freedom Train and the announcement that the Comintern has been revived are an alert signal to all Americans. It will not be long before communist front organizations revive and the mills of subversive action begin to grind.

"Every Elk, every lodge of Elks, individually and collectively, must be ready to fight behind our militant Grand Exalted Ruler to uphold his determination that all the force that Elkdom can muster shall be 'dedicated to the preservation of American rights and American liberties.' "

At the Grand Lodge Session in Philadelphia in 1948, Grand Exalted Ruler Lewis recommended in his annual report the adoption of the following resolution:

"BE IT RESOLVED, That Section 144 of the Grand Lodge Statutes, be and the same hereby is amended by adding at the end of the first paragraph thereof the following words:

"No person shall be accepted as a member of this Order who is directly or indirectly a member or in any way connected or affiliated with the Communist Party, or who believes in the overthrow of our government by force. The official form of application blank shall contain such questions necessary to disclose past or present affiliations with said party or adherence to such beliefs."

This resolution was adopted unanimously.

There was then introduced before the Grand Lodge the following resolution:

"BE IT RESOLVED, That our statutes be and the same hereby are amended by adding thereto the following section:

"Section 84 A. Any member of this Order who is a member of the Communist Party, or who, either directly or indirectly participates in activities of said party, or who advocates the overthrow of our government by force shall be guilty of a violation of his oath and upon being found guilty thereof by action of a subordinate forum shall be expelled from the Order."

The Statutes were thus amended.

When Grand Exalted Ruler George I. Hall made his report to the Grand Lodge Session in Cleveland in 1949 he reminded his audience that he adopted as his slogan for the year "make Democracy work."

He said that he believed that during the year the Order had been successful in building in the minds of the youth of the United States a higher regard for their birthright and a deeper desire to preserve our "American Way of Life." In taking the position that he did Grand Exalted Ruler Hall recognized two fundamental truths:

(1) That building a stronger Democracy is one of the most effective ways to combat subversive elements, and

(2) That teaching true Americanism to the youth is one of the most effective methods of assuring the future strength of Democracy.

An outstanding feature of his program was the Essay Contest throughout the country on the subject "Why Democracy Works," participated in by hundreds of thousands of high school pupils.

This Essay Contest not only had great educational and patriotic influence but possessed major publicity value.

National prizes were:

First prize   — $1,000 United States Bond
Second prize — $ 500 United States Bond
Third prize   — $ 250 United States Bond
Five prizes of — $ 50 each in United States Bonds

The contest was carried on by the Lodge Activities Committee of the Grand Lodge, William J. Jernick, Nutley, N. J., Lodge No. 1290, Chairman, with the cooperation of the Public Relations Director, Otho DeVilbiss.

State Associations and subordinate lodges were requested to cooperate, and they set up the following awards:

State Associations   — $9,045.00
Deputy Districts   —   2,720.00
Subordinate Lodges — 87,976.25

This, added to the national awards, made a total of $101,741.25.

Harold E. Stassen, St. Paul, Minnesota Lodge No. 559, President of the University of Pennsylvania, was Chairman of the Judges.

The other judges were Rabbi Dr. Samuel Belkin, President of Yeshiva University, New York City, and the very Reverend Francis X. Talbot, S. J., President of Loyola University of Baltimore.

National prizes were awarded as follows:

First prize, William Johnson, 17, McAlester, Okla.
Second prize, Dorothy J. Simonds, 17, Lowell, Mass.
Third prize, Grayce Ann Ahern, 17, Middletown, Conn.

Grand Exalted Ruler Emmett T. Anderson in his report at the Grand Lodge Session in Miami, in 1950, said:

"The preamble of our Constitution contains the words:
      'to quicken the spirit of American patriotism'

"Since the inception of our Order, we have demonstrated our faith in our government and the Order of Elks today, as never before, is bringing to the attention of our members and all Americans the dangers of Communism.

"Our definite stand for Americanism has prompted our joining and supporting the newly-formed organization known as the 'All American Conference to Combat Communism.'

"This great American group supports wholeheartedly the basic liberties which are assured by the Constitution of the United States—freedom of speech, freedom of the press, freedom of assembly and freedom of religion."

In accepting his election as Grand Exalted Ruler in 1950, Joseph B. Kyle said:

"Elkdom always has been and always will be the impregnable foe of Communism. Our hatred of Communism comes from a clear understanding of communism's evil nature and evil designs upon the liberties of men and the peace of the world.

"In the early years of its rise to power in Russia, communism's propaganda succeeded in convincing some people, who should have known better, that it was a liberating force destined to bring peace and happiness to millions. Recent history has stripped the mask from communism, and today most of these wishful thinkers of a few years ago now recognize communism for what it was, what it is and what it always will be—a poisonous corruption in the blood-stream of civilization.

"Nevertheless, there are some people who are so stupid, or venal or ambitious that they are willing to sell our country to Moscow. We are in a fight for everything that decent people value and, with the stakes so high, we cannot afford to be tolerant to traitors. They must be sought relentlessly, exposed and punished like any other enemy of society.

"Neither can we afford to tolerate those who are so blind that they cannot see communism for what it has proved itself to be.

"Anyone who persists in collaborating with communist organizations or in parroting communist propaganda should not be surprised to find his fellow men united against him.

"Elkdom will continue to be a militant, dynamic force that lives, preaches and teaches the glory of our Republic. The revolutionary spirit that proclaimed man's inalienable right to life, liberty and the pursuit of happiness flames today in the hearts of more than a million Elks. It lights the Star of Fidelity that blazes above the altars of 1568 Elk Lodges throughout the United States. It is the spirit that urges us to go neither right nor left, but to go ahead.

"I declare that, so great is our devotion to our country and its way of life, we are all determined, as one, that while there is an Elk left on this earth, our country shall never run the slightest risk of prostration beneath the trampling feet of communism or any foreign foe.

"To that we cooperatively pledge."

When Howard R. Davis was elected Grand Exalted Ruler at Chicago in 1951, he said:

"We are Americans all. In these uncertain times, with the threat of an ever-widening war hovering black on the horizon, we, as Elks, have no time for any political philosophy, any national ideology, that subordinates the individual and his freedom of action to rule by the State.

"And we care not what that new rule may be called—fascism, nazism or communism. These are merely different names for the same thing. None of them is American; none of them can find favor in the sight of God; all of them are treasonable to Elks everywhere.

"As Elks we shall not only resist to the utmost any and all threats from without, but we shall be just as quick to combat all attempts to destroy from within. We shall strike to 'Keep America Awake.'

"As Elks and Americans we hold our national heritage to be God-given, and we shall continue to guard it zealously. Twice since the turn of the present century America has saved modern civilization from the efforts of power-mad aggressors to destroy it. For the third time in half a century we again stand guard over the liberties of free men and it is written in the stars that the ultimate fate of Joseph Stalin will be exactly the same as experienced by his blood-thirsty predecessors in their lust for power.

"In these perilous times every resource of the Benevolent and Protective Order of Elks is at the command of our country."

At the Grand Lodge Session in Chicago, Illinois, in 1967, the following resolution was adopted to a rising vote of acclamation:

"WHEREAS *the Benevolent and Protective Order of Elks has been steadfast in upholding the principles of Americanism and its members have served as exemplars of patriotic citizenship and;*

"WHEREAS *the United States has been engaged in a bitter struggle in an underclared but de facto war believed to be manifestation of the 'cold' war with Communist elements;*

"AND, WHEREAS, *subversive groups and individuals within our country have flouted the authority of the United States Government, have sought by illegal means to impede the successful prosecution of the conflict in Vietnam, have desecrated the American flag and thereby committed acts of treason under the shield of rights and freedoms guaranteed by the Constitution of the United States;*

"NOW, THEREFORE, BE IT RESOLVED *that the Grand Lodge of the Benevolent and Protective Order of Elks in convention assembled speaking on behalf of over 1,400,000 members hereby proclaims its complete allegiance to all men in the Armed Forces of the United States of America and strongly condemns all irresponsible and disloyal acts which have a tendency to give aid and comfort to the enemy, to prolong the war, and to impair the morale of the valiant members of our Armed Forces;*

"AND THAT by this reaffirmation of the patriotic principles which guide the destiny of our Order, we solicit and urge the 'support of all other patriotic American citizens and groups in public condemnation of all subversive elements."

During the period from October 1946 to December 1967 the following articles by prominent and informed writers appeared in *The Elks Magazine.*

1. *THE NEED OF THE MOMENT, Owen J. Roberts, October 1946

2. *WE'LL TELL THE WORLD, Dickson Hartwell, November 1946

3. *LAND OF THE FREE, James A. Farley, April 1948

4. *INTERNATIONAL A-BOMB CONTROL, John M. Hancock, June 1948

5. RUSSIA AND US — CAN WE GET ALONG?, William Henry Chamberlin, September 1948

6. KREMLIN BLUEPRINT, Louis J. Alber, July 1950

7. WHAT SHALL WE DO ABOUT CHINA?, Bruno Shaw, August, September 1949

8. *DEMOCRACY — THE AMERICAN WAY, Alben W. Barkley, November 1949

9. MEETING THE COMMUNIST CHALLENGE, George S. Counts, March 1950

10. WHY WE HAVE COMMUNISTS, Bruno Shaw, September 1950

11. FOE TO FREEDOM, J. Edgar Hoover, October 1950

12. RUSSIA'S WEAPON OF SATELLITISM, W. B. Courtney, January 1951

13. *AMI GO HOME, Corey Ford, March 1951

14. DANGER, COMMUNISTS AT WORK, Bruno Shaw, April 1951

15. COMMUNISM — WHAT YOU CAN DO ABOUT IT, T. C. Kirkpatrick and F. J. McNamara, July 1951

16. CRACKING THE IRON CURTAIN, Bruno Shaw, November 1951

17. STALIN'S TROJAN HORSE, Bruno Shaw, November, 1952

18. CAN WE COMPROMISE WITH RED CHINA, Bruno Shaw, July, 1955.

---

*Articles not dealing with Communism directly or principally but in which reference is made to Russia, the Cold War, Soviet partisanship in the UN, etc.

Elks National Headquarters and Memorial Building

In his report to the Grand Lodge in 1920, Grand Exalted Ruler Frank L. Rain said:

"The office of the Grand Secretary is at present located on the seventh floor of an office building in the city of Dubuque, Iowa. The rooms occupied by the Grand Secretary and his assistants are inadequate and inconvenient.

"There are no fireproof vaults in the building and there is not sufficient room in the offices of the Grand Secretary to conduct the affairs of his office, keep lodge supplies and to store the records of the Order and they are consequently stored in the basement of the building. If there should be a fire in the building now occupied by the Grand Secretary, which is the best office building in Dubuque, many records of inestimable value would be destroyed and, in a great many instances, records and miscellaneous articles that could not be duplicated.

"The Order has reached a stage in its history when it should have a permanent place for the offices of the Grand Secretary and National Headquarters. A centrally located city should be selected and suitable headquarters leased, or better still, a building should be built by the Order, for a permanent office for the Grand Secretary and National Headquarters for the Order and, if a building should be built in the future, such a building should be so arranged as to provide room for a printing establishment wherein all of the supplies of the Order could be printed and such an establishment operated by the Order would be a great saving to the Order at present and in the future.

"I recommend that the incoming Grand Exalted Ruler appoint a committee of five to thoroughly investigate the advisability of moving the Grand Secretary's office to a more adequate and permanent location and to ascertain whether it would be advisable to lease office rooms or build a building for a permanent office for the Grand Secretary and National Headquarters for the Order in some centrally located city and report the result of its investigations to the next Grand Lodge Session."

Acting upon this suggestion the incoming Grand Exalted Ruler was directed to appoint a committee whose duty it would be to investigate the advisability of an establishment in some suitable, centrally located city, of a permanent National Headquarters for the Order and to report at the next Grand Lodge Session its recommendations.

The Grand Exalted Ruler, William M. Abbott, entrusted this responsibility to the members of the War Relief Commission.

Reporting to the Grand Lodge Session in Los Angeles in 1921, Grand Exalted Ruler Abbott said:

"Because of the great confidence, standing and ability of the War Relief Commission, I referred the work of the National Headquarters Committee to them. I have attended the most important of their meetings and participated in their labors. Distance, however, has prevented me from attending all of the many meetings held in an endeavor to work out the problems before the committee.

"I shall not attempt to review the work of this committee or to comment upon their report except to say that they have brought to the work of this committee the same high degree of intelligent and unselfish effort as they brought to the work of the War Relief Commission. With painstaking care they have visited, canvassed and considered the claims of all cities desiring recognition.

"The selection of a suitable location for national headquarters was not, however, the only work of this committee as appears from their report. As I stated, I do not propose to comment further upon the report of this committee except to say I concur fully in its recommendations and believe it carries with it the solution of one of the very important problems before the Order and I recommend that the Grand Lodge adopt their report."

At this Grand Lodge Session the Elks National Headquarters Committee made an extensive report on this subject.

Elks National Headquarters and Memorial Building

In that report the Committee said:

"But there is another feature of the National Headquarters Building project which your Committee believes to be of the utmost importance, one which appeals not only to the tenderest sentiments of the Order, but also to its proper sense of obligation and duty.

"It will be remembered that more than seventy thousand members of the Order of Elks were in the service of our country during the World War. More than one thousand of these Brothers made the last supreme sacrifice in that service and laid down their lives in exemplification of their fidelity to the obligation of loyal patriotism and devotion to country which they assumed at our altars.

"No clearer duty, nor one more in accord with every tenet of our Order, lies before us than that of providing a suitable memorial to the valor and sacrifice of these heroes who have shed a radiance of glory over the whole Order.

"That memorial should be not only worthy of the splendid heroism which it would commemorate but also worthy of the great fraternity whose love and pride and grateful memory it would express to the world.

"Of course, the forms which such a memorial might take, are infinite in variety and each suggested form would present an appeal all its own. It might be in the shape of some humanitarian or utilitarian activity. It might be a monument of marble or bronze; an arch, a shrine or temple.

"But in view of the proposed establishment of a National Headquarters of the Order and the erection of a building to be used as such headquarters, it would seem that an opportunity is presented for a combination of the memorial feature with that project in a manner that would be eminently desirable and the results of which would be most effective and satisfactory from every viewpoint.

"The building could itself be of a design and character that would make it a stately memorial; and it could contain definite monumental features and tablets which would fittingly commemorate the service and sacrifice designed to be honored. And at the same time such features would in no way impair its adaptability to the proposed use thereof for headquarters purposes.

"Your Committee is of the opinion that this idea should be carried out in the construction of the Headquarters Building. And it, therefore, recommends that the suggested building be made definitely monumental and memorial in character; that the architectural design be so stately and beautiful, the material of its construction so enduring, its site and setting so appropriate and commanding, and its distinctive monumental features so artistic and dignified, that the attention of all beholders will be arrested, that the heart of every Elk who contemplates it will be thrilled with pride, and that it will, for generations to come, prove an inspiration to that loyalty and patriotism which the Order so earnestly teaches and has so worthily exemplified."

The Commission offered a resolution of which the following is a part:

"BE IT RESOLVED BY THE GRAND LODGE OF THE BENEVOLENT AND PROTECTIVE ORDER OF ELKS OF THE UNITED STATES OF AMERICA:

"1. That there shall be erected, as speedily as practicable, in the city of Chicago, Ill., a suitable building, of such type and character as to be in keeping with the standing and dignity of the Order, to be erected and maintained as a memorial to the members of the Order who were in the service of our Country in the World War, and particularly those who gave their lives in such service; and to be used as the National Headquarters of the Order; for the accommodation of the offices of the Grand Secretary and other Grand Lodge Officers and Committees, the editorial offices of the National publication hereinafter provided for, and for such other purposes as the Grand Lodge may from time to time designate.

"2. That the funds for the purchase of a site for said building, and for the construction, furnishing, equipment and temporary maintenance thereof, shall be derived from such sources, and shall be provided in such amount and in such manner as the Grand Lodge shall provide.

"3. That there be and is hereby created a Commission to be known as 'National Memorial Headquarters Commission,' consisting of nine members to be appointed by the incoming Grand Exalted Ruler, and of which the Grand Exalted Ruler shall be ex-officio a member, and the appointive members of which shall continue to serve thereon until the completion of said building and the filing of the final report hereinafter required."

The Commission further offered the following resolution:

"BE IT RESOLVED BY THE GRAND LODGE OF THE BENEVOLENT AND PROTECTIVE ORDER OF ELKS OF THE UNITED STATES OF AMERICA:

"1. That there be and is hereby appropriated by the Grand Lodge of the Benevolent and Protective Order of Elks of the United States of America the sum of Two and One-half Million Dollars, or so much thereof as may be necessary, for the purpose of purchasing a site and constructing thereon a building, to be erected and maintained as a memorial to the members of the Order who were in the service of our Country in the World War and particularly those who gave their lives in such service, and to be used as the National Headquarters of the Order; for the accommodation of the offices of the Grand Secretary and other Grand Lodge Officers and Committees; the editorial and business offices of such National Journal as may be published by the Grand Lodge; and for such other purposes as the Grand Lodge may from time to time designate.

"2. That the said amount of Two and One-half Million Dollars be raised by assessments against the several Subordinate Lodges in proportion as the membership of each Lodge bears to the total membership of the Order.

"3. That the said assessments shall be made by the National Memorial Headquarters Commission at such times and for such amounts, and to be paid in such manner as the said Commission may determine. Provided: That the said assessments shall not exceed in amount One Dollar per capita in any one calendar year. And, Provided Further: That each of said assessments shall be made against the said Subordinate Lodges upon the basis of the membership of said Lodges upon the first day of April next preceding the date of such assessment.

"4. That each Subordinate Lodge shall be liable for the payment of said assessments in the amounts and at the times specified in said assessments, and for any failure to so make payment of said assessment, the said Lodge so in default shall be liable to all the penalties imposed by statute for failure to pay other indebtedness to the Grand Lodge.

"5. That the several Subordinate Lodges may, if they so desire, and they are hereby specifically authorized and empowered to, collect the amounts of said assessments from their members by special levies upon said members in addition to the annual Lodge dues. But the adoption of such method of raising said assessments by the Subordinate Lodges shall not affect the liability of said Lodge for the payment of said assessment as herein provided.

"6. That in addition to the said appropriation of Two and One-half Million Dollars, there be and is hereby appropriated for the same purposes hereinabove set forth, all the balance of the Elks War Relief Fund remaining in the custody and control of the Elks War Relief Commission as of October 1, 1921. And the said Elks War Relief Commission is hereby directed, on the said first day of October, 1921, to turn over to the said National Memorial Headquarters Commission such balance, in whatsoever form the same shall then exist, and all other property of whatsoever kind or character in its possession or under its control; and the said Elks War Relief Commission shall thereafter be relieved and discharged from any further service, duty or authority. But all the duties, power, and authority heretofore given to or vested in the said Elks War Relief Commission shall be performed and exercised by the said National Memorial Headquarters Commission."

These resolutions were adopted by the Grand Lodge.

———— 1922 ————

At the Grand Lodge Session in 1922, the Commission made another extensive report, the principal items of which were the following:

Acting upon the authority invested in him by the Grand Lodge, Grand Exalted Ruler William W. Mountain had selected as members of the National Memorial Headquarters Commission, the following: Past Grand Exalted Rulers Joseph T. Fanning, John K. Tener, James R. Nicholson, Edward Rightor, Fred Harper, Bruce A. Campbell, William M. Abbott, Rush L. Holland and Frank L. Rain.

The Commission, after a thorough study, by unanimous vote, selected and purchased for the location of the National Memorial Headquarters Building, property at the intersection of Lake View Avenue and Diversey Parkway, in Chicago, fronting Lincoln Park and Lake Michigan, and having a frontage on Lake View Avenue of 393 feet and on Diversey Parkway of 250 feet, at a cost of $375,012.

The Commission determined that it would invite a limited number of architects, of national reputation, to participate in a competition, to be held under the rules of the American Institute of Architects. Seven of the foremost architects of the United States competed.

After careful consideration of all the designs and drawings, the one submitted by Egerton Swartwout of New York City was unanimously selected.

The Commission was advised that it would take several months for these plans and specifications to be prepared. Promptly upon their completion, the Commission invited bids for the construction of the building.

Under the authority conferred upon the Commission by the resolution creating it, an assessment was levied, as of October 1, 1921, upon each subordinate lodge of $1.00 per capita of its membership, from which assessment was realized $762,029.10.

The Commission did not feel it would be necessary to make another assessment, as provided, prior to April 1923.

––––––– 1923 –––––––

At the Grand Lodge Session in 1923, the Commission reported that, after receiving bids from six of the leading construction organizations of the country, it was preparing to enter into a contract with the Hegeman-Harris Company, of New York City, for the erection of the Elks National Headquarters Memorial Building.

At this Session, Past Grand Exalted Ruler Masters was made a member of the Commission.

––––––– 1924 –––––––

The Elks National Memorial Headquarters Commission, at the Grand Lodge Session of 1924, reported that the cornerstone of

290

the building was laid by Grand Exalted Ruler James G. McFarland on June 7th.

———— 1925 ————

At the Grand Lodge Session of this year, the Commission reported that the exterior of the building proper was complete but that there remained the following features to be taken care of, recommended by the architect:

Construction of art glass windows in Memorial Hall;
Decorative painting of dome and interior walls;
Sculpture for exterior niches and in Memorial Hall;
Mural paintings upon interior panels;
Special rugs and furniture for Reception Room;
Special furniture and hangings for other rooms;
Landscaping of the entire grounds.

The estimated cost of these features was $480,000 and the Commission asked that it be authorized to carry out the advice of the architect in respect thereto.

This authority was granted by the Grand Lodge

———— 1926 ————

On July 14, 1926, Past Grand Exalted Ruler Tener, Chairman of the National Memorial Headquarters Commission, reported that the Memorial Headquarters Building was ready for occupancy.

He reported that the sculptures and mural paintings were being made by some of America's foremost artists:

The sculptors:

Adolph A. Weinman

James Earle Fraser

Laura Gardin Fraser

Gerome Brush

The painters:

Edwin Howland Blashfield

Eugene Savage

Chairman Tener referred to these artists as standing at the very top in the field of American Art.

He commended very highly the excellence of the work of:

Egerton Swartwout, the architect
Colonel J. Hollis Wells, advisory architect
Hegeman-Harris Co., Inc., General Contractors and
George C. Smith, Superintendent of Construction

That same day the Elks National Memorial Headquarters Building was dedicated.

The center of the panorama view of those who gathered at the Elks National Memorial Building for its dedication on July 14, 1926.

On this occasion the Building was presented by Chairman John K. Tener of the Elks National Memo-

Chairman Tener presented the building to Grand Exalted Ruler Atwell for the purpose.

The Grand Lodge Officers participating in the ceremony were:

Grand Exalted Ruler—William H. Atwell, Dallas, Texas, Lodge No. 71

Grand Esteemed Leading Knight—Carroll Smith, St. Louis, Mo., Lodge No. 9

Grand Esteemed Loyal Knight—Riley C. Bowers, Montpelier, Vt., Lodge No. 924

Grand Esteemed Lecturing Knight—Walter F. Meier, Seattle, Wash., Lodge No. 92

Grand Secretary—Fred C. Robinson, Dubuque, Iowa, Lodge No. 297

Grand Treasurer—John K. Burch, Grand Rapids, Mich., Lodge No. 48

Grand Tiler—E. W. Kelly, Salt Lake City, Utah, Lodge No. 85

Grand Inner Guard—John McW. Ford, Shreveport, La., Lodge No. 122

Grand Chaplain—Rev. Dr. John Dysart, Jamestown, N. Y., Lodge No. 263

Grand Esquire—William J. Sinek, Chicago, Ill., Lodge No. 4

rial Headquarters Commission to Grand Exalted Ruler
William H. Atwell for the dedication.
   The dedicatory address was delivered by Past Grand
Exalted Ruler Rush L. Holland.
   (Inset photograph is of Grand Exalted Ruler Atwell.)

Grand Trustees:

A Fitting Memorial

The architectural design of the Memorial Building is stately and
beautiful. The material of its construction is enduring. Its setting
is appropriate and commanding. Its memorial features are distinctive and yet artistic.

Competent critics have referred to it as one of the great memorial
buildings of the world. Its marbles have been properly classed as
museum pieces.

Its great frieze, extending around the exterior of the central
rotunda and depicting "Triumphs of War," which perish, on one
side, and "Triumphs of Peace," which endure, on the other side,
is probably the most extensive work of its kind in the world—

*Elks National
Memorial Building
in Chicago, Ill.*

FRATERNITY
*Mural Painting by
Edwin H. Blashfield*

*Elks National
Memorial Building*

Memorial Rotunda of the Elks National Memorial Building

and certainly the finest example of this type of sculpture in America.

Great bronze elks flank the entrance. Bronze groups "Patriotism" and "Fraternity" stand in the facades of the pavilion. A bronze door gives entrance to the rotunda. All these are masterpieces of art.

Within there is the beauty of outstanding murals and the impressive statues emblematic of the four cardinal virtues of the Elks—Charity, Justice, Brotherly Love and Fidelity.

Cost and Source of Funds

The details of cost and source of funds will be found in the Appendix of this History.

Above are three distinguished gentlemen who attended the Order's rededication of the Memorial Building. Left to right are Senator Alben W. Barkley, who delivered the principal address at the ceremonies, Grand Exalted Ruler Charles E. Broughton, who rededicated the Memorial and Past Grand Exalted Ruler Bruce A. Campbell, General Chairman of the Rededication Committee.

Rededication

On September 8, 1946, the National Memorial Building was rededicated in honor of those members of the Order who had served in World War II.

Past Grand Exalted Ruler Bruce A. Campbell, Chairman of the National Memorial and Publication Commission, presided at the ceremony.

The Flag of our Country was raised on the North Flagpole by Jack Bradley, who had raised Old Glory on the Island of Iwo Jima on Feb. 23, 1945. He was a member of Appleton, Wis., Lodge No. 337.

There were addresses by:

Hon. Harold J. Ward, Chief Justice of the Criminal Court of Cook County, representing Mayor Kelly.
Past Grand Exalted Ruler Edward J. McCormick, representing the Elk Veterans of World War I.
Rear Admiral Frederick L. Conklin.
Major General Louis A. Craig.
Grand Exalted Ruler Charles E. Broughton.

Dr. Edward J. McCormick of Toledo, Ohio, Past Grand Exalted Ruler, who, in an address programmed as "Turning Back the Pages of History in Elkdom to World War I," was photographed while delivering his memorable discourse at the rededication ceremonies.

Major Paul Cyr, Gary, Ind., Lodge No. 1152, representing the members of the Order who had served in World War II.

The rededicatory address was delivered by Senator Alben W. Barkley, Paducah, Ky., Lodge No. 217.

In concluding the rededicatory services, Chairman Campbell said:

"This magnificent Memorial Building, the finest of its kind in the world, was dedicated July 14, 1926, as a memorial to the Elks who served and sacrificed in World War I.

"Its erection and dedication were accomplished by equal contributions from each member of the Order.

"More than 70,000 Elks served their country in that great conflict and more than 1,200 of them made the supreme sacrifice in the defense of their country.

"Since that time our country has engaged in another great conflict, in which more than 100,000 Elks served their country in the armed services and 1,678 of them were killed or died in service.

"At its Session in Chicago in 1944, the Grand Lodge resolved that this building be also declared to be a memorial to those of our brothers who served and sacrificed in World War II.

"That is why we are here today.

"It must be distinctly understood that by these rededication services we are not changing, abrogating or detracting from its original dedication as a memorial to our Elk veterans of World War I but are now including also within the scope of the memorial our Elk veterans of World War II so that this great Memorial Building may hereafter be a memorial of love, honor and affection to all of our Elk veterans of both wars, dead or alive, equally and without distinction or class."

On a page of the "Chicago Sunday Tribune" principally devoted to reproduction in color of outside and inside views of the Elks National Memorial Building there appeared the following tribute:

"Among the many well known war memorial buildings in Chicago is the Elks National Memorial Headquarters building on the edge of Lincoln Park at Lake View Ave. and Diversey Pkway., shown in color on this page. It is the main headquarters for 900,000 Elks and their 1500 lodges in America and a memorial to the Elks who served in both World Wars.

"The building was designed by Egerton Swartwout, a New York architect, and the builders were the Hegeman-Harris Company of New York, to whom the contract for construction was awarded in 1923. The cornerstone was laid June 7, 1924, with impressive ceremonies conducted by officers of the Grand Lodge of the Order. On July 14, 1926, the structure was dedicated as a memorial to the Elks who had served in World War I. At a Grand Lodge meeting in Chicago in 1944 it was declared that the memorial was a tribute to the Elks who had served in both World Wars, and on September 8, 1946, the structure thus was rededicated.

"Faced on the exterior with Indiana limestone and finished on the interior largely with colored marble, the building presents an impressive appearance. In its general aspect it is unique. The central dominating unit is circular, massive in proportions, and surmounted by a flattened dome, 115 feet above the main level. Entered by a single great arched doorway, entirely encircled at a height of 38 feet by a stately colonnade, just below which is a belting frieze carved in high relief, this central unit constitutes the distinctively memorial feature of the edifice. On the north and south of the circular unit, and connected with it by column inclosed passageways, are wings of identical, classically simple design, containing administrative offices.

"Of 30 principal murals in the building, 27 are by Eugene Savage, the other three are by Edwin H. Blashfield. Interior sculpture is by James Earl Fraser; the reclining elks in front of the structure by Laura Gardin Fraser. The exterior frieze is by Adolph A. Weinman. who also executed the groups in the niches of the wings."

In this impressive building are located the offices of the Grand Secretary, as well as the offices of the Elks National Foundation.

Since the erection of the building Hubert E. Allen, who was a member of the staff of the contractor responsible for its erection, served as its very capable superintendent until his retirement in 1967.

In 1967, on motion of Past Grand Exalted Ruler Wade H. Kepner, Secretary of the National Memorial and Publication Commission, the Grand Lodge authorized the modernization of the National Memorial Building. It approved the expenditure of

$209,256, plus architect's fees, for the remodeling and air-conditioning of office areas. This made it possible to provide adequate space for the Elks National Foundation operations which had been transferred from Boston, Mass.

THE ELKS MEMORIAL

The following poem is by O. L. Hall, Editor of the "Chicago Daily Journal." He wrote it as a greeting to the Dedication of the Memorial on July 15, 1926.

"There it stands—
Gazing out of golden eyes
At the emerald wood
And at the amethyst sweet-water sea.
It is as the Roman Pantheon was
When the Pantheon was new;
Or it is Greece re-created,
In line as pure as ever was drawn
By Athenian architect to adorn
The high Acropolis.
Upon the very day of its creation
It presents to all the world a classic face;
To all the world it speaks:
'See, thou maker of ugliness,
How readily beauty comes from thy hands
When beauty is in thy dream.'
This is a jewel of peace,
Bought with the blood of heroes;
The calm magnificence of its shining front
Betokens the fraternity
That has everlasting hatred of war.
So lovely a thing it is
That eye may not rest upon it
To be reminded of strife,
But only of beauty."

The Elks Magazine

Up to 1922, actions of the Grand Lodge and messages of the Grand Exalted Ruler were made known to the members in three ways: first, by a report at a lodge meeting from the delegate who had attended the Grand Lodge Convention; second, by an official circular read in a meeting; and third, by miscellaneous publications which, printed in different localities, featured Elk news.

The first and second methods were not altogether satisfactory because no matter how interesting and complete might be a delegate's report, and no matter how timely and informative might be a Grand Exalted Ruler's circular letter, they reached the ears of only a limited number of members for the simple reason that not every member could be expected to be present at every meeting. The third method was not satisfactory because the Elk periodicals were not subscribed to by all Elks, nor were these papers in all cases of a class that made them suitable heralds to spread news of the Order.

In two respects, the need for a dignified, responsible medium of communication was evident. The Order's rank as the leading American fraternity had to be upheld. The usual channels of information had to be supplemented if all members were to be furnished promptly with knowledge of undertakings—if the fraternity, despite size, were to retain its original cohesiveness.

At the Grand Lodge Session in Los Angeles in 1921, the National Memorial Headquarters Commission incorporated the following in its report:

"In the opinion of your Committee the Order has grown to such proportions, and has established itself as so important a part of the fraternal and patriotic life of the country, that the time has arrived when the publication of a national journal is not only a desirable feature of its activities but a real necessity to the full fruitage of those activities.

"Such a journal should be a real magazine of the highest excellence, both in physical makeup and literary contents one which can compare favorably with the best publications of the country. It should contain matter of fraternal interest, of educational value, and literary merit, and of social and family interest, so that it will become a valuable addition to any reading table and a welcome visitor to any home.

"Your committee has given consideration to this matter and has added its recommendations relating thereto in this report as properly incident to the question of establishment of a national headquarters because such a journal should be issued therefrom. Your committee recommends that such a journal be published by the Order; that it be called 'The Elks Magazine'; that it be issued monthly and be sent to every member of the Order to his home address as a paid-up subscription; that its advertising pages be open only to the most reputable advertisers; and that it be financed by the income from advertisements and Grand Lodge dues assessed against the individual members of the Order independently of local lodge dues."

At this Session of the Grand Lodge, Article III, Section 15 of the Consitution of the Order was amended by adding to those items by which the Grand Lodge was authorized annually by resolution to assess each member of the Order annual dues for raising revenue to meet the expenses of the Grand Lodge, including the maintenance of the Elks National Home and the maintenance of the National Headquarters—a provision for it also to include "the expense of publishing and distributing such national journal as the Grand Lodge may provide to be published."

The National Memorial Headquarters Commission, to which was entrusted the responsibility of publishing a national journal, consisted of the following Past Grand Exalted Rulers: John K. Tener, Chairman, Joseph T. Fanning, Secretary, James R. Nicholson, Edward Rightor, Fred Harper, Bruce A. Campbell, William M. Abbott, Rush L. Holland and Frank L. Rain.

The Grand Lodge provided also at that Session for such a national journal to be known as *The Elks Magazine* to be issued monthly beginning with January 1922, or as soon thereafter as arrangements therefor might be made and providing further:

"That the said journal shall be the official organ of the Grand Lodge and shall contain such matter relating to history and purposes of the Order and its activities as may be of general interest to its members, the official announcements and communications of the Grand Exalted Ruler and other Grand Lodge Officers and committees; and such other reading matter of educational value and fraternal, social and family interest as may be determined by the said Commission here and above provided for.

"A copy of each issue of said journal shall be mailed as a paid up subscription to each subordinate lodge and to each member of the Order upon the rolls of the respective subordinate lodges to his home address. And the secretary of each subordinate lodge shall not later than December 1, 1921, furnish the Grand Secretary an accurate roll of members of his lodge with the home address of each member indicated thereon.

"And thereafter the Secretary of each lodge shall each month furnish the Grand Secretary the names and addresses of new members initiated into the respective lodges, together with the names of such members as shall have died, been demitted, expelled or dropped from the rolls, and the new address of each member who shall have changed his address."

Among the powers given to members of this Commission so far as the publication of the Magazine was concerned, was the following:

"To report to the Board of Grand Trustees during each Grand Lodge Session the amount estimated by it to be required for the editing, publishing, and distribution of said journal beyond the estimated receipts of advertising and paid subscriptions therefor; and the said Board of Trustees shall include said amount as an item in the budget presented by them under Section 38 of the Grand Lodge Statutes."

Of the Magazine it has been said:

"The first issue of *The Elks Magazine* was published in June, 1922. Since then its monthly copies have appeared regularly, and they in themselves furnish the best proof of the Magazine's excellence as the organ of the Order. In the quality of cover designs, illustrations, general layout and advertising, the Magazine compares favorably with other established periodicals, and stands unquestionably at the head of publications in the fraternal field. In editorial content, it is a fit magazine, as it was meant by the Order to be, not only for Elks them-

First cover of The Elks Magazine, June, 1922.

selves, but for their families. Manuscripts are scanned for anything of a controversial, sectarian, or political nature that may be offensive to members and their wives, and for anything of a tendency that may be unwholesome for children.

"It is one publication that is looked forward to by parents, not only with interest, but also with confidence. Of course, the separate issues fulfill their prime duty. Carried to his desk, or his easy chair at home, they keep the member who may have been prevented from attending a meeting of his lodge informed of his Order's doings. All official communications and proclamations, all undertakings and activities of national interest in the realm of Elkdom, are contained between their covers for inviting study and future reference.

"From its inception it has been maintained as a magazine of the highest standards, both in physical make up and in literary content. It has achieved its purpose to become a welcome visitor in any home, a valuable addition to any reading table. It has conclusively proved its effectiveness as a medium for conveying to the entire membership the fraternal information the Order desires them to have, the official communications which it is designed they should receive, the news of subordinate lodge activities in which they are naturally interested, and other matters of distinctly fraternal import.

"The foremost writers of the country contribute of their best work to its pages. Its illustrations are from the hands of the most noted artists. Its cover designs are of uniform excellence and distinction, comparing favorably with those of the best periodicals of the country.

"It has established itself as a desirable publicity medium for national advertisers, which is perhaps the best evidence of its popularity. And from this source it derives a revenue which, with its income from subscriptions, including One Dollar per year from each member as a part of his annual dues, has enabled it to show consistent annual net earnings of substantial sums, which have been available to the Grand Lodge."

Commission Personnel

The Commission authorized in 1921 to proceed with the creation and publication of *The Elks Magazine* and consisting of Past Grand Exalted Rulers Tener, Fanning, Nicholson, Rightor, Harper, Campbell, Abbott, Holland and Rain was augmented by the addition of Past Grand Exalted Ruler Mountain in 1922 and Past Grand Exalted Ruler Masters in 1923.

In 1927 Past Grand Exalted Ruler Masters resigned to become Grand Secretary of the Order and Past Grand Exalted Ruler Nicholson resigned to take the chairmanship of the Elks National Foundation Committee.

In 1928 Past Grand Exalted Ruler Rightor resigned to become a member of the Board of the Elks National Foundation Trustees.

At the time of the Grand Lodge Session in Seattle in 1931 the Elks National Memorial Headquarters Commission consisted of the following Past Grand Exalted Rulers: John K. Tener, Joseph T. Fanning, Rush L. Holland, Fred Harper, Bruce A. Campbell, Frank L. Rain, William M. Abbott and William W. Mountain.

In making its report to the Grand Lodge at that Session, the Elks National Memorial Headquarters Commission, making what was its final report, advised in detail relative to the erection and the completion of the Elks Memorial Building, recommended that a Commission be created to be known as the National Memorial and Publication Commission, to be composed of five members whose term of office should be for five years each, and that one be appointed for a term of one year, one for a term of two years, one for a term of three years, one for a term of four years, and one for a term of five years, and that thereafter the Grand Exalted Ruler should nominate a member of said Commission each year for a term of five years.

This report was adopted after it had been amended upon motion of Grand Exalted Ruler Elect, John R. Coen, in the following manner:

"Provided, however, that the Grand Exalted Ruler elected at the Grand Lodge Session held in 1931 shall appoint eight members of said Commission who shall serve until the number thereof is reduced

Members of the Elks National Memorial and Publication Commission at December, 1967.

Left to right: Past Grand Exalted Ruler Earl James, Past Grand Exalted Ruler Emmett T. Anderson, Past Grand Exalted Ruler John S. McClelland, Past Grand Exalted Ruler Wade H. Kepner. Shown in inset and also a member of the Commission is Past Grand Exalted Ruler James T. Hallinan.

by death, resignation or otherwise to five and that at the next ensuing Session of the Grand Lodge after such reduction of membership to five on the first day thereof, the Grand Exalted Ruler shall designate the terms of said five remaining members as follows: one for a term of one year, one for a term of two years, one for a term of three years, one for a term of four years, one for a term of five years. Thereafter the Commissions shall be composed of five members."

There were no more changes in the membership of the Commission until 1936.

On February 18th of that year, Past Grand Exalted Ruler Mountain died. Past Grand Exalted Ruler Fanning died on December 25, 1936, and Past Grand Exalted Ruler Harper passed away on January 4, 1937.

These deaths left the Commission consisting of the following members:

> Past Grand Exalted Ruler Tener, Chairman
> Past Grand Exalted Ruler Campbell
> Past Grand Exalted Ruler Holland
> Past Grand Exalted Ruler Rain
> Past Grand Exalted Ruler Abbott

In that year Past Grand Exalted Ruler Campbell became Chairman of the Commission and Past Grand Exalted Ruler Tener, who had been Chairman, became Executive Director in charge of the publication of *The Elks Magazine*.

The Commission continued to consist of Past Grand Exalted Rulers Campbell, Tener, Holland, Rain and Abbott until 1941. Past Grand Exalted Ruler Abbott passed away on November 13, 1941, and Past Grand Exalted Ruler Rain died on December 24, 1941.

Past Grand Exalted Ruler Michael F. Shannon was appointed to fill the vacancy caused by the death of Past Grand Exalted Ruler Abbott, and Past Grand Exalted Ruler Nicholson was appointed to fill the vacancy of Past Grand Exalted Ruler Rain.

On January 16, 1944, Past Grand Exalted Ruler Holland died and Past Grand Exalted Ruler John R. Coen was appointed to fill the vacancy caused by his death.

On May 19, 1946, Past Grand Exalted Ruler John K. Tener died. The vacancy in the Commission caused by his death was filled by the appointment of Past Grand Exalted Ruler John S. McClelland.

In 1947 Past Grand Exalted Ruler Nicholson resigned from the Commission to become General Manager of *The Elks Magazine* and Past Grand Exalted Ruler James T. Hallinan was appointed to fill the vacancy caused by his resignation.

TYPICAL PAGES FROM THE ELKS MAGAZINE

Militant Articles

Hunting and Fishing Department

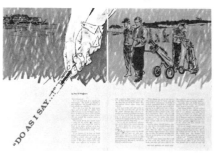

Sports Articles

Inspirational Editorials

Regular Travel Articles

Fiction by leading writers

General Interest Articles

TYPICAL PAGES FROM THE ELKS MAGAZINE

Work of the Elks
National Service
Commission

Reports on Mandatory
Lodge Observances

Special Announcement
to the Order

Subordinate Lodge Activities

Visits of the Grand Exalted Ruler

Report of Grand Lodge Sessions

National Charitable Work of the Order

307

On November 17, 1953 Past Grand Exalted Ruler Shannon passed away. Past Grand Exalted Ruler Emmett T. Anderson was appointed to take his place.

On November 20, 1954 Past Grand Exalted Ruler Coen died and Past Grand Exalted Ruler Wade H. Kepner was appointed to fill the vacancy caused by his death.

On September 29, 1955 Past Grand Exalted Ruler Campbell died and the vacancy was filled by the appointment of Past Grand Exalted Ruler Charles E. Broughton.

On October 31, 1956 Past Grand Exalted Ruler Broughton passed away and Past Grand Exalted Ruler Earl E. James was appointed to fill the vacancy caused by his death.

At the time of filing the annual report of the Commission in 1967 the members were as follows: Past Grand Exalted Ruler John S. McClelland, Chairman, and Past Grand Exalted Rulers Emmett T. Anderson, Vice Chairman; Wade H. Kepner, Secretary; James T. Hallinan, Treasurer, and Earl E. James, Assistant Secretary and Assistant Treasurer.

Personnel

The first editor of *The Elks Magazine* was Past Grand Exalted Ruler Robert W. Brown of Louisville Lodge No. 8, who was an experienced newspaperman and had previously been editor of the "Louisville Times."

Charles Spencer Hart was engaged as business manager. He served in that capacity until elected Grand Exalted Ruler in 1937.

Past Grand Exalted Ruler Brown served as Editor until his death on December 28, 1924.

He was succeeded as Editor by John Chapman Hilder, a man of considerable editorial experience.

John Hilder served in that capacity until February 1930, when he was succeeded by Bruce McClure.

Bruce McClure served until July, 1933, when he was succeeded by James S. Warren.

James S. Warren retained that position until August 1935.

In December, 1935, Neil H. Folwell assumed the editorship. He served in that capacity until September, 1936.

He was succeeded by Coles Phillips, who served in that capacity until July, 1949.

In October, 1949 Lee C. Hickey assumed editorship. He served in that post until September, 1961.

Past Grand Exalted Ruler Joseph T. Fanning was made Executive Director of *The Elks Magazine* at the time of its inception and he continued to serve in that capacity until his death

Last cover of The Elks Magazine before the conclusion date of this History, Dec. 1967.

in 1936. He was succeeded in that position by Past Grand Exalted Ruler John K. Tener who served until his death in 1946.

In 1947 Past Grand Exalted Ruler James R. Nicholson assumed the General Managership of the Magazine. On September 15, 1962, owing to poor health, Past Grand Exalted Ruler Nicholson retired from active participation as General Manager and accepted the post of General Manager Emeritus which he held until his death on August 31, 1965.

On September 16, 1962 William H. Magrath, Controller, was appointed General Manager of the Magazine.

The Magazine staff members as of December, 1967 were:
    William H. Magrath, *General Manager*
    Joseph J. Duhamel, *Auditor*
    James A. Chapman, *Articles Editor*
    John P. Schmitt, *Circulation Manager*

The Advertising Sales Department as of that date consisted of:

    Thomas L. Smith, *Eastern Sales Manager*
    John R. Ryan, *Western Sales Manager*
    Ray C. Watson, *Pacific Coast Sales Representative*
    Lillian Jaffe, *Elks Family Shopper Representative*

At the Grand Lodge Session in Miami Beach, Florida, in July, 1965, the delegates unanimously approved and adopted a resolution offered by the National Memorial and Publication Commission that the Grand Lodge erect, immediately adjacent to the

National Memorial Headquarters Building in Chicago, Illinois, on property owned by the Order, a two story, modern office building and that the offices of THE ELKS MAGAZINE be removed thereto from New York City.

Total cost of project was $798,836.52. Occupancy by the Editorial, Advertising, Circulation and General Administrative Departments of the Magazine, as well as the Grand Lodge Public Relations Department was effected on May 23, 1966.

Earnings of The Elks Magazine
and Disposition of Same

Figures relative to the above will be found in the Appendix of this History.

Elks Magazines——Privately Owned

Prior to the establishment of *The Elks Magazine* many privately owned publications devoted to the news of the Order were published.

Ellis, in his History, says that the first publication of this character was a paper called "The Elk" and that was first published in Hartford, Connecticut, by H. H. Dayton. He states that in the Spring of 1884 it ran for a short time and then was sold to an Elk in Springfield, Massachusetts, where it shortly thereafter ceased to exist.

Apparently the first publication of this character to obtain any general recognition was "The Social Session."

Ellis states that this paper was started by Richard A. McGowan in Chicago and was called "The Elk" and that after running there for a year the publication office was changed to New York City.

He further states that shortly after this move McGowan sold the paper to Allen O. Myers of Cincinnati, Ohio, to which city the new owner moved and changed the publication's name to "The Social Session" and that after a while Myers sold the paper to George Griffith.

Arthur Moreland, the owner and publisher in later years of *"The Elks-Antler,"* is the authority for the statement that Byron W. Orr purchased this publication from Griffith in 1893 and removed it from Cincinnati to Louisville and for the two years prior to the Moreland statement, which was made in 1897, he had been publishing "The Social Session" in Chicago.

In this statement Moreland confirms the origin of the publication as offered by Ellis to the extent of saying that the origin of

"The Social Session" was a paper called "The Elk" published in New York by Richard McGowan.

In 1887 Moreland, then Grand Secretary, offered a resolution in the Grand Lodge that "The Social Session" be recognized as the official organ of the Order and that the Grand Secretary be directed to have Grand Lodge Proceedings printed therein and without charge.

The publication agreeing to print free of charge any official matter for the benefit of the Order and the Grand Trustees being empowered to withdraw this recognition of "The Social Session" if, at any time, its conduct was not in the spirit of Charity, Justice, Brotherly Love and Fidelity to the principles of the Order, this was adopted.

In 1888 the Grand Lodge voted that "the official Proceedings of the Grand Lodge be printed only in 'The Social Session,' the official organ of the body."

In 1889 Exalted Grand Ruler Leach referred to it as the official organ of the Order and the only Elk paper published in the country.

He said:

"While those of you who read the paper know it to be a newsy and well edited sheet, thoroughly disseminating the doctrines of our Order, it is deemed but proper that some recognition be made of the paper's efforts to advance the interests of our fraternity and I therefore recommend The Social Session to this Grand Body."

At that Session the following resolution was adopted:

"Resolved: That the Grand Secretary is hereby instructed to have the proceedings printed in the July number of The Social Session and bound copies of the same should be furnished to the several lodges and the Grand Secretary."

As late as 1895 we find Grand Exalted Ruler Hay referring to "the consideration due The Social Session, the official organ of the Order."

"The Elks—A Monthly Magazine"

While "The Social Session" appears to have had a monopoly in the field of publication of Elk periodicals up to that time, an important competitor appeared in 1893.

In that year there was started the publication of "The Elks—A Monthly Magazine," which was entered in the post office in Erie, Pa., in April and in the post office in Cincinnati in August.

Its masthead showed the following officers: Wm. P. Atkinson, Publisher; John L. Whalen, Business Manager, and Allen O. Myers, Editor.

Allen O. Myers was at that time Grand Secretary of the Order.

Byron W. Orr, who was then Editor and Publisher of "The Social Session," and Business Manager Whalen of "The Elks—A Monthly Magazine," had had some disagreements before "The Elks" was established and when Whalen was promoting an "Annual Elks Register."

There were continuing misunderstandings and altercations between Orr, as publisher of "The Social Session" and those interested in "The Elks," particularly Allen O. Myers.

Finally, in 1894, Orr appealed to the Grand Lodge Session in Atlantic City.

He made the following claims:

That the Grand Lodge of 1893 had ordered the Proceedings of that meeting printed in "The Social Session" as the official organ of the Order.

That the Grand Secretary (Allen O. Myers) had refused to furnish him with a copy of the Proceedings.

That the Grand Secretary advised him that he had been notified by Grand Exalted Ruler Apperly that he had withdrawn all recognition from "The Social Session" for cause.

(One should have in mind in this connection that this was the time when the Grand Exalted Ruler and the Board of Grand Trustees were in disagreement and the former called a Grand Lodge Session at Jamestown and the latter called one in Atlantic City. *See Jamestown Controversy in this History.*)

That an article appearing in the "Louisville Times" contained an announcement that the Grand Exalted Ruler had promulgated a circular to the Order of Elks repudiating "The Social Session" as the official organ of the Order, and that the circular contained the following charges:

That he, Orr, had made false claims as to "The Social Session" being the official organ of the Order.

Had refused to publish any official matter when sent by any of the officials of the Grand Lodge.

Had made "uncalled-for" attacks upon the Grand Secretary.

Had made scandalous attacks upon Grand Lodge members during the Grand Lodge Session at Detroit.

All these charges Orr denied.

In the official circular referred to, Grand Exalted Ruler Apperly stated that he would make public such matters as he may desire through "The Elks," published at Cincinnati by John L. Whalen.

The appeal of Orr was referred to the Committee on Grievances: Daniel A. Kelly, Jay G. Voss and Edmund B. Fuller. That Committee reported that it found as follows:

That at the Grand Lodge Session in 1891 it was voted that "The Social Session" be continued as the official organ of the Order under the direction of the Grand Exalted Ruler and the Grand Trustees, giving them power to withdraw the official patronage if its utterances at any time were objectionable.

That a contract was made between the Grand Trustees and Brother Orr for the publication of the Grand Lodge card for the sum of $35.00.

That this was never paid.

That at the Detroit Session in 1893 it was voted that the Proceedings of the Grand Lodge be published in "The Social Session" at a compensation to be fixed by the Grand Trustees.

That the publisher of "The Social Session" was unable to obtain a copy of such proceedings from the Grand Secretary.

The Committee recommended:

> "That this matter be referred to the Grand Esteemed Loyal Knight and that he be instructed to proffer charges against the Grand Secretary, Allen O. Myers, for willful obstruction of the will of this Grand Lodge."

At this Session the Committee on Laws and Appeals ruled in respect to the powers of the Grand Exalted Ruler and Grand Trustees in the authority given to them by the Grand Lodge regarding the supervisory duties of "The Social Session" that

> "The powers and authority are conferred upon them to act *jointly* and not singly; therefore the Grand Exalted Ruler exceeded his authority in ruling 'The Social Session' not to be the official organ of the Order without the consent of the Trustees."

The controversy involving Allen O. Myers, Cincinnati Lodge and the Grand Lodge was carried on vigorously in the Elk press and in the courts of the Order until finally Cincinnati Lodge, in 1896, expelled Myers. The Grand Lodge to which Myers had appealed, at its next Session, in 1897, confirmed the action of Cincinnati Lodge.

Allen O. Myers had been previously expelled from the Grand Lodge at its Session in 1895.

——————1897——————

In his report in 1897, Grand Exalted Ruler Detweiler said:

> "During the year I have counseled, cautioned and pleaded with the various editors of Elk publications to eliminate from their columns all matters of a personal nature and all articles that would tend to create ill feeling and continue dissensions that have recently distracted the Order.

"I wish to say that they have complied with my request and the result,—the restoration of agreeable feelings that have been most gratifying to myself as Grand Exalted Ruler and chief executive officer of the Order, the duties of which entail great responsibility, ceaseless labor and more than ordinary diplomacy in a period such as we have been going through in trying to restore peace among the conflicting elements."

On February 27, 1895, Arthur C. Moreland entered as second-class matter at the New York Post Office, a publication called "The Antler."

Publication was continued under that name until the issue of August, 1897.

With that issue the name was changed to "The Elks-Antler and Social Session."

Referring to this change of name, Arthur Moreland said, editorially, that Allen O. Myers had, by letter, turned over to him (Moreland) "The Elks," and that at the same time he had entered into a co-partnership with Byron W. Orr, editor and proprietor of "The Social Session," and that the combined publications under the name of "The Elks-Antler and Social Session" would be issued in New York, with Byron W. Orr as business manager and publisher and Arthur Moreland as editor.

The publication of this monthly magazine continued under the name of "The Elks-Antler and Social Session" until the issue of June, 1898, when Editor Moreland announced that, commencing with that issue, the journal would be known only as "The Elks-Antler," and that Byron W. Orr had withdrawn the name "Social Session." It was not apparent at that time that Orr renewed the use of that name in the publication of a magazine, and no evidence was found that the name was in fact later used in that connection.

"The Elks-Antler" continued to be published and edited by Arthur Moreland until his death in 1915, after which it was continued in publication by "The Elks-Antler, Inc.," of which Mrs. Moreland was secretary. On February 8, 1927, Mrs. Moreland advised the Grand Lodge Committee on Good of the Order, which was then studying the question of Elks magazines, privately owned, that the final issue of "The Elks-Antler," had been printed and distributed.

———— 1898 ————

In 1898, Grand Exalted Ruler Detweiler, in his report at the end of his second year, recommended that an official organ be established.

He said that there was not enough diffusion of Elk literature among the members, that in some lodges no Elk paper was taken and the officers and members were in almost total ignorance of the important events transpiring from time to time.

It was his thought that with an official organ all information could be given to the Order in an authoritative manner and in such form as to reach the entire membership promptly.

He recommended that the Grand Exalted Ruler and the Grand Trustees be empowered to designate an official organ and that all official printing placed therein be paid for at a reasonable rate and stated that the other papers could be purchased or consolidated into such a journal.

He called attention to the fact that under the system then prevailing the Grand Lodge had no control over the utterances of the Elk press and that matters, often trivial in themselves, were paraded before the gaze of the world which should never be discussed except in conclaves composed wholly of Elks.

No action was taken.

In 1906 Grand Exalted Ruler Robert W. Brown, in his annual report, referred to the matter of the Elk press.

He stated that no other organization of which he had knowledge granted to its printing affiliates such latitude and said:

> "With no special regulations or restraints of the Grand Lodge laws the publications have been projected and conducted and become mildly epidemic as individual enterprises left entirely to their own conception of editorial and business proprieties."

He recommended that an official paper be issued under the auspices of the Order as a means of information, but also stated that, at that time, he was unwilling to commit himself to such a plan.

―――――― 1913 ――――――

At the Grand Lodge Convention in 1913, Raymond Benjamin, Chairman of the Committee on Judiciary, said:

> "The first matter to be taken up is referred to in the Grand Exalted Ruler's report on pages 10 and 11 with respect to present Elk publications and in regard to future publications of this Order of an official character.

> "I move that that particular matter be taken into consideration by the Board of Grand Trustees for the ensuing year to the end that they may ascertain just what it would cost the Order to institute an official organ, find out how it can be done, and report to the next Grand Lodge."

In the report of Thomas B. Mills in 1913 there appears the following:

> "Elk Publications—

> "It must be apparent to everyone that there are entirely too many magazines and papers published under Grand Lodge sanction. Each

Grand Lodge receives and grants a number of requests to publish these papers. Some of them are never heard of again; some of them make a brave beginning and are soon lost sight of; some of them struggle along in a precarious way for a time and quite a number of them manage to keep the apparently even keel on the sea of somewhat doubtful success. A large portion of these publications are necessarily given over to matters entirely local to the place of publication. The general information contained in any one of them can be found in practically every other one of them, so that a non-resident subscriber gets as far as he is concerned the same information from each of the several papers he may have. I think the time has come for the Grand Lodge to discontinue the granting of licenses for any more of these so called 'Fraternal Papers.'

"Further I believe the Grand Lodge should seriously consider the question of issuing a bulletin for the general information and guidance of the Order at large."

——— 1914-1915 ———

During the period of the service of Raymond Benjamin as Grand Exalted Ruler, he became somewhat disturbed by the extent to which many of these publications would carry articles of a political nature, which might be considered as bringing into the Order matters of a political character, and he communicated with each one of these publications, warning them against continued infractions of that character of the laws of the Order.

A Suggested Official Organ

At the Grand Lodge Session in 1914 at Denver the Board of Grand Trustees, through the Chairman of the Board, Perry A. Clay of Denver Lodge No. 17, to whom was referred the matter of ascertaining just what it would cost the Order to institute an official organ and to find out how it could be done, reported that the Trustees did not believe the Grand Lodge would sanction or the Order consent to the publication of a Magazine which would be sent directly to the Post Office address of every member of the Order, because of great expense involved.

The report then went on to say that the question then arises as to what method to employ best to reach every Elk who not only wishes to keep advised respecting every official proceeding connected with the Order, but at the same time would take pleasure in reading the magazine published by the fraternity to which he belongs, which in addition to Grand Lodge affairs of the Proceedings and the government bodies and officers of our Brotherhood will be filled with said articles of merit and literary gems, all appealing to that which is noblest in speech, and that which is manly in action, to that which causes sympathy in the voice of duty demanded of us; and avoiding all things of a controversial or combative character, the espousing of anyone's candidacy, the denunciation of anyone's candidacy, personality or any matter calculated to engender prejudice, bitterness or strife.

The report then suggested that the Order might with propriety issue a magazine once a month equal in numbers to 5 per cent of the membership and send all the lodges of the Order in the ratio of 5 per cent of the membership of each lodge and one copy of such publication should be addressed to each officer of every subordinate lodge and the balance of the 5 per cent should be addressed to the Club or Reading Room of each lodge, so that every member who so desired could have access to them.

The Trustees estimated that with a membership of 430,000 such a magazine could be sent to 5 per cent of that membership, that is monthly for a year, at a cost of $8,834 and stated that it would require a per capita tax of 2½ cents per member.

However, the Board made no definite recommendation and no action was taken.

——— 1926 ———

Discontinuance of privately-owned Elk magazines:

At the Grand Lodge Session in 1926 the subject of privately-owned Elk magazines was referred to the Committee on Good of the Order, consisting of:

James T. Hallinan, Queens Borough Lodge No. 878, Chairman
Florence J. Schrader, Allegheny, Pa., Lodge No. 339
John F. Hurley, Providence, Rhode Island, Lodge No. 14

for a thorough investigation and study.

The Committee found that, at that time, there were in existence, or had been, the following such publications:

ROCKY MOUNTAIN ELK	James Barton Payne, Denver, Colo.
THE EASTERN ELK	Joseph N. Shafer, Boston, Mass.
NATIONAL ELKS HORN	Norman N. Vaughan, Oklahoma City, Okla.
TRAVELING ELK	A. L. Weinstock, Philadelphia, Pa.
PENNSYLVANIA ELK	Thos. F. Hodges, Pittsburgh, Pa.
JOLLY ELK	Lannie C. Horne, Minneapolis, Minn.

The "Jolly Elk" was established by Robert F. Eldridge of St. Paul in 1900.

PACIFIC COAST ELK	C. Beauregard Poland, Los Angeles, Cal.

THE ELKS-ANTLER	New York City
DAKOTA ELK	Sioux Falls, So. Dak.
SOUTHERN ELK	A. L. Phillips, Nashville, Tenn.
TRANS-MISSISSIPPI ELK	George L. Barton, Omaha, Nebr.
HILLSIDE ELK	Edward H. Stewart, Newburgh, N.Y.
BORDER ELK	J. J. Sullivan, Tucson, Ariz.
BORDER ELK WEEKLY	J. J. Ponder, Texas
CONNECTICUT ELK	M. B. McIntee, Meriden, Conn.
NORTHWESTERN ELK	Portland C. Hunt, Seattle, Wash.
SOUTHWESTERN ELK	High S. Fry, Dallas, Texas
GEORGIAN ELK	C. R. Wright, Macon, Ga.

The Committee stated that it had found it impossible to find any trace of the following:

NORTHWESTERN ELK	SOUTHWESTERN ELK
SOUTHERN ELK	BORDER ELK WEEKLY
CONNECTICUT ELK	HILLSIDE ELK
SOUTHERN BUCK	

The same information previously reported as given to the Committee to the effect that the publication of the "Elks-Antler" had been discontinued was received from:

THE ROCKY MOUNTAIN ELK
THE GEORGIAN ELK
THE DAKOTA ELK
THE TRANS-MISSISSIPPI ELK
THE BORDER ELK

There remained, therefore, the following:

THE EASTERN ELK
NATIONAL ELKS HORN
TRAVELLING ELK
JOLLY ELK
PENNSYLVANIA ELK
PACIFIC COAST ELK

Since that time all of these magazines have ceased publication.

In addition to the publications listed by the Committee on Good of the Order there were also the following publications for varying periods in existence, all of which passed out of existence:

The "Eleven O'clock Toast," started in Cincinnati, Ohio, by John H. Brennen in 1899.

"The Friendly Elk," Detroit, Michigan, L. F. Williams; "Southern Buck," New Orleans, Aubrey Murray.

"The Kentucky Elk," Louisville, Kentucky, Charles J. Croise; "The California Elk," Alex P. Murgotten at San Jose, California.

"The Western Elk," San Francisco, California.

"Interstate Elk," Nat M. Baker, Kansas City, Missouri.

"Tri-State Elk," C. C. Benton, Pittsburgh, Pennsylvania.

"The Purple Ribbon," at Denver, Colorado.

"Hello Bill," at Richmond, Virginia.

"The Purple Book," at Duluth, Minnesota.

"The Golden Elk," at Los Angeles, California.

"The New England Elk," James Mitchell at Lowell, Massachusetts, and later Boston, Massachusetts.

"Elkdom," Memphis, Tennessee.

Restoration of "Old Ironsides"

In 1924 the Congress of the United States provided by resolution for the restoration of the frigate "Constitution," "Old Ironsides," but provided no funds for that purpose and authorized the Secretary of the Navy to gather the funds to carry on the work.

It was the desire of the Secretary of the Navy and President Woodrow Wilson that, for educational purposes, this money be raised through the agency of the school children of the land.

The Secretary of the Navy was then confronted with the problem of how best to reach the school children and get them organized to do this work.

It came to his mind that an agency which would perform this work most creditably was the Benevolent and Protective Order of Elks and he sought to enlist the services of the Elks in organizing the school children to collect necessary contributions, stating that it was not only a great work of patriotism but also a wonderful educational opportunity.

The Secretary of the Navy wired to Grand Exalted Ruler John G. Price as follows:

"Dear Mr. Price:

"It is understood that the Elks have under consideration the active support of the movement to raise funds from the school children to restore the old 'Constitution.' Congress passed an act permitting the Secretary of the Navy to receive donations for this purpose. I am anxious to give the children the first opportunity as a patriotic lesson and educational lesson. The B.P.O.E. has a great record for the welfare of the youth of our country. I hope that your society will decide to give the movement its active support by bringing this before the school children of the country.

"Curtis D. Wilbur

"Secretary of the Navy, Washington"

Grand Exalted Ruler Price replied as follows:

"Hon. Curtis D. Wilbur, Secretary of the Navy
"Washington, D. C.

"Answering your message sent to me at Savannah, am pleased to advise the Benevolent and Protective Order of Elks will cheerfully lend its assistance in the matter of bringing before the school children the movement to raise funds for restoration of historic frigate Constitution. Am preparing a letter to the members of the Order calling for their services. In behalf of the Order, permit me to express appreciation for the opportunity to serve.

"John G. Price

"Grand Exalted Ruler"

Commander Marion Eppley, U. S. N. R., a member of Newport, R. I., Lodge No. 104, donated to the "Save Old Ironsides" fund the sum of $2,500 to be used for the purchase of medals to be presented to the school children within the jurisdiction of each lodge for the best essay on the United States Frigate "Constitution" and the early traditions of the American Navy.

The medals were designed to be distributed as follows:

One bronze medal for each lodge jurisdiction, the obverse of which reads "For excellence in Naval history," and carried other lettering descriptive of the restoration of the frigate "Constitution" for presentation through the lodge to the winning child in elementary school.

One gold medal to be awarded the child writing the best essay of those produced by the children of all the elementary schools in the country.

One silver medal for the child writing the second best essay of those produced by the children of all elementary schools in the country.

One silver medal for the best essay written by a high school student in each state.

One gold medal for the best essay written by a high school student in the nation.

President Calvin Coolidge Participates

President Calvin Coolidge selected topics for the Marion Eppley prizes. He picked for the elementary school essay the subject "Why will the preservation of the U.S.S. Constitution promote patriotism?"

For the high schools he picked the subject "Why did the victory of the United States Constitution contribute so largely to our success in the War of 1812?"

At the Grand Lodge Session in 1925 the following resolution was adopted endorsing the "Restoration of Old Ironsides" movement and calling upon the lodges to do their utmost in this patriotic call:

"WHEREAS the government of the United States through the Secretary of the Navy, recognizing the patriotic character and service of our Order and its previous contributions to the welfare of the children of our country, has requested the Grand Exalted Ruler to appeal to the subordinate lodges to organize the school children of the land for the purpose of raising the necessary funds for the restoration of the frigate Constitution as provided by Congress; and,

"WHEREAS Grand Exalted Ruler Price has pledged the Secretary of the Navy the active co-operation of the Order of Elks in the conduct of the campaign for that purpose and has issued an appeal to the subordinate lodges to respond to this splendid opportunity for patriotic and educational service;

"BE IT RESOLVED, That this Grand Lodge does hereby express its deep satisfaction that the government has again found our Order an acceptable agency for practical patriotic service. That it heartily approves the prompt response made on behalf of the Order by Grand Exalted Ruler Price and endorses the appeal made by him to the members of the Order to thus co-operate with the Secretary of the Navy in the restoration of Old Ironsides, a sacred symbol of Americanism."

The Navy made arrangements for a speaker to broadcast over WEAF on October 18, 1925, to 28 important stations of the country on this subject and the Elks were asked to provide such a speaker.

Grand Exalted Ruler Atwell accepted the assignment.

The Secretary of the Navy was so well pleased with what the Order accomplished that he commissioned Admiral Philip Andrews to attend the Grand Lodge Convention in 1926 as his personal representative to convey his thanks for the work performed by the Elks.

Admiral Andrews said:

"The Secretary of the Navy, Curtis D. Wilbur, has directed me to come here with the kind volition of your Grand Exalted Ruler, and express his thanks to the National Committee for the great patriotic work which you have already done in raising funds for the restoration of the 'Constitution,' the old United States frigate.

"The amount which has so far been raised is approximately one-half the amount needed, or in the neighborhood of $225,000. The amount which has been gathered in from children through the instrumentality of the Elks lodges is about $150,000.

"This campaign is a difficult one. It is very hard to get people to know what is going on and it is a little more difficult to get it into the schools. In many instances this is true because the Superintendent of the Board of Education says that they have a hard and fast rule against campaigning in the schools, so that ends it.

"Some money which you know has been raised has not been turned in, as many lodges have not as yet reported, and quite a few have not as yet functioned, as there have been many difficulties encountered in carrying on this campaign.

"There are 21,000,000 school children in the United States and we have only reached about 4,000,000 of them.

"This insight into the early history of our Country and its principles of good government form a certain and subtle lesson which each child gets in giving its humble means towards this purpose."

The national winner of the elementary school contest was Miss Julia Kochevar. She was 13 years old, the daughter of a machinist's helper of Slavonian background in one of the railroad shops in Grand Junction, Colorado.

This girl was sent to the Grand Lodge by Grand Junction, Colorado Lodge No. 575, and upon presentation read her essay which won over 75 other national competitors who had reached that stage by winning State prizes.

In his report of 1928 Grand Exalted Ruler Malley said:

"The Order accepted the invitation of Secretary of the Navy Wilbur to assist in raising the $500,000, then estimated as to the cost of rebuilding the frigate Constitution (Old Ironsides). The plan advocated by Secretary Wilbur was to raise the money through contributions from school children. Quoting Past Grand Exalted Ruler James R. Nicholson who conducted the Elk campaign in accordance with the policy of the Navy Department, 'It is not so important that the half million dollars that is necessary for the restoration of the old frigate shall be raised, as it is that the school children should be interested in the history of our country at the time "Old Ironsides" was making history.' Unfortunately, the school authorities took a different view. The efforts of the Elks were blocked or embarrassed by the rigid rules of school committees prohibiting the collection of money in the schools. These rules were overcome in many instances but not until enthusiasm had died. Some of the lodges sent checks from their own funds to cover their quotas.

"In spite of these handicaps, the compilation of data received from the United States Navy headquarters at Boston, from which the campaign was and is being directed, shows that 587 subordinate lodges returned a total of $149,590.99, sub-divided as follows:

"Donations from school children $136,436.79
"Donations by Lodges and from individual members   4,804.20
"Plaques placed by Lodges   8,350.00
                                                          _____
                                        Total $149,590.99

"Under date of December 5, 1927, Rear Admiral Philip Andrews, in charge of the nation-wide campaign, wrote concerning the participation of the Elks, 'Their efforts resulted in the collection of about $150,000.' Under date of June 20, 1928, he said that there had been no change in these figures. He further stated that the $500,000 estimate of cost had been found incorrect; that $537,000 had been raised to date (June 20, 1928) and that at least $237,000 additional was needed; that by July 1, 1928, there will have been expended in actual work upon 'Old Ironsides' the sum of $190,000.

"While many agencies have been at work in this campaign since the initial efforts, it is an outstanding fact that the sum of $150,000 acknowledged to have been accumulated and paid in through the efforts of the Elks, is the largest contribution to the total collections of $537,000 which can be credited to the activities of a single agency."

MURRAY HULBERT
1928-29

LAWRENCE H. RUPP
1930-31

WALTER P. ANDREWS
1929-30

JOHN R. COEN
1931-32

Grand Exalted Rulers

SEVENTH DECADE

1928-1938

FLOYD E. THOMPSON
1932-33

WALTER F. MEIER
1933-34

JAMES T. HALLINAN
1935-36

MICHAEL F. SHANNON
1934-35

DAVID SHOLTZ
1936-37

CHARLES S. HART
1937-38

324

S E C T I O N

Seventh Decade

This is the first Decade in which the membership of the Order showed a decrease for the ten-year period.

Even in this instance the decrease ceased and the upturn again was under way before the Decade was over.

For the first eight years (1928 to 1936) there was a decrease of 342,138 (from 808,658 to 466,520) or 42 per cent, while in the last two years of the Decade there was an increase of 2 per cent, making the net decrease for the period 40 per cent.

The reason for this decrease is not difficult to find. In 1929 our country experienced one of the most severe depressions in its history.

Membership in clubs and fraternities bears a very close relationship to economic movements and in that period the membership in the Order of Elks went down with securities quotations, real estate values and commodity prices.

In the same period with this greatest drop in membership the value of the assets of subordinate lodges dropped from

325

$96,529,453.10 to $71,447,782.83, a loss of $25,081,670.27, or 23 per cent.

The number of lodges was reduced from 1,401 to 1,359.

This depression had been preceded by two or three years of cumulative boom, in which extravagant building and wild speculation was the rule.

This spirit, this faith that values were to increase indefinitely, was shared by people in all walks and conditions of life and the subordinate lodges, going along with the tide, found themselves vulnerable when the bubble burst.

Whether a lesson has been learned will never be known unless and until another period of wildly rising and of correspondingly wildly falling values comes again.

In 1932 a very important change was made in the manner of choosing the subordinate lodge representatives to the Grand Lodge.

Whereas previously the provision was that the representative be elected from among the Past Exalted Rulers (the one selected was usually the retiring Exalted Ruler) the amendment provided that the Exalted Ruler then in office automatically be the representative.

This move found its justification in the expectation that the education and inspiration one who had just become an Exalted Ruler would receive at a Grand Lodge Session would be of great value to his lodge.

It was during this Decade that the leaders of the Order began to have an appreciation of the importance of publicity to a fraternal organization as well as an institution, a business or an individual.

In 1931, Grand Exalted Ruler Rupp spoke on the "R.K.O. Theatre of the Air" from the lodge room of New York Lodge.

In 1933, Grand Exalted Ruler Thompson arranged a Memorial Day program broadcast over the Columbia Broadcasting System and the following Flag Day he spoke over the network of the National Broadcasting Company from the home of Thomas Jefferson at Monticello, Virginia.

It was not until 1940, however, that the importance of public relations and publicity was fully recognized by the Grand Lodge by creating the Elks National Defense and Public Relations Commission, the public relations responsibilities of which have continued to be met first by the Elks National Defense and Public Relations Commission, then by the Elks War Commission and then and until the present time by the Elks National Memorial and Publication Commission.

Seventh Decade—1928-1938

GRAND EXALTED RULERS

MURRAY HULBERT, New York, N. Y., Lodge No. 1	1928-1929
WALTER P. ANDREWS, Atlanta, Ga., Lodge No. 78	1929-1930
LAWRENCE H. RUPP, Allentown, Pa., Lodge No. 130	1930-1931
JOHN R. COEN, Sterling, Colo., Lodge No. 1336	1931-1932
FLOYD E. THOMPSON, Moline, Ill., Lodge No. 556	1932-1933
WALTER F. MEIER, Seattle, Wash., Lodge No. 92	1933-1934
MICHAEL F. SHANNON, Los Angeles, Calif., Lodge No. 99	1934-1935
JAMES T. HALLINAN, Queens Borough, N. Y., Lodge No. 878	1935-1936
DAVID SHOLTZ, Daytona Beach, Fla., Lodge No. 1141	1936-1937
CHARLES SPENCER HART, Mt. Vernon, N. Y., Lodge No. 842	1937-1938

GRAND SECRETARIES

At the Grand Lodge Session in Miami, Fla., in July 1928, Past Grand Exalted Ruler J. Edgar Masters, who had been serving out an unexpired term as Grand Secretary, was elected to that office. He continued to be re-elected at each succeeding Grand Lodge Session for the Seventh Decade and continues to have that office as this History is being compiled.

MEMBERSHIP AND CHARITABLE EXPENDITURES

In this Decade the membership of the Order decreased from 808,658 to 479,494. The number of lodges changed from 1,420 to 1,359.

YEAR	MEMBERSHIP	CHARITABLE EXPENDITURES
1928-1929	779,973	$2,449,179.79
1929-1930	761,461	2,640,701.41
1930-1931	707,887	2,677,855.36
1931-1932	640,591	2,321,798.71
1932-1933	556,764	1,869,754.74
1933-1934	500,171	1,402,776.02
1934-1935	468,043	1,290,386.75
1935-1936	466,520	1,304,869.07
1936-1937	472,153	1,400,248.75
1937-1938	479,494	1,417,237.47

The Grand Lodge Sessions in the Seventh Decade were held in the following cities:

1929	Los Angeles, California	1934	Kansas City, Missouri
1930	Atlantic City, New Jersey	1935	Columbus, Ohio
1931	Seattle, Washington	1936	Los Angeles, California
1932	Birmingham, Alabama	1937	Denver, Colorado
1933	Milwaukee, Wisconsin	1938	Atlantic City, New Jersey

At the end of this Decade the assets of the 1,359 lodges amounted to $71,447,782.83.

Public Relations and Publicity

Probably the first time a public relations counsel or publicity agent was employed by the Grand Lodge or any Commission or Committee thereof was when Robert J. Kennedy was engaged to publicize the program and activities of the Grand Lodge.

This service was rendered, however, only at the time of Grand Lodge Sessions. It was continued in this limited form, covering general activities of the Grand Lodge from 1919 to 1937.

July 1930——July 1931

In his report to the Grand Lodge in 1931, Grand Exalted Ruler Lawrence H. Rupp said:

> "On Friday, June 19th, through the courtesy of 'R.K.O. Theatre of the Air' the Order was featured in a nation-wide broadcast. The program was staged at New York Lodge No. 1. It carried the name of our Order throughout the country. I refer to it here since it was the first time our Order has had this kind of publicity. I hope that opportunity will present itself frequently in the future when our Order may reach the audience of a nation-wide broadcast."

(Ed. That Grand Exalted Ruler Rupp was not fully informed when he referred to his national broadcast as the first ever delivered in the name of the Order is indicated by the reference in the article in this History relative to the Restoration of Old Ironsides which tells of Grand Exalted Ruler Atwell accepting the invitation of the Secretary of the Navy to speak on a national broadcast relative to that campaign.)

July 1932——July 1933

Another of the first Grand Exalted Rulers to show an appreciation of the importance of developing good publicity was Floyd E. Thompson. In his report in 1933, he said:

"When I accepted the leadership of this great fraternity it was my hope that I might, in a dignified way, bring its worth to the attention of our fellow citizens in every section of the country."

He then stated that he had enlisted the aid of Charles S. Hart, then business manager of *The Elks Magazine,* and afterwards Grand Exalted Ruler of the Order, in arranging broadcast of the Memorial Day Program, through the courtesy of the Columbia Broadcasting System.

Later, Grand Exalted Ruler Thompson secured the assistance of Past Grand Exalted Rulers Benjamin and Harper in arranging a broadcast of Flag Day exercises from Monticello, Va., the home of Thomas Jefferson.

This was made possible by the cooperation of the National Broadcasting Company.

July 1938——July 1939

In 1938 Grand Exalted Ruler Edward J. McCormick showed appreciation of the value of good publicity and instructed his District Deputies to emphasize its importance to the subordinate lodges.

He retained the publicity department of one of the leading advertising agencies of the country, McCann, Erickson, Inc., and stated in his annual report that he was very much pleased with the results obtained.

He complimented the State Associations upon their cooperation in this work.

He recommended a continuing "publicity program under the direction of able publicity counsel, co-related with the Grand Exalted Ruler, and the Grand Lodge, extending into State Associations and to every subordinate lodge and into communities where there are no lodges."

Elks National Defense and Public Relations Commission

At the Grand Lodge Session in Houston, Texas, in 1940, there was shown evidence that the members of the Grand Lodge, representing the entire membership of the Order, were deeply interested in having action taken in respect to two matters.

The first was the war clouds that were beginning to gather over our country and the second was the desirability that the Grand Lodge take some steps of a continuing nature to develop good public relations and publicity in respect to the patriotic, charitable and humanitarian works of the Order.

The old practice of hiding one's light under a bushel was being abandoned in commercial, industrial and public life at that time and there was strong sentiment in the Order favorable to the Order keeping in step with this development.

There was a general feeling that the Order could pursue its good works much more effectively if the story about them was carried to a larger portion of our people.

And so for the first time the Order was committed to a continuous Public Relations program.

It is not the purpose of this History to tell in detail how this program has been carried out. It does seem, however, that the readers of this History will be interested in knowing something about the methods employed and what were some of the outstanding subjects covered by those having charge of the publicity of the Order.

Public Relations Counsel

Among the first steps taken by the Commission to promote good public relations for the Order was to enter into a contract with Past Grand Exalted Ruler Charles S. Hart (operating as Bureau of Public Relations) to protect the interest of the Order in the matter of Public Relations and Publicity.

This relationship between the Commission and the Bureau of Public Relations continued until October 1941. At that time the Bureau was dissolved as a result of the re-entry of Major (later Lieutenant-Colonel) Hart into the Armed Services.

During that period there was carried out a continuous succession of public relations and publicity activities.

1940——1942

Among these were three outstanding programs worthy of special reference:

> The preparation and presentation of the Uncle Sam poster,
> The essay contest, and the
> "Write 'em a Letter" program.

All of these have been covered in this History in the general report of the activities of the National Defense and Public Relations Commission, and only the publicity feature will be referred to here.

Uncle Sam Poster

A news release carrying a story of the presentation to President Roosevelt of the Uncle Sam poster and his acceptance thereof as a recruiting poster for the Army, and accompanied by a mat of the photograph taken at the White House at the time of the presentation, appeared in over 800 newspapers.

The publishers of Life magazine were so impressed by the

portrait that they published it in the January 15, 1941, issue of the magazine on a full page in two colors.

The subordinate lodges of the Order were advised in advance of the approaching publication of this portrait in Life, with the result that the issue in which it appeared was early sold out.

National Essay Contest

In connection with this contest, hundreds of thousands of American boys and girls of high school age gave thought and study to what Uncle Sam really meant to each of them.

That it had the desired result of developing among them greater appreciation of the rights and privileges of American citizenship cannot be doubted.

It offered an excellent opportunity, of which the Commission took advantage, for the development of worthwhile public relations.

The story of the selection of the national judges of the contest, accompanied by a mat of the Chairman, ex-Governor Cross, of Connecticut, appeared in hundreds of papers as did the general story of the contest.

Write 'em a Letter

In connection with the "Write 'em a Letter" campaign, 650 daily newspapers cooperated in using the prize winning cartoons for 13 weeks.

The Saturday Evening Post published a feature article on the Elks "Write 'em a Letter" program in its issue dated June 20, 1942, and a number of other publications ran features to tie in with the campaign.

Other Programs of the Period

During this period such programs of cooperation with the War and Navy Departments as "Keep 'em Flying," embracing a recruiting campaign for Army and Navy flying cadets, produced a continuous nation-wide stream of publicity.

1942——1946
PERSONNEL

During the period from 1942 to 1946 the Commission employed the services of full-time public relations directors. In the latter year the Commission engaged the services of the Sutton News Service as Public Relations Counsel.

PROGRAMS

The outstanding programs of public relations and publicity during this period, in which E. Mark Sullivan, Frank J. Lonergar

Robert S. Barrett, and Wade H. Kepner served successively as Grand Exalted Ruler, were built around the following subjects:

Diamond Jubilee Anniversary of the Order.
Salutes to the Order were broadcast by the four major radio networks during the Anniversary week.
Newspapers throughout the country carried stories of the founding of the Order.

Cooperation with the Army and Navy in the recruiting campaign for Army Engineers and Navy Seabees.

Cooperation with the Veterans Administration and campaign for the enrollment of nurses.

The work of the Elks in Veterans hospitals.
Prominent in this was a full page pictorial feature in the New York World-Telegram.
A similar four-page feature story (pictorial) covering the work of the California Elks in hospitals, was run by the San Francisco News.

1946——1952

After the close of World War II, when the Elks War Commission made its report in 1946, it recommended that its program of veterans' service be turned over to a new Commission to be known as the Elks National Veterans Service Commission, and that the public relations and publicity work of the Order be placed under the direction of the National Memorial and Publication Commission.

This latter Commission continued to employ the services of the Sutton News Service, which had been engaged by the Defense and Public Relations Commission, until 1948 when Otho DeVilbiss, who had many years experience with public relations and publicity activities, was engaged for full-time service as Public Relations Director of the Order. Mr. DeVilbiss has continued to occupy that position up to the present time.

During the period following the assumption of the responsibility of directing public relations and publicity by the Elks National Memorial and Publication Commission, among the programs and activities of the Order receiving special publicity attention were:

Re-dedication of the Elks National Memorial Building in Chicago in memory of the Elks who served and sacrificed in World War II.

Dedication of a plaque at 193 Broadway as the birthplace of the Order in February 1868, the building then being known as Military Hall.

(Ed. In the Detweiler History there appears the following:

> "The popularity of the new organization soon caused it to over-tax the capacity of the boarding house parlors. Consequently, new quarters were secured in a portion of the building, No. 17 Delancey Street. The new Order of Elks continued to meet in the Delancey Street room for about a month, the initiation fee at that time being $2.00.

> "The rapid increase of the lodge and membership necessitated more extended accommodations. A removal was consequently made to the upper floor of 'Military Hall,' No. 193 Bowery, at which time the fee was increased to $5.00."

Phillips in his "Origin of the Order" says:

> "The revels of this jolly crew became disturbing to the other boarders and Mrs. Giesman finally requested them to forego their Sunday gatherings in her home. Quarters were found at 17 Delancey Street, over a saloon kept by one Paul Sommers, where the meetings were continued."

Ellis in his History says:

> " 'The Corks' only remained at 17 Delancey Street for a period of four weeks or as near as can be ascertained to Sunday, February 2, 1868, when they moved to the upper floor of 'Military Hall' at 193 Bowery.")

Here we have a conflict between Detweiler and Ellis. As the Minutes Book of the period when the Corks changed to Elks was lost, there would appear to be no opportunity at this date definitely to determine the question of the exact location of the birthplace of the Order.

In a letter written by George Guy who was a member of the Jolly Corks but who was not given full credit for having been one of the founding members of the Elks, although Charles W. Young, in a pamphlet written on the Origin of the Order, does include Guy's name as one of the original 15, saying:

> "The Benevolent and Protective Order of Elks was christened in Military Hall on February 16, 1868."

Subversive Groups

An important part of the Order's public relations activities involved the actions of the Elks to protect the country against subversive groups of both the right and the left during the post-war period.

Ku Klux Klan

Grand Exalted Ruler Broughton's condemnation of the resurgent Ku Klux Klan and his campaign against it won support of the press and was helpful in halting the spread of this organization.

Freedom Train

In 1947 Elk publicity exposed the attempt of the Communists to sabotage the Freedom Train program.

A mat carrying a photograph of Grand Exalted Ruler Lewis standing at the Freedom Train in New York City and with the heading "Head of Elks Raps Brazen Communists for Effort to Sabotage Freedom Train" was sent to the Exalted Rulers of all lodges with a mimeographed story of the Grand Exalted Ruler's attack on the Communists, for insertion in their local newspapers.

An Expanded Program

Through educational activities and a vastly expanded youth program supported by every public relations medium, the Elks carried on this battle against the international Communist conspiracy to destroy the United States.

After the 1947 Grand Lodge Session endorsed the Boy Scout Movement, Grand Exalted Ruler Lewis and Scout officials participated in a radio program over the National Broadcasting Company network, and nationwide publicity was given its youth building activity through a matted newspaper feature.

The Order's national essay contest on "Why Democracy Works" received enormous publicity in 1948 and 1949, climaxed when the winner, 17 year old William Johnson of McAlester, Oklahoma, was presented to President Truman at the White House. Newspapers all over the country carried photographs of Grand Exalted Ruler Hall and the boy with President Truman.

Another major promotion of the Public Relations Department was the youth leadership contest and the Elks National Youth Day program under the sponsorship of the Grand Lodge Youth Activities Committee, first established in 1949.

Lodges were supplied with publicity material on these events which related them to the Order's over-all efforts to encourage youth's staunch support of American ideals.

The Elks Magazine published a series of hard-hitting articles by writers exposing the Communist underground's subversive activities.

These were reprinted by many newspapers as a public service, and thousands of reprints were distributed to patriotic organizations and individuals.

National Newspaper Week

Subversive attacks on the free press as a foundation stone of American freedom prompted Grand Exalted Ruler Anderson to call upon Elks lodges to join in observance of National Newspaper Week, and Grand Exalted Rulers Kyle and Davis endorsed this project.

By honoring their home town newspapers and the men and women who staffed them, Elks lodges focused attention upon the vital role the free press plays in our society. This encouragement from the Order won for it great appreciation from the press.

In Grand Exalted Ruler Davis' term the lodges were urged to make their National Newspaper Week observances an appeal in support of the release of William N. Oatis, Associated Press Correspondent, imprisoned by Czechoslovakia on false charges of espionage. Lodges were supplied with copies of a suggested resolution to be adopted by them and forwarded to President Truman urging unremitting pressure to obtain Oatis' freedom and a sheet supplying facts and background of the Oatis case.

The Elks lodge of Marion, Indiana, Oatis' home town, obtained more than 12,000 signatures to a petition on Oatis' behalf. A delegation presented the petition, which consisted of a continuous roll of newspaper print to Joseph Short, White House Press Secretary, in October. Washington newspapers and the Press Associations publicized this event and photos and stories on it were sent to more than 60 Indiana newspapers.

The Millionth Elk

Much favorable publicity was received when the Order's active membership for the first time reached the million mark in 1950. Matted photographs of Grand Exalted Ruler Anderson and the "Millionth Elk," Raymond Cole, of Bay City, Michigan, Lodge No. 89, was released through the lodges, together with stories of the event.

National Service Commission Program

The National Service Commission's Veterans Hospital program, its "Wake Up America," and its "Keep Awake America" programs, designed to alert citizens to the communist menace through community action, its fraternal center program for men in the armed forces, reactivated with the country's rearmament effort, all were backed up with publicity distributed by the Public Relations Department.

Blood Bank

One of the great patriotic activities undertaken by the Order was the Elks Armed Forces Blood Campaign, sponsored by Grand Exalted Ruler Davis (1951-1952), to help relieve the critical shortage of blood for the wounded in Korea.

The Public Relations Department prepared matted photos of the Grand Exalted Ruler pledging to Secretary of Defense Lovett the support of the Elks. These and press releases were distributed to the lodges and were widely publicized along with thousands of stories as the campaign progressed. Local radio stations also carried many programs describing the Elks campaign.

1952——1953

In 1952, the Chanters of Los Angeles Lodge No. 99 were presented in a program of Christmas music over the Mutual Broadcasting System radio network. Grand Exalted Ruler Sam Stern gave a brief Christmas message.

1953——1954

The Department arranged a "Show Your Colors" Flag Day program over the Mutual Broadcasting System radio network in 1954, in which Grand Exalted Ruler Earl E. James participated.

"Report to the President of the United States," an accounting of the Order's youth activities, was prepared for Grand Exalted Ruler William J. Jernick's presentation to President Dwight D. Eisenhower in December, 1954. The Department distributed a mat photo and news story covering the event.

1954——1955

In April, 1955, President Eisenhower received Grand Exalted Ruler Jernick and the winners of the Elks National Youth Leadership Contest at the White House, where the President presented their awards to the youngsters. The Department assisted in arranging the details of the visit and released national and local publicity covering it.

1955——1956

President Eisenhower had invited Grand Exalted Ruler John L. Walker to bring the 1956 Youth Leadership Contest winners to the White House in June, at which time the Grand Exalted Ruler planned to present the President with a special gold medallion from the Order in appreciation of his great interest in youth. The President's illness intervened, and his secretary, Bernard N. Shanley, accepted the award on behalf of the President and presented their awards to the leadership winners. The Department designed the award to the President and covered the event with a newspaper mat photo and story release.

Fred L. Bohn spoke over the National Broadcasting Co. radio network in October, 1956, on behalf of the Elks' "get out the vote" campaign. Publicity aids backing up the drive were supplied to all lodges.

Grand Exalted Ruler Bohn launched a vigorous campaign to expose the so-called "world youth festival" to be held in Moscow in 1957 as nothing but a communist propaganda device. The

Department prepared a presentation of the facts in a letter from the Grand Exalted Ruler to all lodges, requesting their cooperation in bringing the truth to those in their communities. Appropriate publicity materials accompanied this presentation.

1956——1957

With the cooperation of the American Broadcasting Co., the Ted Malone radio network show was devoted to the Order's youth activities in observance of Elks National Youth Day in May, 1957. The program included a message from Grand Exalted Ruler Bohn.

The Department organized a National Flag Day observance in Washington, D. C., presented in Constitution Hall on ^June 14, 1957. Speaker John W. McCormack presided, and seven other Senators and Representatives, all members of the Order, participated with Grand Exalted Ruler Bohn and Acting Grand Chaplain Richard J. Connelly in presenting the Flag Day Ritual. This was followed by a specially written patriotic pageant, starring singers Elaine Malbin and Lanny Ross, supported by the U. S. Army Band and Chorus and assisted by contingents from the military services provided by the Department of Defense. The program was recorded and carried over the Mutual Broadcasting System radio network.

The Public Relations Department supplied material for a feature article published in the CHRISTIAN SCIENCE MONITOR issue of November 23, 1956.

1957——1958

Cooperating with the Board of Grand Trustees, the Department assisted in the production of a sound and color motion picture film entitled "Home Again," a dramatic presentation of the Elks National Home in Bedford. A four-color pamphlet descriptive of the Home also was written and produced for the Board.

In support of Grand Exalted Ruler H. L. Blackledge's 90th Anniversary indoctrination and Open House program, the Department prepared for distribution to the lodges three background articles on the Order. These included a short history of the Order; an article on major Elk benevolent works; and one giving highlights of the Elks National Foundation's Programs.

The boy and girl winners of the 1958 Elks National Youth Leadership Contest were introduced to a nation-wide television audience watching the Ed Sullivan show on the Columbia Broadcasting System network. In connection with Elks National Youth

Day in the same year, the Order's youth activities were featured on Arlene Francis' program on the National Broadcasting Co. radio network, and the Boy Scouts and Elks shared a 15-minute program on "Assignment People" on the Mutual radio network.

1959——1960

Under Grand Exalted Ruler William S. Hawkins' leadership, the Order actively cooperated with the Boy Scouts of America in the observance of that organization's 50th anniversary. Elkdom's long and extensive support of Scouting was stressed in publicity during the year.

The Public Relations Department provided material for a feature on the Order published in the Pageant Magazine issue of August, 1959.

1960——1961

To further publicize the work of the Elks National Foundation, the Department prepared and distributed to the lodges, for use in the newspapers and lodge bulletins, a three-part series of articles on Foundation programs.

The Department supported the work of the New Lodge Committee with a series of five suggested news releases to assist in publicizing the formation of new lodges.

1961——1962

President Kennedy received Grand Exalted Ruler John E. Fenton and the Elks National Youth Leadership Contest winners at the White House in July, 1961, and presented awards to the winners. The Department released national and local publicity on the event.

In May, 1962, winners of the Youth Leadership Contest, accompanied by Grand Exalted Ruler William A. Wall, received their awards from Vice President Lyndon B. Johnson in his office at the Capitol. The Department arranged for news coverage of the presentation ceremony.

Cooperating with the Elks National Service Commission, the Department publicized, through mailings to the lodges, the Order's Cards for the Handicapped Campaign in the Fall of 1961.

In collaboration with the Grand Lodge Americanism Committee, the Department drafted the Order's Declaration of American Principles, distributing copies of it with a covering news story to the nation's press, directly and through the lodges, in September, 1961.

1962——1963

In October, 1962, the Department released a national story on Grand Exalted Ruler Lee A. Donaldson's message to President Kennedy affirming the Order's support of the President's action in the Cuban crisis. Also covered in the story was Americanism Committee Chairman Vincent H. Grocott's request to the lodges to communicate their expressions of support to the President.

The Department assisted Americanism Committee Chairman Grocott in organizing and publicizing the Order's first Freedom Week observance in January, 1963. Freedom Week, honoring all communications media, replaced National Newspaper Week, formerly observed by the Order.

1963——1964

The Public Relations Department worked closely with the Elks National Service Commission in publicizing its second campaign to collect used playing cards for Veterans' Hospitals. In addition to newspaper publicity, we prepared radio and TV spot announcements and supplied them to all lodges.

BPOE Centennial

After the formation of the Grand Lodge Centennial Committee in July, 1965, the Public Relations Department focused largely on the development of Centennial projects and the creation of Centennial publicity materials. These materials, which were announced at the Grand Lodge Convention in July, 1967, included:

1. A publicity guide for Elks lodge publicity chairmen
2. A press packet containing 13 background articles covering every phase of the Order's activities and also photographs and newspaper mats
3. A radio packet consisting of public service spot announcements of various lengths and an electrical transcription containing Centennial salutes from the heads of 14 national organizations on one side and on the other Centennial salutes from 20 prominent Americans
4. A TV packet containing three filmed public service announcements in color featuring Dennis Day; four color slides with text for accompanying public service announcements in various lengths; a suggested script for a 30-minute TV program.

Reproduction of the Founder Certificates
issued by the Elks National Foundation

The Elks National Foundation

The long-established policy of the Order, involving the delegation to subordinate lodges of ordinary local, charitable and benevolent activities and to the State Associations such broader projects as might be deemed appropriate for them to undertake, has demonstrated its wisdom and that general policy is still maintained.

In the early part of 1927, John F. Malley, formerly Chairman of the Committee on Judiciary, who was elected Grand Exalted Ruler at the next Grand Lodge Session, in addressing the lodges of the Order presented a plan which he had conceived, in which the Grand Lodge could assist the subordinate lodges and the State Associations in the promotion of the beneficent projects of their choice.

The plan contemplated the creation and maintenance of a permanent fund under the supervision of the Grand Lodge, the income from which might be used in assisting those local and state units in such of their undertakings as were approved but were found to be unduly burdensome upon their respective resources and also for such independent purposes as the Grand Lodge itself might desire to promote.

Grand Exalted Ruler Charles H. Grakelow endorsed this plan in his report to the Grand Lodge and at the Session of that body held in Cincinnati in 1927 there was adopted the following:

"BE IT RESOLVED: That the Grand Exalted Ruler appoint a committee of five to be known as the Elks National Foundation Committee, to make a survey along the lines suggested by Grand Exalted Ruler Charles H. Grakelow, in his report to the Grand Lodge, assembled in annual convention, in Cincinnati, Ohio, July, 1927, for the establishment of a 'National Elks Foundation,' and that such committee report to the Grand Lodge at the next session, its conclusions and recommendations on the subject.

"BE IT FURTHER RESOLVED: That the Grand Lodge pay such sums as may be necessary to defray the necessary and reasonable expenses incurred by said Committee, subject to the approval of the Grand Exalted Ruler."

Grand Exalted Ruler Malley appointed the following Past Grand Exalted Rulers as members of this committee:

James R. Nicholson, Springfield, Massachusetts, Lodge No. 61, Chairman
Charles E. Pickett, Waterloo, Iowa, Lodge No. 290
Raymond Benjamin, Napa, California, Lodge No. 832
Edward Rightor, New Orleans, Louisiana, Lodge No. 30
James G. McFarland, Watertown, South Dakota, Lodge No. 838

At tne Grand Lodge Session in Miami in 1928, this Committee reported and recommended:

"That there be established by constitutional amendment a permanent trust fund to be known as 'The Elks National Foundation,' the corpus of which shall be invested in income-producing property and securities, and the income of which shall be applied from time to time, and in such manner as the trustees of said Foundation may determine, for the furtherance of such of the charitable, educational and benevolent activities of the Order, or of its subordinate lodges or associations of such lodges, as said trustees may determine; and that the Grand Lodge transfer to said Foundation as an initial appropriation thereto not less than $100,000 from such Grand Lodge funds as may be available to be so transferred and appropriated.

"That there be created by constitutional amendment a body to be known as 'The Elks National Foundation Trustees,' to consist of seven members of the Grand Lodge, to be appointed by the incoming Grand Exalted Ruler; that the said several trustees be appointed for terms of one, two, three, four, five, six and seven years, respectively; and that thereafter, at each annual Grand Lodge session, on the first day there of, the Grand Exalted Ruler shall nominate, and, with the consent of the Grand Lodge, appoint one member of the Grand Lodge to serve as such trustee for the full term of seven years; that vacancies in said body caused by death, resignation or otherwise, may be filled temporarily until the next Grand Lodge session by appointment by the Grand Exalted Ruler, and at the next Grand Lodge session such vacancies shall be filled by the Grand Exalted Ruler with the consent of the Grand Lodge in the same manner as regular appointments.

"That the trustees be given plenary powers to promote, develop and administer the said Foundation to accomplish its charitable, educational and benevolent purposes.

"That the trustees be authorized and empowered to receive from any source, any monies, securities or other property, that may be properly transferred to them, in trust for the purposes for which the Foundation is established; and may either accumulate such monies, securities or other property as a part of the corpus, using only the income thereof, or may use all or a part of such monies, securities, or other property for purposes of distribution, as the respective donors thereof may direct, within the scope of the charitable, educational and benevolent purposes of the Foundation."

The report of the Committee was accepted by the Grand Lodge and its recommendations unanimously adopted.

Thus was established the Elks National Foundation.

Salient Features of the Foundation

Three great outstanding characteristics of the Elks National Foundation are that it is a permanent fund; that this fund is being raised by voluntary gifts or subscriptions without compulsion of any kind—no tax, no levy, direct or indirect; that the entire income of the fund is available for distribution for philanthropic purposes.

Original Trustee Personnel

The original Board of Trustees of the Foundation, appointed by Grand Exalted Ruler Murray Hulbert in December, 1928, consisted of:

Past Grand Exalted Ruler Malley, Springfield, Massachusetts, Lodge No. 61

Past Grand Exalted Ruler Benjamin, Napa, California, Lodge No. 832

Past Grand Exalted Ruler John G. Price, Columbus, Ohio, Lodge No. 37

Past Grand Exalted Ruler James G. McFarland, Watertown, South Dakota, Lodge No. 838

Past Grand Exalted Ruler Charles E. Pickett, Waterloo, Iowa, Lodge No. 290

Past Grand Exalted Ruler Edward Rightor, New Orleans, Louisiana, Lodge No. 30

Past Grand Exalted Ruler Charles H. Grakelow, Philadelphia, Pennsylvania, Lodge No. 2

The Foundation Trustees established the following forms of contributions:

HONORARY FOUNDER CERTIFICATE:

An Honorary Founder Certificate is issued to each contributor of $1,000. Subscriptions for Honorary Founder Certificates may be paid in full or by installments as small as $100 per year.

PERMANENT BENEFACTOR CERTIFICATES:

An Honorary Founder who contributes an additional $1,000 or more becomes entitled to a Permanent Benefacor Certificate. Subscriptions for Permanent Benefactor Certificates may be paid in full or by installments of $100 per year.

PARTICIPATING CERTIFICATES:

A Participating Certificate is given to any member who contributes $100 to the Foundation.

BEQUESTS:

The Elks National Foundation is an admirable agency for perpetuating good works in the charitable, benevolent and educational fields. Anyone planning or advising in respect to the preparation of a will is urged to include a bequest to the Elks National Foundation using this form:

"I give and bequeath the sum of .... dollars to the Elks National Foundation of the Benevolent and Protective Order of Elks of the United States of America, a corporation duly established and existing under the laws of the District of Columbia."

Trustee Personnel

Past Grand Exalted Ruler Malley, who was responsible for the conception of the idea of the Foundation, was chosen as Chairman, a position which he continued to occupy until his death on May 16, 1966, when Past Grand Exalted Ruler Lewis became Chairman and served until his death on October 16, 1966. Past Grand Exalted Ruler Walker was then elevated to the Chairmanship and has since continued in this position.

In 1930, Past Grand Exalted Ruler Murray Hulbert of New York Lodge No. 1 was appointed to fill a vacancy caused by the death of Past Grand Exalted Ruler Pickett.

In 1931, Past Grand Exalted Ruler Lawrence H. Rupp of Allentown, Pennsylvania, Lodge No. 130, was appointed to fill the

Elks National Foundation Trustees—December 1967

Left to right: Past Grand Exalted Ruler Horace R. Wisely, Past Grand Exalted Ruler Hobert L. Blackledge, Past Grand Exalted Ruler John E. Fenton, Past Grand Exalted Ruler Edward J. McCormick, Past Grand Exalted Ruler John L. Walker, Past Grand Exalted Ruler Lee A. Donaldson, Past Grand Exalted Ruler William A. Wall.

vacancy caused by the death of Past Grand Exalted Ruler Price.

In 1936, Past Grand Exalted Ruler Floyd E. Thompson, Moline, Illinois, Lodge No. 556, was appointed to fill the vacancy caused by the death of Past Grand Exalted Ruler Rupp.

In 1946, Past Grand Exalted Ruler Robert S. Barrett of Alexandria, Virginia, Lodge No. 758, was appointed to fill the vacancy caused by the resignation of Past Grand Exalted Ruler McFarland.

In 1949, Past Grand Exalted Ruler L. A. Lewis, Anaheim, California, Lodge No. 1345, was appointed to fill the vacancy caused by the resignation of Past Grand Exalted Ruler Rightor.

In 1950, Past Grand Exalted Ruler Edward J. McCormick, Toledo, Ohio, Lodge No. 53, was appointed to fill the vacancy caused by the death of Past Grand Exalted Ruler Hulbert.

In 1952, Past Grand Exalted Ruler Charles E. Broughton, Sheboygan, Wisconsin, Lodge No. 299 was appointed to fill the vacancy caused by the death of Past Grand Exalted Ruler Benjamin.

In 1953, PGER Sam Stern was appointed to fill the vacancy caused by the resignation of PGER Charles E. Broughton.

In 1959, PGER H. L. Blackledge was appointed to fill the vacancy caused by the resignation in 1958 of PGER Robert S. Barrett.

In 1960, PGER H. L. Blackledge was appointed to a seven year term expiring in 1967.

In 1961, PGER John E. Fenton was appointed to a seven year term to fill the vacancy created by the death of PGER Thompson.

In 1962, PGER John L. Walker was appointed to a seven year term to fill the vacancy created by the death of PGER Grakelow.

In 1966, PGER William A. Wall was appointed to fill the vacancy caused by the death of PGER John F. Malley.

In 1966, PGER Horace R. Wisely was appointed to fill the vacancy caused by the death of PGER L. A. Lewis.

In 1967, PGER L. A. Donaldson was appointed to fill the vacancy caused by the death of PGER Sam Stern.

Relocation of Headquarters

With the thought of better serving our membership from a central location, the Elks National Foundation offices were moved from Boston to the Elks Memorial Building in Chicago during the month of December 1966.

Executive Personnel

From the inception of the Foundation until it was moved to Chicago Miss Katherine Sponagle served most ably and efficiently as Administrative Secretary. Miss Sponagle retired shortly after the office was moved and Miss Alice P. Kavanaugh was appointed Office Manager. Mr. Nelson E. W. Stuart of Cleveland, Ohio resigned as Grand Trustee of the Order to assume the newly created post of Executive Director of the Foundation, effective January 1, 1967 and is acting in this position as this history is being revised.

Powers and Policy of Trustees

The Trustees are clothed with broad powers and wide discretion, including the custody and preservation of the funds of the Foundation; the duties of securing increases thereto and the authority to apply the income therefrom to such charitable, educational and benevolent purposes as they determine.

It was designed that the corpus of the Foundation should continually grow by donations thereto from any source approved by the Trustees, primarily by gifts, legacies and devises from members of the Order and from others interested in the promotion of its objects and purposes. The Foundation has grown steadily since its establishment.

Allocated Scholarships

In order that assistance might be given to students in need of financial aid who do not qualify in the national competition, the Foundation Trustees allocate scholarships in number equal to the quota permitted each state in the "Most Valuable Student" Project so that scholarships may be awarded to students recommended by the scholarship committees of the respective states under rules established by the Foundation Trustees. At the present time these scholarships amount to $600.00 each.

FIELDS OF SERVICE

Most Valuable Student Awards

Each year since 1934, the Foundation has encouraged deserving young men and women of the country who are ambitious to obtain higher education but found it difficult to secure the money

Past Grand Exalted Ruler Raymond Benjamin, Vice-Chairman of the Elks National Foundation, at left, and Past Grand Exalted Ruler John F. Malley, at right, congratulate scholarship award winners Jean Ann Lawson and Gilbert R. Panzer at the 1950 Grand Lodge Session in Miami.

necessary to defray the expenses of a college course, by offering "Elks National Foundation Most Valuable Student Awards" for general excellence in scholarship achievement and extra-curricular work, leadership among their fellow-students, perseverance and other admirable characteristics.

These offers have brought to the attention of the Foundation Trustees many splendid young men and women, and have given the Trustees an opportunity through awards to help towards their ambitions those they considered the most worthy.

State Major Project Grants

From the beginning a major field of activity for the Foundation has been grants to State Elks Associations in support of their major philanthropic project. To date, the Foundation has allocated more than $1 million to these programs. This policy of practical encouragement has been an important factor in the development of philanthropic programs by our State Associations.

Cerebral Palsy

In 1950 the Foundation Trustees, as a result of a survey in which they had long been engaged, came definitely to the conclusion

Chairman John F. Malley of the Elks National Foundation presents a check for Boston's Children's Medical Center, as a Senior Research Fellowship grant to Dr. Sylvia J. Onesti to aid her in the study and treatment of cerebral palsied children in 1951. Center, Dr. Wm. Berenberg, Executive Secretary of the Center's Cerebral Palsy Unit.

that there existed a great need, in meeting which the Foundation should directly engage, and one in which the activities of subordinate lodges and State Associations could be greatly broadened and stimulated to the everlasting benefit of thousands of children of this country.

In April of that year Chairman John F. Malley of the Foundation announced the appropriation by the Trustees of $25,000 to be used in granting fellowships for training doctors, therapists and other qualified personnel to treat the victims of cerebral palsy.

The great value of this activity of the Foundation arose from the fact that the disturbing, delaying factor in coping with this serious affliction is the scarcity of trained personnel in this field. The program has been carried on and expanded. More than 1700 qualified persons have taken courses of specialized training in the treatment of cerebral palsy at leading universities and medical institutions of recognized standing. Many of these have served on staffs of Cerebral Palsy Treatment Centers and clinics and mobile home therapy staffs of State Associations.

Emergency Educational Fund

This fund was established by resolution adopted at the Grand Lodge Session in Chicago, Illinois, in 1944 on the recommendation of then Grand Exalted Ruler Robert S. Barrett, to assist children of Elks killed or incapacitated in World War II. For this purpose a fund of $25,000 was appropriated by Grand Lodge. At the Grand Lodge Session in 1945 this sum was increased to $50,000. In 1954 the scope of the program was broadened in accordance with the following resolution which was adopted at the Grand Lodge Session of that year in Los Angeles:

"That the Emergency Educational Fund heretofore established by the Grand Lodge and all additions thereto shall be part of the Elks National Foundation and shall be administered by the Elks National Foundation Trustees in accordance with the provisions of Article V of the Grand Lodge Constitution; and that said Emergency Educational Fund shall be used by said Trustees to provide for the proper and adequate educacation beyond and supplementary to the usual high or preparatory school courses, of any child, under the age of twenty-three years, of a member of this Order who has lost his life, or been incapacitated, while a member in good standing in the Order, and it appears to the satisfaction of said Trustees that there is need for financial assistance and, in such case, the Trustees, in their discretion may expend the corpus of said fund as well as the income therefrom."

Since that time the fund has been administered by the Foundation and financed from its income. Under this program the Foundation has awarded scholarships totaling approximately $400,000.

It is provided that applications should be made by the student under sponsorship of a parent or guardian or member of the lodge of which the person was or is a member.

The applications are to be filed with the Secretary of the lodge of which the parent is or was a member and referred by such lodge to a special Scholarship Assistance Committee for investigation and report, such report to be submitted to the lodge for approval.

The application with the report of the Committee and the certification and memorandum of the Exalted Ruler and Secretary of the lodge is then to be sent to the Foundation office in Chicago.

Principal and Income

Figures relative to the principal, income and disbursements of the Foundation will be found in the Appendix of this History.

The Antlers

In February 1922, an organization known as The Antlers came into being in San Francisco Lodge No. 3.

It was conceived, founded, organized and promoted by a member of San Francisco Lodge, C. Fenton Nichols.

It was designed to be a junior organization of the Benevolent and Protective Order of Elks. It was planned to consist of lodges of Antlers created by and directed by the individual subordinate lodges of the Order.

Due practically entirely to deep interest and the sustained efforts of Fenton Nichols, Antlers Lodges were established one by one by subordinate lodges in California.

As the result of his efforts to have the Antlers endorsed and adopted by the Grand Lodge, Grand Exalted Ruler Grakelow in his report to the Grand Lodge in 1927 recommended the amendment of the Constitution of the Order to make possible the formation of lodges of Antlers under the sanction and guidance of the Grand Lodge and the drafting of a Ritual for such lodges.

Following this recommendation Section 8 of Article IV of the Constitution was amended to read as follows:

"The Grand Exalted Ruler shall have power to grant permits to subordinate lodges to institute organizations of young men under 21 years of age in the manner prescribed by statute."

This amendment was approved by the subordinate lodges.

Grand Exalted Ruler Malley in 1928, after stating that the Social and Community Welfare Committee had been preparing a ritual for the Antlers, said:

"The policies to be adopted in respect to this innovation require great vision and sound judgment. We must approach the problem dealing with the youth of America with solemn appreciation of the responsibility involved."

At this Grand Lodge Session there was created a Ritualistic Committee and to that incoming Committee was referred such ritualistic matters, relative to the Antlers, as were under consideration by the Social and Community Welfare Committee.

1929

At the Grand Lodge Session in 1929 Grand Exalted Ruler Hulbert endorsed the movement.

Grand Exalted Ruler Hulbert also said that the Committee on Work and Ritual had in preparation, and he hoped would submit to that convention, a Ritual for the institution of "The Antlers," the installation of the officers thereof and the initiation of candidates therein. This was done.

He added that a brief history of the origin and growth of the Order should be incorporated in the Ritual of Initiation.

Prior to this adoption of the Antlers by the Grand Lodge, the list of Elks lodges sponsoring lodges of Antlers continued to grow.

By 1925 there were enough Antlers lodges in California so that there was held that year the first state convention of the organization.

Gradually the program was adopted by lodges in other states, and at the time of the Grand Lodge Session of 1929, previously referred to, there were, in addition to 24 Antlers Lodges in California, 10 lodges in other states, a total of 34 lodges.

1933

Chairman Nichols, the Antlers Counselor, in making a report in 1933 said:

"The Grand Lodge in July 1932, in Convention assembled at Birmingham, Alabama, adopted a resolution authorizing, empowering and requesting the Grand Exalted Ruler to appoint an Antlers Counselor who, subject to his direction and the provisions of our laws, should have supervision and control of lodges of the Antlers, their activities and the advisory councils appointed in connection therewith.

"It was also further resolved that the Antlers Counselor, with the consent and approval of the Grand Exalted Ruler, might prescribe and promulgate rules and regulations for the government of lodges of the Antlers and the members and advisory councils thereof."

Later in the same report he said:

"Since founding the organization in 1922, I have had a continuously pleasant and active association with those fine young men who make up Antler membership. This has been recompense enough. For the privilege of appearing here today and reporting as the first Antlers Counselor and the opportunity heretofore given me to contribute to the work to which I have devoted so many years, I thank the Grand Lodge and our Grand Exalted Ruler."

In 1933 it was reported that there were 45 lodges with a membership of 3,594.

1943

At the Grand Lodge Session in 1943, Homer F. Potter, Chairman of Antlers Council, expressed the regret of the members of the Council that it was necessary to report that practically all of the members of the Order of Antlers had found it necessary to drop their membership for the time being, due to the fact that so many of them were going into the armed services, their ages having been seventeen, eighteen, nineteen, and twenty years.

He stated that because of such conditions many subordinate lodges had asked permission to abandon this activity for the duration of the war.

The Committee recommended that, under those circumstances, the Order of Antlers be dropped as a special Grand Lodge activity.

Chairman Potter also stated it was the belief of the members of the Council that any subordinate lodge which had at that time a lodge of Antlers should be permitted to carry on this work, should it so desire.

The report was adopted by the Grand Lodge.

1944

The Antlers Council reporting in 1944, in reviewing the seventeen-year history of the Antler program, found the following:

At their height the Antlers Councils were composed of 72 lodges which had over 4,500 members.

The subordinate lodges accepted too lightly the responsibility of training the youth of America. The reason for the failure of the Antlers Council in an overwhelming majority of instances can be laid to one of four reasons:

1. Lack of supervision by Big Brother Counselors.

2. Having a member of a lodge assume the Exalted Rulership who was not in sympathy with the Antlers program.

3. Starting a lodge without having the proper men to act as Counselors.

4. Subordinate lodges taking up something because it is new and dropping it when the newness wears off.

The Council stated that due mainly to the war there had been a great curtailment of Antlers lodges during the preceding two years.

While a questionnaire had not brought the council the exact number of Antlers lodges at the time, the returns received indicated between ten and fifteen lodges active.

The report also indicated approximately 75 per cent of the Antlers were in the Armed Forces or in defense work. The Council made the following recommendations:

That subordinate lodges honor the "duration cards" that had been issued by Antlers lodges to their members in the Armed Forces.

That State Associations become really active in Antlers work.

That Antlers quarters be set apart from regular lodge facilities where possible.

That suitable publicity be given the Antlers movement through The Elks Magazine and by State Associations and subordinate lodges through their respective publications and bulletins.

That the age limit be reduced to 14 years.

This report was accepted.

1945

In 1945 the Antlers Council sent out a questionnaire to the Presidents of the State Associations which showed that in the West where the Antlers had been most active, the future was bright, but that this position was reversed in both the Central and the Eastern parts of the country. The Council stated that in the opinion of its members a good boys' program was an asset and that the Antlers program where it had been introduced under proper supervision, had been successful and that the failure of nearly every Antlers lodge could be traced to poor supervision or indifference on the part of the local Counselors.

The Antlers Council reported that a questionnaire sent to the 83 lodges that had sponsored Councils of the Antlers got replies from 60, indicating that of that number 53 had disbanded and 7 were still functioning.

This Antlers Council was of the opinion that the reasons for the discontinuance of the lodges of the Antlers were: lack of competent leadership; lack of suitable quarters; apathy by our membership to the program, and loss of Antlers membership due to war conditions.

The Council stated that it was the opinion of its members that no new lodges of the Antlers should be organized but that such as were now in existence who were desirous of continuing their activities and who obtained the approval of the Grand Exalted Ruler should be permitted to do so.

It was recommended that section 47a and 183a of the Grand Lodge Statutes be repealed. The report of the Council was accepted.

Grand Exalted Ruler Kepner had recommended in his report that Antlers lodges be no longer sponsored by the Grand Lodge. He stated that they had not proved beneficial as a whole but that it was his thought that they might be continued by individual lodges where they had proved successful.

At this same convention the Committee on Judiciary took recognition of the recommendation of the Grand Exalted Ruler and stated that to accomplish that it would be necessary to abolish the Antlers Council of the Grand Lodge, leaving to the subordinate lodges the right to continue the lodges of Antlers which were then in existence.

The Committee therefore recommended that Section 47a of the Grand Lodge Statutes entitled "The Antlers Council" be repealed and that Section 183a be amended to provide that no new Antlers lodges should be organized but that such lodges as were then in existence might continue their activities with the approval of the Grand Exalted Ruler, and that they should be subject to such rules and regulations as might be adopted by the subordinate lodge sponsoring such Antlers lodges, providing that such rules and regulations should first be approved by the Committee on Judiciary.

In 1967, the Grand Lodge repealed Section 183A in its entirety. At the same time, Section 161 was amended to delete the reference to waiving the initiation fee for Antlers joining an Elks Lodge.

EDWARD J. McCORMICK
1938-39

JOSEPH G. BUCH
1940-41

HENRY C. WARNER
1939-40

JOHN S. McCLELLAND
1941-42

Grand Exalted Rulers

E I G H T H   D E C A D E

1938-1948

E. MARK SULLIVAN
1942-43

FRANK J. LONERGAN
1943-44

WADE H. KEPNER
1945-46

ROBERT S. BARRETT
1944-45

CHARLES E. BROUGHTON
1946-47

L. A. LEWIS
1947-48

S E C T I O N

Eighth Decade

Following a setback in the period of depression in the preceding Decade, the Eighth Decade made a striking comeback and not from 1936 to 1952, when this History ends, did any year show a decrease in the membership of the Order.

For the Eighth Decade the percentage of gain was 90, an average membership gain per year of 47,000.

One year, 1945-1946, showed a gain of 86,769.

At the Grand Lodge Session in 1940 there was created the Elks National Defense and Public Relations Commission.

During 18 months of the existence of this Commission under that name its activities were designed to assist in awakening the American people to the danger of approaching war.

Immediately after our entry into the war the name of the Commission was changed to Elks War Commission.

Under one name or the other, the Commission cooperated with the Army and the Navy in establishing refresher schools to prepare young men to take the training course for aviation cadets, providing ground crew men for the Army and engineers for both branches of the service.

Subordinate lodges near mobilization camps assisting, "Fraternal Centers" were established for the convenience, comfort and comradeship of the boys called into service.

When the disabled soldiers were hospitalized comprehensive plans for their entertainment were adopted while services of many kinds were rendered to the members of the fighting forces.

The Elks War Commission made its final report in 1946, its activities in connection with the war having, with one exception, been concluded.

That exception was the program for continuation of the service to the hospitalized veterans.

The Commission recommended to the Grand Lodge that it be discharged but that a new Commission be created to carry on that work.

The Grand Lodge accepted that recommendation and there was created the Elks National Veterans Service Commission which up to the present day has continued with the cooperation of the subordinate lodges to provide comfort, entertainment and good cheer for the disabled soldiers in every War Department or Veterans Administration hospital where they may be found.

In this Decade an amendment to the Ritual was adopted, substituting in the requirement for membership a "belief in God" for the former requirement of a "belief in a Supreme Being."

Eighth Decade—1938-1948

GRAND EXALTED RULERS

During this period there were the following Grand Exalted Rulers:

EDWARD J. McCORMICK, Toledo, Ohio, Lodge No. 53	1938-1939
HENRY C. WARNER, Dixon, Ill., Lodge No. 779	1939-1940
JOSEPH G. BUCH, Trenton, N. J., Lodge No. 105	1940-1941
JOHN S. McCLELLAND, Atlanta, Ga., Lodge No. 78	1941-1942
E. MARK SULLIVAN, Boston, Mass., Lodge No. 10	1942-1943
FRANK J. LONERGAN, Portland, Ore., Lodge No. 142	1943-1944
ROBERT S. BARRETT, Alexandria, Va., Lodge No. 758	1944-1945
WADE H. KEPNER, Wheeling, W. Va., Lodge No. 28	1945-1946
CHARLES E. BROUGHTON, Sheboygan, Wis., Lodge No. 299	1946-1947
L. A. LEWIS, Anaheim, Calif., Lodge No. 1345	1947-1948

Throughout the entire Eighth Decade, Past Grand Exalted Ruler Masters continued to serve as Grand Secretary.

MEMBERSHIP AND CHARITABLE EXPENDITURES

During this period the Order gained in membership, increasing from 479,494 to 925,679.

The number of lodges increased from 1,359 to 1,487.

YEAR	MEMBERSHIP	CHARITABLE EXPENDITURES
1938-1939	473,927	$1,541,005.86
1939-1940	475,599	1,628,660.30
1940-1941	490,417	1,778,075.26
1941-1942	506,887	2,071,324.61
1942-1943	547,718	2,253,091.92
1943-1944	627,513	3,003,974.89
1944-1945	705,570	3,753,800.86
1945-1946	792,339	4,208,533.16
1946-1947	877,271	5,022,896.86
1947-1948	925,679	5,765,239.76

Grand Lodge Sessions during this period were held in the following cities:

1939	St. Louis, Missouri	1944	Chicago, Illinois
1940	Houston, Texas	1945	New York, New York
1941	Philadelphia, Pennsylvania	1946	New York, New York
1942	Omaha, Nebraska	1947	Portland, Oregon
1943	Boston, Massachusetts	1948	Philadelphia, Pennsylvania

At the end of this Decade the assets of the 1,487 lodges amounted to $180,381,479.89.

Elks National Defense and Public Relations Commission

In July, 1940, when the Grand Lodge held its annual Session in Houston, Texas, it was evident to a large percentage of the people of the country that subversive groups were active here and that war was fast approaching our shores.

Joseph G. Buch, Grand Exalted Ruler Elect, reflected the sentiments of millions of Americans when he said in his speech of acceptance:

":We must see that America is safe-guarded from within as well as from without, for in this blessed land there must be no divided allegiance. We who love and would defend America, ask but one simple question of those within our borders: 'Do you, likewise, love America?' The answer should determine the status of every individual enjoying the security and hospitality of our land."

A resolution calling for the appointment of an Elks National Defense and Public Relations Commission was unanimously and enthusiastically adopted.

There was appointed such a Commission composed of the following Past Grand Exalted Rulers: James R. Nicholson, Chairman; James T. Hallinan, Vice Chairman; Edward J. McCormick, Secretary; John R. Coen, Michael F. Shannon, David Sholtz and Henry C. Warner.

Each successive year, as their terms of office expired, succeeding Grand Exalted Rulers were appointed to the Commission.

They were: Joseph G. Buch, John S. McClelland, E. Mark Sullivan, Frank J. Lonergan, Robert S. Barrett and Wade H. Kepner. In 1942, Michael F. Shannon resigned from the Commission and was appointed a member of the Elks National Memorial and Publication Commission. Emmett T. Anderson, Tacoma, Washington, Lodge No. 174, was appointed to the Commission.

The Exalted Rulers of the subordinate lodges were asked to appoint local National Defense Committees. The response of the subordinate lodges to this request was immediate and unanimous.

A similar request from the Commission to Presidents of State Associations also met with complete and enthusiastic compliance.

The Commission communicated with the President of the United States; Secretary of War, Henry L. Stimson; Secretary of the Navy, Frank B. Knox, and Director J. Edgar Hoover of the Federal Bureau of Investigation, offering the services of the Order and the furtherance of the National Defense program.

Expressions of appreciation and suggestions were received from all of them.

July, 1940——December, 1941

THE PROGRAM

The Commission formulated a program designed to place the power and patriotism of the entire membership of the Benevolent and Protective Order of Elks behind the program for National Defense.

Included in this program was a campaign to establish vocational training in the public schools, having in mind the importance of mechanized units for modern warfare, also:

Exempting members of the Order called into the Armed Services from payment of dues.

Urging the use of Elk buildings for community patriotic purposes.

Promoting a general and constant display of our country's flag.

Organizing mothers, wives and daughters for cooperation in the general defense program and for contributing to the comfort of boys in army camps.

Organizing members of lodges for physical culture activities that Elks might be physically fit to meet the responsibility when the country would need the best that each had to give.

The program called upon all Elks to make every possible contribution to the defense of our country and the preservation of our democratic form of government.

SPECIFIED COURSE OF ACTION

It set forth a specified course of action for State Associations and subordinate lodges.

It urged each lodge to hold a patriotic public meeting during the week of October 21, 1940, following this meeting from time to time with others of a like character, these meetings having for their objective the awakening of people everywhere to the necessity of preparation for National Defense.

The Commission urged subordinate lodges to arrange a patriotic program for school children on Washington's Birthday.

To provide dinners and entertainment for men entering the United States Army under the Selective Service Act.

To have a member responsible for each young man entering the Service corresponding with him while in the Service, remembering him on his birthday and at Christmas time.

Supplying medical and legal service gratis to the families of these boys.

Supporting state legislation designed to provide uniform laws for National Defense.

Securing the commitment of lodges and individual members to a full measure of cooperation with local organizations in their communities in the campaigns for funds for the United Service Organizations.

"Keep 'em Flying"

The problem of recruiting young men for the Flying Cadet Corps of our Army offered one of the greatest single opportunities to be of service to our country which had ever been presented to the subordinate lodges of our Order.

In July, 1941, a request was received by the Elks National Defense Commission from representatives of the War Department to inaugurate a program of co-operation with the War Department in securing and assisting in qualifying young men desiring to take the Aviation Cadet Training Course.

Upon assurance of the desire of the Commission and the Order to co-operate, the following telegram was received from the Adjutant General of the Army:

"On behalf of the War Department it is my pleasure to express sincere appreciation to you and the Order of Elks for your splendid National Defense program and current plan of co-operation in the procurement of Army aviation cadets. 'Keep 'em Flying.' "

E. S. Adams, Major-General
the Adjutant General

Immediately thereafter, plans were made for the full participation of the Order in the Army's "Keep 'em Flying" program.

The general program embraced the individual lodges' co-operation with the nearest recruiting office, sponsorship of Cadet rallies at the lodge home, and the operation of special refresher course educational programs designed to enable potential Aviation Cadets to pass the educational requirements for enlistment in this branch of the service.

The subordinate lodges of the Order wholeheartedly co-operated with the program, and more than 400 lodges conducted refresher-course schools.

Thousands of young men were recruited for the Army Air Force and given intensive educational training which not only enabled them to pass the entrance examination but prepared them for the rigorous routine of aviation ground school work. Army officials were high in their praise of the pre-pilot training offered. A large percentage of Elk-trained men passed their examinations and entered the Service.

Uncle Sam Poster

Upon the recommendation of the public relations counsel of the Commission, Past Grand Exalted Ruler Charles Spencer Hart, the service of the well-known artist, C. C. Beal, was engaged to paint a composite portrait of Uncle Sam.

Past Grand Exalted Ruler Hart arranged for this portrait to be accepted by the War Department as a poster design.

Past Grand Exalted Ruler Hallinan, Vice-Chairman of the Commission, arranged through U. S. Senator Robert Wagner, a member of New York Lodge No. 1, for President Roosevelt's personal acceptance of this portrait in behalf of the War Department.

President Franklin D. Roosevelt accepting a poster design for the War Department (a composite picture of Uncle Sam) presented by a group headed by Grand Exalted Ruler Joseph G. Buch (center). Others in the group are, left to right: Past Grand Exalted Ruler James T. Hallinan, United States Senator Robert F. Wagner, Chairman James R. Nicholson of the National Defense Commission and Major Charles S. Hart, afterwards Grand Exalted Ruler.

Accordingly, on January 9, 1941, Grand Exalted Ruler Joseph G. Buch, accompanied by Chairman Nicholson of the Commission, Vice-Chairman Hallinan, Past Grand Exalted Ruler Hart and Senator Wagner, presented the portrait to President Roosevelt at the White House.

The President was very gracious in his acceptance, spoke most appreciatively of the work that the Order was doing in national defense, and with pride of his membership in Poughkeepsie, New York, Lodge No. 275.

National Essay Contest

The Commission decided to use the Uncle Sam poster as the basis for a National Essay Contest, to be participated in by pupils in high schools and schools of the same grade throughout the several states and our territories and possessions.

Plans were evolved for a contest on the following basis:

1. Each subordinate lodge to grant 1st, 2nd, and 3rd awards to contestants within the jurisdiction of such lodge.
2. The best essays of each lodge jurisdiction to be offered in a State, Territory, or Possession contest, with awards for the 1st, 2nd, and 3rd best.

3. The best essays of each State, Territory or Possession to compete in a national contest.

The subordinate lodges and the State Associations provided substantial cash prizes in most instances for 1st, 2nd, and 3rd place, and the Elks National Defense Commission offered cash awards for the national prizes of $1,000, $500, and $250 each.

The National Committee of Awards was composed of:

> Ex-Governor Wilbur Cross of Connecticut, Chairman
> Dr. Ralph B. Wagner of St. Louis University
> Rabbi Edgar F. Magnin of Los Angeles

There was a total of 50 essays submitted for the National Contest, one from each state of the Union (excepting that Maryland, Delaware, and the District of Columbia submitted one essay, inasmuch as they are in one Grand Lodge district) and one each from Alaska, Canal Zone, and Puerto Rico.

The judges selected as the winners of the grand prizes of $1,000, $500, and $250, respectively:

> Miss Grace Langley, Red Wing, Minnesota
> Robert Gilson, Coeur d'Alene, Idaho
> Walter Bierman, Harrisburg, Pennsylvania

A fourth prize of $100 was also awarded to Miss Victoria Lopez of Puerto Rico. The awards were made in U. S. Defense Bonds.

These prizes were presented to the winners at Independence Hall in Philadelphia at the time of the 1941 Grand Lodge Session over a national radio hook-up on which General Pershing spoke from Washington.

The infamous Japanese attack on Pearl Harbor and quick declaration of war on the United States by the Axis powers made us "a nation one and indivisible." It was the spark which set ablaze the fiery determination to win and created a new opportunity for the Benevolent and Protective Order of Elks to live up to its record of patriotic service.

The noise of Japanese bombs had scarcely died away when Grand Exalted Ruler McClelland telegraphed the President of the United States, placing at his disposal the full strength of the Order. A special executive session of the National Defense Commission was called for January 4th, 1942, in the City of New York and in every subordinate lodge in the land a new patriotic fervor to serve burst into flame.

The Elks National Defense and Public Relations Commission became the Elks War Commission at that time.

Elks War Commission (1943). Left to right, standing: Past Grand Exalted Rulers David Sholtz, Joseph G. Buch, John R. Coen, John S. McClelland, former President of the Washington State Elks Association Emmett T. Anderson and Past Grand Exalted Ruler E. Mark Sullivan. Seated: Past Grand Exalted Rulers Edward J. McCormick, James T. Hallinan, Frank J. Lonergan, James R. Nicholson and Henry C. Warner.

Elks War Commission

The necessity for a War Chest to be administered by the Elks War Commission was, of course, immediately recognized. Preliminary contributions were made in the sum of $25,000 by the Elks National Memorial and Publication Commission, $5,000 by the Elks National Foundation and $5,000 by Queens Borough, New York, Lodge No. 878.

Grand Exalted Ruler McClelland approved the Elks War Commission's request to make an appeal to subordinate lodges for contributions to the Commission.

Cables were sent to the District Deputies in Manila, Hawaii, Puerto Rico, Alaska and the Canal Zone, offering the facilities of the Elks National Home at Bedford, Virginia, as a haven for the duration of the war for children of Elks who might be evacuated from our outlying possessions.

Grand Exalted Ruler McClelland issued a proclamation designating the week of March 15, 1942 as "Win the War Week" and directed all lodges to stage a patriotic demonstration during this period.

The Elks War Commission also decided to make an inventory of the potential manpower and resources of the Order and the information gathered was made available to our Government.

Elks War Fund

At the Grand Lodge Session in Omaha, in 1942, the Chairman of the Elks War Commission stated that the members of the Commission felt that they should have at their command a fund of half a million dollars.

Grand Exalted Ruler McClelland, speaking from the floor, moved:

> "That our efforts to raise money for the purpose of prosecution of this war and for the Elks War Fund be in the nature of a voluntary contribution by the Subordinate Lodges of the Order."

The motion was adopted by the Grand Lodge.

At the Grand Lodge Session in Boston, in 1943, the Commission recommended that the representatives of the Grand Lodge pledge additional subscriptions to the Elks War Fund in the amount of $1.00 per member based on lodge membership as of March 31st of that year.

This recommendation was adopted.

Similar action was taken at the Grand Lodge Session in Chicago in 1944.

Army Air Corps Mechanical Personnel Recruiting

In August, 1942, the Adjutant General of the United States Army, impressed by the services performed by the Order of Elks in qualifying men for the Flying Cadet Corps, appealed to the Elks War Commission to assist in the recruiting of other young men for the ground crews of the Army Air Corps.

The Commission unhesitatingly accepted this assignment. All subordinate lodges were supplied with full information as to the requirements necessary for enlistments.

Each lodge was asked to conduct a broad survey to find men qualified for this branch and endeavor to enlist them for the Army. Model programs including local publicity, rallies and personal contacts were carried out by a large percentage of the subordinate lodges.

The Adjutant General asked for 45,000 recruits. The efforts of the subordinate lodges were so successful that in a short time the Adjutant General's office notified the Elks War Commission that 97,000 ground crew men had been obtained and expressed deep appreciation for the part the Elks had taken in this campaign.

Adjutant General Ulio commissioned Major George Foster to attend the 1943 Grand Lodge Session to express the gratitude of the Army for this service rendered by the Order.

Elks Fraternal Centers

At the first conference of the Elks War Commission, it was decided to make a thorough survey of conditions in an effort to establish a program and an adequate policy of cooperation with subordinate lodges adjacent to the larger camps, which would effectually solve the problem of providing hospitality to Elk members and others of the armed forces, retain and strengthen the interest and pride of these brothers in their Elks' membership even though they are distant from their home lodge, and relieve the financial burden on several subordinate lodges resulting from their location adjacent to large military and naval establishments.

The program was inaugurated and expanded until 119 Elks Fraternal Centers were at one time in operation across the country from the Atlantic to the Pacific and from the Great Lakes to the Gulf of Mexico, supplying good fellowship, refreshments and entertainment for hundreds of thousands of our servicemen each month.

In most of the Elks Fraternal Centers the wives, daughters and sisters of members served as hostesses; music was furnished for dancing; there were card games, bingo and community singing. Where space for dancing was not available, a variety of programs was provided, such as barbecues, fish fries, fishing trips, both deep sea and fresh water, depending on the section of the country, which gave wholesome entertainment to a tremendous number.

Of the 119 Fraternal Centers referred to above, several were supported wholly by the subordinate lodges without assistance from the War Commission.

The total number of Fraternal Centers during the period either supported by the War Commission or by the individual Lodges reached 155.

Elks Fraternal Center in New York

The Elks War Commission opened an Elks Fraternal Center in New York City on December 11, 1943, at 39th Street and Madison Avenue, in a former luxurious four-story home.

Although the home was redecorated and remodeled to serve as a recreational center, neither the original charm nor the natural warmth of this fine old residence was sacrificed in the process of renovation.

The Center's overnight lodging accommodations, consisting of 110 beds, laundry facilities and canteen, were a blessing to servicemen who had found the inadequacy of New York's hotel accommodations a serious problem to overcome.

This Center was not restricted to members of the Order or to relatives of members.

Elks Fraternal Center established at Madison Avenue and 39th Street in New York City.

Two interior views of the New York City Fraternal Center

The spacious main lounge with canteen shown in rear.

Christmas — 1945.

The facilities of the Center included the following:

A beautiful lounge where guests might meet their friends, read current magazines, or just rest; a game room for cards, chess, checkers, etc., piano and radio; a canteen containing a snack bar; tables and a free juke box; large bedrooms; adequate shower baths; a laundry containing wash basins, a dryer, an electric iron and pressing facilities; a ping pong room; a powder room for hostesses and women in the armed forces; a library and writing room with free writing paper, shelves of good books and home town newspapers.

The nominal charge for overnight sleeping accommodations was 50 cents. Coffee, tea, cookies and doughnuts were free. There were no charges for any other services.

A serviceman in need of clean linen was welcome to use the laundry when passing through the city whether he stayed over night in the Center or not. He was welcome to make use of the writing room and library, the lounge, and any other facility. The sole aim of the Elks Fraternal Center was to "serve those who serve" and there were no strings attached to that principle. Over 1,000,000 service men and women visited this center and a total of 150,000 service men slept there overnight.

Elks lodges in the New York Metropolitan area assumed the responsibilities of providing volunteer hostesses and junior hostesses to assist in entertaining the Center's guests. Lodges participating in this service on a regular schedule of assignments were New York Lodge No. 1; Brooklyn Lodge No. 22; Bronx Lodge No. 871; Queens Borough Lodge No. 878; Staten Island Lodge No. 841 and Lynbrook Lodge No. 1515.

Naval Air Corps Recruiting

As a result of the successful campaign conducted by the Elks in behalf of the Army Air Corps, Secretary of the Navy Knox requested the assistance of the Elks War Commission in obtaining recruits for the Naval Air Corps. Again the subordinate lodges responded magnificently.

Subordinate Lodges

It is impossible to give a detailed account of the war activities of subordinate lodges. Many turned their homes over for the use of the Red Cross and other community activities. Most all of them engaged in campaigns for the collection of blood plasma; their members and ladies conducted Fraternal Centers wherever sponsored by the Elks War Commission. No lodge failed to enter wholeheartedly and effectively into every community activity bearing upon the war effort including local War Bond sales and drives for funds for the Red Cross and the United Service Organizations.

In addition to their efforts to sell War Bonds, subordinate lodges up to August 1944 purchased $21,787,108 of these bonds.

"G" Boxes——A Suggestion of Grand Exalted Ruler McClelland

The War Commission with the cooperation of the Lodge Activities Committee of the Grand Lodge sponsored and put into operation a plan to send gift boxes to members in the armed forces. Folding boxes were sent to each subordinate lodge to be filled with smoker's supplies, candy, handkerchiefs, shaving equipment and other items. As the boxes were filled they were mailed to lodge members at their military stations.

Thousands were sent to Elks and their buddies in camps overseas.

Write 'em A Letter

Early in the war the Elks War Commission, realizing the importance of letters from home as a preserver of morale, sponsored a "Write 'em A Letter" campaign, designed to increase correspondence between men and women in the Service and their families and friends at home.

Elks Lodges throughout the country responded at once to the "Write 'em A Letter" appeal. Many lodges set up tables in their homes, equipped with writing material, and on meeting nights all who attended were urged to "Write 'em A Letter." Other lodges provided a secretary to do the writing, and more placed boxes in a conspicuous place where letters might be deposited by the writers. These were then collected, properly addressed and mailed by officers of the lodge.

The campaigns of subordinate lodges were supplemented by vigorous publicity from the office of the Elks War Commission. A cartoon contest was conducted throughout Army and Navy camps and prizes offered for the best cartoons based upon the "Write 'em A Letter" theme. For each cartoon selected a prize of $10 was awarded.

> The first prize went to Sergeant Jack O'Brien, attached to the Public Relations Office, Army Flying School, Chico, California
>
> Second prize to Private Bill Mauldin, 45th Division, and the
>
> Third prize to a Navy man, Apprentice Seaman Robert G. Woodcock, Naval Training Station, San Diego, California.

Cigarettes to the A. E. F.

The Elks War Commission in May, 1943, began the purchase and shipment of cigarettes to men of the far-flung battlefronts. Later, in response to requests from pipe smokers and roll-your-own smokers, popular brands of cigarettes were supplemented by tobacco and cigarette papers.

Many subordinate lodges also sent supplies overseas in addition to the shipments made each month by the Elks War Commission. They went to far off places throughout the world, wherever our men had advanced against the foe. And from all these points came back letters expressing gratitude for the smokes and for the thoughtfulness of the folks back home in sending something which was so much appreciated. Thousands of letters were received. They came from Commanding Officers, from Chaplains, and from the men themselves.

This work was carried on at an expense of over $72,000.

In one year alone there were sent 15,640,000 cigarettes and 701,280 packages of tobacco.

Army Engineers——Navy Seabees

An outstanding achievement of the Elks was the part played in the recruiting campaign staged by the Army Corps of Engineers and the Navy Construction Battalions.

When the need for men skilled in the field of construction became urgent, the Army and Navy, for the first time in their history, embarked on a joint campaign to obtain volunteers. The Elks War Commission was asked by the Army and Navy to assist in the drive—the only organization to participate in the campaign.

The Elks War Commission urged all subordinate lodges to wage an intensive drive for recruits for both the Army Corps of Engineers and the Navy Construction Battalions. The lodges displayed so much enthusiasm and efficiency that the required numbers of Army Engineers and Navy Seabees were obtained three months ahead of schedule.

Army and Navy Appreciation

The following communications testify to the success of this effort on the part of the Order:

James R. Nicholson, Chairman   October 8, 1943
Elks War Commission
21 East 40th Street, Room 506
New York 16, N. Y.

Dear Mr. Nicholson:

The support which the Elks lodges gave to the recruiting campaign for construction specialists for the Army Engineers and Navy Seabees brought very gratifying results.

The numbers needed were obtained in record time which resulted in the discontinuance of the campaign sooner than had been originally anticipated.

Since the B.P.O.E. was the only civilian organization actively supporting this campaign, it is entitled to full credit for the success obtained. Assuring you again of my deep appreciation of your fine support in the past, I am,

Sincerely yours,

J. A. Ulio, Major General
Adjutant General

James R. Nicholson, Chairman   September 11, 1943
Elks War Committee
21 East 40th Street, Room 506
New York 16, N. Y.

Dear Mr. Nicholson:

Due to the outstanding efforts of the B.P.O.E., the recruitment of Engineer Specialists has far exceeded our expectations, so much so, that the Engineer requirements have been met three months ahead of schedule, necessitating the immediate suspension of the voluntary induction program.

All special assignment letters issued applicants to date will be honored at reception centers.

The wholehearted cooperation of the Elks in helping to put this program across ahead of schedule has been of inestimable value to the Corps of Engineers and is deeply appreciated.

Reybold, Chief of Engineers
Washington, D. C.

Books for the Merchant Marine

The President of the American Merchant Marine Library Association advised the Commission that the organization needed 600,000 books to provide sufficient reading material for the seamen of the American Merchant Marine Service, greatly expanded because of the war. She asked that the Elks help the library attain its goal.

The Elks War Commission advised the 1,409 Elks lodges of this need for reading matter and suggested that each member, a total of 650,000 throughout the United States, contribute at least one book to the cause.

The appeal met with an instantaneous response among the subordinate lodges which set up special committees for the successful collection program in their respective communities.

In the first few weeks several hundred thousand books had been collected and given to the floating libraries so that amusement and learning might continue to be made available to "the men who go down to the sea in ships."

Slippers for Convalescents

Shortly after our entry into the war, the idea of manufacturing slippers for our hospitalized servicemen was taken up by Columbus, Ohio, Lodge No. 37. Much correspondence with the War Department was necessary before permission was obtained to give slippers to the hospital units of the various branches of the United States armed forces.

Slippers were sent gratis through the efforts of Columbus Lodge to the camps and military hospitals whose commandants made requests for them.

Soon, however, the demand and the task became too great to be met locally. The Elks War Commission stepped into the picture and furnished necessary funds.

The slippers were manufactured by the inmates of the Ohio State Penitentiary and penal institutions in Massachusetts, New York, Washington, and Oregon.

The Elks of Maine, through the cooperation of some shoe manufacturers of their state, contributed several thousand pairs.

Grand Exalted Ruler Robert S. Barrett (left) pledging the aid of the Benevolent and Protective Order of Elks to Brigadier General Frank T. Hines, Administrator, Veterans Affairs.

In acknowledgment of the cooperation of the Order with the Veterans Administration, General Hines wrote as follows:

"Remembering the splendid work of the Elks War Commission in past recruiting programs in the Army and Navy, the Veterans Administration is highly gratified at the recent action of the Grand Lodge in unanimously pledging your great organization to assist in recruiting nurses who are so urgently needed to care for the disabled in our Veterans Hospitals."

Nurses for the Veterans Administration

At the War Conference of the Grand Lodge held in Chicago, July, 1944, Colonel George Ijams, Assistant Administrator of Veteran Affairs, representing the Administrator Brigadier General Frank T. Hines, requested the assistance of the Elks in securing nurses for the Veterans Administration Hospitals.

He explained that the shortage of nurses in Veterans Administration Hospitals had become critical due to the loss of nurses to the armed services and also to the increased demand for beds brought about through our participation in the present war.

Necessarily the recruiting efforts of the Elks had to be directed to those who could not serve with the armed forces. This field naturally was limited, but through the efforts of the Elk lodges, hundreds of nurses who were not practicing their profession were brought back to active duty. Many of these entered the Veterans Administration Hospitals. Some helped by relieving nurses in local hospitals.

Aid for Manila

For the first time in the history of the B.P.O. Elks, two of the lodges of the Order fell into enemy hands. One of these was Manila, Philippine Islands, Lodge which was taken January 4, 1942.

As soon as word flashed to this country of the fall of Manila and its subsequent occupation by the Japanese, the Elks War Commission, prompted by concern for the Brothers there, made immediate inquiries by letters and cable and exerted every effort to send them food and supplies.

During the following three years, while ceaseless attempts were made to penetrate the veil of Jap censorship, little but brief messages and unsatisfactory rumors bridged the gap that existed between members of the Order in the United States and the Americans interned by the Japanese across the Pacific.

Only upon the reoccupation of Manila by American forces and the liberation of the surviving internees, were the stories of the war years disclosed. They were grim tales, most of them, even though they bespoke so much for the fortitude and the humaneness of the American men and women who lived them.

Volumes might be written of the individual tragedies that occurred among the 489 members of Manila lodge and their families, as well as the members and the families of other Elk members who were taken when the Japs occupied the Philippines.

It is gratifying that members of the Order were able to help one another during these trying times and to take some comfort from the fact that there were many thousands of Brothers in the United States who were only too eager to help them whenever and however they might. Slight encouragement, perhaps, but in their plight the unfortunate internees found comfort in the knowledge that they did have friends willing to do what they could.

The Elks War Commission did everything in its power to bring aid and comfort to the internees and actually succeeded in reaching some of those held in the Jap camps with messages from America. Much that the Order would have accomplished in the form of more substantial assistance was denied by the Japanese, despite every attempt the Elks War Commission, together with the Red Cross, made to reach those in custody.

The first real opportunity to render aid to those who were held in Jap internment camps came when the victorious forces of General Douglas MacArthur returned to the Philippines and freed the capital early in 1945.

Without delay, for time was valuable and speed important, the Elks War Commission in early February appropriated $100,000 from its War Fund scarcely before the last Jap had been driven out or killed by the advancing Americans.

Contact was immediately established with the Elk internees, and they were given the assurance that food, clothing, medicine and financial assistance was being made available as speedily as it was humanly possible to do so.

Thomas J. Wolff, a Past Exalted Ruler of Manila Lodge and Past District Deputy, who had been interned along with other members, was appointed by the Elks War Commission to head a relief committee in Manila, and funds were placed at his disposal. Past District Deputy Wolff was well equipped by experience and knowledge of the needs of the other internees to handle the work.

He had a very distinguished military record and had served as an officer under both General Arthur MacArthur and General Douglas MacArthur.

For many years he had been President of the Philippine Red Cross and he continued to function in that capacity even during his imprisonment.

His job was a hard one, and he himself had suffered much at the hands of the Japs during his internment, but he unhesitatingly accepted the task and performed valiant work under difficult conditions.

Pacific Coast Committees

Because some of the former internees were able to leave the Philippines to return to America before aid from the Elks War Commission could reach them, committees were set up in San Francisco and Los Angeles, equipped with necessary funds to meet and assist the arrivals when they landed in this country.

Every incoming ship had been met by the committee, and the

needs of the members and their families, as well as the widows and children of members, had been attended to. This work was under the supervision of Emmett T. Anderson, of Tacoma, Washington, Lodge No. 174, a member of the Commission.

Agana, Guam, Lodge

Agana, Guam, Lodge was taken by the Japs on December 10, 1941; the first lodge of the Order to suffer such a fate.

Members of the Agana Lodge composed mainly of Navy, Marine and government personnel were transferred to prisoner-of-war and internment camps in Japan.

Cables and letters were sent to them by the Elks War Commission at regular intervals, and peculiarly enough, more replies were received from members in Japan than from the internees or prisoners of war in the Philippines. The Elks War Commission also attempted to send relief supplies to the members interned in Japan, but this was not successful due to the lack of co-operation of the Japanese authorities.

Restoration of Manila Lodge

A resolution was adopted at the Grand Lodge Session of 1945 authorizing the Elks War Commission to render full aid and assistance financially and otherwise as in the judgment of said Commission might be deemed necessary to Agana and Manila Lodges that their Elks Homes might be rebuilt and restored to the purposes of the Order.

Accordingly, the Commission advanced to Manila Lodge $250,000 for this purpose with the agreement that such part of that amount as might be received by the Lodge from the Federal government for reimbursement would be repaid to the Commission. Similar assistance was not necessary in the case of Agana Lodge.

Hospital Service

Thousands of disabled soldiers, sailors, and marines were returned home to be cared for in Government hospitals. Many of these boys would be confined for long periods and would require more than medical attention to restore them to a normal condition. Entertainment and recreation would play a very important part in rebuilding their health and morale. Elks in the neighborhood of these institutions were quick to offer their services in entertaining the convalescent veterans.

Notable examples of the unselfish service of brotherly love on the part of Elks in sponsoring hospitalization programs during and following World War II were the activities of 43 State Associations which engaged in this work.

Bedridden patients were supplied with radios, phonographs,

*Certificate issued by the Elks War Commission to
each Subordinate Lodge giving full cooperation.*

books, magazines, cards, games, musical instruments, and material
with which to use their idle hands in creating and producing a
variety of items.

For the boys who were in various stages of rehabilitation and
able to get about, some lodges supplied such items as pool tables,
badminton, ping pong, paddle tennis equipment, boxing gloves,
punching bags, skis, toboggans, fishing tackle, paraphernalia for
basketball, volley ball, football, and softball. Besides this they
supplied tools of many kinds such as drills, planes, hammers, saws,
chisels, squares, rules, paint, clay, etc., to the woodwork shop.

The hours that these returned heroes spent in Government
hospitals grew weary and time dragged heavily on their hands.
They had time to remember and wonder. They had a devil-may-
care attitude, but when you sat down at their bedsides, talked
to them and learned a bit about them, you discovered many things
below the surface. Most of them were young, barely in their twen-
ties; they had mothers and fathers, wives or sweethearts; they
talked of them and their future—they were lonely and homesick.
The days, weeks and months that lay ahead before they could
return home were like a term in prison. Aid and cheer extended
to the veterans by these programs were indeed the personification
of the tenets of the Order; "do unto others as you would they
should do unto you."

Rehabilitation

The restoration of discharged veterans to an ordered civil life was the concern of all our people, for stabilized peace is dependent upon stabilized economy, and this is possible only when the lives, dislocated by the sudden transition from peace to war, have been assured security in the post-war world.

Upon the appeal of the Elks War Commission, rehabilitation committees were organized in every Elks lodge. It was the duty of these committees to keep informed on all legislation, state and federal, affecting the interests of servicemen, to follow closely the rulings and regulations for the administration of the "Servicemen's Readjustment Act," to render personal service whenever needed, and to cooperate with all agencies working for the readjustment of veterans and their restoration to happy community life.

Elks War Commission Finance

A copy of the final financial report of the Elks War Commission will be found in the Appendix of this History.

At the conclusion of the report submitted at the Grand Lodge Session in 1946, the Chairman of the Elks War Commission offered the following statement and resolution:

"The fighting phase of the war is now over and the activities of the Elks War Commission have come to an end. The care, comfort and entertainment, however, of those who fought the war and made the sacrifices that preserved our country is an obligation that will rest upon the Order until the last veteran is served. Therefore, the Veterans Hospital Program, inaugurated by the Elks War Commission, and now carried on by 43 State Associations, must be continued. The Peace Army Enlistment Campaign must also go forward, and provision must be made for such other activities as may remain uncompleted, therefore, be it

"RESOLVED: That the Grand Lodge of the Benevolent and Protective Order of Elks of the United States of America hereby create a Commission consisting of seven members to be known as the Elks National Veterans Service Commission, to serve until such time as the Grand Lodge may otherwise order. This Commission is hereby directed to carry on the Hospital Program, the Peace Army Enlistment Campaign, and all other uncompleted activities now supervised by the Elks War Commission. It shall also be the duty of this Commission to devise such other plans and promote such other activities as may be deemed essential to the aid and comfort of war veterans, and to cooperate with our national government in any movement in which the Benevolent and Protective Order of Elks may contribute to the betterment of conditions affecting the welfare of our veterans; and, in order that the work of the Elks National Veterans Service Commission may be carried forward, the Elks War Commission is hereby

During the Grand Exalted Rulership of Robert S. Barrett, and at his request, there was published by the Elks War Commission a comprehensive and elaborate Report to the Nation, copies of which were presented to the members of the Elks in Congress at a meeting held in the Senate Hearing Room.

The above picture shows a special copy being presented to President Harry S. Truman by a delegation comprising Grand Exalted Ruler Robert S. Barrett, Past Grand Exalted Rulers Raymond Benjamin, James R. Nicholson and David Sholtz, Grand Esquire Joseph B. Kyle and William M. Frasor, Executive Secretary of the Elks War Commission.

authorized and directed to transfer all assets, files and records now in its possession to the Elks National Veterans Service Commission."

Personnel

When the Elks National Defense and Public Relations Commission was first created, Robert C. Jackson was engaged as its Executive Secretary.

He served in that capacity until January, 1944.

In June, 1942, a field force to supervise the creation of fraternal centers and cooperate with the subordinate lodges in their operation was created.

The first representatives in the field were Albert W. Jeffreys, Past Exalted Ruler, Herrin, Illinois, Lodge No. 1146; Floyd Brown, Past Exalted Ruler, Oklahoma City, Oklahoma, Lodge No. 417, and J. Ford Zietlow, Past Exalted Ruler of Aberdeen, South Dakota, Lodge No. 1046, and Past Chairman of the Board of Grand Trustees.

Shortly afterward the field force was increased by the addition of Willliam M. Frasor, Past Exalted Ruler of Blue Island, Illinois, Lodge No. 1331, Past President of the Illinois State Elks Association, and Tom Brisendine, East Point, Georgia, Lodge No. 1617.

Later Tom Brisendine succeeded Robert Jackson as Executive Secretary and William Frasor took charge of all of the activities in the field.

This field force was later expanded as the Fraternal Center activities were extended and the Veterans Hospital activities were established and developed.

To that force was added Arthur D. Bailey, Past Exalted Ruler, Ft. Dodge, Iowa, Lodge No. 306; Daniel J. Honan, Past Exalted Ruler, Winthrop, Massachusetts, Lodge No. 1078, and Robert M. Watkins, Past Exalted Ruler, Seattle, Lodge No. 92.

Later Tom Brisendine resigned to accept the Secretaryship of Atlanta Lodge No. 78, and William Frasor became Executive Secretary in full charge of the conduct of the headquarters office and the field activities.

He served in that capacity until the conclusion of the activities of the Elks War Commission and when the Elks National Veterans Service Commission succeeded the War Commission he became the Executive Secretary of that Commission.

Elks National Veterans Service Commission

Grand Exalted Ruler Charles E. Broughton appointed the following Past Grand Exalted Rulers as members of the Elks National Veterans Service Commission:

James T. Hallinan, Chairman, Queens Borough, N. Y., Lodge No. 878
Edward J. McCormick, Toledo, Ohio, Lodge No. 53
Henry C. Warner, Dixon, Ill., Lodge No. 779
David Sholtz, Daytona Beach, Fla., Lodge No. 1141
E. Mark Sullivan, Boston, Mass., Lodge No. 10
Frank J. Lonergan, Portland, Ore., Lodge No. 142
Wade H. Kepner, Wheeling, W. Va., Lodge No. 28

Wm. M. Frasor, Blue Island, Ill., Lodge No. 1331, who had been Executive Secretary of the Elks War Commission was retained in the same capacity by the new Commission.

July 1946——July 1947

At the Grand Lodge Session in Portland, Oregon, in 1947, Chairman Hallinan reported that during the year the Commission had, with the cooperation of State Associations and subordinate lodges, staged outstanding programs in 152 hospitals in the country, located in 41 states.

He reported that the activities of the Commission during the year that was just closed were financed by the monies contributed to the Elks War Fund by the subordinate lodges, augmented by a contribution of $100,000 by the Elks National Memorial and Publication Commission.

No requests were made for voluntary contributions from the lodges that year, but the Commission received $71,613.72 in contributions from subordinate lodges representing unpaid balances of their quotas to the War Fund for the years 1942 to 1945 inclusive.

During the year the Commission, working through the subordinate lodges of the Order, maintained the splendid record of enlistment previously established in the recruiting of young men for the new regular army.

The Grand Lodge Session voted unanimously to increase the per capita tax 15 cents per member to provide funds to enable the Veterans Service Commission to carry on.

Under the auspices of the Commission, General Mark Clark appeared before the Grand Lodge at that Session and made a most striking address.

During the year 1946-1947, the Commission furnished approximately 2,000 programs at hospitals, not including special entertainment in hospital wards.

July 1947——July 1948
California Elks Program

In its report at the Grand Lodge Session in Philadelphia in 1948, the Commission paid a special tribute to the Elks of California for the outstanding programs they had carried out.

This commendation dealt particularly with the work of the California Elks in developing occupational therapy, supplying materials and instructions to teach the disabled veterans how to repair watches and radios, to carve wood and leather, tie intricate fishing flies and carry on photography, printing and other useful occupations. This work made it possible for many boys who had given up hope of being self-supporting again to operate their own businesses successfully.

At this Grand Lodge Session a great demonstration was staged by the Brothers of California, headed by State Chairman, Robert N. Traver. A delegate from each lodge paraded to the rostrum, each depositing a bundle of tanned hides collected by the Elks of California and donated to the Elks National Veterans Service Commission, to be distributed among the Veterans Administration Hospitals for use in their hobby shops or occupational therapy departments. These hides were valued at $26,000. After serving their purpose at the Convention, they were packed and shipped to the New York office of the Commission and were distributed to 21 Veterans Administration Hospitals from whom the Commission received requests.

In addition to the gift of hides, the Brothers of California also brought 1,700 gavels, made by the disabled veterans, to be distributed one to each lodge of our Order, bearing the following inscription, with proper lodge number:

"B.P.O.E NO. _____

CALIFORNIA ORANGE WOOD

MADE BY VETERANS

Veterans Service Committee
California Elks Association"

These gavels were donated as an expression of gratitude from the hospitalized veterans for what the Order of Elks was doing for them. All gavels that were not distributed at the Convention were shipped from the Commission's New York office to the lodges whose delegates did not receive them at the Convention, with the result that all of our subordinate lodges enjoyed the possession of a gavel made out of California orange wood by the patients in the veterans hospitals of that State.

At the time of this report entertainment for disabled veterans was being carried on in 48 states.

Special Christmas Program

That year a special appeal was made to the subordinate lodges for voluntary contributions to enable the Commission, through the lodges located in the vicinity of hospitals caring for the disabled veterans as patients, to have a Christmas Day celebration in each of the 160 hospitals having as patients 125,000 disabled veterans. It was found that there would be 54,000 of these veterans spending Christmas in the hospitals.

The Commission adopted a program for Christmas Day calling for an expenditure of over $100,000.

The total contributions amounted to $99,000, which left a small deficit that was taken care of as the amount appropriated for certain hospitals was not required.

That year Past Exalted Ruler Emmett T. Anderson, of Tacoma, Wash., Lodge, was added to the membership of the Commission.

At the Grand Lodge Session in Philadelphia in 1948, the Grand Lodge voted an assessment of 20 cents a member for funds for the Elks National Veterans Service Commission for the coming year.

July 1948——July 1949

On May 25, 1949, President Truman appealed to the country to give its young military men "the same sort of treatment they would have received if they had stayed at home." Again, he asked the communities near military camps "to do for them what you would do in war," adding "they are your sons and your neighbors' sons and they are away from home. They need something the armed services can't give them."

The Elks National Veterans Service Commission received word from Army headquarters that the original idea of having only five or six camps had been changed, and at that time there were already approximately twenty-four camps where our young men and women were receiving their training.

The Commission authorized the Chairman to send a letter to all lodges, calling attention to this change in the government pro gram and requesting a voluntary contribution of 25 cents pei member to be available for the purpose of the Commission.

As a result of the splendid response on the part of the lodges, the Commission was in a position to initiate the work of re-establishing former fraternal centers and establishing new ones. Before the close of the year the first center had opened at Columbia, South Carolina, adjacent to Fort Jackson. This had been one of the outstanding fraternal centers conducted by the War Commission during World War II.

The second fraternal center re-opened was at Louisville, Kentucky. This center was re-opened on June 4, 1949, to serve the members of the troops stationed at Fort Knox.

In its report to the Grand Lodge at its Convention in Cleveland in July, 1949, the Commission reported that plans had been completed for re-activating the third fraternal center at Trenton, New Jersey, near Fort Dix, and that plans were under way in North Carolina, Georgia and Texas for the re-opening of fraternal centers in those states.

Manila Lodge

As reported in that part of this History referring to the activities of the Elks War Commission, when word was received that the beautiful home of Manila Lodge was destroyed in the conflict with the Japanese, our Order went on record at two Grand Lodge Sessions to spare no effort in giving aid and finances so that Manila would again be able to enjoy a home.

Accordingly, $250,000 was placed in escrow out of the Order's War Fund to be advanced to Manila Lodge with the understanding that if the United States Government reimbursed Manila Lodge for its losses, such funds advanced by the Elks War Commission were to be returned to the Commission to such extent as such reimbursement allowed. The Veterans Service Commission reported at the Cleveland Convention that all this $250,000 had been turned over in full to Manila Lodge.

The California Elks contributed $30,318 to be applied to the decoration and equipment of the lodge room and library of the new home.

The new home was dedicated on March 25, 1949, the Elks National Veterans Service Commission being represented by Past Grand Exalted Ruler Michael F. Shannon. The other guests at the ceremony included President Elpidio Quirino, his aides and members of his cabinet.

Recruiting

The Commission continued co-operating with the recruiting officers of the Army and the Air Corps in securing volunteers for our peace-time army.

United States Savings Bonds

Upon the appeal of Vernon L. Clark, National Director, United States Savings Bonds Division of the Treasury Department, the Commission sent a representative to a conference in Washington where the heads of the Treasury Department explained the importance of stimulating greater interest on the part of the people in the purchasing of Savings Bonds.

The Commission was made a member of the Advisory Board of the Savings Bond Division of the Treasury Department.

Once more the response of the members of the Order to the appeal sent out by the Chairman of the Commission was outstanding.

At special ceremonies during the 1950 Grand Lodge Convention in Chicago, Chairman James T. Hallinan of the Elks Service Commission, left, with Past Grand Exalted Ruler Michael F. Shannon, right, Chairman R. N. Traver, of the California Elks Veterans Service Commission and other California delegates received a hand-tooled leather wallet from Elk Ray Davis, a disabled California veteran, seated.

Davis presented one of the handsome wallets to each of the former leaders of the Order at the meeting.

These wallets were all made by disabled war veterans with the assistance and under the direction of the California Elks Veterans Service Commission.

At the same Convention disabled Elk Ray Davis presented to Chairman Hallinan a watch which he had constructed from stray parts which had been furnished to him, an outstanding example of the skills developed by disabled veterans with the assistance of the Elks.

Elks National Service Commission

1949——1950

While the Elks National Veterans Service Commission was appointed for the purpose of carrying on the post-war work of the Order, and practically all of its activities were on behalf of the veterans, it was provided in the resolution creating the Commission that it should cover all of the patriotic activities of the Order in co-operation with government agencies, in addition to the veterans' program and the operation of Fraternal Centers.

As these activities broadened, it was deemed advisable to change the name. Accordingly, at the Grand Lodge Session in Cleveland in 1949, this change was approved, and the Commission became known as the Elks National Service Commission.

Fraternal Centers

At the Convention in Miami in 1950, the Commission reported that in addition to the Fraternal Centers previously reported they had added other Fraternal Centers in Columbus, Georgia, adjacent to Fort Benning; Wilmington, North Carolina, adjacent to the Le Jeune Marine Corps base; Tucson, Arizona, and Waukegan, Illinois.

The Commission announced at that time that the center at Columbia, South Carolina, which was of infinite assistance to the government in the building up of the morale of the boys at Fort Jackson while they were stationed there, was discontinued, as the camp had been closed.

"Wake Up, America"

The Commission, mindful of the infiltration of Communists and the development of communistic programs in our country, felt that the Order of Elks should seize the opportunity for launching a program, "Wake Up, America," and an appeal was made by the Chairman to all of the lodges in the Order, under the date of March 9, 1950, to set aside an evening between May 15 and May 31, 1950, for the purpose of holding a "Wake Up, America" program in their lodge room or some other meeting place, to which it was suggested that the citizenry of the various communities be invited. The lodges were urged at that time to arrange a program that would center upon the advantage and benefit of our American way of life.

This appeal met with a ready response.

United States Savings Bonds

When the Bonds Division of the United States Treasury Department decided to conduct another national bond sales campaign, our Order was again invited to participate and the Commission accepted the invitation. Under date of May 15, 1950, Chairman Hallinan sent an appeal to all the lodges of the Order to play an important part in this drive.

In this appeal he called attention of the lodges to the fact that Flag Day, June 14th, was the half-way mark of the independent savings bond drive which the Treasury Department had set up and, as every Elks lodge would hold a Flag Day celebration, he appealed to the lodges to incorporate in their Flag Day celebration a report on the progress the bond drive had made in its community up to that date.

July 1950——July 1951

At the beginning of this Grand Lodge year the United States, responding to the appeal of the United Nations, took a major part in defending Korea from aggression.

This development called for a strengthening and broadening of the program and activities of the Commission.

One of the major activities of the Commission had been its work in behalf of the disabled veterans and now that was necessarily increased to meet the needs and contribute to the comfort of the casualties that began to return home from the Korean front for hospitalization, and it broadened and strengthened its program for the comfort and entertainment of men entering the Service.

Fraternal Centers

Fraternal Centers were opened or reactivated by the following lodges:

    Santa Maria, California, Lodge No. 1538
    Cheyenne, Wyoming, Lodge No. 660
    Kinston, North Carolina, Lodge No. 740
    Hyannis, Massachusetts, Lodge No. 1549
    Geneva, New York, Lodge No. 1054
    Columbia, South Carolina, Lodge No. 1190

This made a total of 12 Centers in action with the assistance and cooperation of the Commission.

"Keep Awake, America"

Encouraged by the success of its "Wake Up America" program, the Commission adopted a follow-up program of "Keep Awake America" which proved a great success.

United States Savings Bonds

In response to a call for additional assistance received from the Savings Bonds Division of the United States Treasury in advancing its payroll savings plan, Chairman Hallinan of the Commission and the Order's representative on the National Organizations Committee for Savings Bonds, sent a strong appeal to all the subordinate lodges.

Such was the response that a letter of commendation and appreciation was received from Vernon L. Clark, National Director of the United States Savings Bonds Division of the United States Treasury.

President Truman receives from Grand Exalted Ruler Kyle the pledge of complete mobilization of the manpower of the Order for Civilian Defense. Standing, left to right: P.E.R. James E. Colliflower and E.R. and Mrs. William H. Cade of Washington, D. C., Lodge, Congressman Russell V. Mack of Aberdeen, Wash., Lodge, Past Grand Exalted Rulers Henry C. Warner and David Sholtz, Mrs. Kyle, P.D.D. Ambrose A. Durkin, Past Grand Exalted Ruler Emmett T. Anderson.

Civil Defense

Realizing the importance of awakening our people to the possibility of an atomic attack and the need for immediate preparedness activities, the Commission appealed to all Elks to become active in Civil Defense programs.

Cigarettes to Korea

During this year the Commission developed its program of sending cigarettes to our servicemen in Korea.

July 1951——July 1952
FRATERNAL CENTERS

During this year Centers were opened at: Honolulu, Hawaii; Ft. Walton, Florida; Key West, Florida, and Okmulgee, Oklahoma.

Centers at Geneva, New York, Okmulgee, Oklahoma, Ft. Walton, Florida, and Columbia, South Carolina, were discontinued, leaving 12 Centers in operation.

Members of the Elks National Service Commission 1951-1952 from left to right: Past Grand Exalted Ruler Charles E. Broughton, Past Grand Exalted Ruler Frank J. Lonergan, Past Grand Exalted Ruler Wade H. Kepner, Past Grand Exalted Ruler E. Mark Sullivan, Past Grand Exalted Ruler James T. Hallinan, Chairman, Past Grand Exalted Ruler David Sholtz, Treasurer, Past Grand Exalted Ruler Henry C. Warner, Vice-Chairman, Past Grand Exalted Ruler George I. Hall, Assistant Treasurer, and Past Grand Exalted Ruler Emmett T. Anderson.

At the Grand Lodge Session in 1952 there were added to the Commission Past Grand Exalted Rulers William H. Atwell, Joseph B. Kyle and Howard R. Davis. At the same Grand Lodge Session, Past Grand Exalted Ruler Charles E. Broughton was transferred to the Elks National Foundation as a Trustee.

EMERGENCY FUND

At the Grand Lodge Session in 1951, a resolution was unanimously adopted authorizing the Board of Grand Trustees, with the approval of the Grand Exalted Ruler, to levy an assessment not exceeding $1.00 per year per member, to be expended under the direction of the Elks National Service Commission in support of our government in the event of a national emergency.

Fortunately the assessment never became necessary but the resolution has been annually adopted with a change made in 1965 so that the assessment might also be expended by the Board of Grand Trustees, with the approval of the Grand Exalted Ruler for the purpose of a major disaster, warranting our aid and assistance.

During this year the Elks National Service Commission developed its veterans' service until such service was in operation in 166 hospitals in 48 states for the benefit of the disabled veterans, many of whom were Korean casualties.

This type of program varied in the several hospitals and always was determined by the local communities and the requirements of the patients. These programs consisted of professional and amateur entertainment, bingo games, card parties, boxing and wrestling, attendance at baseball and football games, theater parties, fishing trips, etc.

In addition, the local committees representing the Commission were cooperating with hospitals sponsoring occupational therapy activities in a most successful manner.

VETERANS ADMINISTRATION CITATION

A citation of which the following is a copy was presented to the Commission in May 1952:

"VETERANS ADMINISTRATION VOLUNTARY SERVICE

"The Veterans Administration, on behalf of the Veteran-patients and domiciliary members gratefully acknowledges the selfless devotion to volunteer duty in the Veterans Administration Voluntary Service Program of members of the

"Benevolent and Protective Order of Elks of
the United States of America

"Your National Organization as a member agency of the Veterans Administration Voluntary Service National Advisory Committee, has worked shoulder to shoulder with the Veterans Administration Staff and with over 40 other great veterans welfare and service groups toward a mutual goal—to provide the best in care and treatment for the men and women disabled in their and our dedicated endeavor—to preserve the American ideal of freedom.

"Your organization's contribution to this nation-wide cooperative mission on behalf of the disabled veterans is an eminently fitting example of our great democracy in action. The leadership and guidance which your national officers have provided and the day-to-day devoted service of your members in communities over the entire country have brought a new and increasingly more meaningful significance to the volunteer spirit in America.

"Carl R. Gray, Jr.,
"Administrator of Veterans Affairs

"Washington, D. C.
"May 21, 1952."

Certificates were also presented to the cooperating subordinate lodges.

Personnel

At the Grand Lodge Session in 1952, Past Grand Exalted Ruler Broughton resigned to accept an appointment as Trustee of the Elks National Foundation.

There were added to the membership on the Commission, Past Grand Exalted Rulers Atwell, Kyle and Davis.

The personnel of the Commission after the changes was as follows:

Past Grand Exalted Ruler James T. Hallinan, Chairman
    "   "   "   "   E. Mark Sullivan, Secretary
    "   "   "   "   Henry C. Warner, Vice Chairman
    "   "   "   "   David Sholtz, Treasurer
    "   "   "   "   George I. Hall, Assistant Treasurer
    "   "   "   "   Frank J. Lonergan
    "   "   "   "   Wade H. Kepner
    "   "   "   "   Emmett T. Anderson
    "   "   "   "   William H. Atwell
    "   "   "   "   Joseph B. Kyle
    "   "   "   "   Howard R. Davis

William M. Frasor, Past Exalted Ruler, Blue Island, Ill., Lodge No. 1331, Past President of the Illinois State Elks Association continued to serve as the Executive Secretary of the Commission, with Floyd H. Brown, Past Exalted Ruler of Oklahoma City Lodge No. 417, covering the service in the field.

Through the years of 1953 to 1967 the program of the Elks National Service Commission continued to operate on a firmly established and well regulated schedule in 172 Veteran Administration hospitals throughout the nation.

At this point in the history of its activities, we review and assess the motivation, aims and purposes of the Elks National Service Commission.

The members of the Commission held the opinion that America's precious freedom was secured at great sacrifice by our military defenders. When the danger of losing this freedom threatened, public attention was focused on the members of our armed forces and the cause for which they were fighting. Enthusiastic and demonstrative appreciation of the military uniform as a symbol of our safety and the priceless value of our national heritage was the patriotic sentiment during times of armed conflict. However, when the battles are fought and the shooting stops the dead are brought home and buried and the sick and wounded are bedded behind hospital walls. Normalcy is established and the fears, anxieties and brutalities of the conflict are things best forgotten. New generations appear on the scene and the war becomes a legend.

To the hospitalized sick and wounded the war remains very real. They suffer from the hurts of war. Many will carry their burdens for a lifetime.

The Commission theorized that particular appreciation is due to the hospitalized veteran. Their basic reason was the fact that to be accepted for service, the volunteer or draftee had to be healthy, strong and fit as a requirement to offer his life and services for our defense. It was the stated opinion of the Commission that it was just ordinary decency to be concerned with the ailing veteran when he needed help. Ill of mind or body is defeat. Health alone was victory for him and we do not want defeated American veterans.

The members of the Commission knew that time dims public memory and concern for the present would relegate wars and the consequence of wars to the recesses of forgetfulness. At the close of World War II a solemn pledge was made: "So Long as There is a Disabled Veteran in Our Hospitals, the Benevolent and Protective Order of Elks Will Never Forget Him."

This pledge was not a mere patriotic gesture made at a time when it was a popular slogan. It was firmly implemented by the establishment of the Elks National Service Commission in 1946 to perform its fulfillment. Funds through per-capita assessment of 35c per member were provided to carry out its promise.

The purpose of the pledge was to communicate to the hospitalized veteran that regardless of his ailment the Order of Elks was behind him in his efforts to regain his health, return to his family and take his place in the community with dignity, to enjoy the freedom for which he served to protect.

Thus, the activities constituted a form of "Companionship Therapy" which takes over when the maximum of medical assistance has been given. The presence of Elks' Committee in the hospital serves to motivate the patient to get well and assist him along the long road to recovery. It has been said of the discouraged hospitalized veteran "It will be lonely to be dead; but it cannot be much more lonely than to be alive." This holds true for the veteran without family or friends to visit him to bring a little cheer and encouragement. He senses the small still voice of gratitude expressed by an Elks visit. It means much to him. He appreciates it. It gives him needed courage in his own fight for existence.

Expressions of remembrance are made in many ways. Our Elks Committees are members of the local hospital's Veterans Administration Voluntary Service. They must have the following qualifications: 1. Sincere interest in people. 2. Sense of responsibility and dependability. 3. Willingness to accept hospital standards of conduct and supervision. 4. Ability to work with people as a group as well as individuals within a group. 5. Tact, patience, congeniality, warmth and kindness. 6. Physical ability to perform volunteer work. 7. Sense of pride in serving others.

Our Committees meet regularly with members of other organizations serving the hospital and care is taken not to duplicate effort.

Veterans Administration hospitals have an average of approximately 119,000 patients with more than 590,000 admissions and 585 discharges during the normal year. There are many types of patients. Nearly 50% of them are suffering from mental disorders. In general medical hospitals some are bedridden. Some are ambulatory. Many are confined to wheel chairs. Domiciliaries take care of the ageing.

Elks programs, therefore, are designed to meet the particular need of any group. They are not occasional or subject to momentary enthusiasm. They are regularly scheduled every week, every month. They are constant year after year.

Live entertainment in the form of auditorium variety shows, ward strollers, etc. are very popular. Bingo games, boxing and wrestling bouts, outdoor carnivals, smokers, picnics, short trips to visit Elks lodges, baseball and football games and sports nights are included. Bedside visits, letter writing, shopping, home phone calls wheel chair pushing, assisting chaplains, assisting in hobby and craft instruction . . . in fact, any service within the capabilities of the Committee workers is perfromed cheerfully for the patient. TV sets for wards and bedside radios are regularly contributed for entertainment between participation programs.

The dedicated Elks and their ladies who carry on this work of mercy are specially gifted persons. They have a zest for helping others and convey their enthusiasm to the patients. They bring the outside world to the bedside. They give lively evidence that the patient will never be relegated to that hopeless limbo of the half forgotten—half remembered. They demonstrate that it is one thing to TELL a veteran who has a serious disability or a long stay in a hospital it doesn't necessarily mean the end of the road. But it is quite another thing to help him see it for himself . . . to help him believe it . . . to restore his enthusiasm for living despite great odds. It is quite another thing to restore confidence, to convince a man he is useful—and can always remain useful so long as he is able to breathe. This is the kind of therapy that is beyond the scope of a busy professional staff. Our

Committees express a love for fellow man and make personal unsung sacrifices which are beyond description. This has been hailed as the exemplification of Charity, Justice, Brotherly Love and Fidelity in the noblest sense. This is patriotism that is deep and fervent. This is Elkdom in its truest benevolence.

Fraternal Centers

War erupted in Korea on June 25, 1950 when the Communist forces in the north invaded the south. Failure to heed the cease-fire request of the United Nations resulted in orders from President Truman to General McArthur to aid the South Koreans. Our ground forces entered the conflict on June 30, 1950.

Our Government engaged in an extensive military man power increase. Army estimates of five or six training areas were changed to more than twenty-five.

President Truman, in an appeal to the communities located near training camps, said, "They are your sons and your neighbors' sons and they are away from home. They need something the armed services can't give them."

In response to this appeal, the Elks National Service Commission reopened many of the Fraternal Centers which were so successful during World War II and added new ones. Again a "Home Away from Home" was provided for our service men in training during a period of emergency.

Occupational Therapy

Commission studies indicated that the hospital day is a long one in the interim of Committee visits. Hospital staffs stated that lethargy retards recovery. Occupational therapy is employed to keep minds active and fingers busy. It is a treatment which helps coordination and gives strength to unused and injured muscles. It teaches new skills to the handicapped. Patients work with wood, plastics, textiles and other materials. Leathercraft is one of the most popular and beneficial projects. Finished hides are always in great demand. Government budgets are always limited and the need for additional leather always exists.

Earlier in this history the story has been told of the hide gathering program of the California Elks. Raw skins were collected at central locations and shipped to a Los Angeles tannery for processing. Finished leather in brilliant colors was made available to local hospitals and the surplus shipped to hospitals in other parts of the country. This was soon adopted actively by neighboring states. Today the Elks in Montana, Wyoming, Oregon, Washington, Alaska, Nevada, North Dakota, Utah, Arizona and New Mexico collect skins for this purpose. With a limited annual budget of less than $6,000 for tanning and shipping costs, hides valued at more than $50,000 are distributed each year. In Massachusetts, leather, textiles and plastics are donated to Elks by many manufacturing firms in the area. "Elks Leather" and other materials are an established and welcome complement in every hospital. In addition, old radios, TV sets, motors, clocks, watches and appliances are collected to encourage skills in mechanical repair.

In Ohio, under the direction of our late State Chairman, Brother Les Strong, an Elks ceramic program was launched. Clay, moulds, decals and kilns are supplied. The idea is rapidly being adopted in other states. It promises to rival the leather program as an exclusive Elks project in hospitals throughout the country.

Courtesy Cards and Duration Stickers

Courtesy cards issued to blood relatives of members of the Order who are under 21 years of age at the time of their induction are available to all lodges by the Elks National Service Commission. By presenting a Courtesy Card duly approved by the members, Exalted Ruler and Secretary, these young servicemen enjoy the gracious hospitality of Elks lodges.

The duration sticker was designed in 1942 and approved by the Grand Exalted Ruler when it appeared desirable to provide a uniform method of assuring that when an Elk serviceman presented a card stating that his dues were paid for the duration there would be no confusion in the mind of anyone examining the card. Supplies are available upon request to the Elks National Service Commission.

The waiving of dues of men in service is an optional courtesy by the member's lodge and is not mandatory.

Cigarettes to Korea and Vietnam

When a shooting war erupted in Korea in 1950 the Service Commission commenced shipping 100,000 cigarettes each month to our troops serving there. The 1953 Armistice stilled the guns but regiments of our armed forces continued their service in this remote country to enforce the truce. The Elks continue to send the cigarettes to the present time. Each pack contains a cheery message of remembrance and the thousands of acknowledgments received express unusual gratitude and demonstrates the morale building value of this activity.

The stepped-up military action in Vietnam and the increased commitments of our fighting men in that area created a need for a similar service. Commencing July, 1965, 100,000 cigarettes have been sent each month to the men in the field and to those in hospitals. Letters of appreciation from recipients proved again the merit of a tangible expression of encouragement from home.

To date, more than twenty-three million cigarettes have been sent by the Commission to our troops in Asia. To this must be added the countless millions sent by individual lodges during the past 17 years.

Finances

To support the program a per capita levy of 35c per member was in force in 1953. This was gradually reduced to 20c per member. A statement of receipts and expenditures from the creation of the Commission (under the name of the Elks National Veterans Service Commission) on July 10, 1946 to the close of the fiscal year ending May 31, 1967 will be found in the appendix of this history.

Emergency Fund

At the Grand Lodge Session in 1951 a resolution was unanimously passed authorizing the Board of Grand Trustees with the approval of the Grand Exalted Ruler to levy an assessment not exceeding $1.00 per member to be expended under the direction of the Elks National Service Commission in support of our government in the event of a national emergency.

Although such an assessment has never been necessary, the resolution was adopted at every Grand Lodge Convention to date.

1953——1954
Fraternal Centers

This year marked the signing of the Armistice in Korea. Nevertheless thousands of service men were still in training here in the United States. The need for Elks Fraternal Centers continued to exist. They were located in Tucson, Arizona; Santa Maria, California; Laredo, Texas; Key West, Florida; Columbus, Georgia; Geneva, New York; Honolulu, Hawaii; Waukegan, Illinois; Louisville, Kentucky; Hyannis, Massachusetts; Trenton, New Jersey; Kinston, North Carolina; Columbia, South Carolina; Sumpter, South Carolina and Cheyenne, Wyoming. They provided a "Home Away From Home" for countless young men and women in uniform. Staffed with experienced personnel, these centers specialized in sympathetic handling of the many problems of adjustment that face the young inductee, many of whom found themselves away from home for the first time. The centers were celebrated for their cordial hospitality and popular off-duty headquarters for young military trainees. Dances, parties and all areas of recreation typified the activities.

Stationery to Korea

Two shipments totaling a quarter of a million letterheads and envelopes bearing the Elks emblem were forwarded to Korea in answer to a reported shortage of writing materials. Thus, it was made possible that thousands of welcome letters were received by anxious parents and loved ones from their fighting men in Korea. As a consequence, some happiness was brought into American homes under the emblem of Elkdom.

Keep in Touch with the Members of the Armed Forces

All Exalted Rulers were requested to use the medium of their lodge bulletins, bulletin boards and meeting announcements to stress the importance of correspondence with our young men and women in uniform.

Manila

The new home of Manila Lodge made possible by an advance of $200,000 by the Elks National Service Commission and $50,000 from Grand Lodge was dedicated in 1949.

Since that time, Manila Lodge filed a claim with the United States Government for war damages. The lodge received an award of $73,789.17.

The Philippine Government passed legislation which provided that any monies taken out of the Philippine Islands would be permitted only upon the government retaining a withdrawal fee which started at 50% and was reduced to 17% by subsequent legislation. The Commission instructed the trustees of Manila Lodge to deposit monies received by them in a special account in the Peoples Bank and Trust Co. to the credit of the Elks National Service Commission to be held for a decision by the Commission.

With the aid and assistance of Brother Thomas J. Wolff, who represented us on the Islands and the efforts of Chairman James T. Hallinan and Treasurer, George I. Hall who held personal conferences with the Philippine Ambassador, Hon. Carlos P. Romulo, the award of $73,789.17 which represented the monies on deposit less the 17% withdrawal fee and $44.28 for stamps was released from Manila and deposited in the Commission account in New York. The withdrawal fee is still subject to protest. The award does not represent the cost of the building destroyed by the Japanese. It represents that portion of the damage allowed by the United States Government.

Per Capita Tax

In 1953, the per capita tax income to the Commission was reduced from 35c per member to 30c.

1954——1955

The fraternal centers program continued to operate in all areas.

The centers as heretofore described, were in operation in the following locations: Tucson, Arizona; Santa Maria, California; Laredo, Texas; Key West, Florida; Columbus, Georgia; Geneva, New York; Honolulu, Hawaii; Waukegan, Illinois; Louisville, Kentucky; Hyannis, Massachusetts; Trenton, New Jersey; Kinston, North Carolina; Columbia, South Carolina; Sumpter, South Carolina and Cheyenne, Wyoming.

Executive Director Brother William M. Frasor was obliged to undergo major surgery in 1953 and post operative complications confined him to bed recuperation which necessitated his retirement in early 1954.

During his illness, his duties were performed by Brother Bryan J. McKeogh, P.E.R. of Queens Borough Lodge No. 878, N.Y. who had conducted the successful operations of the Grand Lodge Convention in New York—1952 and St. Louis—1953. He was appointed to replace Brother Frasor as Executive Director. His qualifications as recorded included the organization and direction of U.S.O. Service Men's Center prior to his induction in World War II where he served for four years in the Morale Activities and Special Services units of the U.S. Army. His activities in the Order commenced in 1939.

1955——1956

The usual hospital and fraternal center programs continued its activities during 1955.

Planning for the Patient's Discharge

For several years the Veterans Administration had been concerned with the rehabilitation of discharged patients. Surveys disclosed that very often a patient returned to the hospital after discharge because of his inability to assume his place in the community by reason of his inability to secure gainful employment.

The Order of Elks was called upon by the Veterans Administration to conduct a pilot program in 13 selected hospitals. Its purpose was the establishment of a nation-wide plan as a guide for other organizations. The plan was briefly as follows:

1. Each lodge was requested to appoint a Veterans Rehabilitation Committee (94% responded immediately).
2. When a patient in need of assistance was discharged from one of the 13 designated pilot program hospitals the lodge nearest the veteran's home was notified.
3. The lodge servicing the patient after his homecoming notified the National Service Commission of the action taken.

At a meeting of the Service Commission held in New York City in February, Chief Director of the Veterans Administration of Medicine and Surgery Department, Vice Admiral Joel T. Boone, U.S.N. M.C. (Rtd) appeared to extend commendations for the pioneer effort of the Elks in the project. The results of the pilot program were most encouraging.

William M. Frasor

It is sorrowfully recorded that the Service Commission's faithful former Executive Director, Brother William M. Frasor died on April 12th, 1956.

Veterans Administration Citation

At the Grand Lodge Convention a citation signed by Harvey Higley, Chief Medical Director of the Veterans Administration was presented in appreciation of the Elks National Service Commission for initiating the first coordinated nation-wide plan of a voluntary organization to assist the Veterans Administration in the planning for the patient's discharge program.

1956——1957

The cessation of hostilities and open warfare in Korea and the reduction in draft inductions diminished the acute need for the Fraternal Center Program greatly. The year 1956 marked the beginning of its gradual closing out of this type of activity for service men.

Civilian Defense

President Eisenhower approved the designation of September 9–13 as America's first Civilian Defense Week.

Mr. Val Peterson, the Administrator of Civilian Defense requested the cooperation of the Elks in attaining the goal of having Civilian Defense Week properly observed in every community in the nation.

All lodges were notified and resultant success of the week's observation and subsequent participation by Elks Lodges in shelter projects of the Civilian Defense Administration demonstrated again the Order's willingness to heed the call of any government agency for assistance.

1957——1958

Remaining Fraternal Centers continued to extend hospitality to service men stationed at the Key West, Florida Naval Base; Fort Benning, Georgia; Great Lakes Naval Training Center and Fort Sheridan, Waukegan, Illinois; Fort Jackson, Columbia, South Carolina; Shaw Air Force Base, Sumpter, South Carolina and Fort Francis E. Warren, Cheyenne, Wyoming.

The Elks Flying Showboat

Presque Island and Loring Air Base located in the extreme northeast boundary of the country in the State of Maine is snow-bound for most of the winter and completely isolated the rest of the time. The first "live" show ever to be seen there was made possible through the efforts of the Maine State Elks Association and the Service Commission. Security clearance from the Pentagon and Air Force transportation for groups of entertainers made this possible.

Entertainment in Europe

The "Hardship Circuit" in France and Germany was described as a chain of lonely outposts manned by small groups of G.I.'s to whom an overnight or weekend pass was meaningless.

Arrangements were made through the Massachusetts Elks State Association to send Manny Williams and his wife, both talented comedy and magic act performers to bring cheer and entertainment to these "forgotten" service men. They, likewise, thrilled hundreds of native French and German villagers who had never before witnessed a live magic act, thus, extending American Good Will to sections of Europe.

1958——1959

Fraternal Centers

The six fraternal centers in operation during 1957 continued activities during the first months of 1958. It became increasingly evident that the reduced draft calls and weekend passes to allow time for short trips to visit family and friends away from the base greatly diminished the acute need for the Fraternal Center program. Consequently, the remaining six centers were closed down before the end of 1958.

1959——1960

Civilian Defense

In 1959 the Commission again urged lodges to participate in the Civilian Defense program. It was pointed out that other than the defense phase of the appeal, a trained emergency corps is essential to every community. Dangers of disaster by explosion, fire, flood, tornado and riot among others are always present as past experience has proved.

Per Capita Assessment

Through prudent and careful management of Commission funds, program expenditures were held to a minimum. The very splendid financial assistance contributed locally by lodges and State Associations to augment Commission allocations were also a factor in reducing the per capita assessment from 30c to 25c per member.

1960——1961

Public Relations

In 1960 hospital committees were requested to acquaint their local newspapers, radio and TV news broadcasters with their activities. A volume of newspaper clippings received from all parts of the country gave ample testimony of the "good-will" value of the Elks efforts for hospitalized veterans.

1961——1962

There were no changes in the established routine of the Commission's program during 1961–62.

Per Capita Assessment

As a result of the discontinuance of the Fraternal Center program, the strict and careful management of the Commission funds and the continued financial aid by lodges and State Associations on a local level, the per capita income of 25c was reduced to 20c per member at the July Grand Lodge Convention.

In 1961, having passed the age of 65, Brother Floyd H. Brown retired on pension.

1962——1963

The regular activities of the Commission remained in constant action during 1962–63.

Used Playing Cards Collection

In many hospitals throughout the country, our Committee discovered a need for playing cards—new or used—so long as it was a complete deck. Hospital authorities agreed that card games had a group therapy value through incidental conversation sharing mutual problems.

A drive to collect "Cards For the Handicapped" was launched. Each lodge was requested to appoint a Committee. To acquaint the entire country with our efforts, arrangements were made for effective publicity in daily and weekly newspapers, magazines, radio and television stations.

For example, announcements were made on Championship Bridge Tournament network television shows. Radio network stars of the stature of Arthur Godfrey, together with local radio and TV broadcasters pushed the drive on their shows. Network wire services and and syndicated columnists carried our appeal. Elk Public Relations Director, Brother Otho DeVilbiss prepared special news release forms and suggestions which were supplied to every lodge. Specially inscribed cartons for placement in lodges and public places as collection depots were supplied to each lodge. Newspapers and radio stations gave the public special instructions for mailing cards to the nearest lodge. All parts of the United States in every news media were covered in this extensive publicity operation.

At the conclusion of the drive, special Elks donor stickers for the cards and shipping instructions to the nearest Veterans Administration hospital were sent to each lodge.

More than a quarter of a million decks of cards with a value of more than $50,000 resulted from the drive.

An important fringe benefit was the priceless national publicity given to the Elks programs in Veterans Hospitals.

1963——1964

Used Playing Cards

The "Cards for the Handicapped" collection continued in 1963–64 resulting in more than 50,000 decks donated and distributed to Veteran Administration hospitals.

All other programs continued without change.

Annual Report Award

The annual printed report of the Elks National Service Commission is published with the sole intent of advising our membership of the aims, purposes, progress and results of the national program for hospitalized veterans. Its yearly acceptance by the membership is the primary intent.

Unusual recognition from a group of experts not affiliated with the Order is extremely gratifying. The Printing Industries of Metropolitan New York, Inc. selected our report from among thousands submitted by industries, banks, corporations, etc. and nominated by printers as being one of the best of their production for the year ending 1962.

1964——1965

The used playing cards drive, as well as all other permanent programs of the Commission continued.

Ohio Ceramics Program

A new Elks sponsored program was established in Ohio. Hospitals were furnished with clay and other materials to further a ceramics project in the Occupational Therapy Departments.

Publicity

The collection of "Cards For the Handicapped" again resulted in nation-wide publicity for the Elks National Service Commission's interest in hospitalized veterans.

1965——1966

Veterans Administration Voluntary Service Award

Highlighting the activities in 1965–66 was the presentation of a citation by the Veterans Administration at the annual meeting of the Veterans Administration Voluntary Service held in Washington, D.C. It read:

"In Recognition of and Grateful Appreciation for TWO DECADES OF SERVICE on the Twentieth Anniversary of V A Voluntary Service, we of the Veterans Administration acknowledge with sincere appreciation the valued assistance of BENEVOLENT AND PROTECTIVE ORDER OF ELKS. As a member of the Veterans Administration Voluntary Service National Advisory Committee, your organization has played a major role in helping us to plan and develop our nationwide program of volunteer participation in the medical care and treatment of patients.

"Your organization's contributions—along with those of the other members of our national volunteer advisory committee—to the recovery and rehabilitation of veteran-patients have brought a new dimension to citizen volunteer participation.

"In addition, your organization's work with us has given a new meaning and significance to the working together of government and our country's private voluntary organizations in a common cause—our endeavoring to assure the best in care and treatment for our country's sick and disabled veterans."

William J. Driver
Administrator of Veterans Affairs

Washington, D.C., April 18, 1966

Vice President Hubert H. Humphrey personally extended the appreciation and commendation of the national government to the Elks National Service Commission.

Letters from Home

With over 400,000 of our troops fighting a cruel war in Vietnam, the nation witnessed the spectacle of draft card burnings and demonstrations against the nation s policy to halt communist aggression in Asia. The Defense Department was concerned with the threat to the morale of our fighting men. Consultation with Defense Department officials determined that the effect of civil disobedience at home could be counteracted by letters of encouragement and assurance to men overseas in all areas. The assistance of the Elks was requested.

All lodges were immediately contacted and requested to use their lodge bulletins and newspaper announcements to solicit the names and correct addresses of service men so that personal letters could be sent by members of a lodge committee. The idea was enthusiastically adopted. In addition to letters, gift packages, home newspapers, cigarettes, etc. were sent to the individual service man.

The idea that a home town neighbor whom he might not even know thinks enough of his sacrifices to write him in appreciation was the intent of the morale boosting campaign. Publicity Director Brother Otho DeVilbiss assisted in preparing the necessary forms for newspaper publicity which were supplied to all the lodges.

1967——1968

All permanent programs during 1967–68 continued as scheduled.

Plaque at Pearl Harbor

P.G.E.R. Horace Wisely brought the Commission's attention to the fact that it would be appropriate for the Elks National Service Commission to provide an Elks memorial plaque for the U.S.S. Arizona memorial which is erected on the wreckage of the only battleship totally lost in the Japanese attack.

Accordingly, P.G.E.R.'s Horace Wisely and R. Leonard Bush, represented the Commission at ceremonies at Pearl Harbor where the plaque was presented to Rear Admiral Henry S. Persons, Commandant of the 14th Naval District.

The plaque bearing the Elks emblem reads as follows:
"Lest we forget..............
Let the tragic death of these heroes ever remind us of the great sacrifice at which freedom is bought."

Vietnam Casualties

A survey of the Vietnam casualties indicated a large number of wounded men treated at the Naval hospital in Guam prior to their return to mainland service hospitals. A hospital program was instituted by Agana, Guam Lodge #1281 with financial support from the Commission.

Personnel

The personnel of the Elks National Service Commission in 1952 was recited earlier in this history. Since then Past Grand Exalted Rulers David Scholtz, E. Mark Sullivan, Henry C. Warner, Joseph B. Kyle, Frank J. Lonergan, William H. Atwell, and Howard R. Davis passed away and Past Grand Exalted Ruler Wade H. Kepner resigned in 1957 to devote his time to membership on the Elks National Memorial and Publication Commission.

In 1967, the Commission was composed of the following members:

Past Grand Exalted Ruler, James T. Hallinan, *Chairman*
Past Grand Exalted Ruler, George I. Hall, *V-Chairman*

Past Grand Exalted Ruler, William J. Jernick, *Treasurer*
Past Grand Exalted Ruler, John L. Walker, *Secretary*
Past Grand Exalted Ruler, Emmett T. Anderson
Past Grand Exalted Ruler, Fred L. Bohn
Past Grand Exalted Ruler, William A. Wall
Bryan McKeogh remains as *Executive Director*

Finances

A statement of the receipts and expenditures from the creation of the Commission (under the name of the Elks National Veterans Service Commission) on July 10, 1946 to the close of the fiscal year ending March 31, 1967, will be found in the Appendix of this History.

S E C T I O N

Ninth Decade

A distinction characterizing this Decade was the attainment of a membership of over 1,000,000.

The 1,000,000th Elk was Raymond Cole of Bay City, Michigan, Lodge No. 89.

At the Eighty-Second Anniversary Banquet of New York Lodge No. 1, in 1950, he was presented by Grand Exalted Ruler Anderson with a watch commemorating the occasion.

This is the Decade in which we found ourselves engaged in a war on the other side of the World—in Korea.

It was fortunate that in the Elks National Service Commission we had an organization in being already serving the hospitalized veterans, prepared to extend these services to the disabled in the additional Veterans Administration Hospitals needed and erected.

GEORGE I. HALL
1948-49

EMMETT T. ANDERSON
1949-50

JOSEPH B. KYLE
1950-51

HOWARD R. DAVIS
1951-52

SAM STERN
1952-53

Grand Exalted Rulers

NINTH DECADE

1948-1958

Earl E. James
1953-54

William J. Jernick
1954-55

John L. Walker
1955-56

Fred L. Bohn
1956-57

Hobert L. Blackledge
1957-58

This Commission also was prepared to and did renew the important Fraternal Centers service so successfully conducted in World War II and took advantage of other opportunities to be helpful to the boys in service.

An important change of the Ritual was made in this period when it was unanimously voted at the Grand Lodge Session that the use of a blindfold in initiation be discarded.

In 1956 the treatment of the American Flag in our Ritual was changed, removing the Flag from our alter and substituting an altar cloth.

In this Decade, several new Committees of the Grand Lodge were created as follows: "The Committee on Youth Activities," a "Convention Committee," a "Pension Committee," and a "Membership and New Lodge Committee."

In Section "F" of this History there has been told the story of "The Order and the American Youth" from the Fifth to the Eighth Decades.

In this (the Ninth) Decade is told the story of the "Committee on Youth Activities" from its inception to the end of this Decade.

This period marked the Silver Anniversary of the Elks National Foundation for it was established at the Grand Lodge session in Miami in 1928. Its history and proud record of accomplishments are recited elsewhere in this History.

Grand Exalted Rulers

During this period there were the following Grand Exalted Rulers:

George I. Hall, Lynbrook, N. Y. Lodge No. 1515	1948-1949
Emmett T. Anderson, Tacoma, Wash. Lodge No. 174	1949-1950
Joseph B. Kyle, Gary, Ind. Lodge No. 1152	1950-1951
Howard R. Davis, Williamsport, Lodge No. 173	1951-1952
Sam Stern, Fargo, N. D. Lodge No. 260	1952-1953
Earl E. James, Oklahoma City, Okla. Lodge No. 417	1953-1954
William J. Jernick, Nutley, N. J. Lodge No. 1290	1954-1955
John L. Walker, Roanoke, Va. Lodge No. 197	1955-1956
Fred L. Bohn, Zanesville, Ohio Lodge No. 114	1956-1957
H. L. Blackledge, Kearney, Neb. Lodge No. 984	1957-1958

Grand Secretary

Past Grand Exalted Ruler J. Edgar Masters was re-elected as Grand Secretary at the 1954 Convention but he passed away on

August 6, 1954, after serving in the office for 25 years. Lee A. Donaldson, Etna, Pa. Lodge No. 932 was appointed by Grand Exalted Ruler Jernick to fill his unexpired term and served as Grand Secretary for the balance of the Decade.

Elks National Home

After having served as Superintendent of the Elks National Home for twenty six years, Robert A. Scott resigned and in September of 1953, Thomas J. Brady of Brookline, Mass. Lodge No. 886 assumed the position and served through this Decade.

Membership and Charitable Expenditures

During these years up to March 31, 1958, the Order grew in membership to 1,214,163. The number of lodges had increased to 1,832.

Year	Membership	Charitable Expenditures
1948-1949	965,387	$5,878,042.14
1949-1950	1,004,985	6,104,373.18
1950-1951	1,041,264	6,025,613.89
1951-1952	1,069,868	5,750,956.73
1952-1953	1,097,003	5,699,774.80
1953-1954	1,122,803	6,061,327.43
1954-1955	1,149,613	6,285,567.85
1955-1956	1,173,494	6,489,021.41
1956-1957	1,195,509	6,607,580.34
1957-1958	1,214,163	6,620,407.89

Grand Lodge Sessions during this period were held in the following cities:

1949	Cleveland, Ohio
1950	Miami, Florida
1951	Chicago, Illinois
1952	New York, New York
1953	St. Louis, Mo.
1954	Los Angeles, Cal.
1955	Philadelphia, Pa.
1956	Chicago, Ill.
1957	San Francisco, Cal.
1958	New York, New York

Youth Movement

In his report to the Grand Lodge Session in Cleveland, in 1949, Grand Exalted Ruler Hall referred to the inspiration that had come to him from the support given by the subordinate lodges to the programs inaugurated during his year on behalf of the youth of our country.

He then stated:

> "It is my recommendation that an additional Committee of the Grand Lodge be appointed and to it assigned the duties of the preparation and carrying through of programs on behalf of our youngsters, which I feel confident will receive unanimous support of all our members."

The Committee on Judiciary recommended that Section 47D of the Grand Lodge Statutes be amended to read as follows:

> "The Youth Activities Committee shall prepare, supervise and carry on all Elks programs on behalf of the youth of our country, and shall have charge of the supervision of such matters as shall be referred to it by the Grand Exalted Ruler or the Grand Lodge pertaining to the youth program of our Order."

This recommendation of the Committee was adopted.

Grand Lodge Youth Activities Committee

The first Committee (appointed in 1949) consisted of

John F. Scileppi, Queens Borough, New York, Lodge No. 878
Edward A. Spry, Boston, Massachusetts, Lodge No. 10
H. H. Russell, Warrensburg, Missouri, Lodge No. 673
Raymond C. Crowell, Pasadena, California, Lodge No. 672
Boyce A. Whitmire, Hendersonville, North Carolina, Lodge No. 1616

1949——1950

The members of this first Committee recognized that their most important responsibility was to lay a solid foundation for the future; building the moral and physical character of the American boys and girls, the leaders of tomorrow.

A three-color poster of Grand Exalted Ruler Anderson with two typical American youngsters was sent to each Elks lodge, its intended purpose being to make all Elks "Youth Conscious."

Each lodge was urged to appoint a Youth Committee and a program of youth activities was recommended to each lodge.

At the same time all lodges were asked to answer a questionnaire as to its present youth activities.

The results were:

442 lodges reported that they had adopted youth programs for the first time. Presumably there were more.

The number and character of the activities were impressive.

A major activity of the Committee, under the chairmanship of Past Exalted Ruler John F. Scileppi, Queens Borough, New York, Lodge No. 878, was an educational one and embraced scholarship awards to eleven boys and girls selected for qualities of leadership and located in eleven different zones into which the Committee divided the country.

These awards were financed by the Elks National Foundation and amounted in total to $3,300.

Certificates were also awarded to eleven other youths.

1950——1951

The members of the Committee of 1949-1950 were reappointed.

The Committee estimated that 500,000 more boys and girls were reached by the subordinate lodges cooperating with the Committee at an additional expenditure of $750,000.

The Committee stated that 1,094 lodges reported carrying on youth programs, an increase of 231 lodges over those engaged in youth work the preceding year and that hundreds of lodges expanded their existing programs.

The Committee presented each lodge sponsoring a youth program with the official Youth Committee "Participation Certificate."

In addition the lodge selected as the one which promoted the outstanding youth program in each state or territory was awarded an official Youth Committee plaque and the lodge providing the most outstanding youth program in the nation a National Championship achievement trophy.

Hellgate Lodge No. 383, Missoula, Montana, was the winner of the national award.

The Committee continued support of the Boy Scout program. The number of Boy Scout troops sponsored by Elks lodges increased to 591.

The Committee also endorsed the work of the Girl Scouts and urged all lodges to support it.

The Committee, with the cooperation of 34 State Associations, promoted a National Youth Leadership Contest in which $3,500, representing $4,600 in Savings Bonds, was awarded to boys and girls in all sections of the country who displayed outstanding qualities of leadership in their service to their communities. The Elks National Foundation provided the funds for these awards.

In addition to the 34 national awards, State Associations and individual lodges made awards to state and local winners.

At the request of the Committee, Grand Exalted Ruler Kyle designated March 24, 1951, as Elks National Youth Day.

In this connection, hundreds of lodges held appropriate ceremonies in honor of American youth generally and those worthy of individual recognition particularly.

The Committee reported that extensive newspaper, radio and television coverage was accorded these programs honoring thousands of American boys and girls.

1951——1952

The Grand Lodge Youth Activities Committee for 1951-1952, with Edward A. Spry, Boston, Mass., Lodge No. 10, as Chairman, reported that more than 2,000,000 boys and girls were served by Elks lodges and State Associations at an estimated cost of $2,600,000.

This indicated that approximately 80 per cent of the subordinate lodges and 90 per cent of the State Associations engaged in youth works of one form or another.

The Committee provided a "Participation Certificate" for each lodge engaged in youth work, a plaque for the outstanding youth program in each state or territory, and a National Championship trophy for the outstanding youth program in the country. The Committee also awarded a prize to the State Association doing the most outstanding work in promoting the Committee's program.

The National Lodge Champion was Kelso, Washington, Lodge No. 1482.

The State Champion was Colorado.

Youth Leadership Awards

This Committee repeated the Youth Leadership awards program of its predecessors.

The Elks National Foundation has provided the funds for these Youth Leadership Awards since the Program's beginning. Such awards to date, total approximately $150,000.

There were first, second and third awards to boys and the same to girls and an award to the winner in each of the 46 states participating.

Boy Scouts

The Committee reported an increase of the number of Boy Scout troops sponsored by subordinate lodges to 619, an increase of 366 in five years.

William Johnson (center), 17-year-old McAlester, Oklahoma, high school student whose essay on "Why Democracy Works" won first prize of $1,000 Defense Bond smiles happily as he receives congratulations from President Truman at the White House. Sharing the handclasp is George I. Hall of New York, Grand Exalted Ruler of the Benevolent and Protective Order of Elks, sponsor of the contest in which $101,000 in prizes were awarded.

Make May Day American

Grand Exalted Ruler Howard R. Davis designated May 1, 1952, as Elks National Youth Day and called upon all the lodges of the Order to pay tribute to American youth on that date.

The Committee submitted to each subordinate lodge a comprehensive and detailed program for participation in the celebration of the day.

In its report to the Grand Lodge Session in 1952, the Committee said:

"The Committee cannot even attempt to report here the wonderful results of this epoch-making day. However, we do feel safe in saying that every delegate to this Convention, and every Elk reading this report participated in this outstanding event by some act, word or deed.

Grand Exalted Ruler Emmett T. Anderson making a Presentation at the Anniversary Banquet of New York Lodge No. 1 in 1950 to Raymond Cole of Bay City, Michigan, Lodge No. 89, the One Millionth Elk.

"Elks lodges all over the country held their ceremonies in lodge rooms, auditoriums, schools, parks and other public places, and joining wholeheartedly in this movement, to take proper recognition of Youth, were prominent leaders in the public, civic and spiritual life of our communities.

"Elks National Youth Day was a thrilling and magnificent demonstration of public patriotic fervor and a manifestation of our faith in the Youth of America."

During the following years the Chairmen of the Youth Activities Committee were as follows:

1952-1953 P.E.R. Benjamin F. Watson, Lansing, Mich. Lodge No. 196

1953-1954 P.E.R. Jay H. Payne, Ann Arbor, Mich. Lodge No. 325

1954-1956 P.E.R. Dewey E. S. Kuhns, Charleston, W. Va. Lodge No. 202

1956-1957 P.E.R. C. P. Hebenstreit, Huntington Park, Cal. Lodge No. 1415

1957-1958 P.E.R. Charles E. Bowie, San Benito, Texas Lodge No. 1661

The National Judges of the Youth Leadership Contest during the same period were as follows:

1953 U.S. District Judge Allen B. Hannay of Houston, Texas
Clyde E. Jones, Ottumwa, Iowa
Michigan Supreme Court Justice John R. Dittmore

1954   Vice President Richard M. Nixon
        Mrs. Eleanor Roosevelt
        Hon. J. Edgar Hoover, Director Federal Bureau of Investigation

1955   Governor Christian A. Herter, Massachusetts
        Governor Robert B. Meyner, New Jersey
        Hon. James A. Farley, formerly Postmaster General

1956   Governor Thomas B. Stanley, Virginia
        Governor Dennis J. Roberts, Rhode Island
        Governor Victor E. Anderson, Nebraska

1957   This year the judging was done by the Youth Activities Committee of the Grand Lodge.

1958   Hon. Harry F. Byrd, United States Senator, Virginia
        Hon. Barry M. Goldwater, United States Senator, Arizona
        Hon. Roman H. Hruska, United States Senator, Nebraska

1952–1953

At the Grand Lodge Session of 1953, Chairman Watson, P.E.R. of Lansing, Mich. Lodge No. 196, stated that this year the Committee again featured a "Three Pronged" Program policy:

1. Conducting of Youth Leadership Contests at local, state and national levels.
2. Designation of May 1, 1953 as "Elks National Youth Day" featuring the slogan "Keep May Day American."
3. Insistent urging that each subordinate lodge of the Order institute, foster, activate and maintain a year-round Youth Program in its area.

Every lodge was forwarded a questionnaire to fill out and return to the Committee. The purpose of this was to obtain the name of the subordinate lodge Youth Chairman and call to the attention of the Exalted Rulers the need for a Committee in each lodge. Over six hundred lodges responded and, as a result, many local Youth Committees, were appointed.

A booklet was distributed to every Exalted Ruler, local chairman, state president, and state chairman. The booklet was a handbook of the aims of the Committee and how they could be accomplished.

Upon orders from lodges and State Association Committees, over 15,000 Youth Leadership contest entry blanks were distributed.

Each State Association was authorized to submit a winning boy and girl entrant in the State Competition as contestants in the national contest. Every state submitted entries. The Youth

Leadership Awards, totaling $6,000, in U.S. Savings Bonds were made in cooperation with the Elks National Foundation.

Recognizing that when May Day is red, it is the antithesis of American principles, the Committee continued the practice of timing Elk National Youth with May 1st. The response was splendid. Governors of States issued proclamations designating May 1st as Elk National Youth Day and extolling the program. President Eisenhower wrote to Grand Exalted Ruler Stern emphasizing his belief in the merit of our Youth Day. Mayors of cities signed resolutions lauding the day and events. "However, above and beyond all this stirring of governmental approbation was the response of the lodges," said Chairman Watson.

The Committee was gratified to note the gradual but steady growth of long-term boy and girl programs. High on the list is Scout Troop sponsorship. The Committee estimated that in this lodge year about 650 lodges are sponsors of Scout Troops of one type or another, aggregating nearly 675 units, several lodges sponsoring more than one troop. Chairman Watson stated that he believed the subordinate lodges disbursed in the neighborhood of $2,500,000 on behalf of the Youth of our country during the year.

To stimulate subordinate lodge participation in the Youth Program, handsome plaques were again awarded this year. From each State Association, the Committee selected a lodge as outstanding for its work during the year.

Chairman Watson introduced Commander Thomas J. Keane Director of Civic Relationships of the Boy Scouts of America, who spoke of the extremely important role of the Elks in this great Youth Activities Program. He then presented John F. Killebrew, Exalted Ruler of Nashville, Tenn. Lodge and announced the presentation of a trophy to that lodge for its outstanding Boy Scout work. This lodge not only saved the Boy Scout Troops in Nashville but built them to the point where they were one of the most outstanding districts in the country. Elkdom's direct cooperation with the Boy Scouts of America was initiated at the Grand Lodge Session in Portland, Oregon, when L. A. Lewis was elected Grand Exalted Ruler, and, therefore, Commander Keane asked Mr. Lewis to make the presentation of the trophy to Exalted Ruler Killebrew of the Nashville Lodge.

The South Dakota Elks State Association was judged as the State which best carried on its Youth Programs.

1953–1954

At the Grand Lodge Session of 1954, Judge Jay H. Payne, Chairman, reported that a questionnaire was sent to every State

Association President and the Exalted Rulers of all lodges with the result that direct contact was made with the Youth Activities Chairman of about 1400 of the 1680 Subordinate Lodges, a record of more than 81%.

The Committee made out a certificate of participation and a "Youth Program Booklet" with detailed information and suggestions for an effective year-round program, including full information about the Youth Leadership Contest.

While no definite figures could be determined, the Committee expressed the conviction that possibly more than 2,000,000 to 4,000,000 contacts were made with our country's youth.

At the request of Grand Exalted Ruler James, this year's Youth Program included special help and rehabilitation awards for the under-privileged child as well as social, recreational and educational projects for healthy and normal children.

No less than 30,000 Youth Leadership Contest entry blanks were distributed to the Committees. Ninety-eight boys and girls representing every state and territory of this country were entered in the finals of this contest.

By special grant from the Elks National Foundation, a U. S. Savings Bond with maturity value of $100 was presented to each top state winner, in addition to the $1600 Bonds presented to the National Winners.

The Wisconsin Elks State Association was selected as the State Association which had done the most outstanding Youth Activities work during the year.

1954–1955

In his acceptance speech at the meeting of the Grand Lodge in Los Angeles, Grand Exalted Ruler Jernick said, "Through our Youth Activities, we can and must provide that experience, that moral foundation, that guidance which will guarantee the proper development of our citizens of tomorrow for as Elkdom-Sows, America Reaps."

Through our Committee our Grand Lodge Youth Activities attained new heights of participation and accomplishment. In addition to the State Association Award for the most outstanding work in promoting our Youth Program an additional award was made to the best and most comprehensive State Youth Day Program.

The State winner for the best promotion and greatest participation was the Arizona Elks State Association and the State Youth Day Contest was won by Maine Elks State Association.

On December 20, 1954 Grand Exalted Ruler Jernick presented to President Eisenhower, a report of the work which our Order

had done on behalf of the Youth of America, over a period of many years. The President was greatly impressed and interested. At the time of his visit arrangements were made with the President for the presentation of the Youth Leadership Awards which he made the following April to the winners.

1955–1956

Dewey E. S. Kuhns, chairman of the Committee on Youth Activities, stated at the Grand Lodge Session of 1956 that the Committee had based its program this year on three points:

1. Promotion of year-round Youth Program in subordinate lodges
2. Youth Leadership Contest
3. The promotion of Youth Day on May 1 to impress on the minds of our young people, the countless benefits and blessing of freedom, such as we have in America and to dispel any thought that this was a day to be used for furthering communism.

417

Brother Kuhns reported an outstanding response of our lodges, investing more than $3,000,000 in programs in which over 1,000,-000 of the Youth of our Country participated. He also reported that the entries in the Youth Leadership Contest exceeded 50,000, with $8600 in Bonds made available by the Elks National Foundation.

For the second straight year, the Maine Elks State Association won the State Youth Day Program and the award for the State having best all around Youth Program was won by Wisconsin Elks State Association.

1956–1957

In making his Report to the Grand Lodge Convention in 1957 Chairman Hebenstreit said, "At the outset of this year in July 1956, it was made clear that Grand Exalted Ruler Bohn was most sincere and determined to devote a major portion of his program to the most valuable part of our Nation, the American Youth."

The Committee therefore, decided to again adopt the same three point program used in the past several years and it met with increased participation and enthusiasm. Again the Bonds for the winners of the various contests were provided by the Elks National Foundation.

Again the Wisconsin Elks State Association was named the State winner of the "Best Youth Program" with the Youth Day award going to Maine for the third time.

At the Convention of 1957 a report of Partnership between the Benevolent and Protective Order of Elks and the Boy Scouts of America was read as follows:

Nearly 30,000 American boys belonged to the 683 Scout units sponsored by Elks Lodges as of December 31, 1956. This represented a net gain of 30 Scout units during the year, more than keeping pace with the net gain of 30 Elks Lodges. Subordinate Lodges now sponsor 120 Cub packs for boys eight through ten, 359 Boy Scout troops for boys eleven through thirteen, and 204 Explorer units for young men fourteen through seventeen. The percentage of Scout units sponsored to total Subordinate Lodges rose from 37.3% to 38.4%.

States showing a net gain of three or more Scout units were California (11), Texas (7), Illinois (5), Washington (4), and Rhode Island, Alaska, South Carolina, and West Virginia (3). States showing greatest improvement in standing were South Carolina (45th to 24th), Hawaii (18th to 14th), and West Virginia (37th to 26th), and Arkansas (50th to 41st).

The attractive eight page promotion folder in two colors entitled "The Elks and the Boy Scouts" was released in June, 1956, by the

Grand Lodge Youth Activities Committee. Distribution was made to every Subordinate Elks Lodge by the Grand Lodge and to each of the 540 local Boy Scout councils by the Civic Relationships Service of the Boys Scouts of America. This folder proved to be an immediate success and has done much to improve mutual understanding and interest locally.

Appreciation is expressed to Mr. Dewey E. S. Kuhns, former chairman, and Mr. C. P. Hebenstreit, present chairman of the Grand Lodge Youth Activities Committee and the Order's Public Relations Director, all of whom worked diligently to produce this popular piece of literature. Because of the great demand, supplies of this piece are nearly exhausted and a request for a second printing has been forwarded to the committee.

Scouts representing local councils continued to provide honor guards for the Grand Exalted Ruler upon his visits throughout America.

Elks continued to hold many top Scouting leadership positions in the 540 local Scout councils in the U.S.A.

The rapid increase in boy population presents a challenge to the Benevolent and Protective Order of Elks and the Boy Scouts of America to extend our partnership to reach still more boys with the character building and citizenship training values of Scouting program.

The Boy Scouts of America are proud to have served as your partner in this important enterprise and looks forward to still greater cooperation in the interest of American boys.

> Prepared by: George K. Myers, National Director
> Civic Relationships Service
> Boy Scouts of America

The renowned commentator, Ted Malone and American Broadcasting Company paid tribute to our Youth Work by dedicating his program of May 1 to Elks National Youth Day.

1957-1958

Chairman Charles E. Bowie, at the Grand Lodge Session of 1958, summarized the projects his Committee had undertaken. The first was an endeavor to encourage our lodges to have a sound, well balanced year-round Youth Program, rather than working on an intermittent basis. The second project was the Youth Leadership Contest, which this year had outstanding national response with more than 50,000 contest entry blanks received by the subordinate lodges. The third project was to promote Elk National Youth Day on May 1, using the theme "Keep it American."

Again the Elks National Foundation made available a $1,000 United States Bond as first place awards to the boy and girl winner on a national level. Our two first place winners were introduced to the nation by Ed Sullivan on his television show, resulting in favorable publicity for the Order and its Youth Program.

This year the Committee reprinted 6,000 copies of a booklet entitled "The Elks and the Boy Scouts." The lodges in our Order were now sponsoring 720 Scout units and were contributing some $250,000 annually to scouting. The Nebraska Elks State Association won the award for the best State Youth Activities and the Ohio Elks State Association was the winner of the Youth Day Contest.

Korean War and Elks Armed Forces Blood Campaign

Grand Exalted Ruler Howard R. Davis making his pledge to Robert A. Lovett, Secretary of Defense, that the members of the Benevolent and Protective Order of Elks would contribute one million pints of blood as their part of the campaign for gathering three million pints of blood necessary for the protection of the members of our Armed Forces in Korea.

Blood Bank

The outstanding contribution of the Order to the success of the Korean War commitment of our country, up to the date of the closing of this History, aside from activities of the Elks National Service Commission referred to in the chapter of this History

420

devoted to that Commission, started in September, 1951.

The latter part of that month request was received from the United States Department of National Defense that the Order of Elks participate in a campaign for gathering the 3,000,000 pints of blood necessary in the following year for the protection of the members of our Armed Forces serving in the Korean War.

Through the Public Relations Department of the Order an engagement was made for a conference between the Grand Exalted Ruler and Robert A. Lovett, Secretary of Defense.

At that conference Grand Exalted Ruler Davis made the promise that the Elks would provide "a million pints of blood from a million Elks by July 1, 1952, for use of the members of our Armed Forces."

The Grand Lodge State Associations Committee was given charge of this program by the Grand Exalted Ruler.

In the annual report Grand Exalted Ruler Davis submitted at the Grand Lodge Session in 1952 he said that while exact figures were not available at the writing of that report, it was evident that the Order had reached the half million pints in blood given and another quarter of a million pints volunteered and pledged.

He referred to the fact that the American Red Cross had been cooperative in this program but that it had lacked the facilities of taking blood as fast as the Elks were prepared to offer it.

He suggested that only a lack of sufficient facilities for taking blood prevented the Elks from reaching the full goal set for the period ending July 1st, 1952.

At the Grand Lodge Convention, General David N. W. Grant, Director of the American Red Cross National Blood Campaign, praised the Elks for their outstanding work in this vital effort to assure that every wounded veteran in the Korean conflict would receive full benefit.

He said that he would appreciate it if the members present would pass on to all Elks the hearty concurrence of the Department of Defense in giving thanks for the pledge of one million pints of blood by the Order and the enthusiastic endeavor of all Elks to fulfill the pledge, constituting the greatest single effort in the program.

He said that the Elks' contribution already had had a salutary effect upon the entire Blood Program which he referred to as an "all-over defense effort."

When Sam Stern became Grand Exalted Ruler he decided to continue the Armed Forces Blood Donor Campaign. It was so successful that at the 1953 Grand Lodge Convention our Order was awarded the United States Defense Department's Meritorious award by Major General Clark L. Ruffner.

NATIONAL FLAG DAY OBSERVANCE

The Grand Lodge organized an observance of Flag Day in Washington, D.C., June 14, 1957. The observance, which took the form of a pageant based on the Flag Day ritual, was presented in the D.A.R. Auditorium with Grand Exalted Ruler Fred L. Bohn and members of the Order from both Houses of Congress participating. These included Speaker John W. McCormick, Boston Lodge No. 10, former Speaker Joseph W. Martin, Jr., No. Attleboro, Mass., Lodge No. 1011, Senator Karl E. Mundt, Madison, S.D. Lodge No. 1442, House Members Russell V. Mack, P.E.R., Aberdeen, Wash., Lodge No. 593, Ben F. Jensen, Atlantic, Ia. Lodge No. 445, John F. Baldwin, Jr., Pittsburg, Calif. Lodge No. 1474, Frank J. Becker, P.E.R., Lynbrook, N.Y. Lodge No. 1515 and John J. Rooney, P.E.R., Brooklyn Lodge No. 22.

Music was provided by singers Elaine Malbin and Lanny Ross supported by the U.S. Army Band and Chorus.

The Mutual Broadcasting Co. presented a half-hour broadcast of the program over a coast-to-coast network.

Prior to the Flag Day observance, members of the Order in Congress and in the Executive and Judicial branches of the Government and their wives were guests at a reception and dinner at the Willard Hotel.

INDOCTRINATION

At the end of his year in reporting to the Grand Lodge, Grand Exalted Ruler Walker said "One of the basic factors in the problem of lapsation is our failure to indoctrinate new members with a knowledge and understanding of Elkdom and the achievements and the great contributions to the public welfare that the Grand Lodge, the State Associations and the subordinate lodges are making. Some of the lodges are acutely aware of this fact and have developed excellent indoctrination programs that have been of invaluable assistance to them in eliminating and curtailing lapsation."

In 1957, Grand Exalted Ruler Blackledge named as one of his major objectives the adoption by every lodge of a planned, comprehensive and intelligent indoctrination of new members. He offered various suggestions and ideas for this program and at his suggestion a Section was added to our Statutes at the 1957 Convention, making it mandatory that a committee on Indoctrination be named in every lodge to prepare, supervise and conduct a planned program of indoctrination for all newly initiated members.

At the 1961 Convention, Grand Exalted Ruler Fenton reported to the Grand Lodge that a committee of which Past Grand Exalted Ruler L. A. Lewis was chairman had prepared and distributed to all lodges a splendid set of Visual Indoctrination Slides and an accompanying commentary, narrated by Vincent Grocott, Santa Barbara, Cal. Lodge No. 613.

He further stated "The purpose of this program was to furnish to each Subordinate Lodge condensed material which should be used by the lodge in the indoctrination of new candidates for membership and also to increase pride of membership in present members. These slides and narration can be used also at public meetings of the lodge or before service and civic club meetings.

"These slides and narration graphically portray Elkdom in action and depict all of the magnificent programs of the Order. Youth Service, Veterans Service, Elks National Home, The Elks Magazine, Elks National Foundation, Elks Memorial Building, State Association Major Projects, Family participation and the myriad programs carried on by our Lodges for civic and community betterment and for youth, patriotic and benevolent purposes.

"The slides were first shown at the Exalted Rulers' luncheon in Dallas and received a most enthusiastic reception. They were also shown at each District Deputy Conference.

"This program has been notably successful and already has had the expected profound effect of not only increased pride in membership but of setting before the public the record of the wonderful, good works of our Order."

Every year since the slides were first sent to our lodges, the Committee has sent a few additional slides to update them.

H. R. WISELY
1958-59

JOHN E FENTON
1960-61

WILLIAM S. HAWKINS
1959-60

WILLIAM A. WALL
1961-62

Grand Exalted Rulers

TENTH DECADE

1958-1968

LEE A. DONALDSON
1962-63

RONALD J. DUNN
1963-64

R. LEONARD BUSH
1965-66

ROBERT G. PRUITT
1964-65

RAYMOND C. DOBSON
1966-67

ROBERT E. BONEY
1967-68

424

S E C T I O N

TENTH DECADE

In this decade great emphasis was placed on efforts to improve the administration of lodges and clubs. The Grand Lodge produced numerous manuals on such subjects as membership control, lapsation and club management to name a few and supplied them to lodge officers to assist them in the performance of their duties. The Stray Elk program was developed, family participation was strongly encouraged, and preparations were begun for the observance of the Order's Centennial in 1968.

In 1958, the Board of Grand Trustees engaged the Merchants National Bank of Boston as Investment Counselors and began to diversify the investments of Grand Lodge. This program has resulted in a much greater yield than our previous policy of investing these funds in government savings bonds.

At the Grand Lodge Session, an amendment was made in Section 117 of our Statutes so that in the discretion of a lodge, the ceremony of installation of officers might be public.

At the same session the name of the "Auditing Committee" was changed to the "Auditing and Accounting Committee" and because of the constant increase in our membership, the number of our lodges and the magnitude of our Grand Lodge Programs, the membership of all but three of our Grand Lodge Committees was increased to eight members.

At the 1961 Grand Lodge Session, the "Committee on Americanism" was created, to implement the patriotic activities of the Order and its lodges. This year the number of Grand Trustees was increased from five to eight and the term was reduced from five to four years.

On recommendation of the Grand Lodge "Pension Committee" at the 1962 Grand Lodge Session, this Committee was abolished and the administration of the Employees Pension Plan of the Grand Lodge was placed in the hands of the Board of Grand Trustees.

A change was made in 1960 in the procedure for the appointment of District Deputies. Theretofore, the Deputies had been appointed in July and they were brought to the Convention at the end of their term of office. The new procedure provided that the "District Deputy Grand Exalted Ruler shall be designated for the next grand lodge year, by the Grand Exalted Ruler, not later than June 1st of each year and directed to attend the forthcoming session of the Grand Lodge. The District Deputy Grand Exalted Rulers shall be installed in office by the Grand Exalted Ruler, following his election and installation, by taking and subscribing to the oath, after which they are declared duly appointed and installed."

FIRST NINE YEARS OF THE TENTH DECADE 1958–1967

Grand Exalted Rulers

During this period there were the following Grand Exalted Rulers:

Horace R. Wisely, Salinas, Cal. Lodge No. 614	1958-1959
William S. Hawkins, Coeur d'Alene, Idaho Lodge No. 1254	1959-1960

John E. Fenton, Lawrence, Mass. Lodge No. 65	1960-1961
William A. Wall, West Palm Beach, Fla., Lodge No. 1352	1961-1962
Lee A. Donaldson, Etna, Pa. Lodge No. 932	1962-1963
Ronald J. Dunn, Oneida, N. Y. Lodge No. 767	1963-1964
Robert G. Pruitt, Buckhead (Atlanta) Ga. Lodge No. 1635	1964-1965
R. Leonard Bush, Inglewood Cal. Lodge No. 1492	1965-1966
Raymond C. Dobson, Minot, N. D. Lodge No. 1089	1966-1967
Robert E. Boney, Las Cruces, N. Mex. Lodge No. 1119	1967-

Grand Secretary

Lee A. Donaldson served as Grand Secretary in the first four years of this Decade until 1962 when he was elected as Grand Exalted Ruler. Franklin J. Fitzpatrick, Lynbrook Lodge No. 1515 was then elected as Grand Secretary and as this history is being written is still in this office.

Elks National Home

Thomas J. Brady passed away on September 8, 1964 after having served as superintendent of the Elks National Home since 1954. Doral E. Irvin, Lynchburg Lodge No. 321 was named as his successor and continues in that capacity.

Membership and Charitable Expenditures

During these years up to March 31, 1967 the Order grew in Membership from 1,214,163 to 1,417,435.

The number of our lodges had increased from 1,832 to 2,091.

Year	Membership	Charitable Expenditures
1958-1959	1,232,007	$6,910,541.23
1959-1960	1,260,007	7,028,698.27
1960-1961	1,280,524	7,040,518.89
1961-1962	1,294,604	7,006,293.47
1962-1963	1,315,319	6,994,566.38
1963-1964	1,333,482	6,950,298.21
1964-1965	1,361,455	7,706,968.65
1965-1966	1,388,561	7,924,983.99
1966-1967	1,417,435	8,119,745.95

Grand Lodge Sessions during this period were held in the following cities:

1958   New York, New York
1959   Chicago, Illinois

1960   Dallas, Texas
1961   Miami Beach, Florida
1962   Chicago, Illinois
1963   San Francisco, California
1964   New York, New York
1965   Miami Beach, Florida
1966   Dallas, Texas
1967   Chicago, Illinois

YOUTH MOVEMENT

The committee on Youth Activities continued the three point Youth Program which had been so well received and successful in the past six years. During these years the Chairmen of the Committee were as follows:

1958-1959   P.E.R.   Charles E. Bowie, San Benito, Tex, Lodge No. 1661
1959-1960   P.E.R.   W. L. Hill, Great Falls, Montana Lodge No. 214
1960-1961   P.E.R.   E. Gene Fournace, Newark, Ohio Lodge No. 391
1961-1962   P.E.R.   Joseph F. Bader, Lyndhurst, New Jersey Lodge No. 1505
1962-1965   P.E.R.   E. Gene Fournace, Newark, Ohio Lodge No. 391

1965-1967   P.E.R.   Mellville J. Junion, Green Bay, Wis. Lodge No. 259

During this period, the National Judges were as follows:
1959   Hon. J. Edgar Hoover, Director Federal Bureau of Investigation
       Mrs. Ivy Baker Priest, Treasurer of the United States
       Congressman John W. McCormick, Massachusetts, Majority Leader
1960   Hon. Frank Church, United States Senator, Idaho
       Hon. Spessard L. Holland, United States Senator, Florida
       Hon. Prescott S. Bush, United States Senator, Connecticut
1961   Hon. Maurine B. Newberger, United States Senator, Oregon
       Hon. Jessica McCullough Weis, Congresswoman, New York
       Hon. Margaret Stitt Church, Congresswoman, Illinois
1962   Vice President Lyndon B. Johnson
       Hon. Thomas H. Kuchel, United States Senator, California
       Hon. Edmund S. Muskie, United States Senator, Maine
1963   Hon. John W. Byrnes, Congressman, Wisconsin
       Hon. Robert Secrest, Congressman, Ohio
       Hon. William Cramer, Congressman, Florida
1964   Hon. Bourke B. Hickenlooper, United States Senator, Iowa
       Hon. Roman L. Hruska, United States Senator, Nebraska
       Hon. Clinton P. Anderson, United States Senator, New Mexico

1965 Hon. John O. Pastore, United States Senator, Rhode Island
Hon. William Proxmire, United States Senator, Wisconsin
Hon. Warren S. Magnuson, United States Senator, Washington
1966 Hon. Thomas H. Kuchel, United States Senator, California
Hon. Lee Metcalf, United States Senator, Montana
Hon. Gaylord Nelson, United States Senator, Wisconsin
1967 Hon. Milton R. Young, United States Senator, North Dakota
Hon. Philip A. Hart, United States Senator, Michigan
Hon. Edward M. Kennedy, United States Senator, Massachusetts

State Winners

Best Overall Youth Program	Best Youth Day Program
1959 Ohio Elks State Association	Ohio and New York Elks State Associations (tied)
1960 Ohio Elks State Association	Pennsyvania Elks State Association
1961 Nebraska Elks State Association	Ohio Elks State Association
1962 Nebraska Elks State Association	New York Elks State Association
1963 Ohio Elks State Association	Pennsylvania Elks State Association
1964 Nebraska Elks State Association	Pennsylvania Elks State Association
1965 Florida Elks State Association	Pennsylvania Elks State Association
1966 Nebraska Elks State Association	Massachusetts Elks State Association
1967 Nebraska Elks State Association	Pennsylvania Elks State Association

AMERICANISM

At the Grand Lodge Convention in 1961 at Miami Beach, a Committee on Americanism was created and charged with "implementing the patriotic activities of the Order and its subordinate lodges."

The original members of this Committee were as follows:

Vincent H. Grocott, Chairman
   Santa Barbara Lodge No. 613
W. Edgar Porter, Sr.
   Salisbury Lodge No. 817

Charles W. Claybaugh,
Champaign Lodge No. 398
J. A. McArthur, Lewiston Lodge No. 896
Bert Harkness, Plattsburg Lodge No. 621
Clarence H. Dietz, Sapulpa Lodge No. 1118
Arvey E. Diettert, Cincinnati Lodge No. 5
W. B. Wagenheim, Norfolk Lodge No. 38

Immediately following the activation of the Committee, Grand
Exalted Ruler Wall dispatched a telegram to President John F.
Kennedy telling him of the creation of the Committee "to launch
a program of Militant Patriotism and Aggressive Anti-Commu-
nism" and assuring our President that our Order was prepared
to undertake any program or project in the service of our
country that he might request.

The first major task of the Americanism Committee was to
produce a "Declaration of American Principles" which stated in
clear and concise language the position of our Order.

A DECLARATION OF AMERICAN PRINCIPLES

The Benevolent and Protective Order of Elks is dedicated to the welfare of the United States of America. One of our Order's purposes is
"to quicken the spirit of American patriotism." To that end our
Order has striken to advance the principles that guide our Nation,
and has opposed all attacks upon them from whatever quarter.

Freedom, the historic goal of mankind, is our Nation's basic principle. Freedom has been under steady attack by international communism for many years. Now, freedom and communism are engaged in a
struggle for survival. This struggle is not of our choosing, but has been
forced upon us. Free men have no choice but to accept the challenge.
The Americanism Committee of the Grand Lodge of Elks believes
that freedom too long has stood on the defensive. The time has come
for us who believe in freedom to take the initiative, fight for what we
believe in and stand against those who are against us until freedom
has defeated those who would destroy it. To rely on military power
alone in this ideological struggle would be illusory and fatal. Our
paramount necessity is internal strength which can come only from
unity of understanding and purpose and a willingness to place our
Nation's safety and welfare above personal interest.

Appealing, as did our Founding Fathers, to the Supreme Judge of the
World for the rectitude of our intentions, we submit to our Brothers
this Declaration of American principles on which we shall challenge
the enemies of freedom, and to which we invite our fellow citizens to
subscribe:

1. Moral values are the basis of our society and the responsibility of
   each citizen to live by these moral values is fundemntal to the welfare and progress of our society. These moral values include hon-

esty of word, deed and purpose; brotherly love that requires us to be fair with our fellow men and just in our relations with them; faithful performance of our labor in every honorable calling; and a recognition that each of us has the duty to contribute to the best of his ability to the advancement of the general welfare.

2. Freedom has made America. Not just political freedom, but the whole environment of freedom is resopnsible for the tremendous progress of our Nation since its revolutionary birth in 1776. Freedom encourages initiative, experiment, invention, enterprise. Freedom lets citizens choose their work, encourages individuals to discover their talents and make the most of them. In consequence we have a standard of living higher than any Nation has enjoyed, a material abundance more widely shared among all our people than ever before, and a high level of intellectual and cultural attainment. Every citizen is the beneficiary of the freedom that has unleashed the abilities of the American people and provided the incentive for their maximum use.

3. Inherent in the American concept of freedom is the integrity of the individual. Individualism makes each person primarily responsible for himself, his welfare, his success or failure. Freedom lays upon each person the individual responsibility and duty of citizenship. A free society will emphasize individualism and individual responsibility as the sure way to produce democratic leadership and preserve freedom.

4. Self-government presupposes the duty of every citizen to obey the established government, and to employ only those lawful methods of reason and persuasion that are open to all of us to achieve political action. It follows that government by the majority must be reasonable in the exercise of its authority and protect the rights and interests of the minority.

5. Our ability to change our institutions and practices, through orderly process of law, to accommodate to changing needs has helped our Nation to develop, as it will in the future. All proposals for change in our institutions should be weighed carefully by all citizens to determine whether such change will reduce or add to our freedom. Our goal should be more freedom, not less. We must guard against the growth of governmental power through surrender of civil right and individual freedom for contemporary gain at the expense of future generations.

6. The tendency of groups to seek preferential treatment from government breeds rivalries dangerous to political stability, is harmful to genuine economic growth and leads to fragmentation of society rather than to unity and strength. All groups of citizens ought to measure political and economic proposals advanced in their own interest against their effect on the whole Nation.

7. We believe that the time has come when all citizens who believe in these principles should speak up for them and set an example by applying them fully in their daily lives. We urge those in positions of leadership and influence—clergymen, educators, business execu-

tives, holders of public office, leaders of labor, intellectuals, editors, radio and television producers, motion picture producers and all others—to assume a greater responsibility for the wider understanding of these principles and their practical application in the day to day lives of the people.

The Declaration was mailed to all subordinate lodges with the request that it be read at a regular meeting and adopted and that wide publicity be given the "Declaration" in the lodge bulletins, local newspapers and in releases to radio and television outlets. At the 1961 Convention, Chairman Grocott reported that the majority of our lodges had responded and that many newspapers throughout the country had editorialized the "Declaration."

In 1963, the Committee announced the following programs and urged their adoption by all lodges of the Order:

"Know Your America Week"; "Bill of Rights Day"; "Freedom Week"; "Freedom of speech—Freedom of the press"; "Birthday observances of Washington and Lincoln"; "Memorial Day"; "Flag Day"; "Let Freedom ring on July 4th."

The "Let Freedom Ring Program" was conceived by Mr. Eric Sloane, a painter, meteorologist and writer from Warren, Connecticut and Mr. Eric Hatch, a writer from Litchfield, Connecticut. It was a new program adopted by our Americanism Committee and the idea caught on like wildfire and has been enthusiastically supported by many of our lodges.

Messrs. Sloane and Hatch along with their wives were in attendance at our 1964 Convention in New York and at this time the Americanism Chairman gave them a memento of our Order's appreciation in the form of a miniature Liberty Bell. Mr. Hatch responded by thanking the Elks, saying "I think really due to the Elks there has been created a sound that has never before been heard since the beginning of time, and that was the sound of three million miles of bells ringing a united sound of freedom." In his response Mr. Sloane said that on July 4 he would remember the B.P.O.E. as "Bells Peal over Elkdom."

At the 1964 Convention a budget item of $35,000 was adopted for the production of an Americanism film and Joseph A. McArthur of Lewiston, Idaho Lodge succeeded to the Chairmanship of the Committee. In his report in 1965, he announced that the film had been produced under the supervision of Past Grand Exalted Ruler Lewis and a copy of it sent to every lodge. He also expressed his pleasure in being able to report on the favorable response with which it had been met when used by our lodges in their indoctrination Programs and shown to other groups. He further stated the film was selling Americanism and helping to destroy the complacent, lethargic attitudes into which we, as Americans, sometimes slip.

At the Dallas, Texas Convention in 1966, the Americanism Committee inaugurated the practice of having the State Presidents enter the Convention at the opening ceremonies each bearing the Flag of his State and proceeding to the platform where the Flags were placed on display. A film entitled "Freedom Mine," was shown. It was awarded the George Washington Honor Medal by Freedoms Foundation at Valley Forge. The awards jury had this to say about the film: " 'Freedom Mine' is a stirring record of American Freedoms and their universal validity for each individual citizen of our nation."

In the 1966–67 year, the Americanism Committee enlarged its program of patriotic activities to include an Eagle Scout Recognition Ceremony. The Committee urged all lodges to conduct special public programs honoring Boy Scouts who attain the highest rank in Scouting, and presenting each with a certificate and an American Flag.

Creation of the Americanism Committee in 1961 met an important need at a critical time in our history. The Committee provided our lodges with constructive programs for strengthening the spirit of American patriotism in their communities, and vigorously promoted their use. The response of our lodges was prompt and enthusiastic and the result has been a tremendous expansion in the Order's patriotic activities and a major contribution to the security of the Nation.

CUBAN CRISIS

In the early evening of October 22, 1962 the eyes of all Americans were glued to their television sets or their ears attuned to radios to hear the following words from President Kennedy:

"Because of the rapid build-up of missiles in Cuba, I have directed that the following initial steps be taken immediately:
"1. A strict quarantine on all offensive military equipment under shipment to Cuba is being initated.
"2. I have directed the continued and increased close surveillance of Cuba and the Military build-up."
The President concluded with these solemn words:
"Our goal is not a victory of might, but the vindication of right; not peace at the expense of freedom, but both freedom and peace in this hemisphere and we hope around the world. God willing, that goal will be achieved".

President Kennedy's action in the Cuban crisis won immediate, strong and united support from our Order. The day after the President's nationally televised announcement of the impending blockade of Cuba, Grand Exalted Ruler Lee A. Donaldson sent the following wire to the White House:

"1,300,000 members of the Benevolent and Protective Order of Elks applaud your action in respect to the Cuban situation and pledge their wholehearted support which will be confirmed by telegrams you will receive from our various lodges."

At the same time, Vincent H. Grocott of Santa Barbara, Calif., Chairman of the Grand Lodge Americanism Committee, telegraphed the Order's 2,006 lodges, requesting that they wire messages of support to the President. Brother Grocott's telegram follows:

"President Kennedy has spoken decisively. Urgently request your lodge dispatch wire to him pledging support of action taken. Mail copy of wire to undersigned."

Reaction was immediate as a flood of telegrams from Elks lodges throughout the country poured into the White House, leaving no doubt where members of the Order stood in the crisis. Here are excerpts from some of the Elk messages to the President, reflecting the strong support for the President's action throughout the Order.

"Pledge 100 per cent support. All members are in agreement with action taken regarding Cuba and Soviet Union."
"Join with 2,000 other Elk lodges in approving decision on Cuba and pledge efforts to help uphold sovereignty of our nation."
"Actively support you. Lodge properties placed at disposal of local CD for use as they deem necessary."
"Soundly endorse your Cuban action. Our prestige among free people around the globe will certainly be bolstered by your firm stand. While inherent risks are great, such a decision shows true leadership in the defense of our great heritage."
"Your stand is in keeping with the great American ideals of protection of our God-given rights as free men."
"Whatever sacrifices we may ultimately be required to make are completely justifiable under the circumstances."
"Blockade now in affect reaffirms our Monroe Doctrine. No foreign domination in this hemisphere. We pledge full support."
"Support you to fullest extent in action you have taken."
"Strongly support your stand in present crisis and will cooperate with any suggested program to fullest possible extent."

"We must keep the flame of freedom alive throughout the world and go forth to serve America."

"Unanimously and enthusiastically approve your recent action relative to Cuba."

The tremendous outpouring of support for President Kennedy's determined stand also produced from our lodges commendation for the action taken by the Grand Exalted Ruler and the Americanism Committee to unite the Order in the national emergency. A number of lodges pledged their support for any further measures deemed necessary by the Order in the defense of America, and stated that they had stepped up their Americanism Program activity.

Grand Exalted Ruler Donaldson received the following from the White House:

"THE WHITE HOUSE

Mr. L. A. Donaldson, Grand Exalted Ruler,

Benevolent and Protective Order of Elks

Dear Mr. Donaldson:

The President has asked me to convey to you his appreciation and thanks for the generous message of confidence you have sent him during the current international crisis.

He has asked me to extend to you and to the members of the Benevolent and Protective Order of Elks his gratitude for this expression of common purpose and unity. I can assure you that your message is most heartening to the President and his associates.

With all best wishes,

Sincerely,

Ralph A. Dugan
Special Assistant to the President"

THE ALASKA DISASTER

The news of the disastrous earthquake in Alaska on March 27, 1964 distressed every American citizen and caused concern among Elks for the welfare of our brothers, their homes and their families. Grand Exalted Ruler Dunn immediately contacted Past Grand Exalted Ruler Anderson asking him to investigate the situation and determine how best the Grand Lodge could help in the devastated area and to assure the Elks of Alaska that help would be immediately forthcoming. The services of Richard Harpole, President of the Washington State Elks Association were enlisted for this purpose. He flew to Alaska and reported that Kodiak Lodge had been completely demolished and severe damage had been suffered by Anchorage and Seward Lodges.

Grand Exalted Ruler Dunn then sent a letter to every lodge of our Order asking for financial assistance with the funds to be placed in an "Elk Disaster Fund" so that any excess of the needs for Alaska could be kept in a permanent fund, for use in similar circumstances.

Almost immediately the Elks National Foundation forwarded a check for $10,000. The National Memorial and Publication Commission voted a contribution of $20,000; the Elks of Manila Lodge, who were assisted in a similar way after World War II sent the sum of $25,000. The Contributions received from numerous lodges and State Associations brought the total amount raised to over $161,000. In addition to this almost $5,000 was sent directly to Alaska Lodges by Elk Lodges and individuals.

At the 1964 Convention a resolution was adopted empowering the Grand Exalted Ruler, the Grand Secretary, the Chairman of the Board of Grand Trustees and Past Grand Exalted Ruler Anderson, in their discretion, to make any and all disbursements in connection with the Alaska Elks Disaster and Relief Fund. Pursuant to this resolution, the Committee after careful investigation and appraisal of losses distributed $155,000 of the available funds as follows: Anchorage Lodge $5,000, Kodiak Lodge $130,000, and Seward Lodge $20,000.

In 1967 disaster struck Fairbanks Lodge in the form of a flood which completely inundated the lodge Home and rendered it unuseable. Following a visit and survey by Grand Exalted Ruler Robert E. Boney, a check for $1,000.00 was sent to Fairbanks Lodge.

PREPARING FOR OUR 100th YEAR

The Grand Lodge, meeting in Miami Beach, Fla., in 1965, adopted a resolution creating a Centennial Committee with the responsibility for planning the observance of the Order's hundredth anniversary in 1968.

The Committee, as appointed then and later enlarged, consisted of these Past Grand Exalted Rulers: Emmett T. Anderson, Tacoma, Wash., Lodge, Chariman; Robert G. Pruitt Buckhead (Atlanta), Georgia, Lodge, Secretary; George I. Hall, Lynbrook,

N.Y., Lodge, Horace R. Wisely, Salinas, Cal., Lodge, John E. Fenton, Lawrence, Mass., Lodge and R. Leonard Bush, Inglewood, Cal., Lodge.

The program drafted by the Committee included these major features:

1. Production of a half-hour motion picture in color to tell the story of the Order's first hundred years
2. Design of a Centennial Medallion
3. A narrative history of the Order, by a professional writer, to be published serially in The Elks Magazine
4. A special U.S. postage stamp commemorating the Centennial
5. Production and distribution to all lodges of Centennial publicity materials for newspapers, magazines and radio and television stations
6. Erection of a bronze tablet in the new Federal building on Foley Square during the 1968 Centennial Grand Lodge Convention in New York City marking the site of the house at 188 Elm Street where the actors and entertainers held the Sunday night meetings out of which grew the BPO Elks in 1868.

The Grand Lodge Centennial Committee strongly recommended that each Subordinate Lodge create a special Centennial committee to plan local Centennial features and to coordinate the local program with the national program.

Conclusion

As this history was concluded, the Order of Elks was nearing the end of its first century. We have linked the destiny of our Order with the destiny of our country, and because of this, we have grown with America and prospered with America.

While the Elks take just pride in the services that they have rendered to their country and to their fellowmen in this first century, they look not to the past but to the future, young in heart, with enthusiasm and with confidence that even greater accomplishments lie ahead.

It is to the future that this history is dedicated.

Edward W. McCabe
1968-69

Frank Hise
1969-70

Glenn L. Miller
1970-71

E. Gene Fournace
1971-72

Grand Exalted Rulers

ELEVENTH DECADE

Francis M. Smith
1972-73

1968-1978

Robert A. Yothers
1973-74

Gerald Strohm
1974-75

Willis C. McDonald
1975-76

George B. Klein
1976-77

Homer Huhn, Jr.
1977-78

438

S E C T I O N

ELEVENTH DECADE

Ritual modifications, changes in membership requirements, institution of additional youth programs and a surge in contributions to the Elks National Foundation were highlights of the 11th decade.

Elkdom observed its Centennial and the nation marked its Bicentennial, and all the while, the Order continued to stress that as long as there is a veteran in the Hospitals the Elks will never forget him.

The Elks National Memorial in Chicago was rededicated to include those who fought in the Korean and Vietnam conflicts.

Grand Exalted Rulers

During this period there were the following Grand Exalted Rulers:

Edward W. McCabe, Nashville, Tenn., Lodge No. 72	1968-69
Frank Hise, Corvallis, Ore., Lodge No. 1413	1969-70
Glenn L. Miller, Logansport, Ind., Lodge No. 66	1970-71
E. Gene Fournace, Newark, Ohio, Lodge No. 391	1971-72
Francis M. Smith, Sioux Falls, S.D., Lodge No. 262	1972-73
Robert A. Yothers, Seattle, Wash., Lodge No. 92	1973-74
Gerald Strohm, Fresno, Calif., Lodge No. 439	1974-75
Willis C. McDonald, New Orleans, La., Lodge No. 30	1975-76
George B. Klein, Lincoln, Neb., Lodge No. 80	1976-77
Homer Huhn, Jr., Mount Pleasant, Pa., Lodge No. 868	1977-78

Grand Secretary

With the death of Grand Secretary Franklin J. Fitzpatrick in 1970, Grand Lodge Controller Frank Vossel agreed to assume the office until a successor could be found. Brother Vossel resigned the office early in 1971 and Homer Huhn, Jr. was appointed to succeed him by Grand Exalted Ruler Glenn L. Miller. Brother Huhn was elected Grand Secretary at the 107th Grand Lodge Session, 1971, in New Orleans. He served until being elected Grand Exalted Ruler at the 113th Grand Lodge Session, 1977, in New Orleans. At this same session Stanley F. Kocur, East Chicago, In., Lodge No. 981, past President of the Indiana Elks Association, Inc. and secretary of his Elks Lodge for 25 years, was elected Grand Secretary, and re-elected to the office in 1978.

Centennial Observance

The Order of Elks returned to the city of its origin, New York, for its 100th birthday.

Elkdom followed through with the plans recommended by the Centennial Committee.

New York Mayor John V. Lindsay proclaimed July 14-18 as Elks Days in New York City as a tribute to the 104th Grand Lodges Session.

One of the features of the Centennial Convention was the unveiling of a bronze tablet in the new Federal Building in New York. The plaque commemorates the founding of the Order a short distance from the site. GER Boney dedicated the tablet which was accepted by Edward V. Kline, Regional Administrator of the General Services Administration. Presiding at the ceremonies was PGER Anderson, chairman of the Centennial Committee. Vocal selections were provided by the Girl Scout Chorus directed by Miss Patricia Lano. The invocation and benediction were by Grand Chaplain Rev. Fr. Francis P. Fenton. From the left are Brothers Anderson and Boney, and Mr. Kline.

In addition to the Centennial observance session in New York City in 1968, the Grand Lodge Sessions during this period were held in the following cities:

1969	Dallas, Texas	1974	Miami Beach, Florida
1970	San Francisco, California	1975	Dallas, Texas
1971	New Orleans, Louisiana	1976	Chicago, Illinois
1972	Atlantic City, New Jersey	1977	New Orleans, Louisiana
1973	Chicago, Illinois	1978	San Diego, California

Membership and Charitable Expenditures

Year	Membership	Charitable Expenditure
1968-1969	1,480,412	$ 8,670,304.77
1969-1970	1,508,050	9,240,646.16
1970-1971	1,520,731	9,543,134.62
1971-1972	1,531,912	9,861,849.82
1972-1973	1,541,784	10,642,881.26
1973-1974	1,558,772	11,311,271.18
1974-1975	1,582,735	12,484,756.00
1975-1976	1,611,139	13,880,602.00
1976-1977	1,624,702	14,257,597.00
1977-1978	1,634,488	15,198,029.00

Charitable Contributions

A total of $2,000 was appropriated from the Emergency Charity Fund in the 1968-69 Grand Lodge year to assist those involved in disastrous floods in North Dakota.

The news media issued high commendations to the Idaho State Elks for donating $13,000 to help Ricks College in Rexburg, Idaho, who took in refugees from destructive flood waters loosed by the Teton Dam disaster. Ricks College is on high ground and the little institution served nearly 400,000 free hot meals and provided 100,000 nights of free lodging to those left homeless and hungry by the disaster.

The 1969-70 Grand Lodge year was marked by a grant of $2,000 from the Emergency Charity Fund to the Washington State Elks Association for the Don Guthrie Kidney Fund and $25,000 to Gulfport, Miss., Lodge No. 978 to rehabilitate the lodge home which was destroyed by hurricane Camille.

AMERICANISM PROGRAM

Elkdom's 100 years of patriotism was highlighted in the Order's Centennial year. Serving as chairman during the decade were:

1968 - Joseph A. McArthur of Lewiston, Idaho, Lodge No. 896.
1969 - William J. Windecker of Orange, N.J., Lodge No. 135.
1970-71 - Edward L. Harbaugh of Roswell, N.M., Lodge No. 969.
1971-73 - Dan Davis of Van Nuys, Calif., Lodge No. 2028.
1974 - Alex McKnight of Dallas, Texas, Lodge No. 71.
1975-76 - William H. Collisson of Linton, In., Lodge No. 866.
1977-78 - James W. Damon of John Day, Ore., Lodge No. 1824.

At the 105th Grand Lodge Session in Dallas, Texas, Elks adopted a strong, militant resolution dedicated to law, order and justice.

The following year, delegates adopted a resolution presented by PGER H. L. Blackledge urging maximum penalties be imposed on those convicted of rioting, looting, arson and other crimes.

Under GER Glenn L. Miller flag decals, Eagle Scout certificiates, expanded Flag Day ceremonies, Law and Order Nights were urged to stimulate appreciation of our national heritage.

GER E. Gene Fournace urged drug abuse education.

Bicentennial of the Nation

As America approached its 200th birthday, Elkdom appointed a special committee consisting of Past Grand Exalted Rulers, Raymond C. Dobson, Chairman; Robert E. Boney; R. Leonard Bush; George I. Hall; Robert G. Pruitt; William A. Wall, and John L. Walker.

The committee stressed that each Subordinate Lodge should originate or participate in every possible way in their communities in glorifying the nation's birthday.

The Americanism Committee carried the load of observing the Bicentennial.

Elks enthusiastically endorsed a resolution calling for a National Patriotism Week after hearing a plea from a 16-year-old Scottsdale, Arizona girl, Lori Cox.

Elks Memorial Rededicated

It was a triply important date for Elkdom...July 4, 1976.

It marked the 200th birthday of the United States, the 50th anniversary of the Elks Memorial Building and the opening day of the 112th Grand Lodge Session in Chicago.

Once again the Memorial Building was rededicated, this time to the memory of those who served and died in Korea and Vietnam and to the hospitalized veterans the Order has long served through the Elks National Service Commission.

The formal rededication was by GER Willis C. McDonald. "We rededicate this building," he said, "hoping that it may in some small measure recognize the debt which we acknowledge to all those who served so nobly, so well and so unselfishly."

Featured speaker was PGER Francis M. Smith

"This magnificent structure was conceived from the union of the spirit and the body of an organization devoted to patriotic purposes," he said. "It was born and it lives as a memorial to those of our Brothers who gave so much that we may now observe this birthday."

PGER Raymond C. Dobson who acted as Master of Ceremonies, referred to the occasion and the Memorial edifice as "typifying the reverence of the Elks of America have for those who have preserved our liberties."

He introduced a special recorded message by the President of the United States, Brother Gerald R. Ford of Grand Rapids, Mich., Lodge No. 48.

The President lauded the Order for its patriotic programs, its service to veterans, scholarships and youth projects.

"I extend to you the thanks of Americans everywhere for your unselfish and constructive efforts," he said.

PGER William J. Jernick, Chairman-Treasurer of the Elks National Service Commission, unveiled a bronze plaque which was placed in the Memorial Building.

The plaque read:

1976 Grand Lodge Convention
Renewal of Pledge
July 4, 1976

In observance of our nation's glorious Bicentennial celebration and in tribute to the gallant defenders of our flag whose sacrifice guaranteed America's freedom, we solemnly renew our promise to those who are now sick and handicapped.

"So long as there is a disabled veteran in our hospitals, The Benevolent and Protective Order of Elks will never forget him."

Instrumental music was provided by the Racine, Wisconsin, Lodge No. 252, Youth Band, under the direction of brothers, Harry Abramowitz and Lee Shannon.

The colors were advanced by a Marine Corps color guard. The U.S. and Elks Bicentennial flags were hoisted to the top of the two flagpoles by a veteran of the Korean conflict, Col. Wesley W. Waterhouse, President of the Illinois Elks Association, and Brother Richard Stetler, a paraplegic veteran of Vietnam and a member of Chicago (South) Lodge No. 1596.

The Pledge of Allegiance to the Flag was led by PGER Wade H. Kepner, chairman of the Elks National Memorial and Publication Commission.

The invocation and benediction were by Grand Chaplain, Rev. Msgr. Henry F. Speck of Owatonna, Minn.

Vocal selections were by George Balbach of Queens Borough (Elmhurst), N.Y., Lodge No. 878.

The Memorial Rededication Committee was made up of Homer Huhn, Jr., then Grand Secretary, and John R. Ryan, publisher-general manager of *The Elks Magazine.*

Decorating of the Memorial Building was supervised by Brother Merton Ephraim of Chicago who assisted his father, the late Max M. Ephriam, PER of Chicago, Il. No. 4 at the 1946 rededication. Bro. Max was also responsible for the building's exterior decoration for the 1926 dedication ceremony.

ELKS NATIONAL MEMORIAL AND PUBLICATION COMMISSION

When the report for 1968 was filed, the commission consisted of John S. McClelland, chairman; Emmett T. Anderson, vice chairman; James T. Hallinan, treasurer; Wade H. Kepner, secretary, and Earl E. James, assistant secretary and treasurer, all past Grand Exalted Rulers.

William H. Magrath served as General Manager of *The Elks Magazine.*

He retired in 1975 after having served the magazine for 48 years. He was succeeded by John R. Ryan, a member of Waukegon, Il., Lodge No. 702. He previously was advertising director.

Serving on the commission in 1978 were:

Past Grand Exalted Rulers, Wade H. Kepner, chairman; R. Leonard Bush, vice chairman; Edward W. McCabe, treasurer; Raymond C. Dobson, secretary, and Robert E. Boney, assistant secretary-treasurer.

They had succeeded to the posts over the years when their predecessors had been called by death.

When Otho DeVilbiss, who had served as Public Relations Director since 1948, retired in 1971, the post was assumed by Martin Karant, a P.E.R. of Kingsport, Tenn., Lodge No. 1833.

In 1976, this office and duties were moved from the Memorial and Publications Commission office and placed under the supervision and jurisdiction of the Grand Secretary, with offices in the Memorial Building.

Robert E. Sconce then assumed the office.

Since its inception in 1922 the subscription price of the *The Elks Magazine* was $1 per year. However, due to rising costs of paper and production plus postal rates, delegates in 1973 voted to increase the price to $1.25 effective the following year.

ELKS NATIONAL FOUNDATION

Assets as well as disbursements from the Elks National Foundation continued to climb. The 50th anniversary of the Foundation was observed in addition to the Centennial of Elkdom. The Most Valuable Student and the Elks Leadership Contests were combined.

As Elkdom entered its second century, the Elks National Foundation Board of Trustees consisted of PGERs John L. Walker, chairman; H. L. Blackledge, vice chairman; John E. Fenton, secretary; Edward J. McCormick, M.D., treasurer; Lee A. Donaldson; William A. Wall, and Horace Wisely.

Nelson E. W. Stuart of Cleveland No. 18 continued as executive director.

Members of the board 10 years later were:

PGERs John L. Walker, chairman; William A. Wall, vice chairman; Horace R. Wisely, secretary; E. Gene Fournace, treasurer; Glenn L. Miller, assistant treasurer; Robert A. Yothers, assistant secretary, and Willis C. McDonald.

Brother Stuart remained as executive director.

Death had claimed PGERs Donaldson, Blackledge, Fenton, and McCormick. In 1974, PGER Francis M. Smith was appointed to the unexpired term due to the death of PGER Fenton. In 1975, PGER Smith was named to a full seven-year term. He resigned, however, in 1977 to assume the chairmanship of the Grand Lodge Advisory Committee.

Contributions

During the term of GER Edward W. McCabe, in 1968-69, contributions to the Foundation soared to over $2.3 million in a year's time. This was more than one-sixth of all contributions for the previous 40 years.

This was partially as a result of a $1.2 million bequest from the estate of Mrs. Leah J. Baum, of Jackson, Tennessee.

Past Chairman of the Board of Grand Trustees, Hugh W. Hicks of Jackson, Tenn., Lodge No. 197 who was instrumental in arranging the gift, was presented a special citation.

Centennial Bottle

During the 100th anniversary of the Benevolent and Protective Order of Elks, arrangements were made with the Jim Beam Distillery Corp. and Regal China Corp. for a special Elks Centennial bottle. Assisting in this was Vern R. Huck of Los Angeles, Calif., Lodge No. 99, a member of the Grand Lodge State Associations Committee.

At the 106th Session in San Francisco, Calif., in 1970, it was announced that the Jim Beam Co. so far had turned over to the Foundation $658,417.73 from the sale of the Centennial Bottles.

Brother Huck was presented an engraved testimonial certificate for his efforts.

Foundation Awards

As the "Hoop Shoot"® Free Throw Contest continued its fantastic growth, a decision was made to combine the Elks "Most Valuable Student" Scholarship Contest and the Elks Leadership Contests — along with Financial Need.

The Grand Lodge Youth Activities Committee Leadership Contest was therefore discontinued after the 1973-74 fiscal year.

"Most Valuable Student" contest awards increased from a total of $295,600 to 421 students at the start of the decade to $808,800, with 1,100 students benefiting in the 1978-79 academic year. Award-offers ranged from $1,500 to first-place boy and girl winners during this same period to $3,000, $2,500 and $2,000 for the first three boy-girl students.

These top-three awards are extended annually over a four-year period so that they accumulate to $12,000, $10,000 and $8,000 in respective undergraduate school periods for a total of $60,000 distributed to three boys and three girls in this special category.

Application blanks are to be made available only to graduating high school students. College students and High School juniors are not eligible to enter the contest henceforth. Merit standards to prevail in the 1975 scholarship-leadership competition are to be as follows:

$$
\begin{array}{lr}
\text{Scholarship} & 450 \text{ points} \\
\text{Leadership} & 350 \text{ points} \\
\text{Financial Need} & \underline{200} \text{ points} \\
& 1,000 \text{ points}
\end{array}
$$

At the end of the 50-year span from July 11, 1928 through March 31, 1978 a cumulative total of $32,387,997.14 had been contributed to the Foundation with $19,616,236.45 of these gifts being received in the 10-year spand from April 1, 1968 through March 31, 1978.

Distributions over 50 years in the form of grants to State Associations, Emergency Educational scholarship assistance, Cerebral Palsy and other special and vocational training grants, together with Scholarship and special achievement awards totaled $16,313,473.60. The sum of $10,779,561.78 was distributed in these general areas during this 1969-1978 decade.

Condensed versions of the Foundation's annual reports were introduced in an effort to grain wider distribution to Lodges in respective Grand Lodge areas at reduced percopy printing and mailing costs.

Investment Counselors

As the principal fund of the Foundation continued to grow, it was decided in 1973 to redistribute holdings by engaging the following investments counselors for the next three years to manage the following percentages of the Foundation portfolio:

—40 percent to New England Merchants National Bank of Boston, Mass.

—40 percent to Loomis Sayles and Co. of Milwaukee, Wis.

—20 percent to Omnivest Reseach Corp. of Tampa, Fla.

In 1974, approval was given for Stein Roe & Co. of Chicago to handle 20 percent of the principal fund portfolio in place of Omnivest.

Foundation office accounting procedures were switched from manual to computer effective April 1, 1975.

Mandatory Committee

In 1974, Grand Lodge delegates approved a statutory provision providing for the Exalted Ruler of each subordinate lodge to appoint an Elks National Foundation committee of not less than three members to publicize the Foundation, promote the programs, activities and charities, and to encourage and solicit contributions. The committee does not have jurisdicition over scholarship contests or other activities sponsored by the Foundation trustees.

50th Anniversary

The year 1978 marked the 50th anniversary of The Elks National Foundation. A special bottle patterned around the Elks National Foundation seal was prepared by the Jim Beam Distillery Co.

Issuance of 50th Anniversary "50" Heart Lapel Pinettes and Heart Charms began on April 1, 1978, recognizing initial payments on formal participating membership and/or honorary Founder and permanent benefactor pledges.

ELKS NATIONAL SERVICE COMMISSION

Elks continued to be dedicated to their pledge that "So long as there is a disabled veteran in our hospitals, the Benevolent and Protective Order of Elks will never forget him."

From 1968 to 1978, the Elks' program operated in 207 Veterans Administration Hospitals.

At the beginning of the period the Commission consisted of: James T. Hallinan, Chairman; George I. Hall, Vice Chairman; William J. Jernick, Treasurer; and John L. Walker, Secretary; Emmett T. Anderson, Fred L. Bohn, and William A. Wall, all Past Grand Exalted Rulers. Bryan J. McKeogh was director with offices in New York City.

When PGER Hallinan died in 1969, PGER Jernick was named both Chairman and Treasurer. He continued his service and at the end of the decade in 1978, in addition to PGER Jernick, the commission members were: PGERs Hall, Vice Chairman; Homer Huhn, Jr., Secretary; Ronald J. Dunn; Frank Hise; Gerald Strohm, and George B. Klein.

Deaths and resignations to serve on other Elks commissions resulted in changes in the commission membership.

In addition to the above, others serving during the 10-year period were: Robert E. Boney, Robert G. Pruitt, E. Gene Fournace, and Francis M. Smith.

During 1969-70 George M. "Bud" Hall, who had been serving as part-time accountant, was employed as full-time assistant because of the increased volume of work in the expansion of the the programs. Previously he had been employed in the Accounting Department of Union Carbide Corp. for 28 years.

In 1977-78, George Malekian, a PER of Valley Stream, NY, Lodge No. 2164, a Past District Deputy, state officer of the New York State Elks Association, and state National Service Chairman, was engaged to assist in the activities of both the Service Commission and Convention Committee.

1968-1969
An Unusual Program for Returning Vietnam Wounded

The First Aeromedical Staging Area at the Scott Air Force Base in Illinois was a transfer point for Vietnam wounded. It is sometimes a long wait. Time hangs heavily when you are sick and disabled. Back in 1968, the officers of nearby Belleville, Ill. Lodge No. 481 became concerned about the comfort of these wounded youngsters.

Upon inquiring, the hospital staff advised that they could not solicit Elks aid. Belleville Elks, however, soon discovered what was needed and acted promptly. They started with stainless steel carts and buckets for passing refreshments both in the hospital and near the flight line where men rest before continuing on. To this was soon added stereo records, games, record players and entertainment.

Those permitted to travel were hosted at barbecues, football games and Lodge dance parties.

Garden lounge chairs, razors, electric shavers, mirrors, shaving necessities and toilet articles were supplied.

Thousands of wounded have enjoyed a respite from the pain of their wounds and injuries because the Belleville Elks and Lodges in the Illinois Southwest District were mindful of the Elks solemn pledge and hastened to keep it when the occasion arose. The program was financed by the local Lodges.

1969-1970
Soap For Seattle-Tacoma Airport Military Lounge

A shortage of soap developed in the USO military lounge in the Seattle-Tacoma, Wash., airport. About 700 men per month used the showers there.

Elks quickly made arrangements for 12,500 individual hotel size soap bars in a distinctive wrapper bearing the message, "Courtesy of the Elks National Service Commission."

Air Conditioning For Honolulu Tripler Army Medical Center

Critically wounded Vietnam vets lay sweltering in their own sweat in the Tripler Army Medical Center in Honolulu. There was no air conditioning.

The Commission promptly purchased 24 much-needed air conditioners. They were installed and each had a plate inscribed, "Donated by the Benevolent and Protective Order of Elks of the United States of America."

Rest and Recreation Huts at Guam Naval Hospital

The Navy Hospital on Guam was a crowded facility caring for Vietnam casualties preparatory to their return to the United States.

Hospital space was at a premium. The need was for an outdoor shelter. Assistance was requested through Agana, Guam, Lodge No. 1281.

The Navy supplied Seabee manpower and the Elks through the Commission, provided the necessary materials. Not one but two, pavilions were built plus barbecue pits for each.

1970-1971
Cigarettes to Vietnam Discontinued

Because of the reduced number of troops in Vietnam and the U.S. Surgeon General's warning of a health hazard, it was decided to discontinue the shipments of cigarettes to military personnel in Vietnam as of Sept. 21, 1971.

Since the outbreak of World War II, courtesy cards to members of the Armed Forces in basic training or assigned to the United States were issued to sons and daughters of Elk members to identify them for any courtesies a Lodge might be in position to provide.

Naturally some of these cards were issued to service personnel under 21. Due to restrictions in some areas concerning minors it was decided to end the issuance of courtesy cards.

1971-1972
National Service Committee Mandated in Every Lodge

A resolution making it mandatory for every Lodge to appoint a National Service Committee was approved in the 1970 Grand Lodge Session in San Francisco.

It provides that each Exalted Ruler appoint no less than three members to this committee to implement the commission's programs.

A further aim was to also increase participation by women, retired Elks, and others in veterans' programs.

Lodges at a distance from hospitals collected books, playing cards and conducted fund-raising projects for special veterans' programs.

It was an opportunity for all Lodges to participate in the fulfillment of the Elks' pledge.

Elks Do Remember

Vietnam vets were young. Elks, however, did not neglect the young Vietnam returnees. Typical of some of the programs were as follows:

—In its "Project Amputee," the Lodges of the Orange Coast of California had a group of wounded veterans flown from Letterman Army and Oakknoll Navy hospitals in San Francisco to Southern California for a whirlwind tour of Lodges and points of interest. It was a weekend stay which included lunches, dinner, breakfasts and a final banquet at which clock radios were presented. PGERs Horace R. Wisely and Leonard Bush were on hand to greet the patients. Famed comedienne Martha Raye helped welcome the boys.

—Bordentown No. 2085 and other New Jersey Lodges periodically entertained groups of Vietnam veterans at the Lodge. Unsolicited letters of enthusiastic thanks gave evidence of the great pleasure derived from Elks' hospitality.

—Tracy, Calif. Lodge No. 2031 orginated a pheasant hunt for wounded servicemen. Most patients were amputees in wheelchairs. Lunch, dinners and gifts were provided.

1972-1973
Jobs for Vietnam Veterans

In the belief that Elks had a responsibility and in an effort to secure employment for Vietnam veterans, Lodges were requested to give individual support in any area where employment was available and where an Elk had influence.

Lodges were urged to run classified ads in the help wanted columns of the local newspapers urging employers to give consideration to Vietnam vets.

Arts and Crafts Competition

Because of the long-time association of the Elks with occupational therapy, the Veterans Administration Voluntary Services requested that the Order conduct a nationwide arts and crafts competition in all Veterans Administration hospitals. The contest was part of the 25th Anniversary of the voluntary service program.

The competition took place on three levels: Local, state and national, with cash awards on all levels as follows:

National: First place, $150; second place, $100; third place, $75; fifteen Honorable Mentions at $25 each.

State: First place, $100; second place, $75; third place, $50.

Local Hospitals: First place, $50; second place, $30; third place, $15; five Honorable Mentions at $10 each.

The entries were judged by hospital and other professionals with emphasis on the therapeutic value of the effort that went into the production of the craft and creativity of the design, rather than the quality of the finished product.

The contest was an overwhelming success. The prizes for the national winners were awarded by PGER William J. Jernick at ceremonies held in Washington, D.C., in connection with the observance of the 25th Anniversary.

Although the national awards were furnished by the Elks National Service Commission, over $32,000 in prizes were provided on the local and state levels by Lodges and state associations. Hospital officials acclaimed the effort because of the benefits to the thousands of patients who participated.

This contest has been continued every year since its inception. However, because of the complicated details involved, the national awards were eliminated.

Many states still conduct state competition. The balance is on a hospital level. All cash prizes were provided by the Lodges or state associations.

Grand Exalted Ruler's Proclamation.

When Francis M. Smith served as Grand Exalted Ruler in 1972-73 he began what was to become another Elk tradition. He issued a proclamation naming November as Elks Veterans Remembrance Month. These proclamations have been repeated annually.

PROCLAMATION

Whereas: The Benevolent and Protective Order of Elks made a solemn pledge!

"So long as there is a disabled veteran in our hospitals, the Benevolent and Protective Order of Elks will never forget him."

Whereas: The fulfillment of this pledge is the obligation of every Elk, as set forth in Section 134i of the Grand Lodge Statutes, and

Whereas: Service to hospitalized veterans is an expression of patriotism in its purest sense.

Now, Therefore: By virtue of the authority of the office of Grand Exalted Ruler: I hereby proclaim the month of November as "National Veterans Remembrance Month" and hereby request all Lodges to observe this month of recollection of the debt we owe to hospitalized veterans in the manner which has been recommended by the Elks National Service Commission in its communication to all Lodges.

ELKS RITUAL

After the 1952 ritual change when it was voted to discontinue the use of the blindfold, no changes were made until 1956 when the Esteemed Leading Knight was given a charge to deliver when he presented the flag to the Esquire in the opening ceremony.

Then in 1963, the number of raps of the gavel to call up the Lodge was reduced from four to three. In earlier rituals, the three raps were the signal to remove the blindfold. The four raps have been indicative of the four cardinal virtues of the Order.

Significant Changes

In 1969, several significant changes were made in addition to some slight word changes.

The Pledge of Allegiance was transferred from the closing to the opening ceremony and "God Bless America" was approved to be sung as an optional substitute for the Opening Ode.

The major change, not in the ritual language but in its placement, was to have the Esquire's instructions on procedures moved from the end of the initiation ceremony to a position following the penalty of the obligation. It thus permitted the initiation to be closed with the tribute to and the presentation of the flag. The Esquire's instructions were previously delivered at this point in the initiation in the early years but was changed during the 1900's.

Ritual Chairmen

The following served as chairmen of the Ritual Committee during the 10 year period:

1966-68 — Lloyd Chapman, Eldorado, Kan., Lodge No. 1407
1969-70 — C. Wallace Ericson, Glendale, Calif., Lodge No. 1289
1970-72 — Charles P. Bender, Wabash, Ind., Lodge No. 471
1972-74 — William H. Whaley, Buckhead (Atlanta), Ga., Lodge No. 1635
1974-76 — J. Arthur Drehle, Littleton, Colo., Lodge No. 1650
1976-78 — Duncan McPherson, Ballard (Seattle), Wash., Lodge No. 827

Ritual Winners

The following were the National Ritualistic Champions:

Year	Lodge	Score
1968	Albany, Ore., Lodge No. 359	94.986
1969	Tucson, Ariz., Lodge No. 385	94.641
1970	Wellington, Kan., Lodge No. 1167	94.2054
1971	Huntington, N.Y., Lodge No. 1565	93.151
1972	Huntington, N.Y., Lodge No. 1565	93.795
1973	Orlando, Fla., Lodge No. 1079	93.219
1974	Huntington, N.Y., Lodge No. 1565	92.7148
1975	Huntington, N.Y., Lodge No. 1565	93.340
1976	Greeley, Colo., Lodge No. 809	94.0139
1977	Kingsport, Tenn., Lodge No. 1833	94.2466
1978	Muskegon, Mich., Lodge No. 274	91.2011

PER CAPITA TAX

In 1967, the per capita tax was $2. With rising costs and inflation the amount was gradually increased by 25-cent increments. At the session in 1978, delegates approved a per capita tax of $3 to take effect in 1979.

The increase effective in 1975 provided that the yearly subscription of *The Elks Magazine* would be $1.25, up 25 cents from $1. This was the first increase in subscription price since the magazine's inception in 1922.

WHITE REQUIREMENT

The record isn't exactly clear how or when the word "white" crept into the requirements for membership in the Order.

It was probably simply taken for granted since the Order was formed in the immediate years following the Civil War.

The word "white" as a requirement did show up in the statutes of 1890.

Under pressures of a changing world, the word with reservations was eventually dropped in the early 70s.

Action to eradicate the requirement began in 1968, when it was defeated. It was defeated again in 1970. Only 22 voted in favor of it.

The following year, 1971, delegates enacted a statute giving the Grand Exalted Ruler the power to suspend the word "white" as a membership requirement with respect to any Lodge located on government property.

This was intended to provide relief for two Lodges located in the Panama Canal Zone which were being faced with federal government action in regard to civil rights laws.

Delegates also voted to give the Grand Exalted Ruler standby authority to suspend the "white" membership requirement until the next Grand Lodge Session should he deem such action to be in the best interest of the Order.

An attempt in 1972 to remove the word was again defeated.

Then at the Grand Lodge Session in 1973, delegates approved, and Lodges later ratified a change in the constitution and statutes deleting the word "white" with reservations. The action on the floor of the Session came after a report by Edward C. Alexander of Great Falls, Montana, Lodge No. 214, chairman of the Committee on Judiciary.

The amendment "shall be effective only until the Supreme Court of the United States shall decide that the right of the people to form associations and to determine membership qualifications shall not in any way be abridged, limited or denied, or until an amendment to the Constitution of the United States shall be adopted which will guarantee that such rights shall not in any way be abridged, limited or denied."

In connection with this action a change was also made in Section 202 relative to the rights of a member to visit and attend another Lodge.

Prior to 1973, any member of the Order was entitled to visit another Lodge meeting upon presenting a paid up membership card and passing an examination.

No such entitlement was extended concerning clubroom privileges.

At the 1973 Grand Lodge Session in Chicago, this section was amended to also make consent of a visited Lodge necessary to attendance to Lodge meetings.

YOUTH ACTIVITIES

Elkdom's concern for youth increased in the 10-year period.

A most successful "Hoop Shoot"® Free Throw contest was added, the "Youth Leadership" program was combined with the "Most Valuable Student" contest, a drug abuse program was emphazed and a new program, "Teen-Ager of the Month" and "Teen-Ager of the Year" was added.

Chairmen of the Committee during the period were as follows:

1967-68 Melville J. Junion, Green Bay, Wisc., Lodge No. 259. (He had served since 1965.)

1968-70 Michael J. McNamara, Brockton, Mass., Lodge No. 164.

1970-72 Horace E. Miller, Jr., Charleston, S.C., Lodge No. 242.

1972-73 Gerald L. Powell, Peru, In., Lodge No. 365.

1973-75 Miland H. Dunivent, Grand Junction, Co., Lodge No. 575.

1975-77 Norman S. Lien, Watsonville, Calif., Lodge No. 1300.

1977-79 John T. Traynor, Devils Lake, N.D., Lodge No. 1218.

Drug Abuse Program

Elks' concern over drug addiction and other antisocial conduct among the nation's youth prompted the establishment of a Drug Abuse Program.

At the 108th Grand Lodge Session in Atlantic City in 1972, famed entertainer Art Linkletter addressed the convention. His comments brought enthusiastic and prolonged applause.

Mr. Linkletter's daughter died as a result of a drug overdose.

"Hoop Shoot"® Free Throw

The Elks "Hoop Shoot"® Free Throw contest was begun in Corvallis, Ore., a number of years ago and eventually became a state project.

In 1970, when Frank Hise served as Grand Exalted Ruler, the program was instituted by the Youth Activities Committee as a state project and about 100,000 participated.

The program grew rapidly and in 1972 GER Francis M. Smith asked the committee to conduct a national contest.

The first National Finals were held in Kansas City and there were 24 boys entered from eight regionals throughout the United States.

The following year nine regional sites were set up and 27 boys were entered in the National Finals.

A National Director was appointed and Gerald L. Powell of Peru, In., Lodge No. 365 became the first to serve.

Girls were included in the program and participation grew to approximately two and one-half million youths each year.

In 1975, Elks were honored to have the winners names enshrined in the Basketball Hall of Fame in Springfield, Mass.

GER George B. Klein made the orginal dedication, in the fall of 1976.

The Elks National Foundation finances the national program.

By the end of the decade 72 winners of 12 regional contests took part in the national event. An estimated 2.6 million youngsters were involved.

Two-time National "Hoop Shoot"® winner Kelly Lane of Vincennes, IN, Lodge No. 291

"Teen-Ager of the Month and Year"

When E. Gene Fournace became Grand Exalted Ruler in 1971, he asked the Grand Lodge Youth Activities Committee to institute a "Teen-Ager of the Month" and "Teen-Ager of the Year" program.

The first year some 400 Lodges successfully conducted the program, and over the years it continued to expand.

Overall Youth Programs

In overall programs, the number of youths touched by Elkdom's projects continued to swell. The costs for the widely-diversified youth programs were estimated at more than $3.335 million. The man-hours expended by Elks were almost unbelieveable.

Elks Honored

At the 110th Session in 1974 at Miami Beach, Fla., the then U.S. Sen. Walter Mondale of Minnesota lauded the concern of Elks for American's youth.

"The Elks' charitable efforts are a classic example of the way it should be done with 100 percent of the money going to charity," the senator said, speaking of the Elks National Foundation.

Sen. Mondale at the time was chairman of the Senate Subcommittee on Children and Youth.

DECADE ENDED

As the decade ended, Elks were expressing concern with rising prices and inflation and their effect on the Lodges.

Plans were being made to form a Government and discussions were under way to elevate the Grand Lodge Convention Committee to a commission status.

The future looked bright for the Order and its programs as Elks sought to continue to build a better America.

Elks Centennial Medallion
1868-1968

Leonard J. Bristol
1978-1979

H. Foster Sears
1980-1981

Robert Grafton
1979-1980

Raymond V. Arnold
1981-1982

Grand Exalted Rulers

TWELFTH DECADE

1978-1988

Marvin M. Lewis
1982-1983

Kenneth V. Cantoli
1983-1984

John T. Traynor
1985-1986

Frank O. Garland
1984-1985

Peter T. Affatato
1986-1987

Ted Callicott
1987-1988

458

S E C T I O N

TWELFTH DECADE

Several significant happenings occurred during the twelfth decade. For the first time in the organization's history, a Grand Lodge Session was held outside the continental limits of the United States. The 119th Session was held in Honolulu, Hawaii, in July, 1983.

Work of previous years on changing the Grand Lodge Convention Committee to the "Elks National Convention Commission" was completed in 1979. A five-member commission was set up, with duties assigned, approved by the Grand Lodge.

In 1979, the "Government Relations Committee" was formed with Yubi G. Separovich of Sacramento, California, Lodge No. 6 as chairman. Aims of the committee were to "preserve, protect and defend Elks' rights from an infringement or limitation from any source." This important work continues.

In 1981, membership showed a loss for the first time in 40 years and continued to decrease during the decade. However, the number of Lodges increased each year, and charitable contributions showed a tremendous increase; more than doubling during 1984 from $25 million to more than $53 million, and continuing to grow during the remaining years of the decade.

In response to President Reagan's call for volunteer help, Grand Exalted Ruler Raymond V. Arnold in a letter dated September 25, 1981, wrote that he was asking members "to rededicate themselves to our principles and to redouble our efforts to provide volunteer dollars and service . . ." A response from the President dated December 18, 1981, stated: "It gives me great pleasure to commend the Benevolent and Protective Order of Elks for their voluntary service to others . . ."

The Elks Drug Awareness Education Program was adopted in 1983 and continues today as one of the most important programs of the Grand Lodge. *The Elks Magazine* in each issue carries outstanding articles on the program and its accomplishments.

By resolution at the 1983 Session in Honolulu, the Grand Lodge endorsed the United States "Liberty Centennial Campaign" and pledged one million dollars to the restoration of the Statue of Liberty (see Americanism).

The Elks Hall of Fame Basketball Classic was instituted in conjunction with the 1984 National "Hoop Shoot" Finals. The game featured two teams of All-Stars, coached by well-known collegiate basketball coaches.

Grand Exalted Rulers

During the twelfth decade the Grand Exalted Rulers were:

Leonard J. Bristol, Saranac Lake, NY, Lodge No. 1508	1978-1979
Robert Grafton, North Palm Beach, FL, Lodge No. 2069	1979-1980
H. Foster Sears, Macomb, IL, Lodge No. 1009	1980-1981
Raymond V. Arnold, Jackson, MI, Lodge No. 113	1981-1982
Marvin M. Lewis, Brawley, CA, Lodge No. 1420	1982-1983
Kenneth V. Cantoli, Hasbrouck Heights, NJ, Lodge No. 1962	1983-1984
Frank O. Garland, Centralia-Chehalis, WA, Lodge No. 2435	1984-1985
John T. Traynor, Devils Lake, ND, Lodge No. 1216	1985-1986
Peter T. Affatato, Hicksville, NY, Lodge No. 1931	1986-1987
Ted Callicott, Paris, TN, Lodge No. 816	1987-1988

Grand Secretary

Stanley F. Kocur, East Chicago, IN, Lodge No. 981 continued to serve as Grand Secretary through the twelfth decade.

Membership and Charitable Expenditures

Year	Membership	Charitable Expenditure
1978-1979	1,644,496	$16,573,351
1979-1980	1,649,267	17,725,618
1980-1981	1,640,247	39,417,815
1981-1982	1,631,508	46,969,197
1982-1983	1,621,356	53,484,787
1983-1984	1,613,647	57,116,231
1984-1985	1,594,954	61,008,951
1985-1986	1,560,825	64,035,646
1986-1987	1,529,871	71,315,100
1987-1988	1,500,665	77,576,641

Grand Lodge Sessions during this period were held in the following cities:

1979	Dallas, Texas		1984	Houston, Texas
1980	New Orleans, Louisiana		1985	Seattle, Washington
1981	Las Vegas, Nevada		1986	Denver, Colorado
1982	Chicago, Illinois		1987	Atlanta, Georgia
1983	Honolulu, Hawaii		1988	Las Vegas, Nevada

Vincent R. Collura (right), Coordinator of B.P.O. Elks fund-raising for the Statue of Liberty Restoration with National Chairman Lee Iacocca on Ellis Island.

AMERICANISM PROGRAM

"LIBERTY NEEDS OUR HELP." Resolution:

WHEREAS the Benevolent and Protective Order of Elks of the United States of America is committed by the provisions of its Constitution and the will of its members to quicken the spirit of American patriotism, and

WHEREAS the Order has a glorious record of achievement in furtherance of that commitment, and

WHEREAS the Liberty Centennial Campaign now being launched has for its purpose the rehabilitation of the Statue of Liberty and Ellis Island, and

WHEREAS the Statue of Liberty symbolizes the concept of freedom of the person which is so precious to the American way of life, and

WHEREAS the Benevolent and Protective Order of Elks with its more than 1,600,000 proud Americans in over 2,200 Lodges is peculiarly endowed by its members and its purposes to add strength and vigor to the campaign,

NOW, THEREFORE BE IT RESOLVED by the delegates of its 119th Grand Lodge Session that the Benevolent and Protective Order of Elks endorses the Liberty Centennial Campaign and pledges its full support thereto.

Done this 26th day of July, 1983, in the City of Honolulu, the State of Hawaii.

To implement these eloquent sentiments was the job given to Vincent R. Collura, Chairman of the Grand Lodge Americanism Committee. A pledge of one million dollars was made and fulfilled by July of 1986 with a total of $1,380,759.61. Collura, a PER of Lincoln, Nebraska, Lodge No. 80, served as Coordinator of the Statue of Liberty Restoration, after serving two years as chairman of the Americanism Committee. Brother Collura had authored the Eagle Scout Recognition program that was adopted by the Grand Lodge in 1966. He was elected Grand Trustee in 1987.

Chairmen of the Americanism Committee During the Decade

1978-1979	Robert L. Smith of McAlester, OK, Lodge No. 533
1979-1981	Dominic P. Dululio of Leominster, MS, Lodge No. 1237
1981-1983	J. W. Wortman, Jr. of Albany, GA, Lodge No. 713
1983-1985	Vincent R. Collura of Lincoln, NE, Lodge No. 80
1985-1987	Dan Davis of Van Nuys, CA, Lodge No. 2028
1987-1988	Arthur W. Bartunek of Ponca City, OK, Lodge No. 2002

ELKS NATIONAL HOME

The Elks National Home in Bedford, Virginia, once termed "The Elks' Best Kept Secret" kept up its splendid record of caring for those Brothers choosing to live at the Home. Over the years the Home has undergone continuous improvements, both to buildings and grounds.

Doral Irvin, Executive Director since 1964, retired in September, 1985, and William P. Pickett of Butler, PA, Lodge No. 170, assumed that post and continues in that capacity.

The Elks National Home and the city of Bedford have enjoyed the reputation of being the "Christmas Capital of Virginia." Each Christmas holiday season the Home is transformed into a spectacular display of lights depicting the spirit of Christmas. During the 1986 season, 15,334 vehicles passed through the grounds, carrying visitors to enjoy the display.

ELKS NATIONAL MEMORIAL AND PUBLICATION COMMISSION

At the end of 1987-1988 Grand Lodge year, the members of the Elks National Memorial and Publication Commission were Wade H. Kepner, Chairman Emeritus; George B. Klein, Chairman; R. Leonard Bush, Vice-Chairman; Raymond C. Dobson, Past Chairman; Edward W. McCabe, Treasurer and Past Chairman; and H. Foster Sears, Secretary.

The Elks Magazine celebrated its 60th anniversary in June 1982. Because of sharply increasing postage rates, it was decided to distribute the Magazine via third class mail rather than continue to pay the second class rate. Postage costs had also been a factor in the decision in 1980 to reduce the frequency of publication to ten issues a year with combined December-January and July-August issues.

In October, 1986, John R. Ryan, Publisher and General Manager of the Magazine, retired after 22 years. Ryan was instrumental in organizing the Grand Lodge computer department used by the Grand Secretary's office and the National Foundation as well as the Magazine. Fred D. Oakes became Executive Editor of the Magazine and continued in that position through the decade.

ELKS NATIONAL FOUNDATION

In the beginning of the twelfth decade the Trustees of the Foundation consisted of PGER's John L. Walker, Chairman; William A. Wall, Vice-Chairman; Horace R. Wisely, Secretary; E. Gene Fournace, Treasurer; Robert A. Yothers, Assistant Secretary; Glenn L. Miller, Assistant Treasurer; and Willis C. McDonald.

Nelson E. W. Stuart of Cleveland, OH, Lodge No. 18 continued as Executive Director. Because of ill health, John L. Walker resigned in February of 1980 and William A. Wall succeeded him as Chairman; Horace R. Wisely became Vice-Chairman; Willis C. McDonald, Secretary; E. Gene Fournace, Treasurer; Robert A. Yothers, Assistant Secretary; Glenn L. Miller, Assistant Treasurer; and John L. Walker.

That was to be the end of long tenures of chairmen. From 1928 through 1980 there were only three chairmen. Thereafter the chairmen would only serve four one-year terms.

Death invaded the ranks of the Trustees with the passing of John L. Walker on August 20, 1982. PGER Homer Huhn, Jr., was appointed to the unexpired term and subsequently appointed to a full seven-year term. In July of 1984, William A. Wall resigned as a Trustee and was elected Chairman Emeritus. Robert A. Yothers resigned also to assume the Chairmanship of the Grand Lodge Advisory Committee. PGER Robert Grafton was appointed to a full seven-year term to replace William A. Wall's seat and PGER Francis M. Smith was appointed to the unexpired term of Robert A. Yothers.

The Board reorganized as follows: Homer Huhn, Chairman; Willis C. McDonald, Vice-Chairman; Francis M. Smith, Secretary; E. Gene Fournace, Treasurer; Robert Grafton, Assistant Secretary; Glenn L. Miller, Assistant Treasurer; and Horace R. Wisely.

Once again death invaded and claimed the life of E. Gene Fournace, Treasurer, on October 21, 1985. PGER Kenneth V. Cantoli was appointed to the unexpired term and elected as the Treasurer.

In July of 1987, Horace R. Wisely resigned as a Trustee due to poor health and PGER Marvin M. Lewis was appointed to the unexpired term and subsequently appointed to a full seven-year term. Death invaded again on September 14, 1987, with the passing of Horace R. Wisely.

In 1988, the Trustees were Willis C. McDonald, Chairman; Kenneth V. Cantoli, Vice-Chairman; Robert Grafton, Secretary; Francis M. Smith, Treasurer; Marvin M. Lewis, Assistant Secretary;

Glenn L. Miller, Assistant Treasurer; Homer Huhn, Jr., and William A. Wall, Chairman Emeritus.

On June 1, 1981, Nelson E.W. Stuart, the first Executive Director of the Foundation since January 1, 1967, retired. He was succeeded by James C. Varenhorst of Ludington, MI, Lodge No. 736 who continued in that position through the decade. A. Patricia Kavanaugh who had been serving as Office Manager, was promoted to the responsibility of Controller and continued in that position through the decade.

Per capita contributions to the Foundation continued to grow from $1.895 in 1980 to $2.735 in 1988. Total donations in 1987-88 were $4,183,084.23.

In 1978, the Elks National Foundation offered $840,000 in scholarship awards for students entering the "Most Valuable Student" contest in 1979. In 1987 the Foundation offered $2,500,000 for students entering the contest in 1988. This does not include those monies given for vocational grants, Eagle Scout scholarships, and other awards from the Foundation.

The Elks National Foundation Trust Fund now exceeds $100 million. Distributions in 1987-88 totaled $7.8 million.

In 1984, the Foundation initiated the Vocational Grant program to provide educational assistance to those adults who were being removed from the labor market due to new technologies. The program is designed to provide two years of training at a community college or voc-tech school. Grants of $1,000 a year for two years are awarded through a contest format.

Initially, 50 grants were awarded. In the fall of 1987, the Foundation offered 269 grants worth a total of $538,000. In 1984, the Foundation also began awarding Eagle Scout Scholarships through a program conducted by the National Headquarters of the Boy Scouts of America. Six four-year scholarships of $1,000 per year are awarded, one in each of the six Eagle Scout regions.

During the decade, the Foundation began to directly fund major programs which it had previously funded through the Grand Lodge. These included the Elks National Service Commission, the national "Hoop Shoot" and Drug Awareness Programs, and a substantial portion of the budget of the Elks National Home.

ELKS RITUAL

Serving as Chairmen of the Ritualistic Committee during the decade were:

1978-1979	Dale Blanton, San Rafael, CA, Lodge No. 1108
1979-1982	Ted Callicott, Paris, TN, Lodge No. 816
1982-1983	Robert F. Kauphusman, Jamestown, ND, Lodge No. 995
1983-1985	G. Lester Von Bargen, Lewiston, ID, Lodge No. 896
1985-1987	Joseph DeLitta, Mamaroneck, NY, Lodge No. 1457
1987-1988	Homer Oberst, Lakewood, WA, Lodge No. 2388

National Ritualistic Champions of the Decade

Year	Lodge	Score
1979	Greeley, CO, Lodge No. 809	95.0195
1980	Greeley, CO, Lodge No. 809	93.7792
1981	Kearney, NE, Lodge No. 984	94.5142
1982	Laramie, WY, Lodge No. 582	95.5863
1983	Ocala, FL, Lodge No. 286	94.7139
1984	Laramie, WY, Lodge No. 582	95.8886
1985	Ogallala, NE, Lodge No. 1760	95.1560
1986	Ogallala, NE, Lodge No. 1760	95.0443
1987	Ocala, FL, Lodge No. 286	95.8022
1988	Wellington, KS, Lodge No. 1167	95.6209

There were no significant changes in the ritual or procedures during the decade.

DRUG AWARENESS PROGRAM

The Elks Drug Awareness Program inaugurated in 1983 has seen yearly growth in all phases. *The Elks Magazine* has given generously of its space to the furtherance of the program. In 1988, Subordinate Lodges numbering 1,883 were participating. There were 3,559 programs involving three million children, with $1.8 million spent on local, state and national levels.

Distribution of bumper stickers, book covers, pamphlets and books and videotapes for schools has been carried out by local Lodges. Subordinate Lodge members have devoted many hours to the program, arranging and making presentations to school assemblies and to many other audiences of children and parents. Many Lodges participate in the national "Just Say No" Walks Against

Drugs each year in May. In all of these efforts, the Elks Drug Awareness Program has received strong support from local media.

The Order of Elks continues to co-sponsor the annual PRIDE World Drug Conference, an international conference on drug-use prevention. Attending the 1988 Conference were 52 Elks, including 40 State Drug Awareness Chairmen. Additionally, Elks Lodges and State Associations sponsored more than 300 youths, parents and teachers who attended. During her years as First Lady, Nancy Reagan attended and actively participated in the PRIDE Conferences.

In 1988, Dick Herndobler of Ashland, OR, Lodge No. 944, national director of the Elks Drug Awareness Program, was appointed by President Reagan to serve as a member of the White House Conference for a Drug Free America. Each Grand Exalted Ruler, when he has visited the nation's capitol, has given his pledge to the nation's leaders that the Elks will work diligently to prevent drug use by young people.

1978-1979

The Veterans Administration presented a certificate to Bryan McKeogh, Director of the Elks National Service Commission, in recognition of his 25 years of service to the commission.

The Elks Magazine concludes a two-year series on the Major Projects of each State Association in its December 1979 issue. Major Project stories continued to be featured in the Magazine during the remaining years of the decade.

1980-1981

GER Robert Grafton sent a telegram to President Carter expressing support for actions to obtain release and return of American prisoners in Iran.

Grand Lodge Statutes were amended to require Exalted Rulers to appoint a Government Relations Committee and a Public Relations Committee.

A Resolution was passed recognizing the American Red Cross as "one of the great humanitarian organizations in history."

The Benevolent and Protective Order of Elks float captured the coveted Sweepstakes Award in the 1982 Pasadena Tournament of Roses Parade. The Elks were first invited to participate in 1980.

GER Marvin Lewis completed a two-day whirlwind tour of Washington, D.C., meeting with Senators and Congressman from 21 states and other high government officials.

The Kansas Elks Training Center for the Handicapped received national recognition from President Reagan for "creativity, initiative and tenacity in forging successful public-private partnerships in the community."

A national survey of mayors by all Exalted Rulers revealed "a critical need for volunteers" to deal with the challenges of drug abuse, for community clean-up, and for programs for elderly and youth recreation.

"We believe drug abuse poses today's greatest threat to our country's most precious resource: its youth," said Grand Exalted Ruler Kenneth V. Cantoli to members of Congress in announcing the new National Drug Awareness Education Program on November 9, 1983. Cantoli sought congressional endorsement of the program at a reception for the 91 members of Congress who were Elks.

Bryan J. McKeogh, who served as Director of the Elks National Convention Commission for 32 years, retired. His duties were assumed by George G. Malekian and Reg Christmas. Malekian resigned in August, 1984, and Christmas continued during the decade as director.

A renovation plan for the Elks National Home was approved in 1984; work began on Phase One, with an estimated cost of $1,148,526 in 1985. On Sunday, December 1, 1985, thirty-two residents of the Home were honored for having served in World War I.

The Elks Basketball Hall of Fame Classic was inaugurated at the 1984 "Hoop Shoot" National Finals at Market Square Arena in Indianapolis, Indiana. Ray Meyer, former DePaul coach, headed the Nationals and Eddie Sutton of Arkansas headed the American squad. The Nationals won 77-72.

In April 1985 the Grand Lodge co-sponsored the PRIDE International Conference on Drug Abuse in Atlanta, Georgia. Mrs. Nancy Reagan attended along with visiting First Ladies of fifteen other nations.

At the PRIDE International Conference on Drugs held in Atlanta, Georgia, Dick Herndobler (right), director of the Grand Lodge Drug Awareness Program, was recognized by First Lady Nancy Reagan for the Elks' considerable contribution to the fight against drug abuse. Also pictured is Roberto Goizueta, chairman of the board of Coca-Cola. This was the second year that the Elks co-sponsored the conference. (Photo courtesy of Reis Birdwhistell.)

The Elks National Service Commission observed its 40th Anniversary. It remains true to the promise that, "So long as there are veterans in our hospitals, the Benevolent and Protective Order of Elks will never forget them."

During the visit of GER Ted Callicott to the nation's capitol he met with many of the nation's leaders. Discussion focused on major Elks programs relating to Drug Awareness Education, youth activities and veterans service.

Upon the death of Grand Treasurer Robert D. Moore of Fairfield, Iowa, Marlin J. Haack of Bemidji, Minnesota, was appointed to complete the remainder of Moore's term, and subsequently was elected and served as Grand Treasurer for the 1987-1988 year.

The Lodge Development Committee of Grand Lodge, established in 1958 and charged with membership promotion and lapsation control, underwent a name change in 1987 to more clearly define its nature as the Membership Committee. At the same time, those functions relating to the formation of new Lodges were transferred to the auspices of the Grand Lodge State Associations Committee.

END OF DECADE

As the decade drew to a close, the Elks, though concerned about a gradual, continuing decline in membership, took great pride in the continued growth of their charitable programs. The 1987-1988 Grand Lodge year was the most successful ever for the Elks National Service Commission. At the same time, the Drug Awareness Program continued to expand, and over three million boys and girls took part in the Elks "Hoop Shoot" Free Throw Program.

APPENDIX

IT HAS SEEMED desirable to disasso-
ciate from the body of this History
certain financial reports and statistics;
several such items will be found in this
Appendix.

This material includes financial
reports of several Grand Lodge Commissions and of the Elks National Foundation, and statistics relative to lodge
membership, Grand Lodge Sessions and
Officers, which it is hoped will be of
sufficient reference value to justify their
being incorporated in this History.

NUMBER OF LODGES BY YEARS

Year	Lodges	Year	Lodges	Year	Lodges
1868-1870	1	1914	1264	1954	1677
1871-1875	2	1915	1287	1955	1720
1876	3	1916	1284	1956	1755
1877	8	1917	1286	1957	1791
1878	10	1918	1280	1958	1832
1879	11	1919	1280	1959	1866
1880	10	1920	1300	1960	1919
1881	11	1921	1321	1961	1966
1882	14	1922	1350	1962	2006
1883	20	1923	1366	1963	2022
1884	26	1924	1386	1964	2034
1885	34	1925	1403	1965	2049
1886	49	1926	1407	1966	2071
1887	66	1927	1404	1967	2091
1888	92	1928	1420	1968	2108
1889	114	1929	1401	1969	2124
1890	158	1930	1421	1970	2146
1891	196	1931	1420	1971	2164
1892	222	1932	1362	1972	2175
1893	264	1933	1388	1973	2179
1894	287	1934	1384	1974	2191
1895	320	1935	1370	1975	2201
1896	350	1936	1356	1976	2212
1897	379	1937	1346	1977	2214
1898	442	1938	1359	1978	2228
1899	514	1939	1366	1979	2240
1900	602	1940	1376	1980	2253
1901	725	1941	1393	1981	2263
1902	806	1942	1398	1982	2265
1903	879	1943	1409	1983	2271
1904	932	1944	1402	1984	2283
1905	983	1945	1418	1985	2286
1906	1042	1946	1433	1986	2295
1907	1081	1947	1463	1987	2300
1908	1119	1948	1487	1988	2296
1909	1155	1949	1521		
1910	1150	1950	1557		
1911	1185	1951	1586		
1912	1226	1952	1607		
1913	1255	1953	1642		

YEAR OF INSTITUTION OF FIRST 100 LODGES

	New York, N. Y., No. 1	Feb. 12, 1871
	Philadelphia, Pa., No. 2	Feb. 19, 1871
NOTE 1	San Francisco, Cal., No. 3	1876
	Chicago, Ill., No. 4	1876
	Cincinnati, Ohio, No. 5	1877
NOTE 2	Sacramento, Cal., No. 6	1877
	Baltimore, Md., No. 7	1877
NOTE 3	Louisville, Ky., No. 8	1877
	St. Louis, Mo., No. 9	1878
	Boston, Mass., No. 10	1878
	Pittsburgh, Pa., No. 11	1878
NOTE 4	California No. 12	1879
	Indianapolis, Ind., No. 13	1881
	Providence, R. I., No. 14	1882
	Washington, D. C., No. 15	1882
NOTE 5		
	Denver, Colo., No. 17	1882
NOTE 6	Cleveland, Ohio, No. 18	1883
	Hartford, Conn., No. 19	1883
	Peoria, Ill., No. 20	1883
	Newark, N. J., No. 21	1883
	Brooklyn, N. Y., No. 22	1883
	Buffalo, N. Y., No. 23	1884
	Rochester, N. Y., No. 24	1885
	New Haven, Conn., No. 25	1884
	Kansas City, Mo., No. 26	1884
	Memphis, Tenn., No. 27	1884
	Wheeling, W. Va., No. 28	1885
	Little Rock, Ark., No. 29	1885
	New Orleans, La., No. 30	1885
	Syracuse, N. Y., No. 31	1886
	Marion, Ohio, No. 32	1885
	Utica, N. Y., No. 33	1885
	Detroit, Mich., No. 34	1885
	Meriden, Conn., No. 35	1885
	Bridgeport, Conn., No. 36	1885
	Columbus, Ohio, No. 37	1885
	Norfolk, Va., No. 38	1886
	Omaha, Nebr., No. 39	1886
	St. Joseph, Mo., No. 40	1886

NOTE 1 — San Francisco, Cal. — In 1885 San Francisco Lodge No. 3 was united with California Lodge No. 12 to make one lodge, Golden Gate Lodge No. 6.
In 1897 Grand Exalted Ruler Detweiler replaced Golden Gate Lodge No. 6 by a lodge known as San Francisco Lodge No. 3.

NOTE 2 — Sacramento, Cal. — This charter was surrendered in 1878. In 1896 Sacramento was re-established with the number 328.
In 1908 the old number 6 was restored to the lodge.

NOTE 3 — Louisville, Ky. — This charter was forfeited in 1882 and restored in 1883.

NOTE 4 — California — As noted above, in 1885 this lodge was united with San Francisco Lodge No. 3 to make one lodge, Golden Gate Lodge No. 6.
In 1904 the number 12 was given to Harrisburg, Pa., Lodge, which up to that time had had the number 241.

NOTE 5 — Illinois — In December, 1882, Exalted Grand Ruler Garrett advised that he had granted a dispensation for Illinois Lodge No. 16, located in Chicago, but as very little was done under the dispensation, he recommended that the Grand-Lodge call in the dispensation. This was done.

NOTE 6 — Cleveland, Ohio — This charter was surrendered in 1884 and restored in 1886.

	Lockport, N. Y., No. 41	1887
	Little Falls, N. Y., No. 42	1886
NOTE 7	Adrian, Mich., No. 43	1886
	Minneapolis, Minn., No. 44	1886
	Richmond, Va., No. 45	1886
	Milwaukee, Wis., No. 46	1886
NOTE 8	East Saginaw, Mich., No. 47	1886
	Grand Rapids, Mich., No. 48	1886
	Albany, N. Y., No. 49	1886
	Kalamazoo, Mich., No. 50	1887
	Springfield, Ohio, No. 51	1886
	Chillicothe, Ohio, No. 52	1887
	Toledo, Ohio, No. 53	1886
	Lima, Ohio, No. 54	1887
	Youngstown, Ohio, No. 55	1886
	Mansfield, Ohio, No. 56	1886
	Fond du Lac, Wis., No. 57	1886
	Dayton, Ohio, No. 58	1886
	Saint Paul, Minn., No. 59	1887
	Paterson, N. J., No. 60	1887
NOTE 9	Springfield, Mass., No. 61	1887
	Elmira, N. Y., No. 62	1887
	Cumberland, Md., No. 63	1887
	Rockford, Ill., No. 64	1887
	Lawrence, Mass., No. 65	1887
	Logansport, Ind., No. 66	1887
	Erie, Pa., No. 67	1888
	Canton, Ohio, No. 68	1887
	New Castle, Pa., No. 69	1887
NOTE 10	Binghamton, N. Y., No. 70	1888
	Dallas, Texas, No. 71	1888
	Nashville, Tenn., No. 72	1887
	New Bedford, Mass., No. 73	1887
	Hoboken, N. J., No. 74	1888
	Findlay, Ohio, No. 75	1888
	Delaware, Ohio, No. 76	1888
	Circleville, Ohio, No. 77	1888
	Atlanta, Ga., No. 78	1888
	Birmingham, Ala., No. 79	1889
	Lincoln, Nebr., No. 80	1888
	Glens Falls, N. Y., No. 81	1888
	Portsmouth, Va., No. 82	1888
	Upper Sandusky, Ohio, No. 83	1888
	Burlington, Iowa, No. 84	1888
	Salt Lake City, Utah, No. 85	1888
	Terre Haute, Ind., No. 86	1888
	Lowell, Mass., No. 87	1889
	Bay City, Mich., No. 88	1888

NOTE 7 — Adrian, Mich. — This lodge was instituted in 1886 and its charter was forfeited in 1887.

NOTE 8 — In 1892 the name of this Lodge was changed to Saginaw.

NOTE 9 — Springfield, Mass. — In 1894 the charter of Springfield, Massachusetts Lodge No. 61 was suspended.
In 1900 a new lodge was instituted with the number of 561.
In 1907 Springfield Lodge was allowed to take the number of the first lodge in that city—Number 61.

NOTE 10 — Binghamton, N. Y. — This lodge was instituted in 1888 and its charter was forfeited in 1894, but later the lodge was re-instituted as Lodge No. 852.

Lexington, Ky., No. 89..1888
Pueblo, Colo., No. 90 1888
Chattanooga, Tenn., No. 91 1888
Seattle, Wash., No. 92 1888
Hamilton, Ohio, No. 93 1888
Tiffin, Ohio, No. 94 1889
Vicksburg, Miss., No. 95 1888
NOTE 11   Rome, N. Y., No. 96 1888
Portsmouth, N. H., No. 97..1888
Des Moines, Iowa, No. 98..1889
Los Angeles, Calif., No. 99 1889
Quincy, Ill., No. 100..1889
NOTE 11 - Rome, N. Y. - This charter was surrendered in 1898 and later restored.

MEMBERSHIP BY YEARS

The Order of Elks started on February 16, 1868, with a membership of 15.

Its growth in membership in the first four years is not definitely stated in the early records.

In the Ellis History it is stated that as of December of 1868, 1869 and 1870, the membership figures were 76, 149 and 289, respectively.

However, there is added the qualifying note that from these figures there should be deducted suspensions, the number of which is not on record.

The recorded figures starting with 1871 are as follows:

Year		Year		Year	
1871	243	1911	359,677	1951	1,041,264
1872	271	1912	384,026	1952	1,069,868
1873	268	1913	408,281	1953	1,097,003
1874	385	1914	428,479	1954	1,122,803
1875	376	1915	442,658	1955	1,149,613
1876	418	1916	453,516	1956	1,173,494
1877	*not reported	1917	474,690	1957	1,195,509
1878	820	1918	493,733	1958	1,214,163
1879	929	1919	527,522	1959	1,232,007
1880	1,060	1920	645,678	1960	1,260,007
1881	1,339	1921	767,661	1961	1,280,524
1882	1,806	1922	812,657	1962	1,294,604
1883	2,400	1923	826,825	1963	1,315,319
1884	3,051	1924	839,429	1964	1,333,482
1885	3,949	1925	832,083	1965	1,361,455
1886	5,511	1926	825,960	1966	1,388,561
1887	7,334	1927	816,000	1967	1,417,435
1888	8,952	1928	808,658	1968	1,452,187
1889	10,549	1929	779,973	1969	1,480,412
1890	13,067	1930	761,461	1970	1,508,050
1891	15,472	1931	707,887	1971	1,520,731
1892	18,424	1932	640,591	1972	1,531,912
1893	21,844	1933	556,764	1973	1,541,784
1894	22,068	1934	500,171	1974	1,558,772
1895	27,610	1935	468,043	1975	1,582,735
1896	32,025	1936	466,520	1976	1,611,139
1897	36,515	1937	472,153	1977	1,624,702
1898	44,252	1938	479,494	1978	1,634,488
1899	60,129	1939	473,927	1979	1,644,496
1900	77,351	1940	475,599	1980	1,649,267
1901	99,827	1941	490,417	1981	1,640,247
1902	128,679	1942	506,887	1982	1,631,508
1903	155,434	1943	547,718	1983	1,621,356
1904	177,527	1944	627,513	1984	1,613,647
1905	199,370	1945	705,570	1985	1,594,954
1906	225,016	1946	792,339	1986	1,560,825
1907	254,532	1947	877,271	1987	1,529,871
1908	284,321	1948	925,679	1988	1,500,665
1909	304,899	1949	965,387		
1910	331,228	1950	1,004,985		

---

* In the proceedings of 1877 there appeared no figures of membership. In this connection the paragraph with which Henry P. O'Neil, Grand Secretary, closed his report, is of interest: "The minutes here given are as full as the rough minutes of the outgoing Grand Secretary rendered possible and are submitted with the reservations indicated."

GRAND LODGE SESSIONS
(Place and Year of)

With the exception of the Session of 1877, which was held in Philadelphia, the Grand Lodge from the date of its organization in 1871 met in New York City until 1890, after which it was held in these cities:

1890 Cleveland, OH	1926 Chicago, IL	1962 Chicago, IL
1891 Louisville, KY	1927 Cincinnati, OH	1963 San Francisco, CA
1892 Buffalo, NY	1928 Miami, FL	1964 New York, NY
1893 Detroit, MI	1929 Los Angeles, CA	1965 Miami Beach, FL
*1894 Atlantic City, NJ	1930 Atlantic City, NJ	1966 Dallas, TX
*1895 Atlantic City, NJ	1931 Seattle, WA	1967 Chicago, IL
1896 Cincinnati, OH	1932 Birmingham, AL	1968 New York, NY
1897 Minneapolis, MN	1933 Milwaukee, WI	1969 Dallas, TX
1898 New Orleans, LA	1934 Kansas City, MO	1970 San Francisco, CA
1899 St. Louis, MO	1935 Columbus, OH	1971 New Orleans, LA
1900 Atlantic City, NJ	1936 Los Angeles, CA	1972 Atlantic City, NJ
1901 Milwaukee, WI	1937 Denver, CO	1973 Chicago, IL
1902 Salt Lake City, UT	1938 Atlantic City, NJ	1974 Miami Beach, FL
1903 Baltimore, MD	1939 St. Louis, MO	1975 Dallas, TX
1904 Cincinnnati, OH	1940 Houston, TX	1976 Chicago, IL
1905 Buffalo, NY	1941 Philadelphia, PA	1977 New Orleans, LA
1906 Denver, CO	1942 Omaha, NE	1978 San Diego, CA
1907 Philadelphia, PA	1943 Boston, MA	1979 Dallas, TX
1908 Dallas, TX	1944 Chicago, IL	1980 New Orleans, LA
1909 Los Angeles, CA	1945 New York, NY	1981 Las Vegas, NV
1910 Detroit, MI	1946 New York, NY	1982 Chicago, IL
1911 Atlantic City, NJ	1947 Portland, OR	1983 Honolulu, HI
1912 Portland, OR	1948 Philadelphia, PA	1984 Houston, TX
1913 Rochester, NY	1949 Cleveland, OH	1985 Seattle, WA
1914 Denver, CO	1950 Miami, FL	1986 Denver, CO
1915 Los Angeles, CA	1951 Chicago, IL	1987 Atlanta, GA
1916 Baltimore, MD	1952 New York, NY	1988 Las Vegas, NV
1917 Boston, MA	1953 St. Louis, MO	
1918 Atlantic City, NJ	1954 Los Angeles, CA	
1919 Atlantic City, NJ	1955 Philadelphia, PA	
1920 Chicago, IL	1956 Chicago, IL	
1921 Los Angeles, CA	1957 San Francisco, CA	
1922 Atlantic City, NJ	1958 New York, NY	
1923 Atlanta, GA	1959 Miami Beach, FL	
1924 Boston, MA	1960 Dallas, TX	
1925 Portland, OR	1961 Miami Beach, FL	

At the session referred to above as being held in Philadelphia in 1877, the Grand Lodge, after full debate upon the subject, resolved that the only legal place for the communications of the Grand Lodge, under the laws, was the city of New York, and that, therefore, the next communication should be there.

It was also determined by vote of the Grand Lodge that the communication be resumed in New York City in order to cure any illegalities or objections that might thereafter arise and that all the legislation recorded therein be repassed.

This was done after the return of the constitutional number to New York.

* (See also JAMESTOWN CONTROVERSY - p. 172)

GRAND LODGE SESSIONS ATTENDANCE

DATE	COMMUNICATION	SESSION	ATTENDANCE
Feb. 12, 1871	1st	1st (A)	10
Feb. 19, 1871	1st	2nd	11
Apr. 9, 1871	1st	3rd	10
June 11, 1871	2nd	4th	10
Dec. 10, 1871	3rd	5th	
Dec. 17, 1871	3rd	6th	
Dec. 24, 1871	3rd	7th	(B)
June 9, 1872	4th	8th	
June 16, 1872	4th	9th	
June 23, 1871	4th	10th	
Dec. 8, 1872	4th	11th	11
Dec. 15, 1872	4th	12th	11
Mar. 9, 1873	4th	13th	8
June 8, 1873	5th	14th	11
June 15, 1873	5th	15th	7
June 22, 1873	5th	16th	10
Dec. 7, 1873	5th	17th	13
Dec. 14, 1873	6th	18th	7
Feb. 1, 1874	6th	19th	19
Mar. 8, 1874	6th	20th	17
Apr. 12, 1874	6th	21st	11
June 14, 1874	7th	22nd	8
June 28, 1874	7th	23rd	9
Dec. 13, 1874	8th	24th	20
June 13, 1875	9th	25th	12
Dec. 12, 1875	10th	26th	14
June 11, 1876	11th	27th	15
Dec. 10, 1876	12th	28th	21
Dec. 9, 1877	13th	29th	(B)
Dec. 8, 1878	14th	30th	40
Dec. 14, 1879	15th	31st	44
Dec. 12, 1880	16th	32nd	68
Dec. 11, 1881	17th	33rd	68
Dec. 10, 1882	18th	34th	83
Dec. 9, 1883	19th	35th	95
Dec. 14, 1884	20th	36th	101
Dec. 13, 1885	21st	37th	102
Dec. 12, 1886	22nd	38th	133
Dec. 11, 1887	23rd	39th	204
July 10, 1888	24th	40th	275
July 9, 1889	25th	41st	(B)
July 8, 1890	26th	42nd	207

In 1891 the designation "Session" was substituted for the designation "Communication" and the meeting of that year was referred to as the "27th Session."

YEAR	SESSION	ATTENDANCE	YEAR	SESSION	ATTENDANCE
1891	27th	203	1940	76th	1480
1892	28th	222	1941	77th	2071
1893	29th	243	1942	78th	1422
1894	30th	193	1943	79th	1607
1895	31st	232	1944	80th	1767
1896	32nd	285	1945	81st	337(C)
1897	33rd	358	1946	82nd	3313
1898	34th	298	1947	83rd	2229
1899	35th	533	1948	84th	2475
1900	36th	622	1949	85th	2490
1901	37th	813	1950	86th	2288
1902	38th	662	1951	87th	2601
1903	39th	933	1952	88th	2816
1904	40th	1320	1953	89th	2411
1905	41st	1252	1954	90th	2693
1906	42nd	1255	1955	91st	2675
1907	43rd	1912	1956	92nd	2724
1908	44th	1050	1957	93rd	2573
1909	45th	1258	1958	94th	3084
1910	46th	1951	1959	95th	2753
1911	47th	1880	1960	96th	2680
1912	48th	1236	1961	97th	2916
1913	49th	1735	1962	98th	2893
1914	50th	1351	1963	99th	2899
1915	51st	1216	1964	100th	3214
1916	52nd	1662	1965	101st	2914
1917	53rd	1712	1966	102nd	2747
1918	54th	1368	1967	103rd	3077
1919	55th	1684	1968	104th	3302
1920	56th	1945	1969	105th	2842
1921	57th	1469	1970	106th	3178
1922	58th	1615	1971	107th	3291
1923	59th	1382	1972	108th	3486
1924	60th	2534	1973	109th	3564
1925	61st	1329	1974	110th	3261
1926	62nd	1890	1975	111th	3258
1927	63rd	1878	1976	112th	3382
1928	64th	1282	1977	113th	3837
1929	65th	1770	1978	114th	4010
1930	66th	1713	1979	115th	3475
1931	67th	1303	1980	116th	3647
1932	68th	1208	1981	117th	3846
1933	69th	1788	1982	118th	3758
1934	70th	1346	1983	119th	4414
1935	71st	1794	1984	120th	3228
1936	72nd	1540	1985	121st	3926
1937	73rd	1642	1986	122nd	4118
1938	74th	1975	1987	123rd	3982
1939	75th	1646	1988	124th	4735

(A) The first meeting of the Grand Lodge was held at 114-116 East 13th Street, New York City, on February 12, 1871.

The ten members present were:

George J. Green	Hugh P. O'Neil
Antonio Pastor	Fernando Pastor
J. C. Pinckney	S. K. Spencer
Claude Goldie	Henry P. O'Neil
A. H. Mulligan	E. G. Browne

George J. Green presided and E. G. Browne acted as Secretary.

(B) No reference in minutes to exact attendance.

(C) In 1945, due to war-time restrictions on travel, attendance was limited to the minimum necessary for a quorum.

COMMUNICATIONS AND SESSIONS

At the beginning of the Grand Lodge what are referred to now as Grand Lodge *Sessions* were called *Communications,* and adjournments of *Communications* were called *Sessions.*

Communication No. 1 was held on February 12, 1871. This was also called the First Session.

There was a total of three Sessions to this Communication, the others being held on the following dates:

Session No. 2	Feb. 19, 1871
Session No. 3	Apr. 9, 1871

Thus Communication No. 2 was Session No. 4. This was held on June 11, 1871.

Communication No. 3 started with Session No. 5, held on Dec. 10, 1871. This Communication also had the following Sessions:

Session No. 6	Dec. 17, 1871
Session No. 7	Dec. 24, 1871

Communication No. 4 comprised the following Sessions:

Session No. 8	June 9, 1872
Session No. 9	June 16, 1872
Session No. 10	June 23, 1872
Session No. 11	Dec. 8, 1872
Session No. 12	Dec. 15, 1872
Session No. 13	Mar. 9, 1873

Communication No. 5 comprised the following Sessions:

Session No. 14	June 8, 1873
Session No. 15	June 15, 1873
Session No. 16	June 22, 1873
Session No. 17	Dec. 7, 1873

Communication No. 6 comprised the following Sessions:

Session No. 18	Dec. 14, 1873
Session No. 19	Feb. 1, 1874
Session No. 20	Mar. 8, 1874
Session No. 21	Apr. 12, 1874

Communication No. 7 comprised the following Sessions:

Session No. 22	June 14, 1874
Session No. 23	June 28, 1874

This is the last Communication to have more than one Session. Thus we have Communication and Session numbers running as follows:

Communication No. 8	Session No. 24	Dec. 13, 1874
Communication No. 9	Session No. 25	June 13, 1875
Communication No. 10	Session No. 26	Dec. 12, 1875
Communication No. 11	Session No. 27	June 11, 1876
Communication No. 12	Session No. 28	Dec. 10, 1876
Communication No. 13	Session No. 29	Dec. 9, 1877
Communication No. 14	Session No. 30	Dec. 8, 1878
Communication No. 15	Session No. 31	Dec. 14, 1879
Communication No. 16	Session No. 32	Dec. 12, 1880
Communication No. 17	Session No. 33	Dec. 11, 1881
Communication No. 18	Session No. 34	Dec. 10, 1882
Communication No. 19	Session No. 35	Dec. 9, 1883
Communication No. 20	Session No. 36	Dec. 14, 1884
Communication No. 21	Session No. 37	Dec. 13, 1885
Communication No. 22	Session No. 38	Dec. 12, 1886
Communication No. 23	Session No. 39	Dec. 11, 1887
Communication No. 24	Session No. 40	July 10, 1888
Communication No. 25	Session No. 41	July 9, 1889
Communication No. 26	Session No. 42	July 8, 1890

In 1891 the Grand Lodge proceedings referred to the "27th Annual, Forty-Third Session." This was the first year in which the word "Communication" was dropped. In 1892 the reference was to "28th Annual Session." Of course the word "annual" was not correctly used, as the Grand Lodge was then only 21 years old. In 1893 the reference was to the "29th Session," the word "annual," quite properly, being eliminated.

It will be noted that the word "Session" was now being substituted for the term "Communication" and there was no further use of the term "Session" to indicate an adjourned meeting of what had previously been called "Communications."

In 1894 the reference was to the "30th Session."

In 1895 the reference was to the "31st Annual Session."

In 1896 the reference was to the "32nd Annual Session."

In 1897 the reference was to the "33rd Annual Session."

In 1898 the reference was to the "34th Annual Session."

In 1899 the reference was to the "35th Annual Session."

In 1900 the reference was to the "36th Annual Session."

In 1901 the reference was to the "37th Annual Session."

In 1902 the reference was to the "38th Annual Session."

In 1903 the reference was to the "39th Annual Session."

In 1904, however, someone must have detected the error, as the Session in that year was referred to as the "40th Session," and since that time the word "annual" was not applied in the Proceedings.

CHARITABLE EXPENDITURES

Year	Amount	Year	Amount
1880	$ 4,440.64	1936	1,304,869.07
1881	5,553.01	1937	1,400,248.75
1882	5,073.30	1938	1,417,237.47
1883	8,163.65	1939	1,541,005.86
1884	10,085.73	1940	1,628,660.33
1885	8,246.67	1941	1,778,075.26
1886	9,336.75	1942	2,071,324.61
1887	11,716.77	1943	2,253,091.92
1888	7,761.64	1944	3,003,974.89
1889	16,427.22	1945	3,753,800.86
1890	13,131.74	1946	4,208,533.16
1891	14,978.63	1947	5,022,896.86
1892	28,339.27	1948	5,765,239.76
1893	28,962.17	1949	5,878,042.14
1894	53,385.46	1950	6,104,373.18
1895	32,893.08	1951	6,025,613.89
1896	35,810.99	1952	5,750,956.13
1897	47,138.71	1953	5,699,774.80
1898	46,774.47	1954	6,061,327.43
1899	53,075.43	1955	6,285,567.85
1900	80,683.73	1956	6,489,021.41
1901	225,867.34	1957	6,607,580.34
1902	189,018.19	1958	6,620,407.89
1903	143,072.26	1959	6,910,541.23
1904	237,021.29	1960	7,028,698.27
1905	244,654.97	1961	7,040,518.89
1906	276,613.92	1962	7,006,293.47
1907	376,491.37	1963	6,994,566.38
1908	351,670.09	1964	6,950,298.21
1909	365,404.90	1965	7,706,968.65
1910	401,091.25	1966	7,924,983.99
1911	458,301.86	1967	8,119,745.95
1912	467,698.53	1968	8,454,643.14
1913	516,176.53	1969	8,670,304.77
1914	592,404.35	1971	9,240,646.16
1915	625,633.14	1971	9,543,134.62
1916	656,245.97	1972	9,861,849.82
1917	714,611.81	1973	10,642,881.26
1918	925,532.41	1974	11,311,271.18
1919	1,049,206.73	1975	12,484,756.00
1920	1,285,560.16	1976	13,880,602.00
1921	1,566,234.63	1977	14,257,597.00
1922	2,044,218.97	1978	15,198,029.00
1923	2,017,561.11	1979	16,573,351.00
1924	2,432,641.50	1980	17,725,618.00
1925	2,484,250.18	1981	39,417,815.00
1926	2,407,008.10	1982	46,969,197.00
1927	2,497,923.97	1983	53,484,787.00
1928	2,556,634.44	1984	57,116,231.00
1929	2,449,179.79	1985	61,008,951.00
1930	2,640,701.41	1986	64,035,646.00
1931	2,677,855.36	1987	71,315,100.00
1932	2,321,798.71	1988	77,576,641.00
1933	1,869,754.74		
1934	1,402,776.02	Total	$834,406,472.66
1935	1,290,386.75		

EXALTED GRAND RULERS AND GRAND EXALTED RULERS

*Deceased.

†Grand Leading Esteemed Knight Davies filled out the unexpired term of Exalted Grand Ruler Maguire, who died before the expiration of his official term.

*1904-1905 Wm. J. O'Brien, Jr.
Baltimore, MD
Lodge No. 7
*1905-1906 Robert W. Brown
Louisville, KY
Lodge No. 8
*1906-1907 Henry A. Melvin
Oakland, CA
Lodge No. 171
*1907-1908 John K. Tener
Charleroi, PA
Lodge No. 494
*1908-1909 Rush L. Holland
Colorado Springs, CO
Lodge No. 309
*1909-1910 J. U. Sammis
LeMars, IA
Lodge No. 428
*1910-1911 August Herrmann
Cincinnati, OH
Lodge No. 5
*1911-1912 John P. Sullivan
New Orleans, LA
Lodge No. 30
*1912-1913 Thomas B. Mills
Superior, WI
Lodge No. 403
*1913-1914 Edward Leach
New York, NY
Lodge No. 1
*1914-1915 Raymond Benjamin
Napa, CA
Lodge No. 832
*1915-1916 James R. Nicholson
Springfield, MA
Lodge No. 61
*1916-1917 Edward Rightor
New Orleans, LA
Lodge No. 30
*1917-1918 Fred Harper
Lynchburg, VA
Lodge No. 321
*1918-1919 Bruce A. Campbell
East St. Louis, IL
Lodge No. 664
*1919-1920 Frank L. Rain
Fairbury, NE
Lodge No. 1203
*1920-1921 Wm. M. Abbott
San Francisco, CA
Lodge No. 3
*1921-1922 W. W. Mountain
Flint, MI
Lodge No. 222
*1922-1923 J. Edgar Masters
Charleroi, PA
Lodge No. 494
*1923-1924 James G. McFarland
Watertown, SD
Lodge No. 838
*1924-1925 John G. Price
Columbus, OH
Lodge No. 37
*1925-1926 William H. Atwell
Dallas, TX
Lodge No. 71

*1926-1927 Charles H. Grakelow
Philadelphia, PA
Lodge No. 2
*1927-1928 John F. Malley
Springfield, MA
Lodge No. 61
*1928-1929 Murray Hulbert
New York, NY
Lodge No. 1
*1929-1930 Walter P. Andrews
Atlanta, GA
Lodge No. 78
*1930-1931 Lawrence H. Rupp
Allentown, PA
Lodge No. 130
*1931-1932 John R. Coen
Sterling, CO
Lodge No. 1336
*1932-1933 Floyd E. Thompson
Moline, IL
Lodge No. 556
*1933-1934 Walter F. Meier
Seattle, WA
Lodge No. 92
*1934-1935 Michael F. Shannon
Los Angeles, CA
Lodge No. 99
*1935-1936 James T. Hallinan
Queens Borough, NY
Lodge No. 878
*1936-1937 David Sholtz
Daytona Beach, FL
Lodge No. 141
*1937-1938 Charles Spencer Hart
Mt. Vernon, NY
Lodge No. 842
*1938-1939 Edward J. McCormick
Toledo, OH
Lodge No. 53
*1939-1940 Henry C. Warner
Dixon, IL
Lodge No. 779
*1940-1941 Joseph G. Buch
Trenton, NJ
Lodge No. 105
*1941-1942 John S. McClelland
Atlanta, GA
Lodge No. 78
*1942-1943 E. Mark Sullivan
Boston, MA
Lodge No. 10
*1943-1944 Frank J. Lonergan
Portland, OR
Lodge No. 142
*1944-1945 Robert S. Barrett
Alexandria, VA
Lodge No. 758
*1945-1946 Wade H. Kepner
Wheeling, WV
Lodge No. 28
*1946-1947 Charles E. Broughton
Sheboygan, WI
Lodge No. 299
*1947-1948 L. A. Lewis
Anaheim, CA
Lodge No. 1345

---

*Deceased

484

*1948-1949 George I. Hall
Lynbrook, L.I., NY
Lodge No. 1515
*1949-1950 Emmett T. Anderson
Tacoma, WA
Lodge No. 174
*1950-1951 Joseph B. Kyle
Gary, IN
Lodge No. 1152
*1951-1952 Howard R. Davis
Williamsport, PA
Lodge No. 173
*1952-1952 Sam Stern
Fargo, ND
Lodge No. 260
*1953-1954 Earl E. James
Oklahoma City, OK
Lodge No. 417
*1954-1955 William J. Jernick
Nutley, NJ
Lodge No. 1290
*1955-1956 John L. Walker
Roanoke, VA
Lodge No. 197
*1956-1957 Fred L. Bohn
Zanesville, OH
Lodge No. 114
*1957-1958 H. L. Blackledge
Kearney, NE
Lodge No. 984
*1958-1959 Horace B. Wisely
Salinas, CA
Lodge No. 614
*1959-1960 William S. Hawkins
Coeur d'Alene, ID
Lodge No. 1254
*1960-1961 John E. Fenton
Lawrence, MA
Lodge No. 65
*1961-1962 William A. Wall
West Palm Beach, FL
Lodge No. 1352
*1962-1963 Lee A. Donaldson
Pittsburgh, PA
Lodge No. 932
*1963-1964 Ronald J. Dunn
Oneida, NY
Lodge No. 767
1964-1965 Robert G. Pruitt
Atlanta, GA
Lodge No. 1635
1965-1966 R. Leonard Bush
Inglewood, CA
Lodge No. 1492
*1966-1967 Raymond C. Dobson
Minot, ND
Lodge No. 1089
*1967-1968 Robert E. Boney
Las Cruces, NM
Lodge No. 1119
1968-1969 Edward W. McCabe
Nashville, TN
Lodge No. 72
1969-1970 Frank Hise
Corvallis, OR
Lodge No. 1413

1970-1971 Glenn L. Miller
Logansport, IN
Lodge No. 66
*1971-1972 E. Gene Fournace
Newark, OH
Lodge No. 391
1972-1973 Francis M. Smith
Sioux Falls, SD
Lodge No. 262
1973-1974 Robert A. Yothers
Seattle, WA
Lodge No. 92
1974-1975 Gerald Strohm
Fresno, CA
Lodge No. 439
1975-1976 Willis C. McDonald
New Orleans, LA
Lodge No. 30
1976-1977 George B. Klein
Lincoln, NE
Lodge No. 80
1977-1978 Homer Huhn, Jr.
Mount Pleasant, PA
Lodge No. 868
1978-1979 Leonard J. Bristol
Saranac Lake, NY
Lodge No. 1508
1979-1980 Robert Grafton
North Palm Beach, FL
Lodge No. 2069
1980-1981 H. Foster Sears
Macomb, IL
Lodge No. 1009
1981-1982 Raymond V. Arnold
Jackson, MI
Lodge No. 113
1982-1983 Marvin M. Lewis
Brawley, CA
Lodge No. 1420
1983-1984 Kenneth V. Cantoli
Hasbrouck Heights, NJ
Lodge No. 1962
1984-1985 Frank O. Garland
Centralia-Chehalis, WA
Lodge No. 2435
1985-1986 John T. Traynor
Devils Lake, ND
Lodge No. 1216
1986-1987 Peter T. Affatato
Hicksville, NY
Lodge No. 1931
1987-1988 Ted Callicott
Paris, TN
Lodge No. 816

---

*Deceased

485

GRAND SECRETARIES

At the first regular Session of the Grand Lodge of the Benevolent and Protective Order of Elks held in New York, February 12, 1871, E. G. Browne was elected Grand Secretary. At that meeting William Coffin acted as Secretary pro tem. E.G. Browne served until December 10, 1871, when A. Hamilton Mulligan was elected Grand Secretary.

At a Session of the Grand Lodge held on June 16, 1872, Thomas G. Gaynor, a Past Exalted Ruler of New York Lodge, was elected Grand Recording and Corresponding Secretary.

At that meeting at which Thomas G. Gaynor was elected, Henry P. O'Neil acted as Grand Secretary pro tem.

William Coffin was elected Grand Secretary in December, 1972, and he served until, at a Session of the Grand Lodge held in December, 1877, Henry P. O'Neil was elected Grand Secretary.

At a Session of the Grand Lodge held in December, 1878, R. S. Martin, who was for many years Secretary of New York Lodge No. 1, was elected Grand Secretary.

In December, 1881, Arthur C. Moreland was elected Grand secretary and for the first time the Grand Secretary had an office and suitable records.

He served until 1890.

Allen O. Myers, of Cincinnati, Ohio, Lodge No. 5, served as Grand Secretary from 1890 to 1894.

In 1894, George A. Reynolds, of Saginaw, Michigan, Lodge No. 47, was elected Grand Secretary in Atlantic City, New Jersey.

Due to the Jamestown Controversy and the resulting elections held by two Grand Lodges, also elected as Grand Secretary (by those at Jamestown, New York) in 1894 was Clate A. Smith, who obtained possession of the Grand Lodge files and supplies, and transacted affairs of office until the two Grand Lodges reconciled in Buffalo, New York, on May 20, 1895. Grand Secretary Reynolds' legal action to secure these records was one of many suits filed in connection with the schism, and the records' absence hampered his activities until the fall of 1895, when he resumed as the Order's sole Grand Secretary until the Grand Lodge Session of 1904.

At that Session Fred C. Robinson of Dubuque, IA, Lodge No. 297 was elected Grand Secretary. He served in that capacity until September, 1927, when he resigned.

Upon the resignation of Fred C. Robinson, J. Edgar Masters of Charleroi, PA, Lodge No. 494, was appointed to the position.

Brother Masters was re-elected at each succeeding Grand Lodge until 1954. He passed away in September of 1954 and Lee A. Donaldson was appointed to complete the unexpired term and he continued to serve in this capacity until he was elected as Grand Exalted Ruler in 1962.

Franklin J. Fitzpatrick, Lynbrook Lodge No. 1515, was elected in 1962 and served until his death in 1970.

Controller Frank Vossel agreed to assume the office until a successor could be found. He resigned in early 1971 when Homer Huhn, Jr. was appointed to the post.

Brother Huhn served until 1977 when he was elected Grand Exalted Ruler. At the same time, Stanley F. Kocur, East Chicago, IN, Lodge No. 981 was elected Grand Secretary. He was re-elected to the office in 1978. Brother Kocur served all ten years of the twelfth decade as Grand Secretary.

GRAND TREASURERS

At the organization meeting of the Benevolent and Protective Order of Elks held on February 16, 1868, H. Vandemark was elected Treasurer.

At the meeting of February 21, 1869, William H. Brown was elected Treasurer.

In 1870 the Treasurer was Charles T. White.

Previously the word "Treasurer" had been used, but in 1870, White was referred to as "Grand Treasurer."

This was for the First Degree; for the Second Degree William Coffin was Grand Treasurer.

At the first meeting of the Grand Lodge, February 12, 1871, Hugh P. O'Neil was Grand Treasurer.

In 1872 the Grand Treasurer was Charles T. White. He served in that office until 1884. He was succeeded by the following:

Joseph F. Waring, New York, NY, Lodge No. 1	1884-1886
Hugh P. O'Neil, New York, NY, Lodge 1	1886-1889
James O. Gray, Lowell, MA, Lodge No. 87	1889-1891
William F. Bechel, Omaha, NE, Lodge No. 39	1891-1895
Percy G. Williams, Brooklyn, NY, Lodge 22	1895-1896
Edward S. Orris, Meadville, PA, Lodge No. 219	1896-1902
Samuel H. Needs, Cleveland, OH, Lodge No. 18	1902-1904
John K. Tener, Charleroi, PA, Lodge No. 494	1904-1907
Edward Leach, New York, NY, Lodge No. 1	1907-1913
Charles A. White, Chicago, IL, Lodge No. 4	1913-1919
P. J. Brennan, Dension, TX, Lodge No. 238	1919-1923
John K. Burch, Grand Rapids, MI, Lodge No. 48	1923-1926
Fred A. Morris, Mexico, MO, Lodge No. 919	1926-1929
Lloyd Maxwell, Marshalltown, IA, Lodge No. 312	1929-1932
James F. Duffy, Providence, RI, Lodge No. 14	1932-1935
Edward J. McCormick, Toledo, OH, Lodge No. 53	1935-1938
Robert South Barrett, Alexandria, VA, Lodge No. 758	1938-1941
George M. McLean, El Reno, OK, Lodge No. 743	1941-1944
John F. Burke, Boston, MA, Lodge No. 10	1944-1947
Joseph B. Kyle, Gary, IN, Lodge No. 1152	1947-1950
William J. Jernick, Nutley, NJ, Lodge No. 1290	1950-1952
Edward A. Dutton, Savannah, GA, Lodge No. 183	1952-1954
Robert G. Pruitt, Buckhead (Atlanta), GA, Lodge No. 1635	1954-1955
Edward A. Spry, Boston, MA, Lodge No. 10	1955-1957
Robert G. Pruitt, Buckhead (Atlanta), GA, Lodge No. 1635	1957-1959
Arthur M. Umlandt, Muscatine, IA, Lodge No. 304	1959-1962
John B. Morey, Palo Alto, CA, Lodge No. 1471	1962-1965
Chelsie J. Senerchia, Miami, FL, Lodge No. 948	1965-1968
Edwin J. Maley, New Haven, CT, Lodge No. 25	1968-1971
H. Foster Sears, Macomb, IL, Lodge No. 1009	1971-1974
Frank V. Archibald, Fargo, ND, Lodge No. 260	1974-1977
George J. Balbach, Queens Borough (Elmhurst), NY, Lodge No. 878	1977-1978
William H. Collisson, Linton, IN, Lodge No. 866	1978-1981
Edward M. Schlieter, New Braunfels, TX, Lodge No. 2279	1981-1984
Leonard E. Bennett, Rifle, CO, Lodge No. 2195	1984-1986
Robert D. Moore, Fairfield, IA, Lodge No. 1192	1986-1987
Marlin J. Haack, Bemidji, MN, Lodge No. 1052	1987-1988

CHAIRMEN OF THE BOARD OF GRAND TRUSTEES

The Charter granted by New York State incorporating the Grand Lodge of the Benevolent and Protective Order of Elks provided that "the persons particularly named in the first section of the act shall be the first Trustees of said corporation." As George J. Green, who was the first Exalted Ruler was the first one named in the list of Trustees, it can be assumed that he was also the first Chairman of the Board of Grand Trustees.

William Sheppard, New York, NY, Lodge No. 1	1871-1872
Hugh P. O'Neil, New York, NY, Lodge No. 1	1872-1873
Henry P. O'Neil, New York, NY, Lodge No.1	1873-1874
George F. McDonald, New York, NY, Lodge No. 1	1874-1875
Joseph C. Pinckney, New York, NY, Lodge No. 1	1875-1876
Antonio Pastor, New York, NY, Lodge No. 1	1876-1877
Lewis R. Kean, Louisville, KY, Lodge No. 8	1877-1878
Antonio Pastor, New York, NY, Lodge No. 1	1878-1879
William E. Lex, Philadelphia, PA, Lodge No. 2	1879-1880
L. C. Waehner, New York, NY, Lodge No. 1	1880-1882
Antonio Pastor, New York, NY, Lodge No. 1	1882-1883
William Bowron, New York, NY, Lodge No. 1	1883-1884
David T. Lynch, Brooklyn, NY, Lodge No. 22	1884-1885
Edward H. Warker, New York, NY, Lodge No. 1	1885-1889
Charles A. Wilson, Providence, RI, Lodge No.14	1889-1890
Willard C. VanDerlip, Boston, MA, Lodge No. 10	1890-1896
Jerome B. Fisher, Jamestown, NY, Lodge No. 263	1896-1898
B. M. Allen, Birmingham, AL, Lodge No. 79	1898-1899
Joseph T. Fanning, Indianapolis, IN, Lodge No. 13	1899-1903
Henry W. Mears, Baltimore, MD, Lodge No. 7	1903-1904
Robert W. Brown, Louisville, KY, Lodge No. 8	1904-1905
John D. O'Shea, Lynn, MA, Lodge No. 117	1905-1907
W. H. Haviland, Butte, MT, Lodge No. 240	1907-1909
Charles C. Schmidt, Wheeling, WV, Lodge No. 28	1909-1910
Thomas F. McNulty, Baltimore, MD, Lodge No. 7	1910-1911
Thomas B. Mills, Superior, WI, Lodge No. 403	1911-1912
Alfred T. Holley, Hackensack, NJ, Lodge No. 658	1912-1913
Perry A. Clay, Denver, CO, Lodge No. 17	1913-1914
James R. Nicholson, Springfield, MA, Lodge No. 61	1914-1915
Cary L. Applegate, Owensboro, KY, Lodge No. 44	1915-1916
John J. Faulkner, East St. Louis, IL, Lodge No. 664	1916-1917
Samuel V. Perrott, Indianapolis, IN, Lodge No. 13	1917-1918
J. Edgar Masters, Charleroi, PA, Lodge No. 494	1918-1920
George D. Locke, Rogers, AR, Lodge No. 1223	1920-1921
Patrick T. Powers, Jersey City, NJ, Lodge No. 211	1921-1922
C. F. J. McCue, Cambridge, MA, Lodge No. 839	1922-1923
W. E. Drislane, Albany, NY, Lodge No. 49	1923-1924
John Halpin, Kansas City, MO, Lodge No. 26	1924-1925
R. A. Gordon, Atlanta, GA, Lodge No. 78	1925-1926
Robert A. Scott, Linton, IN, Lodge No. 866	1926-1927
Edward W. Cotter, Hartford, CT, Lodge No. 19	1927-1929
Clyde Jennings, Lynchburg, VA, Lodge No. 321	1929-1930
Ralph Hagan, Los Angeles, CA, Lodge No. 99	1930-1932
John K. Burch, Grand Rapids, MI, Lodge No. 48	1932-1933
A. Charles Stewart, Frostburg, MD, Lodge No. 470	1933-1934
James S. Richardson, Cincinnati, OH, Lodge No. 5	1934-1935

Lloyd Maxwell, Marshalltown, IA, Lodge No. 312	1935-1937
Henry A. Guenther, Newark, NJ, Lodge No. 21	1937-1938
John S. McClelland, Atlanta, GA, Lodge No. 78	1938-1939
J. G. Buch, Trenton, NJ, Lodge No. 105	1939-1940
William T. Phillips, New York, NY, Lodge No. 1	1940-1941
J. Ford Zietlow, Aberdeen, SD, Lodge No. 1046	1941-1942
Fred B. Mellmann, Oakland, CA, Lodge No. 171	1942-1943
Joseph B. Kyle, Gary, IN, Lodge No. 1152	1943-1944
Wade H. Kepner, Wheeling, WV, Lodge No. 28	1944-1945
C. E. Broughton, Sheboygan, WI, Lodge No. 299	1945-1946
John E. Drummey, Seattle, WA, Lodge No. 92	1946-1948
Hugh W. Hicks, Jackson, TN, Lodge No. 192	1948-1950
Sam Stern, Fargo, ND, Lodge No. 260	1950-1951
D. E. Lambourne, Salt Lake City, UT, Lodge No. 85	1951-1953
Thomas J. Brady, Brookline, MA, Lodge No. 886	1953-1954
Fred L. Bohn, Zanesville, OH, Lodge No. 114	1954-1955
Nick H. Feder, Belleville, IL, Lodge No. 281	1955-1956
Ronald J. Dunn, Oneida, NY, Lodge NO. 767	1956-1957
Arthur M. Umlandt, Muscatine, IA, Lodge No. 304	1957-1958
William A. Wall, West Palm Beach, FL, Lodge No. 1352	1958-1960
Dewey E. S. Kuhns, Charleston, WV, Lodge No. 202	1960-1961
Edward A. Spry, Boston, MA, Lodge No. 10	1961-1962
Jacob L. Sherman, Denver, CO, Lodge No. 17	1962-1963
Edwin J. Alexander, Aberdeen, WA, Lodge No. 593	1963-1964
R. Leonard Bush, Inglewood, CA, Lodge No. 1402	1964-1965
Edward W. McCabe, Nashville, TN, Lodge No. 72	1965-1966
Robert E. Boney, Las Cruces, NM, Lodge No. 1119	1966-1967
Joseph F. Bader, Lyndhurst, NJ, Lodge No. 1505	1967-1968
Vincent H. Grocott, Santa Barbara, CA, Lodge No. 613	1968-1969
Francis P. Hart, Watertown, NY, Lodge No. 496	1969-1970
Francis M. Smith, Sioux Falls, SD, Lodge No. 262	1970-1971
H. Beecher Charmbury, State College, PA, Lodge No. 1600	1971-1972
John B. Morey, Palo Alto, CA, Lodge No. 1471	1972-1973
W. Edward Wilson, Newton, MA, Lodge No. 1327	1973-1974
George B. Klein, Lincoln, NE, Lodge No. 80	1974-1975
Alton J. Thompson, Salt Lake City, UT, Lodge No. 85	1975-1976
Robert Grafton, North Palm Beach, FL, Lodge No. 2069	1976-1977
Leonard J. Bristol, Saranac Lake, NY, Lodge No. 1508	1977-1978
H. Foster Sears, Macomb, IL, Lodge No. 1009	1977-1978
Frank O. Garland, Centralia-Chehalis, WA, Lodge No. 2431	1978-1979
Marvin M. Lewis, Brawley, CA, Lodge No. 1420	1979-1980
Alex M. Harman, Jr., Pulaski, VA, Lodge No. 1067	1980-1981
John T. Traynor, Devils Lake, ND, Lodge No. 1216	1981-1982
Robert J. Tancredi, Toledo, OR, Lodge No. 1664	1982-1983
Gerald L. Powell, Peru, IN, Lodge No. 365	1983-1984
Peter T. Affatato, Hicksville, NY, Lodge No. 1931	1984-1986
Bob J. Bybee, Idaho Falls, ID, Lodge No. 1087	1986-1987
Lester C. Hess, Jr., Wheeling, WV, Lodge No. 28	1987-1988

CHIEF JUSTICES OF THE GRAND FORUM

Charles E. Pickett, Waterloo, IA, Lodge No. 290	1907-1908
Morse Rohnert, Detroit, MI, Lodge No. 34	1908-1909
William H. Moore, Seattle, WA, Lodge No. 92	1909-1910
Thomas J. Cogan, Cincinnati, OH, Lodge No. 5	1910-1911
Robert W. Brown, Louisville, KY, Lodge No. 8	1911-1912
Perry A. Shanor, Sistersville, WV, Lodge No. 333	1912-1913
Edward Rightor, New Orleans, LA, Lodge No. 30	1913-1914
Henry L. Kennan, Spokane, WA, Lodge No. 228	1914-1915
Thomas J. Cogan, Cincinnati, OH, Lodge No. 5	1915-1916
Robert W. Brown, Louisville, KY, Lodge No. 8	1916-1917
John H. Mitchell, St. Paul, MN, Lodge No. 59	1917-1918
Albert T. Brophy, Brooklyn, NY, Lodge No. 22	1918-1919
Henry L. Kennan, Spokane, WA, Lodge No. 228	1919-1921
Robert W. Brown, Louisville, KY, Lodge No. 8	1921-1922
William J. Conway, Wisconsin Rapids, WI, Lodge No. 693	1922-1923
John G. Price, Columbus, OH, Lodge No. 37	1923-1924
Henry L. Kennan, Spokane, WA, Lodge No. 228	1924-1925
Thomas J. Lennon, San Rafael, CA, Lodge No. 1108	1925-1926
John J. Carton, Flint, MI, Lodge No. 222	1926-1927
William J. Conway, Wisconsin Rapids, WI, Lodge No. 693	1927-1928
Walter P. Andrews, Atlanta, GA, Lodge No. 78	1928-1929
Andrew J. Casey, Newburyport, MA, Lodge No. 909	1929-1930
Walter P. Meier, Seattle, WA, Lodge No. 92	1930-1931
Floyd E. Thompson, Moline, IL, Lodge No. 556	1931-1932
Dwight E. Campbell, Aberdeen, SD, Lodge No. 1046	1932-1933
Arthur S. Tompkins, Haverstraw, NY, Lodge No. 877	1933-1934
John S. McClelland, Atlanta, GA, Lodge No. 78	1934-1935
Frank J. Lonergan, Portland, OR, Lodge No. 142	1935-1936
Wilbur M. Alter, Victor, CO, Lodge No. 367	1936-1937
Clayton F. Van Pelt, Fond Du Lac, WI, Lodge No. 57	1937-1938
Benn Kenyon, Auburn, NY, Lodge No. 474	1938-1939
Marshall F. McComb, Los Angeles, CA, Lodge No. 99	1939-1940
E. Mark Sullivan, Boston, MA, Lodge No. 10	1940-1941
James M. Fitzgerald, Omaha, NE, Lodge No. 39	1941-1942
Daniel J. Kelly, Knoxville, TN, Lodge No. 160	1942-1943
John M. McCabe, Toledo, OH, Lodge No. 53	1943-1944
Henry G. Wenzel, Queens Borough, NY, Lodge No. 878	1944-1945
George W. Bruce, Montrose, CO, Lodge No. 1053	1945-1946
Allen B. Hannay, Houston, TX, Lodge No. 151	1946-1947
John E. Mullen, Providence, RI, Lodge No. 14	1947-1948
Clyde E. Jones, Ottumwa, IA, Lodge No. 347	1948-1949
Alto Adams, Tallahassee, FL, Lodge No. 937	1949-1950
Benjamin F. Watson, Lansing, MI, Lodge No. 196	1950-1951
S. D. McKinnon, Miles City, MT, Lodge No. 537	1951-1952
John E. Mullen, Providence, RI, Lodge No. 14	1952-1953
Henry S. Lindsley, Denver, CO, Lodge No. 17	1953-1954
John L. Walker, Roanoke, VA, Lodge No. 197	1954-1955
John F. Scileppi, Queens Borough, NY, Lodge No. 878	1955-1956
J. Paul Kuhn, Aurora, IL, Lodge No. 705	1956-1957
Glen S. Paterson, Watertown, SD, Lodge No. 839	1957-1958
John C. Cochrane, Toledo, OH, Lodge No. 53	1958-1959

John F. Scileppi, Queens Borough, NY, Lodge No. 878	1959-1960
A. F. Bray, Richmond, CA, Lodge No. 1251	1960-1961
Alfred E. LaFrance, Racine, WI, Lodge No. 252	1961-1962
Joseph O. Spangler, Greybull, WY, Lodge No. 1431	1962-1963
Robert G. Pruitt, Buckhead, (Atlanta), Ga, Lodge No. 1635	1963-1964
Donald K. Quayle, Alameda, Ca, Lodge No. 1015	1964-1965
Benjamin F. Watson, Lansing, MI, Lodge No. 196	1966-1967
Thad Eure, Raleigh, NY, Lodge No. 735	1967-1968
Harold J. Field, Brookline, MA, Lodge No. 886	1968-1969
John T. Raftis, Colville, WA, Lodge No. 1753	1969-1971
Thomas F. Rhodes, Jr., Hamilton, NJ, Lodge No. 2262	1971-1972
Willis C. McDonald, New Orleans, LA, Lodge No. 30	1972-1973
Bernard Lawler, Redondo Beach, CA, Lodge No. 1378	1973-1974
Hal M. Randall, Salem, OR, Lodge No. 336	1974-1975
Thomas A. Goodwin, Wheeling, WV, Lodge No. 28	1976-1977
Alex M. Harman, Jr., Pulaski, VA, Lodge No. 1067	1977-1978
Edward C. Alexander, Great Falls MT, Lodge No. 214	1978-1979
William J. Steinbrecher, New Hyde Park, NY, Lodge No. 2107	1979-1980
Sidney J. Nicholson, Florence, OR, Lodge No. 1858	1980-1981
Robert B. Webb, Santa Ana, CA, Lodge No. 794	1981-1982
Donald F. Nemitz, St. Charles, MO, Lodge No. 690	1982-1983
Edward W. Connolly, Livingston, NJ, Lodge No. 1855	1983-1984
George J. Balbach, Queens Borough, NY, Lodge No. 878	1984-1985
William Keylor Smith, Walla Walla, WA, Lodge No. 287	1985-1986
Eugene F. Costello, Denver, CO, Lodge No. 17	1986-1987
Robert J. Sabin, Arlington Heights, IL, Lodge No. 2048	1987-1988

CHAIRMEN OF COMMITTEE ON LAWS AND SUPERVISION, LAWS AND APPEALS, AND COMMITTEE ON JUDICIARY

At the meeting of the Grand Lodge on March 5, 1871, Exalted Grand Ruler Green appointed a Committee of three on Laws and Supervision, of which he made Thomas Grattan Riggs the Chairman.

In December, 1872, the Chairman was L. Nevers.

On March 8, 1874, several Committees were appointed but the Proceedings make no reference to the appointment of a Committee on Laws and Supervision.

In the Proceedings of December 13, 1874, however, there is reference to the report of a Committee on Laws and Supervision by Henry P. O'Neil as Chairman.

At the end of that same meeting a Committee on Laws and Supervision was appointed of which Joseph C. Pinckney was Chairman. Pinckney was continued as Chairman for the Committee for the year 1876.

1877, Henry P. O'Neil.
1878, Henry P. O'Neil.
1879, Henry P. O'Neil.
1880, Edwin A. Perry, Boston Lodge No. 10.
1881, G. Howard Jones, Boston Lodge No. 10.
1882, Willard C. VanDerlip, Boston Lodge No. 10.
1883, Willard C. VanDerlip, Boston Lodge No. 10.
1884, Willard C. VanDerlip, Boston Lodge No. 10.
1885, W. C. Jones, St. Louis Lodge No. 9.
1886, Willard C. VanDerlip, Boston Lodge No. 10.
1887, Willard C. VanDerlip, Boston Lodge No. 10.
1888, Leroy Andrus, Buffalo Lodge No. 23.
1889, Willard C. VanDerlip, Boston Lodge No. 10.
1890, Charles A. Wilson, Providence, R. I., Lodge No. 14.

In 1891 the name of the Committee on Laws and Supervision was changed to Committee on Laws and Appeals. The first Chairman, for the year 1891, was L. M. Hadden, Cincinnati, Ohio, Lodge No. 5.

1892, L. M. Hadden, Cincinnati, Ohio, Lodge No. 5.
1893, Lewis E. Griffith, Troy, N. Y., Lodge No. 141.
1894, Lewis E. Griffith, Troy, N. Y., Lodge No. 141.
1895, M. A. Foran, Cleveland, Ohio, Lodge No. 18.
1896, M. A. Foran, Cleveland, Ohio, Lodge No. 18.
1897, Thomas F. Turner, Canton, Ohio, Lodge No. 68.
1898, Thomas F. Turner, Canton, Ohio, Lodge No. 68.
1899, Charles H. Smith, Jackson, Mich., Lodge No. 113.

In 1899 the name of the Committee was changed to the Committee on Laws. The first Chairman of the Committee under that name and acting for the years 1899-1900 was Charles H. Smith, Jackson, Mich., Lodge No. 113.

1900-1901, Charles H. Smith, Jackson, Mich., Lodge No. 113.
1901-1902, Charles H. Smith, Jackson, Mich., Lodge No. 113.
1902-1903, Charles H. Smith, Jackson, Mich., Lodge No. 113.
1903-1904, John Galvin, Cincinnati, Ohio, Lodge No. 5.
1904-1905, J. U. Sammis, LeMars, Iowa, Lodge No. 428.
1905-1906, J. U. Sammis, LeMars, Iowa, Lodge No. 428.

In 1907 the name of the Committee was changed to the Committee on Judiciary, which name it has retained up to the time of this History. The first Chairman of the Committee under that name for the years 1907-1908 was J. U. Sammis, LeMars, IA, Lodge No. 428.

1908-1909,	J. U. Sammis, LeMars, IA, Lodge No. 428
1909-1911,	Charles P. Bates, Sioux Falls, SD, Lodge No. 262
1911-1912,	Edward Rightor, New Orleans, LA, Lodge No. 30
1912-1913,	Raymond Benjamin, Napa, CA, Lodge No. 832
1913-1914,	Albert R. Brophy, Brooklyn, NY, Lodge No. 22
1914-1915,	Edward Rightor, New Orleans, LA, Lodge No. 30
1915-1918,	Frank L. Rain, Fairbury, NE, Lodge No. 1203
1918-1919,	William M. Abbott, San Francisco, CA, Lodge No. 3
1919-1922,	J. G. McFarland, Watertown, SD, Lodge No. 838
1922-1923,	Lawrence H. Rupp, Allentown, PA, Lodge No. 130
1923-1926,	John F. Malley, Springfield, MA, Lodge No. 61
1926-1929,	Lawrence H. Rupp, Allentown, PA, Lodge No. 130
1929-1930,	John R. Coen, Sterling, CO, Lodge No. 1336
1930-1931,	James T. Hallinan, Queens Borough, NY, Lodge No. 878
1931-1932,	Walter F. Meier, Seattle, WA, Lodge No. 92
1932-1936,	E. Mark Sullivan, Brookline, MA, Lodge No. 886
1936-1938,	Daniel J. Kelly, Knoxville, TN, Lodge No. 160
1938-1940,	Guy T. Tou Velle, Lincoln, NE, Lodge No. 80
1940-1941,	Martin J. Cunningham, Danbury, CT, Lodge No. 120
1941-1942,	Philip U. Gayaut, Washington, DC, Lodge No. 15
1942-1944,	Clyde E. Jones, Ottumwa, IA, Lodge No. 347
1944-1945,	Clayton F. Van Pelt, Fond du Lac, WI, Lodge No. 57
1945-1946,	John E. Mullen, Providence, RI, Lodge No. 14
1946-1947,	Robert S. Farrell, Jr., Portland, OR, Lodge No. 142
1947-1948,	J. C. Travis, Omaha, NE, Lodge No. 39
1948-1952,	Earl E. James, Oklahoma City, OK, Lodge No. 417
1952-1953,	John C. Cochrane, Toledo, OH, Lodge No. 53
1953-1955,	H. L. Blackledge, Kearney, NE, Lodge No. 984
1955-1957,	William S. Hawkins, Coeur d'Alene, ID, Lodge No. 1254
1957-1960,	John E. Fenton, Lawrence, MA, Lodge No. 65
1960-1962,	Benjamin F. Watson, Lansing, MI, Lodge No. 196
1962-1965,	John T. Raftis, Colville, WA, Lodge No. 196
1965-1969,	Glenn L. Miller, Logansport, IN, Lodge No. 66
1969-1972,	Thomas A. Goodwin, Wheeling, WV, Lodge No. 28
1972-1974,	Edward C. Alexander, Great Falls, MT, Lodge No. 214
1974-1977,	George J. Balbach, Queens Borough (Elmhurst), NY, Lodge No. 878
1977-1978,	Edward W. Connolly, Livingston, NJ, Lodge No. 1855
1978-1980,	Raymond V. Arnold, Jackson, MI, Lodge No. 113
1980-1982,	Eugene F. Costello, Denver, CO, Lodge No. 17
1982-1983,	Robert J. Sabin, Arlington Heights, IL, Lodge No. 2048
1983-1985,	Seymour Nathanson, Portland, ME, Lodge No. 188
1985-1986,	Robert Bean, Coolidge-Florence, AZ, Lodge No. 2350
1986-1988,	John J. Delworth, Jr., Rochester, IN, Lodge No. 2120

ELKS WAR RELIEF COMMISSION, WORLD WAR I

RECEIPTS

Elks War Relief Fund, per capita assessment of $2.10 Cash received from Grand Treasurer	$ 973,932.21	
Liberty Bonds received in payment	25,850.00	
	$ 999,782.21	
Donation of Brother Edward W. Cotter, Hartford, Conn., Lodge No. 19	$ 100.00	$ 999,882.21
Refunds of Advances for Vocational Education		598,690.91
Receipts from Returned Items account Loan Fund		1,805.08
Receipts from Motion Picture Contracts		8,841.23
*Interest on Deposits of Commission		21,897.35
*Interest on Liberty Bonds in Safety Deposit Vault		2,365.27
		$1,633,482.05

*Interest on Deposits of Commission	$ 21,897.35	
*Interest on Liberty Bonds, Safety Deposit Vault	2,365.27	
Interest on Deposits of Grand Secretary office	3,648.10	
Total Interest Earned	$ 27,910.72	

DISBURSEMENTS

July 12th, 1917, to July 1st, 1918	$ 223,906.65	
July 1st, 1918, to June 14, 1919	466,103.45	
June 14th, 1919, to June 5th, 1920	489,611.91	
June 5th, 1920, to June 15th, 1921	191,733.92	
	$1,371,355.93	
Cash in Banks ...$236,276.12		
Liberty Bonds in Safety Deposit Vault....$ 25,850.00	$ 262,126.12	$1,633,482.05

N. B.—Revolving Loan Fund account for disabled soldiers, sailors and marines:		
Repayments received to date	$ 598,690.91	
Payments made to date	503,000.00	
Balance	$ 95,690.91	
Amount expended on account of Support Cases to May 31, 1921	$ 60,671.78	
Total Appropriations to Loan and Support Funds for disabled soldiers, sailors and marines	$ 200,000.00	

ELKS WAR RELIEF COMMISSION, WORLD WAR I—*Continued*

ASSETS

Cash on Hand	$ 236,276.12
Liberty Bonds, par value	25,850.00
Reconstruction Hospital, Boston, Mass.	308,355.45
Balance due from outstanding Loans to disabled ex-service men	38,018.45
Moving Pictures, negatives (2), prints (55) and balance due on contracts	7,540.00
	$ 616,040.02

These remaining assets were turned over to the Elks National Headquarters Commission.
The amount realized on the Reconstruction Hospital in Boston was $ 100,000.00

ELKS NATIONAL HEADQUARTERS AND MEMORIAL BUILDING

DETAILS OF COST

Land	$ 375,012.00
Building Construction	
General Contract	2,037,103.33
Architects' Fees	182,336.13
Premium on Contractor's Bonds	29,710.51
Preliminary Expense	12,969.89
General Expenses	83,309.13
Insurance (Indemnity, Liability, etc.)	16,478.92
Special Assessments—City of Chicago	39,628.31
Murals, Paintings, Sculptures, Statues, Decorative Paintings, Interior Furnishings, Furniture, Rugs, Landscaping, etc.	519,222.24
Maintenance and Administration to date of Dedication—July 1926	141,728.38
Transferred to Publication Fund	7,027.78
TOTAL	$3,444,526.62

SOURCE OF FUNDS

War Relief Fund	$ 356,895.06
First Per Capita Assessment	770,749.71
Second " " "	537,116.70
Third " " "	831,924.00
Fourth " " "	371,234.50
Interest on Deposits and Assessments	87,726.77
Miscellaneous Receipts	8,630.00
Elks Magazine	480,249.88
TOTAL	$3,444,526.62

THE ELKS MAGAZINE

EARNINGS OF THE ELKS MAGAZINE AND DISPOSITION OF SAME

DISPOSITION OF EARNINGS

To Grand Lodge for reduction of per capita tax and other Grand Lodge uses..........	$ 8,336,366.00
To National Memorial Headquarters Commission to cover cost of art features-National Memorial Building, Chicago..........	480,000.00
To National Memorial Headquarters Commission to cover maintenance, taxes, city improvements, and administrative costs-National Memorial Building, Chicago..........	2,477,338.00
To Grand Lodge for additions and new buildings-Elks National Home, Bedford, Virginia..........	350,000.00
To Grand Lodge-to defray cost of District Deputy visits..........	24,413.00
To Elks War Commission-for furtherance of war effort programs..........	50,000.00
To Elks National Veterans Service Commission for furtherance of post-war veterans rehabilitation programs..........	100,000.00
To Elks National Foundation for furtherance of philanthropic activities..........	125,000.00
To Grand Lodge-for creation of emergency reserve fund..........	520,000.00
To Grand Lodge to defray costs of rededication exercises, Elks National Memorial Building, Chicago 1946..........	15,649.00
To Grand Lodge as a contribution to "Elks Disaster Fund"..........	20,000.00
To Grand Lodge for partial funding of Grand Lodge Computer Department..........	412,959.00
	$12,911,725.00
Honorarium, 1976..........	15,000.00
Honorarium, 1985..........	23,400.00
Honorarium, 1986..........	5,000.00
Surplus at June 1, 1988..........	2,874,438.00
Aggregate Earnings-June 1, 1922 to May 31, 1988...	$15,829,563.00

ELKS NATIONAL FOUNDATION
CONTRIBUTIONS AND DISTRIBUTIONS

CONTRIBUTIONS

From the date of its inception to March 31, 1988, donations had been received by the Foundation from various sources as follows:

Grand Lodge	$ 200,000.00
State Associations, subordinate Lodges, individuals and miscellaneous donations	70,169,651.07
	$70,369,651.07

ELKS NATIONAL FOUNDATION - Continued

Distribution of income received by the Foundation is as follows:

State Charities Grants / Major Projects	$19,671,025.00
Scholarship and Grant Programs	29,399,772.99
Elks National Home	4,100,000.00
"Hoop Shoot" Free Throw Competition	2,756,740.77
Drug Awareness Program	1,106,909.23
National Service Commission	786,400.00
Youth Leadership & Cerebral Palsy Grants	1,408,061.09
Miscellaneous & Achievement Awards	225,203.81
Boy Scouts of America/Eagle Scout Awards	24,000.00
Total	$59,478,112.89

SUMMARY OF DONATIONS TO THE ELKS NATIONAL FOUNDATION
60-Year Cumulative since Inception-1928 thru March 31, 1988

States/Areas	Members in State 4-1-87	Donations By—Individuals	Lodges	Associations State/Distr.	Group Totals 3-31-88	Average per Member	Bequests	Grand Total of Donations
Alabama	8,641	109,482.86	85,152.25	4,600.00	199,235.11	23.056		199,235.11
Alaska	12,514	483,005.77	101,623.59	5,030.00	589,659.36	47.119	900.00	590,559.36
Arizona	34,489	1,610,723.52	337,153.27	39,805.32	1,987,682.11	57.632	320,806.45	2,308,488.56
Arkansas	7,076	258,616.40	83,515.50	4,300.00	346,431.90	48.958	39,832.51	386,264.41
California	164,154	7,699,303.60	1,930,800.08	71,323.85	9,701,427.53	59.099	641,802.26	10,343,229.79
Colorado	50,354	1,445,207.42	531,918.96	7,359.93	1,984,486.31	39.410	48,173.32	2,032,659.63
Connecticut	32,531	1,029,936.14	190,959.72	31,700.00	1,252,595.86	38.504	37,752.37	1,290,348.23
Florida	86,664	1,655,352.85	670,076.64	12,100.00	2,337,529.49	26.972	149,730.86	2,487,260.35
Georgia	11,581	260,059.63	105,251.16	2,810.00	368,120.79	31.786		368,120.79
Guam Island	323	9,993.00	12,570.00		22,563.00	69.854		22,563.00
Hawaii	4,121	261,630.25	74,481.15		336,111.40	81.560	3,011.51	339,122.91
Idaho	17,162	228,872.52	93,833.88	5,950.32	328,656.72	19.150		328,656.72
Illinois	55,390	2,005,564.07	413,474.81	34,791.80	2,453,830.68	44.300	580,853.19	3,034,683.87
Indiana	46,090	1,395,148.39	357,527.10	26,219.00	1,778,894.49	38.596	213,657.08	1,992,551.57
Iowa	22,537	793,425.13	160,250.25	13,533.08	967,208.46	42.916	10,268.73	977,477.19
Kansas	19,564	643,747.23	130,985.50	14,667.00	789,399.73	40.349	35,912.25	825,311.98
Kentucky	7,766	244,861.44	62,920.10	6,250.00	314,031.54	40.436	4,100.00	318,131.54
Louisiana	3,923	145,402.68	62,249.28	2,700.00	210,351.96	53.620		210,351.96
Maine	12,431	699,000.84	108,994.67	10,075.00	818,070.51	65.808	1,100.00	819,170.51
Maryland, Delaware & District of Columbia	25,643	816,323.26	329,077.46	5,687.00	1,151,087.72	44.888	43,677.39	1,194,765.11
Massachusetts	62,947	1,918,192.91	829,121.97	119,948.57	2,867,263.45	45.550	93,577.63	2,960,841.08
Michigan	58,084	2,867,131.52	182,783.70	17,116.00	3,067,031.22	52.803	306,282.90	3,373,314.12
Minnesota	18,889	464,612.25	65,407.50	4,100.00	534,119.75	28.276	60,357.61	594,477.36
Mississippi	4,708	172,343.91	58,230.75	3,300.00	233,874.66	49.676	1,000.00	234,874.66
Missouri	25,833	619,932.89	192,417.49	4,027.70	816,378.08	31.602	16,190.58	832,568.66
Montana	22,614	366,766.99	91,200.39	9,329.40	467,296.78	20.664	943,890.96	1,411,187.74
Nebraska	27,934	884,278.86	141,597.37	6,729.93	1,032,606.16	36.965	6,447.50	1,039,053.66

Nevada	6,843	379,999.58	76,213.69	9,562.00	465,775.27	68.065	13,436.56	479,211.83
New Hampshire	9,763	283,662.12	73,251.50	7,500.00	364,413.62	37.325	13,806.14	378,219.76
New Jersey	54,316	1,944,702.86	627,701.99	15,282.00	2,587,686.85	47.641	90,587.06	2,678,273.91
New Mexico	15,930	528,336.86	187,240.72	7,601.05	723,178.63	45.397	76,592.01	799,770.64
New York	85,724	2,309,865.31	811,496.82	27,454.70	3,148,816.83	36.732	51,513.45	3,200,330.28
North Carolina	14,915	1,063,537.93	197,951.71	16,392.40	1,277,882.04	85.677	1,100.00	1,278,982.04
North Dakota	27,956	515,647.33	163,881.44	5,515.00	685,043.77	24.504	8,125.00	693,168.77
Ohio	65,650	1,509,881.11	618,348.57	42,851.56	2,171,081.24	33.070	74,319.40	2,245,400.64
Oklahoma	20,708	890,782.00	187,179.22	5,100.00	1,083,061.22	52.301		1,083,061.22
Oregon	76,322	1,816,744.96	371,795.38	46,010.00	2,234,550.34	29.277	147,078.75	2,381,629.09
Panama Republic	1,236	46,829.79	37,596.60		84,426.39	68.306		84,426.39
Pennslyvania	84,459	1,925,887.40	546,156.57	65,619.68	2,537,663.65	30.046	35,078.35	2,572,742.00
Philippines Republic	248	56,515.00	17,700.00		74,215.00	299.254		74,215.00
Puerto Rico	324	26,007.25	13,757.00		39,764.25	122.729		39,764.25
Rhode Island	7,122	406,291.75	99,512.66	8,805.00	514,609.41	72.256	183,059.24	697,668.65
South Carolina	6,777	257,308.43	30,846.10	10,326.00	298,480.53	44.043		298,480.53
South Dakota	13,914	577,503.22	58,928.50	9,350.00	645,781.72	46.412	59,504.10	705,285.82
Tennessee	14,705	522,734.15	205,117.10	15,110.00	742,961.25	50.524	1,237,318.54	1,980,279.79
Texas	25,346	832,666.33	208,209.91	8,972.94	1,049,849.18	41.420		1,049,849.18
Utah	11,388	536,381.45	116,929.67	9,959.00	663,270.12	58.242	5,500.00	668,770.12
Vermont	10,097	345,265.91	206,559.00	7,150.02	558,974.93	55.360	100.00	559,074.93
Virginia	13,626	703,948.67	168,856.20	7,415.00	880,219.87	64.598	193,055.40	1,073,275.27
Washington	69,668	1,061,573.51	333,964.65	22,434.00	1,417,972.16	20.353	164,467.47	1,582,439.63
West Virginia	14,080	288,366.36	112,512.50	32,990.00	433,868.86	30.814	13,667.20	447,536.06
Wisconsin	21,671	890,931.18	240,503.83	5,329.16	1,136,764.17	52.455	91,938.51	1,228,702.68
Wyoming	13,337	379,698.68	90,275.81	12,000.30	481,974.79	36.138	9,995.74	491,970.53
	1,530,088	$49,189,985.47	$13,206,061.68	$862,183.71	$63,258,230.86	$41.342	$6,029,568.02	$69,287,798.88
Miscellany								1,081,852.19
Cumulative Total for 60 Years								$70,369,651.07

ELKS NATIONAL FOUNDATION

GEOGRAPHICAL ANALYSIS OF DISTRIBUTIONS

From Inception - 1928 to March 31, 1988

State	State Association Projects	Allocated Awards	Most Valuable Student Awards	Emergency Educational Fund Grants	Vocational Training Grants	Youth Leadership & Cerebral Palsy Awards/Grants	Totals
Alabama	$58,947.00	$43,950.00	$36,650.00	$16,550.00	$3,668.00	$15,702.50	$175,467.50
Alaska	176,663.00	77,204.50	49,183.30	13,025.00	13,000.00	6,987.50	336,063.30
Arizona	694,838.00	363,188.05	338,950.00	46,828.45	33,000.00	21,003.50	1,497,808.00
Arkansas	100,515.00	73,137.92	88,903.92	2,250.00	5,000.00	8,635.00	278,441.84
California	2,920,399.00	1,423,258.17	1,300,007.95	303,994.00	102,500.00	74,179.50	6,124,338.62
Colorado	640,416.00	300,949.42	235,071.66	274,537.55	35,333.00	40,366.00	1,526,673.63
Connecticut	361,002.00	228,958.75	202,100.00	139,227.80	22,537.21	30,377.00	984,202.76
Florida	752,395.00	271,305.00	205,300.00	45,755.75	27,000.00	25,360.93	1,327,116.68
Georgia	134,593.00	62,400.00	75,000.00	50,523.00	11,000.00	24,245.50	357,761.50
Guam/Island	13,059.00	1,800.00	1,400.00			150.00	16,409.00
Hawaii	98,785.00	43,550.00	32,500.00	600.00	6,200.00	4,001.00	185,636.00
Idaho	116,461.00	65,350.00	63,853.35	4,520.00	7,000.00	27,927.66	285,112.01
Illinois	820,983.00	619,925.00	613,120.11	141,279.44	50,667.00	45,763.50	2,291,738.05
Indiana	543,441.00	341,793.10	320,283.85	185,372.65	29,768.50	15,991.50	1,436,650.60
Iowa	276,601.00	176,400.00	208,316.81	248,941.37	20,000.00	42,465.90	972,725.08
Kansas	222,299.00	163,600.00	183,675.00	69,080.00	14,000.00	18,753.80	671,407.80
Kentucky	87,400.00	58,700.00	47,100.00	70,765.00	10,080.42	12,118.75	286,164.17
Louisiana	65,202.00	41,100.00	24,793.05	19,570.00	6,000.00	12,787.83	169,452.88
Maine	249,007.00	112,400.00	78,150.00	104,564.00	12,000.00	21,402.50	577,523.50
Maryland, Delaware & District of Columbia	358,158.00	167,700.00	136,950.00	84,722.92	22,000.00	23,455.60	792,986.52
Massachusetts	811,209.00	548,350.00	421,950.00	690,084.01	37,951.25	80,873.22	2,590,417.48
Michigan	972,148.00	487,316.00	459,707.00	140,338.50	49,100.00	49,689.50	2,158,299.00
Minnesota	192,591.00	110,431.00	92,790.50	62,252.55	8,411.60	14,952.50	481,429.15
Mississippi	66,289.00	46,850.00	31,600.00	6,675.00	6,603.13	20,648.50	178,665.63
Missouri	244,050.00	123,450.00	95,650.00	36,967.00	9,000.00	20,641.50	529,758.50
Montana	374,140.00	269,881.60	312,346.30	39,477.00	23,834.40	13,646.85	1,033,326.15
Nebraska	281,147.00	206,650.00	269,100.00	332,996.97	18,000.00	53,334.28	1,161,228.25
Nevada	139,210.00	89,710.00	82,263.05	31,697.56	7,344.50	9,431.50	359,656.61
New Hampshire	98,530.00	69,900.00	60,900.00	65,900.00	13,000.00	16,078.25	324,308.25
New Jersey	771,296.00	375,985.00	379,638.00	387,912.73	27,000.00	40,001.05	1,981,832.78
New Mexico	231,024.00	152,650.00	138,600.00	21,998.00	11,000.00	16,336.80	571,608.88

New York	903,793.00	512,870.00	464,983.34	762,784.62	49,000.00	166,282.85	2,859,713.81
North Carolina	358,020.00	215,689.00	185,835.34	109,892.41	20,000.00	22,053.75	911,490.50
North Dakota	215,267.00	153,300.00	175,700.00	29,069.50	12,000.00	14,645.00	599,981.50
Ohio	641,601.00	343,596.34	459,800.00	160,132.40	32,433.70	52,104.40	1,689,667.84
Oklahoma	307,448.00	159,790.00	143,857.88	24,258.00	18,457.77	12,550.80	666,362.45
Oregon	683,737.00	343,100.00	313,052.75	55,473.69	33,000.00	19,174.50	1,447,537.94
Panama Republic	20,528.00	22,100.00	14,800.00			5,887.50	63,315.50
Pennslyvania	725,242.00	580,309.56	523,903.67	263,012.00	34,725.00	51,234.13	2,178,426.36
Philippines/Republic	26,473.00	18,350.00	10,400.00			75.00	55,298.00
Puerto Rico	13,538.00	12,450.00	19,700.00			3,075.00	48,763.00
Rhode Island	191,952.00	172,220.33	121,356.00	11,700.00	10,000.00	11,797.50	519,025.83
South Carolina	86,315.00	81,950.00	74,900.00	151,110.68	12,000.00	8,427.50	414,703.18
South Dakota	194,817.00	127,533.00	150,350.00	54,120.00	10,000.00	15,344.50	552,164.50
Tennessee	394,502.00	440,217.65	456,741.05	30,028.15	35,766.63	11,752.50	1,369,007.98
Texas	303,620.00	164,835.68	147,512.50	38,992.40	16,000.00	40,115.00	711,075.58
Utah	188,086.00	121,433.00	201,992.00	18,320.00	14,667.00	49,172.50	593,670.50
Vermont	171,244.00	99,200.00	89,034.00	80,225.00	11,000.00	12,850.00	463,553.00
Virginia	304,072.00	163,619.00	166,301.25	57,070.00	20,000.00	24,570.92	735,633.17
Washington	460,315.00	210,276.65	250,625.00	129,119.00	29,148.73	35,170.48	1,114,654.86
West Virginia	127,529.00	93,300.00	78,850.00	45,652.50	7,000.00	21,416.50	373,748.00
Wisconsin	341,968.00	210,850.00	228,700.00	20,480.50	22,000.00	16,573.75	840,572.25
Wyoming	138,160.00	99,150.00	77,525.00	29,300.00	10,000.00	6,487.50	360,622.50
	$19,671,025.00	$11,463,983.72	$10,941,773.63	$5,709,057.10	$1,039,197.84	$1,408,061.09	$50,233,098.38

SPECIAL DISTRIBUTIONS:

The Elks National Home	4,100,000.00
Drug Awareness Program	1,106,909.23
"Hoop Shoot" Free Throw Competition	2,726,740.77
Naismith Memorial Basketball Hall of Fame, Inc.	30,000.00
Eagle Scout Awards	24,000.00
Elks National Service Commission	786,400.00
Scholarship Management	245,760.70
Special Achievement Awards and Miscellaneous	43,378.21
Nathan O. Noah Scholarship Trust Fund - Grants in accordance with terms of will	108,494.85
T. L. Bear Fund - Grants for Special Training	73,330.75
	$59,478,112.89

ELKS WAR COMMISSION
FINAL REPORT

At the Grand Lodge Session in New York City in 1946 the Elks War Commission made its final report.

In this report was recorded a statement of the financial transactions of the Commission as follows:

RECEIPTS AND DISBURSEMENTS—ELKS WAR COMMISSION
Jan. 4, 1942—May 31, 1946

RECEIPTS

Donations to War Fund from:

Subordinate Lodges—net	$ 1,605,451.48
National Memorial and Publication Commission	50,000.00
Elks National Foundation	5,000.00
Miscellaneous	2,577.00
Donations to Manila Lodge and Elk Internee Relief Fund	710.00
TOTAL DONATIONS	$ 1,663,738.48
Received from Grand Lodge on account of appropriations	60,111.50
Less expenses charged to Grand Lodge appropriation (per schedule)	60,068.19
	$ 43.31
	$ 1,663,781.79

ELKS WAR COMMISSION—Continued

DISBURSEMENTS

Fraternal Centers program	$	472,209.51
Veterans' Hospital Service program		323,555.00
New York Fraternal Service Center—less income		140,734.54
Manila Lodge and Elks Internee relief program		107,391.97
A.E.F. cigarette and equipment program		72,562.58
Other Elks War programs		125,053.37
Elks Report to the Nation		15,000.00
General administrative expenses		68,437.34
TOTAL DISBURSEMENTS	$	1,324,944.31
EXCESS RECEIPTS OVER DISBURSEMENTS	$	338,837.48

During the period of the operation of the Elks National Defense and Public Relations Commission and the Elks War Commission the membership of the Order averaged about 500,000 so that the subordinate lodge subscriptions amounted to about $3.20 per capita.

The books of the Elks War Commission, however, were not closed until September 30, 1946. The financial transactions between May 31, 1946 and September 30, 1946 were as follows:

Balance on hand, May 31, 1946	$	338,837.48

RECEIPTS

Donations to War Fund from Subordinate Lodges		14,766.81
TOTAL	$	353,604.29

DISBURSEMENTS

Fraternal Centers	$	8,193.33
Veterans Hospitals		46,667.60
New York Fraternal Center		10,021.21
Manila Lodge and Elks Internee Relief		885.98
Slipper Campaign		1,000.00
Medal of Valor Program		642.58
Rehabilitation Program		749.01
Other War Programs		780.80
Administrative Expenses		14,042.04
		82,982.55

Balance turned over to Elks National Veterans Service Commission $270,621.74

STATEMENT OF OPERATIONS
AND FUND BALANCE

ELKS NATIONAL SERVICE COMMISSION,
BENEVOLENT AND PROTECTIVE ORDER OF ELKS
OF THE UNITED STATES OF AMERICA

(For The Period From July 10, 1946 to March 31, 1988)

RECEIPTS

Grand Lodge per capita contribution	$ 11,483,020.00
Appropriations from Grand Lodge for expenses	598,000.00
Appropriations from National Foundation	776,400.00
Interest Income	1,226,969.00
Contributions	8,725.00
Donations for various inactive or discontinued programs (net)	637,821.00
Miscellaneous	8,616.00
TOTAL REVENUES	14,135,933.00

EXPENDITURES

Veterans' Hospital service program	13,472,373.00
Various inactive or discontinued programs	663,560.00
TOTAL EXPENDITURES	14,135,933.00

EXCESS OF REVENUES OVER EXPENDITURES
(EXPENDITURES OVER REVENUES) .... $ 603,618.00

SUMMARY OF EXPENDITURES

Veterans' hospital service program:

Donations to lodges and state associations	$ 10,483,362.00
Wages	1,122,212.00
Travel expense	283,233.00
General office	118,683.00
Printing and stationary	268,780.00
Veterans remembrance awards	76,325.00
Leather expenses--tanning and freight	317,108.00
Postage, express, etc.	59,412.00
Furniture, fixtures and equipment	25,582.00
Promotion expense	48,869.00
Telephone and telegraph	79,012.00
Payroll taxes and hospitalization	108,836.00
Auditing and accounting	84,285.00
Rent	169,211.00
Veterans Administration meeting - hospital committee conferences	180,786.00
Special convention exhibit	24,601.00
Office insurance	9,970.00
Miscellaneous	12,106.00
	13,472,373.00

Various inactive or discontinued programs	663,560.00
TOTAL EXPENDITURES	$14,135,933.00

INDEX

D

E

H

I

J

K

L

M

N

O

P

Q

R

S

T

V

W

Y

PERSONAL INDEX